Conceptions
of
Postwar
German Masculinity

Conceptions
of
Postwar
German Masculinity

Edited by

Roy Jerome

with an Afterword by
Michael Kimmel

State University of New York Press

Cover Painting: *Trauriger Europäer*, 1977, Rudolf
Hausner (1914–1995)

Published by
State University of New York Press, Albany

For information, address State University of New York Press,
90 State Street, Suite 700, Albany, N.Y. 12207

Production by Michael Haggett
Marketing by Patrick Durocher

Library of Congress Cataloging-in-Publication Data

Conceptions of postwar German masculinity / edited by Roy Jerome.
p.   cm.
Includes bibliographical references and index.
ISBN 0-7914-4937-8 (alk. paper) — ISBN 0-7914-4938-6
(pbk.: alk. paper)
1. Masculinity — German — History — 20th century.
I. Jerome, Roy, 1964–

BF692.5 .C66   2001
155.3'32'094309045 — dc21   00-053151

10 9 8 7 6 5 4 3 2 1

For Julian

Contents

Acknowledgments

With gratitude to Carl Pietzcker and Klaus Theweleit for their early support of this project during my DAAD Post-Doctoral Fellowship at the Albert-Ludwigs-Universität Freiburg—to Carl for his inexhaustible knowledge of German literature and intense interest in furthering knowledge about gender and to Klaus for teaching me the history of the privatization of knowledge and the fallacy of single authorship; to Harry Brod, Sander Gilman, Michael Kimmel, and Daniel Purdy for serving as readers and helping me place this work within current research on men and masculinity. Without Harry Brod and Michael Kimmel, there would be no such thing as American Men's Studies. For their writings, I am deeply grateful; to Carin Companick for her diligent and erudite copyediting skills and for helping give this difficult subject its rich texture and quality; to the translators of these chapters, for their undaunted efforts in bringing this anthology to an English-speaking audience: Katherine Bower (University of Virginia), Jerry Heidenreich, Christoph Holzhey (Columbia University), and Elizabeth Pennebaker (Oxford University); to Wolf Sohlich, whose very life has shown me the complexity, struggle, failure, and triumph that is German manhood. His uninstrumentalized words, "Go with it, baby! I'll be your cheerleader!" did more to further my understanding of men and masculinity than did my entire graduate education; to Elke Liebs, for her wisdom and capacity to make sense of my chaotic thoughts. Her ability to dig into the deep layers of the self in an effort to understand masculine identity makes her truly remarkable; and to my family: Larry, Diane, Jim, Tracy, JoAnn, Lenny, and Tina.

With special gratitude to Kathrin, for listening to me ramble, make excuses, complain, throw temper tantrums, procrastinate, and become depressed/euphoric, and for enduring all of the other wonderful emotions that academic people subject their partners to when writing. This book is also dedicated to her.

Julian, the love of my life, it is for you that I write this book. I hope that one day you will read these words and understand that this is for you.

New York City, January 2001

Part I

Introductory Considerations

Introduction

Roy Jerome

Like many recent explorations into the nature and content of masculine identity, as well as into specific sociohistorical and cultural conditions informing the construction of contemporary masculinity in American society, this anthology frames its analysis by asking, "What is a German man?" Those familiar with key American Men's Studies scholars and their attempts to explore the properties of male consciousness understand that this seemingly perennial question is neither innocent nor academically arcane. Rather, it concerns itself with analyzing the shifting ethical, moral, and psychological contents of masculine identity in an effort to expose how patriarchal society employs conceptions of masculinity to exploit men for economic and political gain, and it uncovers the means by which men as a group maintain power over women and other less powerful groups. The question "What is a German man?" or, better still, how does he perform the power relations afforded to him as the privilege of his body—what Foucault has called "the political economy of the body"—thus concerns itself with examining a complicated existence that is at once privileged, exploited, and, most important, invisible.

Directing our attention to the production of masculine identity in postwar German society, we are confronted with a consciousness that may appear self-evident and stable, yet when analyzed through Men's Studies theories, it immediately reveals itself as being historically in crisis, fragile as well as constructed. Only very recently has the German academy begun to question the lack of attention given to masculinity—the logic governing its invisibility—and its constant crisis. In doing so, a steady challenge to the "unity" of masculine identity has emerged in the German academy as a feminist intervention aimed at further challenging patriarchal structures. The possibility that theories of masculinity, or

Men's Studies, can serve as a form of feminist intervention becomes most clear in the analyses of literary masculinity, which constitute the final half of this book. But even before the academic theorizing of the middle and late 1990s, German boulevard newspapers and periodicals publishing special editions on "hidden masculine dilemmas" were already laying the groundwork for later scholarship on German men and masculinity. The need to begin with "common knowledges" about masculinity has always been central to Men's Studies. Here it is continued in the chapters of Klaus-Michael Bogdal and Klaus-Jürgen Bruder, who read popular and mass culture—translating it into what the Self Psychologist Heinz Kohut has termed "experience near metapsychological abstraction"—as "reliable seismographs for registering the processes of cultural change in everyday life," to borrow an expression from Bogdal.

In their analyses, the writers of this anthology make explicit that masculine identity is neither stable nor intransitory but rather is historically determined, thus subject to the material conditions of class, ethnicity, sexual orientation, and religion. As Men's Studies scholars as diverse as Michael Kimmel, Harry Brod, and Elisabeth Badinter have stressed—and as Bogdal, Bruder, and Tilmann Moser also show here—an analysis of masculine identity must include an investigation of specific sociohistorical events that have conditioned that identity. By undertaking such examinations, we achieve a greater understanding of how historical events have affected men's lives. Moreover, we obtain an indispensable critical revision of why individual men, male-dominated organizations, and *Männerbünde* have reacted differently to destabilizing events. In short, we arrive at paths that lead to a conception of men's history.

The authors' stance vis-à-vis Germany's recent past forms a thread that runs throughout this collection. In order to make clearer the determinants and, consequently, the possible transformations of masculine identity in postwar society, the authors implicitly or explicitly take as their point of departure the psychic and material legacies of the Third Reich. This is not to undermine Moray McGowan's assertion that analyses of Turkish-German masculinities test the boundaries by which we can maintain that National Socialism has affected all men in Germany, for that is certainly the case. Nevertheless, in reading Moser's transcribed therapy sessions with a fifty-six-year-old son of an SS officer still fleshing out his relationship with his father, it becomes painfully obvious that one cannot talk of German masculine identity after 1945 without talking about fascism. Describing a trip to the concentration camp Sachsenhausen, where his father was stationed during World War II, Moser's patient relates:

I wanted to find some sort of trace and this is . . . (begins to cry silently again, sighs.)
Somehow it is really . . .
Coughs, sounds as if he needs to throw up.
It is as if he never returned again after '45, although he was still there till a year and a half ago and I gave speeches on his birthdays. (He senses the extent to which there exists an unknown, lost part of his father.) I was just reading your book, *Der Erlöser* (The savior). And you ask this patient what you would have to say in order for you to be, for a moment, an ideal father for him. I apparently had a momentary debilitation with this sentence (laughs a little) and had to read it about five times. The sentence is perhaps a little complex, but this is no reason why I should be slow in catching on. I thought then of what I would really want from my ideal father.
There is somehow . . .
He pauses, breathes very deeply, sobs once, then a loud scream appears to want to come out, which he suppresses however.
Therapist: Allow a sound to come out, too. These are almost sounds of panic, or cries of pain, that I believe I hear. Screams perhaps, or a type of high-pitched crying.
(Patient sobs loudly and convulsively, breathing and crying mix together. Yells, full of despairing rage:)
Patient: That you would talk to me for once!
(He cries again, but no longer silently as in the beginning; he shudders from crying. Though it seems he wants to calm himself as quickly as possible, he cries for a long time.) I don't want to hear anything about your past! (He wants to say: Don't be afraid. I won't dig up your guilt!) But you should talk to me for once: what affects you, what you think about me, what makes you happy. I never heard anything that came from inside of you.
He no longer sounds enraged now, rather resigned and sad.
I always had to guess what you . . .
He sighs, it sounds as if he feels sick, one senses suppressed crying in his voice.

This dense portrayal of the psychic legacies of National Socialism constitutes our first departure into a masculine problematic that is specifically German.

Further, Moser's and Bruder's analyses of the psychic legacies of National Socialism in postwar German society bring to light the historical conditions informing masculine identity and accordingly situate the investigator within this recent history. Perhaps even more telling than the interpretations of literary images of masculinity in themselves are the forces informing the literary analyses. This becomes apparent only in reading the theoretical chapters of this book against the literary interpretations of masculine identity. Because the interpretation of literary images of masculinity are mediated by the postwar development of theory itself, we must also situate the investigator, and the investigator's methodologies, historically. By doing so, we begin to more closely define and chart postwar German masculine identity itself. Consequently, while Inge Stephan's analysis of the Cassandra motif in the works of Hans-Erich Nossack reveals a particular conservative reaction on the part of German men to the restructuring of gender relations in early postwar society, reading Moser against Stephan produces some surprising results.[1] Moser's theories would suggest that Nossack's depoliticizing, dehumanizing, and deintellectualizing of the literary character Cassandra (not to mention his strong identification with her) become simultaneously descriptive of the failure of the postwar German male intellectual himself—a failure in his masculinity kept silent by his masculinity. Suggesting that "Cassandra is the prototype of the intellectual," and that both Cassandra and Odysseus "mark the endpoints of a spectrum" of power, Stephan's chapter explores the questions of why postwar male intellectuals—of which the two most striking examples are Peter Handke and Botho Strauß—turn conservative and renounce earlier, more emancipatory political philosophies, why they ignore radical theories of political processes in favor of the aestheticizing of the political, and why their works become critiques of language and not of power structures themselves. As Stephan's reading of Nossack's Cassandra suggests, and as Moser and Carl Pietzcker demand we consider, conservative conversions provide psychic compensation for narcissistic crises occasioned by the intellectual's inability to affect political processes. Finally, reading Moser's chapter against Stephan's, and against Barbara Kosta's analysis of the *Väterliteratur*, we see that this malaise, this conservative conversion of male intellectuals of the early postwar period and the '68 movement, is not really present in German women. German postwar feminist writing has yet, however, to seriously embrace the notion that the contents of male intellectuality—of which conversion to conservativism is probably the most easily recognized—may be conditioned by crises in masculinity.

By reading the theoretical examinations against the literary analyses, we also gain insight into the literary representation of the feminine in, among others, the works of the male writers Nossack, Borchert, Böll,

Andersch, and Meckel. It seems to me that the reason lies—and Stephan, Hans-Gerd Winter, and Russell West suggest this—in the relationship between the representation of the "feminine" and in the nature of trauma itself: identification with the phantasized maternal/feminine offers men a form of psychic compensation that guards against the painful fragmentation of the self in the moment of traumatization, and also later during potential moments of reliving traumatic experience. Union, merging, dreams of feminine love—these coping mechanisms enable the male, through dissociation, to create psychic cohesion in the moment of traumatic exposure. Bruder and West hold that, for men, the "meaning" of traumatization ("meaning" being, I contend, the transformation of somatic experience, that is, behaviors, flashbacks, intrusive thoughts, and so on, into linguistic and symbolic structures, into declarative or narrative memory) may only be reconstituted as a form of femininity precisely because it does not fit within culturally accepted models of masculinity: the hero, the nationalist-warrior, the neo-Nazi, the son of an SS man or any other military man for that matter, the sons of an entire generation of German men. Trauma remains split off from the self in the form of femininity.

Following Nossack's experience of the bombing of Hamburg, Borchert's portrayal of war, and Böll's description of returning home, the sexualization of female relations also provides psychic cohesion during subsequent occurrences of fragmentation. Paradoxically, however, the experience of trauma destroys the potential for building a mature erotic relationship. Trauma extinguishes any real opportunity for mature erotic contact and replaces it with an axis of power relations—characterized by a rigid, extreme polarity—around which interactions turn. Sexualization becomes a means of keeping the self alive while also providing an agency for controlling the Other—an Other who might remind the subject of his traumatization, his lack of manliness. This might explain why Nossack both sexualizes and deeroticizes the character of Cassandra. Certainly, Borchert's and Böll's powerful maternal imageries raise serious questions about the relationship between the portrayal of the feminine and the nature of trauma. Although sexualization is possible in Borchert's texts, mature erotic contact is not, because merging with the Other, surrendering the self and allowing the boundaries of the self to become permeable without losing the self, is remindful of the original traumatic exposure itself. This is the paradox of the traumatized man who uses his masculinity to mask fragmentation—the maintenance of manhood at the expense of women. The psychic cohesion maintained through the feminine during type II traumatization—the humiliation, the crystalline image of the event, the comeliness aiding the dissociative response, itself an aspect of the biphasic response—the sexualization guarding the subject against decompensation, perhaps a coping mechanism itself, brought on by flashbacks, intrusive thoughts, somatic sensations and dreams, the man fleeing his lover before union because her saving grace reminds him of original attempts to master incoming stimuli. As Moser and Winter make clear, and as Kosta and Stephan begin to suggest, traumatic exposure is one important factor informing the masculine identity of two generations of German men: the "National Socialist generation," and its sons.[2]

By further reading the theoretical against the literary with an eye for the possible forces informing theoretical and literary examinations of masculinity, we must consider the subject of the study of masculinity in the German academy and Bogdal's chapter, "Hard-Cold-Fast: Imagining Masculinity in the German Academy, Literature, and the Media." For Bogdal, contemporary images of masculinity—of which the hypermasculinity of the nationalist-warrior is perhaps the most easily recognized—cannot simply be traced back to "the spirit of submission that characterized Wilhelminian society and fascism. Rather, these images have their roots in the eighteenth-century beginnings of bourgeois society." And while it is important to understand that masculine identity is the product of sociohistorical processes reaching back to eighteenth-century German society and the constitution of the small family through the privatization of property and the accumulation of capital,[3] Bogdal reminds us that it is also necessary to historically situate the postwar scientific investigation of the sociohistorical processes of masculinity itself: its methodologies, assumptions, hypotheses, and dominant critical theories. Reading Bogdal, Kosta, and Moser together, we can conclude that German men of the '68 generation still struggle with conflicts shaped by an educational tradition that publicly disavowed the persistence/importance of the image of the fascist hero, and at the same time forbade both educators and students to openly admit their fascination with the beauty and strength of the soldier-father. This prohibition did not lead to a working through of the attachment to the idealized image of the father but rather to a "derealization" (the Mitscherlichs) through a "strengthening" of ego processes.[4] This is one explanation for why the male '68 generation is unable to break fully with the image of the fascist hero. Turning our attention toward the portrayal of the masculine in Moser's chapter "Paralysis, Silence, and the Unknown SS-Father," he offers another answer to the question of why German men of the "National Socialist generation" and their sons were unable to break fully from fascist or conservative patriarchal conceptions of the hero. In my interview with Moser, he concludes that the '68 generation could not break with the fathers because such an act was forbidden by both fascism and the Christian commandment to honor thy father.

Furthermore, Bogdal's analysis of "Men's Studies" in the German academy compels us to ask what is at stake when the German university system marginalizes Men's Studies—if it is studied at all—by placing it under the moderation of "Gender Studies" or even "Feminist Studies." As long as the study of masculinity in Germany remains buried within Gender Studies or Feminist Studies, that is, as long as this form of criticism endures as women's labor, from which men are excluded, German men do not have to become the objects of their own investigation, and the constitution of masculinity in postwar society fails to be brought to their attention. This is why the practice of German feminism in the academy offers men a certain comfort—the comfort of not having to consciously confront themselves.

By reading Bogdal's examination of the German academy against Kosta's, we also see that the psychoanalytic literary criticism of the *Väterliteratur* must necessarily have its own history. Those familiar with the history of literary criticism surrounding the *Väterliteratur* realize, as Kosta does, that 1980s' and 1990s' literary critics have marshaled divergent psychoanalytic theories in order to interpret and diagnose the relationship between the generation of men responsible for the Holocaust and that generation's sons. Reading Bogdal against Kosta, we begin to discover historical moments in postwar society when theorists attempted postmortem to account for the transformation of conceptions of masculine identity from hard-cold (helpless) providers to "Softies" and back again.

Certainly, in the five years during which I have worked with the contributors to this anthology, it has become evident to me just how much work remains to be done in theorizing German masculinities and in creating social programs that employ Men's Studies to expose the traumatic etiologies of patriarchy.[5] This anthology, like any edited volume, is incomplete. Initiating a much needed area of study, it will, I hope, serve as an invitation to more enumerated analyses of postwar German masculinity. Clearly, more work must be done in the field of German-Jewish masculinities; such work could take its cue not only from the writings of Sander Gilman and Jeffrey Peck but also from the work of American-German Jewish writer Harry Brod, who clearly shows that the children of the National Socialist generation and the children of Holocaust survivors have so much in common.[6] Comprehensive research into the sociopolitical and cultural conditions of gay men in postwar Germany likewise needs to be undertaken. I contend that Hans-Georg Stümke, in his work at the *Rosa Hilfe*, has made a profound inroad into the governmental wastelands that determine the lives of gay men in Germany. He has created a needed point of departure for researchers wishing to examine the political conditions under which gay men live.[7] I have often asked myself how an anthology on postwar German masculinity could be possible without an analysis of East German men, without considering the effects of forty years of East German socialism and its defeat. Perhaps future researchers will make forays into postwar East German history as literary critic Julia Hell has done.[8] Then, what about men of other—non-Turkish—ethnic minorities living in Germany?

Space also prevents me from representing analyses of class, labor, and globalization, and their effects on German men in Germany, yet such analyses are extremely important to Men's Studies. Exciting work is being done by economist and sociologist Maria Mies and political scientist Claudia von Werlhof in their analyses of Third World labor, workers' rights for women, the German military industrial complex, the global economy, and the role the German army will play in defending economic interests abroad in the form of "humanitarian," out-of-area deployments—what we might call a German "military humanism." The current transformation of German civil society from a social democracy to a privatized, deregulated, market-driven economy (in which German citizens will have only a restricted voice in the constitution of domestic and foreign policy) will not only have deep effects on the constitution of German labor in a federalized Europe but, more important, latent, militaristic, fascist identities will once again be required to protect German economic interests, if not to pave the way for enhanced German capital markets overseas. The globalization of German capital requires the militarization of German civil society in order to compensate male workers who are dispossessed of their ability to provide for their families, precisely because globalization necessitates that German labor be modeled according to Third World standards. The "perfect" German worker thus becomes a fifteen- to twenty-year-old female, uninsured, un-unionized, and vulnerable to industrial toxins—one who might, for example, work in Manhattan's garment district.

Additionally, as Maria Mies has shown, economic and military arming for globalization requires not only political and technical instruments but, above all, societal and *ideological acceptance*. First, it necessitates the normalization of war and brutality within German society under the longed-for belief that German society, free of its Nazi past, should be allowed to protect itself. Second, it demands economic gain through a strengthened military and weapons industry (ironically, this is obtained by proclaiming that a strong military will bring about the equality of the sexes by allowing women to enter the *Bundeswehr* and take part in combat). Finally, it requires a defeated German male worker; it requires a Rambo.[9] Germany is currently the world's fifth largest manufacturer and exporter of weapons.[10] This is worth thinking about. It seems to me that investigations of how men maintain power over women and other less powerful groups must include examinations of class, labor, globalization, and militarization—analyses that were central to any creditable critique of German society and politics during the 1960s. Given more space, this anthology would have included works by von Werlhof and Mies,[11] for these two scholars have made it painfully clear that there can be no real critique of masculinity without a critique of capital.

NOTES

1. Current Men's Studies scholarship tends to link historical crises in masculinity to renegotiations of gender relations as occasioned by changes in the structure and content of labor, in sociopolitical conditions, and so on. Historically, men have reacted to this restructuring in three ways: (1) *Pro-Male Backlash* is understood as a strengthening of political, economic, and cultural organizations favoring men's status in society; (2) *Anti-feminist backlash* is understood as men's attempts to take away women's rights through social, political, educational, and cultural programs; (3) *Pro-feminist support of women's causes* may be understood as political, economic, and private support by men of women and their causes. See Michael Kimmel, ed., *Changing Men: New Directions in Research on Men and Masculinity* (Newbury Park, Calif.: Sage, 1987), or Harry Brod, ed., *The Making of Masculinities: The New Men's Studies* (Boston: Allen & Unwin, 1987).

2. Additionally, the long and complex reforms that German society has employed since 1945 in order to rebuild itself and maintain its present-day democratic and capitalistic structures in post-unified society have required that German men assume different public and private roles in the everyday social reality of German postwar society. The generation of German males who blueprinted fascism or were its victims differed greatly from its children, who experienced at a young age the brutality of a total war as well as the reconstruction of German society during the Adenauer era. Still different from the German male who was old enough to take part in National Socialism and the '68 generation is a generation of German males born into a divided Germany of the 1960s and 1970s. Consequently, several broad typologies of masculine identity emerge from what is also an intergenerational analysis of the constitution of masculinity in postwar society.

3. George Mosse argues along similar lines when he shows how the "standard" for modern, aesthetic conceptions of normative, straight masculinity, of male beauty, may be traced back to eighteenth-century conceptions of Greek art as put forth in the writings of

Johann Joachim Winckelman. See George Mosse, *The Image of Man: The Creation of Modern Masculinity* (New York: Oxford University Press, 1996).

4. See Dan Bar-On, *Legacy of Silence: Encounters with Children of the Third Reich* (Cambridge, Mass.: Harvard University Press, 1989) and Rafael Moses, ed., *Persistent Shadows of the Holocaust: The Meaning to Those Not Directly Affected* (Madison, Wisc.: International University Press, 1993).

5. A wonderful example of a program that considers conceptions of masculinity is "Kind im Zentrum," created by Klaus-Jürgen Bruder in Berlin. "Kind im Zentrum" is dedicated to therapeutically treating both the victims and the perpetrators of child sexual abuse.

6. See Harry Brod, *Gender and Judaism: The Transformation of Tradition* (New York: New York University Press, 1995), or *A Mensch among Men: Explorations in Jewish Masculinity* (Freedom, Calif.: Crossing Press, 1988).

7. See Hans-Georg Stümke, *Homosexuelle in Deutschland. Eine politische Geschichte* (München: Beck, 1989).

8. See Julia Hell, *Post-Fascist Fantasies: Psychoanalysis, History, and the Literature of East Germany* (Durham, N.C.: Duke University Press, 1997).

9. See Maria Mies, "Globalisierung-Militarisierung-Ramboisierung," *Wieder "Helm ab zum Gebet"? Nein! Protest auf der Domplatte. Gegen Soldatengottesdienst, Aufrüstung und die Militarisierung der Gesellschaft*, Kay Hecht, ed. (Köln: Selbst Verlag, 1998).

10. *Stockholm International Peace Research Institute*, February 21, 2000, <http://www.sipri.se/>.

11. See Claudia von Werlhof, *Herren-Los. Herrschaft, Erkenntnis, Lebensform* (Frankfurt a.M.: Peter Lang, 1996); Maria Mies and Claudia von Werlhof, *Frauen, die letzte Kolonie* (Zürich: Rotpunktverlag, 1992); Maria Mies, *The Subsistence Perspective: Beyond the Globalised Economy* (London: Zed Books, 1999) and *Patriarchy and Accumulation on a World Scale: Women in the International Division of Labour* (London: Zed Books, 1991).

Hard-Cold-Fast: Imagining Masculinity in the German Academy, Literature, and the Media

Klaus-Michael Bogdal

Mass media and advertising are reliable seismographs for registering the processes of cultural change in everyday life. Relying as they do upon the effects of repetition and recognition, they react more quickly to symbolic shifts in social relations than, for example, does literature. Some of the most conspicuous alterations in Germany today belong to the representation of "images of masculinity."[1] Sociologists and cultural theorists are engaged in a heated debate over whether our "New Man" is simply the long-overdue answer to the "New Woman" of the '80s, or if he signals a postmodern "liberation" of men from a conception of gender roles in place since the eighteenth century.[2] Interpretations by professional observers in our society are positive, sometimes even suspiciously emphatic. One reads and speaks of the (re-)discovery of the "Male Sex Object" (*Stern*) and of the return of hedonism to a world alienated from sensual pleasures by a masculine work ethic. Even normally cautious researchers such as Ulf Preuss-Lausitz are claiming "that the 'old Adam,' that mixture of patriarchal dominance, repression of self and others, and incapacity for love, is dying out, and the 'new men'[3]—more democratic, more gentle, more aware of the feelings of others (and themselves more sensitive), more in tune with themselves and more friendly—have long been on the scene. That isn't a bad sign at all!"[4]

Despite similar observations in everyday life, I would like to claim here that the opposite is true. There is indeed a proliferation of "masculine" and "feminine" cultural and social signifiers. But this multiplicity poorly masks a simultaneous tendency toward the reactivation of traditional gender behaviors in a social environment that is confusing

---

Translated by Elizabeth Pennebaker.

and without overview (*unübersichtlich*). This tendency has become noticeably stronger in the everyday lives of young people over the past ten years. Needs and fears that were still articulated in the 1970s, as well as problems and conflicts that were once frequently expressed, are today increasingly regulated by young adults between the ages of fifteen and twenty-five through habituation, that is, through a broad set of "masculine" and "feminine" behaviors. All that is really new is that the male body is now described, phantasized, and made into a discourse—and indeed to such an extent that one might even speak of a "somatic culture."[5]

This chapter moves beyond superficial description to critical analysis. First, it is clear that in an era apparently shaped by "New Men," the cultural typology of the *hero* is still the dominant "male image," and it continues to offer the strongest potential for identification. Additionally, *Männerbünde*, in their myriad forms, continue to figure the collective image of the "masculine." One has only to think of social micro-organizations—from sports clubs to big-city cliques and gangs to men's organizations in the German provinces. Even today, for many men, the initiation rituals and masculine ideologies of these organizations play a decisive role in the development of their gender identities. Second, one can observe the return of the historically and sociologically "sunken" masculine topoi of the *nationalist-warrior*. The new national discourse in Germany excludes civility and democracy as "feminine" and finds itself in the grammar and lexicon of heroic-martial masculinity, up to and including the grotesque historical costume play of the New Right. This is clearly connected to the militaristic core of nationalism, as Susan Jeffords shows in her analysis of American culture and politics during the Reagan era.[6] In Germany, the mass media speaks of "our boys in Somalia" or "our boys in Bosnia," and in a graveside ceremony, former Chancellor Kohl officially celebrates with ostentatious symbolism the masculine virtues of erstwhile national leaders such as Friedrich II. On the streets, right-wing youths exhibit their masculinity with pieced-together uniforms stemming from different nationalist traditions. And in Botho Strauß' hit play *Ithaca* (with Bruno Ganz in the leading role), Odysseus, returning to his *Heimat*, rids his court of strangers through bloody slaughter. It would be too simplistic, however, to trace the masculine image of the nationalist-warrior back to the spirit of submission that characterized Wilhelminian society and fascism. Rather, this image has its roots in the eighteenth-century beginnings of bourgeois society. Hence we read in Friedrich Schiller's *Die Räuber* (1781), a drama written in the spirit of rebellion:

Thus it is that cowards and petty criminals lead the regiments and shatter men's swords.—Peace in Germany!—Go forth, this newspaper has forever branded you black.—Quill pens instead of swords.—No!—I don't want to think of it—I must confine my breast within a corset and bind my will with laws.—Peace in Germany! Cursed be the peace, which reduces to the slow path of the snail what should have been the flight of an eagle.— Peace hasn't yet created a great man, but war brings forth colossi and heroes. . . . Ah! that the spirit of Hermann still glowed in the ashes! Put me before an army of men like myself, and from Germany—from Germany. . . .[7]

It is in this sense that "great" men of history are once again enjoying a revival, despite, or perhaps because of, the rapid loss of respect for the political elite. This can clearly be seen in the high sales of the biographies of such men. A corollary to the political-literary mythology of "great" men is always the devaluation and forgetting of the real, historical achievements of the majority of the members of society, regardless of their gender.

On the other hand, neologisms such as *Softi* (softy) and *Schlaffi* (wimpy) indicate an erosion of traditional gender attributes. Many people disregard the fact, however, that this side of the image of masculinity, now visible in everyday life, has actually always been present in German literature. Goethe's Werther, for example, a powerful male type of the intellectual elite, confesses: "She [the woman] is holy to me. All desire is silent in her presence." This is the "loving man" speaking, who must subject his "true" feelings and sensibilities to the prevailing masculine norms if he does not want to endanger his public position of power, which is, in the final analysis, also a familial-private one.

A critical analysis of the representation of masculine identity in postwar German society must take as its point of departure the contradictions and convergent aspects of images of masculinity, inquiring into their history *and* into their respective cultural and social functions. This field of investigation pushes literary analysis to the limits of its possibilities, yet it likewise yields exciting and abundant results. The vital first step in any literary analysis of masculine identity is to distinguish literary patterns of representation, as well as masculine typologies, within a complex bundle of aesthetic, sociological, biopolitical, cultural, ethnological, anthropological, psychological, and historical factors.[8] Although important work has been done in feminist research in literary studies, these methods and results cannot simply be transferred or applied to the representation of masculinity. Literary-analytical forays into images of masculinity should first concentrate on three central questions: In what way is "man" "born" in literary texts? What meaning is "attributed" to him? And how? That these questions should be asked and answered has, until now, been anything but self-evident. While numerous studies on the subject of women in German literature have been published—particularly since the feminist interventions of the 1970s in the humanities and social sciences—and have, over time, reached a high degree of specialization, attention to images of masculinity has been limited to "deviant figures" such as androgynes, eccentrics, or homosexuals. In literary studies up to the present day, "man" has been equated with "human" in the tradition of the Enlightenment, and, consequently, characteristics of gender identity only seldom come into view. Thus, to take only one example, theorists of narrative and drama recognize the "hero" as an analytic category, without taking into consideration the fact that within this terminology specific historical images of masculinity with distinct implications for masculine identity unconsciously course into the analysis. In answering the three central questions regarding the constitution of, and attribution of meaning to, male subjects in literary texts, I define and employ a number of different levels of analysis. Even though these levels clearly stand in close relationship to one another, current research has not, in my opinion, systematically connected them, at least not without breaks or contradictions.

The first level of an analysis of masculinity in German literature requires *knowledge* of the (symbolic) forms of representation of the masculine as it is archived and systematized in current humanistic theories. One must ask how various and, to some extent, competing, scientific approaches to the question of gender identity and gender relations constitute their object of inquiry, what perspective they offer to literary analysis, and what relationship they have to one another. Further, one might, in an analogy to feminist approaches derived from French poststructuralism, consider whether it is possible to have genuine access to images of masculinity through literary criticism, and then attempt to locate specifically masculine *écriture* in authors such as Jean Genet or Wolf Wondratschek. To me, the existence of such *écriture* seems highly unlikely. Literary discourse in regard to literary traditions, intertextuality, and the cultural power of images is simply too complex to be reduced to an existence mediated through authorship.

The second level concerns the images of masculinity that have arisen since the eighteenth century, an archive of which has been handed down to us through literary texts. Through the *history* of these images, we find ourselves at the center of bourgeois society, whose core phantasies, assumptions of identity, and power relationships have been—and continue to be—recorded in literature.[9]

I. CATEGORIES OF KNOWLEDGE

The Sociological Approach

In the German-speaking world, the sociological term *social role*, theoretically grounded in the work of Talcott Parsons, gained broad acceptance in the postwar era.[10] By the early 1960s, Parsons's theories had gained entrance to the German academy and had moved to its theoretical center. Parsons's functionalist term *ability to act* rested on the belief in a capable and independent subject that had arisen in the discontinuation of the image of the authoritarian personality of National Socialism. Contemporaneously, the term *role* attained a particular attractiveness through comprehensive educational reforms. Investigations into the requirements of socialization were viewed as the key to the construction of equal educational opportunities, which were, in turn, portrayed as an indispensable precondition for the modernization of the economy and of science. Because role theory placed the internalization of social ideas of norms in the foreground and intoned the adaptation of the individual in the face of the opportunity to actively shape the self, it led to objections by, above all, the proponents of critical theory, as well as to modifications even before the political and cultural movement of 1968.

Due to the influence of Max Horkheimer's study, "Autorität und Familie" (Authority and the family), which first appeared in 1936 while Horkheimer was living in exile in the United States, role theory was transformed into an instrument for social criticism.[11] The term *role* was—at least within the narrow framework of family sociology—further differentiated through the use of the term *sex role*.[12] With the aid of this term, the social structures, actions, images, and dynamics of dominance resulting from gender relations were to be more precisely described. The first large-scale sociological examination of men's sex roles did not appear in West Germany until 1978, however, when the first poststructuralist theories of "femininity" and patriarchy gained attention in the United States and in France.[13] According to Helge Pross, the author of one of West Germany's first inclusive studies on male sex roles, *Die Männer*, sex roles are *"general behavioral rules"* which are added to the biological given 'man' and the biological given 'woman'. . . . The rules contained within

sex roles indicate *which positional roles a man should normally assume,*
which a woman should assume. Furthermore, these rules indicate the
way in which each should behave within their positional roles, and
which gender-determined coloration each should give the roles."[14] In this
study, Pross takes as her point of departure the observation that in the
society under examination—namely, West German postwar society—
biological equality is effaced by social inequality, despite the assumption
of democratic principles. The different socialization of boys and girls
provides the site where these gender inequalities are created. In her
book, Pross attempts to describe the contemporary male sex role using
interactionist premises. To do so, she places men's professional and familial roles at the center of her analysis and empirically researches their
self-understanding in regard to work, marriage/sexuality, and fatherhood.
The result is hardly surprising:

> At the core of the prevailing definition of the man is the prem-
> ise of his superiority. According to the majority of masculine
> opinion, men possess stronger nerves than women and have su-
> perior muscular strength. Physically better equipped, the man
> is also intellectually superior and psychically more highly qua-
> lified. . . . In addition, the man possesses a greater self-
> confidence; he interacts more confidently with the world and is
> better able to assert himself.[15]

Studies such as the one by Helge Pross raised the question of whether
it was possible to gradually eradicate social inequality between the genders through altered familial and public practices in child rearing. The
goal of Pross's endeavor was the equalization of feminine and masculine
sex roles in professional and family life. One must remember that West
German postwar society found itself facing a twofold dilemma in the
early 1950s. On the one hand, it had enormous difficulty mentally processing the modernizing impulses in the areas of economic life, development of infrastructure, construction of cities, and so on. Until the
1960s, these alterations, which were symbolized as "Americanization,"
were assimilated through a conservatism in interpersonal relations (family structures, public forms of interaction in schools, institutions, universities, etc.). Continuity between present and past family structures, as
well as public forms of interaction, could not be represented openly,
since the motifs of family, the male hero, *Heimat,* and so on were tainted
by their association with National Socialism. Consequently, a hybrid

society arose, one that was forced to give its everyday practices a "modern" (democratic) face. This had particular consequences for gender relations. Furthermore, the sciences, insofar as they understood themselves to be critical and democratic like postwar sociology as a whole, possessed enough authority in postwar society to direct the way toward the adaptation of everyday life to (democratic) forms of representation. In the process, sociological role theory took on an important function. It could "prove" that social inequalities, or inequalities conditioned by sex/gender differences, were not "natural" but rather the result of (alterable) socialization processes. Within a favorable historical constellation—economic development was threatening to stagnate, because the reserves of educated workers (traditionally men from the middle classes) were exhausted—sociological role theory was able to propose that men from the lower classes and women in general could, through changes in patterns of socialization, be recruited to the elite in economics, science, and politics. Sociological role theory simultaneously became, for this reason, a program of social advancement in the so-called Brandt Era.

By the beginning of the 1970s, sociological role theory was already being criticized for its belief that it purported to know what was "real" role behavior, that is, reflective and emancipatory, and what was "false" role behavior, that is, conformist and unreflective. Additionally, it often generalized as normative a middle-class-oriented set of behaviors.[16] It was not this critique, however, that caused the pedagogical and literary concepts based on role theory to appear obsolete. Rather, role theory ran aground on a changed social reality: through the dissolution of social stratification, innovations in communication technology, and changes in gender relations.[17] Today, for example, young people possessing an almost narcissistic awareness of their gender identities (in new German, *boys* and *girlies*) paradoxically present these gender identities in the traditional "pre-emancipatory" polarity of "masculine" and "feminine" while simultaneously refusing to accept inequalities. When young students find themselves confronted with teaching materials developed in the 1970s, materials containing role ideals characterized by a conspicuous neutralization of the visible signs of gender differences, they tend to be amused rather than irritated. In light of the current differentiation (*Ausdifferenzierung*) within sex roles—which can be traced back to the loss of the normative effects of those areas that socialization theory placed at the center of its analysis (namely, family and professional life)—one must seriously question what sociological role theory can offer to the description of contemporary life and the examination of history.

The Psychoanalytical Approach

In 1978, a dissertation in literary studies appeared in a small press and quickly exploded into a best-seller. The immense success of this dissertation was based not only on its "unacademic" presentation, a collage of illustrations/images, quotes, and scientific commentaries, but rather on its provocative attack on the constitutive image of masculinity in twentieth-century German history. Through its mastery, Klaus Theweleit's *Männerphantasien* (*Male Fantasies*) became a catchphrase in debates on gender relations as well as in confrontations on equal rights. In his description of "folkist," nationalist, and pre-fascist writers, Theweleit asks why the Freikorp soldiers, who sought to destroy the Weimar Republic after the First World War with civil war-like battles, felt the impulse to write down their experiences. These texts, remembrances, stories, diaries, and novels are less justifications of their illegal actions than they are attempts to compensate for the loss of the old order (the *Kaiserreich*) through phantasies and phantasms of a strong masculine body, as well as through the rejection and destruction of a threatening feminine body. The real (putative) political helplessness in the narrative moment leads to the exaggeration and outbidding of the warrior image of masculinity, one that is recognized from a contemporary perspective as a proto-fascist image.

The analysis of the "soldierly man" and not simply the proto-fascist subject is, however, at the center of Theweleit's book.[18] In the tradition of Margaret Mahler, Theweleit conceives of "masculinity" as the specific expression of ego-identity. According to Mahler and, subsequently, Theweleit, becoming a man—and thereby attaining adult status—is dependent upon overcoming symbiotic unity with the mother. In every male's development, individuation must be struggled for through concrete actions and "tests of masculinity." Symbolically and in actuality, such actions help form the foundations for achieving the independence necessary for survival. At the same time the infant carries these actions out, he continually resists regressive desires that could lead him back to symbiosis with the mother.

Under normal circumstances, these fears are more or less overcome between the second and third years of life through the discovery of the self and the acceptance of separation from the mother. Soldierly men, however, "have in all probability not yet reached this developmental stage."[19] Theweleit interprets the physical, violent phantasies of soldierly men as a defense against the infantile fear of reengulfment, as well as a simultaneous and contradictory longing for it. He postulates that their initial early childhood socialization within the family caused these males to grow up "without a feeling of certainty about external boundaries, without the psychic authority of the 'ego' in the Freudian sense."[20] In the "normal case" of male socialization described by Freud, the boy is able, in the process of individuation, to overcome the Oedipal phase and thus to accept the father/authority figure and later take his place. In contrast to Theweleit, the particular emphasis on masculinity is explained by Freud as the unconscious reaction to the castration anxieties caused by Oedipal traumata. Consequently, hypermasculinity compensates for castration anxieties. Theweleit not only examines early childhood, to which Freud restricts himself, but also concentrates, with reference to Adorno and Horkheimer's concept of the "authoritarian character," on the boy's subsequent development. According to Theweleit, it is the "second" socialization, that is, the social drills practiced in the schools and barracks, based on humiliation, obedience, physical beatings, and sexual oppression, that makes a socially functioning man out of the "not-yet-fully-born" male whose "soft" ego is held together by an armor of commandments. Theweleit reads literary images of masculinity as the conscious/unconscious result of the maintenance, repression, and projection mechanisms of ego-weak men.

In *Muttersöhne* (Mother's boys)—a book typical of the 1980s, employing the findings of other authors in order to create a spectacular thesis—the "men's writer" Volker Elis Pilgrim also takes as his starting point the hypothesis of the not-yet-fully-born man. He simplifies this psychoanalytical concept into the typology of the "mother's boy" and comes to the conclusion that: "Growing up under a constricting mother and a fragmentary father torpedoes the constitution of the boy's ego and inhibits his male gender identity."[21] While Theweleit convincingly locates the self- and other-images of the soldierly man as stemming from phantasies of creating male power and dominance, Pilgrim decodes these phantasies as being, in the final analysis, those of overpowering mothers and thus as female phantasies from which men must free themselves. For Pilgrim, a pioneer of the German men's movement, mother's boys (he examines Hitler and Stalin as examples) are the incarnate revenge of women who have been relegated to childbearing and betrayed by their own men to a patriarchal society in which only men—here, the sons—can act effectively. "Being bound to the mother engenders in a man the susceptibility to the temptations of power and exposes his violent tendencies," Pilgrim concludes.[22] Unfortunately, Pilgrim entirely neglects to mention the possibility that male violence also may have other causes.

While Pilgrim's moralizing approach produces little more than clichés about men, Theweleit's sharp, precise observations represent an almost inexhaustible discovery of twentieth-century images of masculinity. Nonetheless, it must be added that Theweleit's speculative application of the findings of individual psychology to the study of collective processes remains problematic.

Even more strongly than Theweleit, sociopsychological approaches have concerned themselves with the function of the adolescent phase in the development of masculine identity and images of masculinity. In 1987, the influential journal *Psychosozial* published a volume on "heroes," which, along with current and historical problems, investigated the representation of the hero in literature and the media, ranging from Robinson Crusoe to Rambo. All of its contributions posed questions concerning "which unconscious conflicts, fears, hopes, longings, which unseen interests and needs . . . find their condensed symbolic expression in a hero figure and his history."[23] Similar to Theweleit, sociopsychological approaches interpret the extroverted behavior of the male heroes, their lack of consideration for others and willingness to be violent, as a "regression to the omnipotence phantasies of earliest childhood."[24] These approaches connect heroism and the veneration of heroes primarily to the male adolescence phase, in which the young man—in a state of crisis—must separate himself a second time from an adult world that appears overpowering. In this stage, identification with the hero, or more precisely, admiration of his "physical strength and beauty, sexual success or social glamour, riches, unscrupulous career, fame in the areas of sport, art, science, business, finance or in the political world, or even in the criminal world," is particularly strong due to the fear of ego dissolution.[25] From a sociopsychological perspective, heroes represent a psychic misdevelopment in the process of male socialization: "Their development is a total failure, civilization has been unable to shape them in the slightest. They are anti-social. Undisguised, irrational, destructive tendencies break through. Bodily strength and vitality—as well as the ability to 'endure'—become the decisive factors."[26] In the final analysis, postwar researchers who combine psychological and sociological techniques, such as Horst E. Richter, have in mind the typology of the National Socialist "blond beast" when they speak about heroes: the man chosen as the *Übermensch*, who counters the complexity of modernity with a reduction to a "pure" male image.[27] In Germany, this male typology is, rightly, the demon image of every science concerned with gender relations. As a result, these sciences have done everything in their power to prevent this hero from becoming a model for postwar society. They were successful until unification—at least as far as publicly controlled discourse was concerned. The hero in postwar Germany was forced to descend into the nadir of mass culture and the suburban martial arts schools.

On the other hand, humans continually require a narcissistic over-valuing of the self in order to cope with powers and conditions that appear overwhelming. Historically, and in terms of individual psychology, sociopsychological approaches in Germany see a predomination of the destructive functions of the hero. Fifty years after the end of the war, this approach ultimately views heroes as social risk factors; they must be publicly criticized and exorcised from individuals through therapy. From the point of view of literary study, we must ask ourselves where literature would be without these "false developments."

The Ethnological Approach

In general, sociology and psychology direct their inquiries toward the European (or North American) man, mostly of the urban-bourgeois type. In contrast, recent ethnological studies of images of masculinity work from a perspective that is both multicultural and historical. This is certainly true for Klaus E. Müller's study, *Die bessere und die schlechtere Hälfte. Zur Ethnologie des Geschlechterkonflikts* (The better and the worse halves: On the ethnology of gender conflict).[28] Müller takes ethnological research on "otherness" as his point of departure and defines gender conflict as a "power struggle" between respective male and female self- and other-groups.[29] Even at this early stage one can see clearly how much the ethnological approach departs from the (bourgeois European) family orientation of gender sociology and social psychology. The "struggle for power" constitutes one of the fundamental hypotheses in a comparative analysis of the function of "typical" images of masculinity in hunter-gatherer, agricultural, nomadic-herding, farming, and urban civilizations in America, Africa, Asia, and Europe. In contrast to discursive-analytical and constructivist approaches, Müller thoroughly incorporates issues of "biological survival" into his study.[30] He appropriately describes the function of images of masculinity as "protective and defensive mechanisms for securing the male identity."[31] In addition to finding *Männerbünde* as a universal organizational form for the self-group, Müller also discovers mechanisms that recur in all cultures and include "the monopolization of gender-specific typical activities, dress, objects of use and decoration, forms of behavior" as well as "specific moral norms."[32] Accompanying these strictly male behaviors in the self-group, he also finds "the weakening and demeaning of the other gender," the other-group of women.[33] Finally, on a symbolic level, a mystification and an overinterpretation of masculinity may be universally observed. This is true of the paternalistic organization of most religions as well as of the unquestioned nineteenth-century assumptions that progress and civilization were male achievements.

The American ethnologist David D. Gilmore postulates an entirely different scenario in his book *Manhood in the Making: Cultural Concepts of Masculinity*, which also has received great attention in Germany.[34] According to Gilmore, masculinity is regarded in all cultures as anything but a "natural," biological state of maturity; rather, it is a "symbolic category," precisely because most societies seek to transcend biological dispositions through social organization.[35] Gilmore describes this "primal scene" of symbolic masculinity as constitutive of the "dilemma of masculinity." By this, he refers to

> the often dramatic ways and means by which cultures construct
> a masculinity suitable for their purposes and the way in which
> they represent the male role "in images." Particularly noteworthy is the continually recurring belief that real masculinity cannot be equated with simple anatomical masculinity. . . . [The]
> belief that masculinity is problematic, a decisive threshold,
> which the young must cross by passing tests, can be found at all
> levels of socio-cultural development, regardless of other possible/
> acceptable alternative roles. [This belief] can be found among
> the simplest hunters and fishers, among farmers and educated
> city dwellers; it can be found on all continents, in every environment.[36]

According to Gilmore, masculinity is connected to an accomplishment or ability that men must produce in order to be socially recognized. On the one hand, this situation produces (collective) cultural models of manhood, but on the other hand there results a constant worry and fear on the part of the individual about his masculinity. Images of masculinity, according to Gilmore, result from tests and rites of manhood, self-imposed challenges, and individual masculine symbols. In nearly all of the societies he examines, he finds three universal imperatives for "real" men: in order to be recognized as a man, one must impregnate women, protect dependents from danger, and care for the entire family.[37] Based on these premises, it appears—and, I would add, this was still absolutely the case in premodern society—that the loss of masculine identity is worse than death. The social pressure toward the legitimization of masculinity through competitive situations does not resolve the "dilemma of masculinity" for the adult man either; rather, it creates further dilemmas and new behavioral imperatives and rules, of which the duel is perhaps the most spectacular.[38]

The results of ethnological research have been impressively and accessibly brought together in the two-volume catalogue for the exhibition *Männerbande-Männerbünde. Zur Rolle des Mannes im Kulturvergleich* (Male bands-*Männerbünde*: On the role of the man in cultural comparison).[39] The contributions to this volume in politics, religion, education, crafts, sport, military, art, and literature in Europe, Asia, Africa, and America paint a nuanced picture of male group behavior throughout history and in the contemporary world.[40] The female creators of the exhibition chose with the term *Männerbünde*—for which there is no English equivalent—a very broad, vague description for male social organizational forms from early times to the present day. Their thesis is that men are allied in the goal of "maintaining male dominance in society." As a consequence, *Männerbünde* become quite diverse and may extend from religious duties to securing influence and prestige.[41] Contrary to popular opinion, the female exhibitors come to the conclusion "that the number and power of *Männerbünde* increased with the complexity of the society."[42] In addition to the description of and investigation into male self-organizations, the exhibition also devoted itself to "emotional relationships" that "developed between the members of a *Männerbund.*"[43] These included homoerotic moments, but various initiation rituals that have lasting effects on respective images of masculinity also became visible. With regard to the representation of images of masculinity in German literature, the chapters concerning themselves with the formation of *Männerbünde* in the nineteenth century and the role of *Männerbünde* in politics (the SS, among others) are of particular interest. Although the individual contributions follow various theoretical approaches (ethnological, sociological, historical), the exhibit directed its knowledge and interest—for the first time in gender studies within Germany—toward the elucidation of the function of gender-specific masculine organizational forms in differing societal forms.

The Discursive-Analytical Approach

The examination of images of masculinity has, until now, occupied only a small part of feminist studies devoted to researching gender differences, for which the term *gender studies* has become internationally recognized. While gender studies in the United States has asserted itself as a broad university-level research and teaching program, it occupies a more marginal position in Germany.[44] Increasing numbers of projects at German universities are christened as "gender studies," but this often is because female researchers in institutions dominated by men are seeking a socially acceptable, or a milder, substitute for the still-discredited term *feminist studies.*

Nevertheless, the discursive-analytical approach remains present in the German debate, despite the fact that scientific, philosophical, and political objections are continually leveled against (for example) Althusser and Foucault, whose works have had great influence on gender studies. Productive reception in Germany is made still more difficult by the fact that the term *gender* is pragmatically derived from the repertoires of various theoretical traditions, and, as a "constructivist" category, it is at first sight reminiscent of the phenomenological and system-theoretical approaches that have been and continue to be quite influential in the German humanities and social sciences. Finally, in Germany, the term *gender* has, in contrast to the biological term *sex*—in German there is a single word for both, *Geschlecht*—convincingly taken on the meaning of a socially and culturally determined gender identity. Gender in discourse analysis, however, is neither an a priori "natural" given nor a social role but rather a form of representation for the subject, determined by social power structures and knowledge.

In his historical study *Auf dem Leib geschrieben. Die Inszenierung der Geschlechter von der Antike bis Freud* (Making sex: Body and gender from the Greeks to Freud), Thomas Laqueur radicalizes the approach of gender studies by attempting to prove that the still unquestioned biological (medical) gender definition has been, contrary to belief, socially and culturally determined since antiquity.[45] Past societies (pre-Enlightenment), however, have "interpreted" the bodies of men and women very differently, and not always according to the dichotomy of masculine versus feminine: "Being a man or a woman meant having a social status, a place in society and perceiving a cultural role, but not, however, *being* one or the other of the two organically incomparable expressions of the sexes."[46]

Laqueur demonstrates that gender identities are "ways of reading," and not the reflection of "natural," that is, anatomical or biological, givens. It is only through "representation"—and thus also through literature—that gender differences gain meaning: "Literary texts not only bring out and structure attitudes towards gender differences; texts create the difference between genders."[47]

In sharp contradiction to the ethnological findings of Gilmore, who predicates a social and psychic instability in men that is laid down during adolescence, Laqueur concludes that the forms of representation of the masculine are characterized by the "fundamentally unproblematic, stable male body," which until recently has been recognized as the universal standard for the human body.[48] This is true, however, only in the general sense of the cultural symbolization of the biological alterations of the (male) body from "boy" to "youth" and from "man" to "elder." Individualized images of masculinity are characterized by instability even in the mythology of antiquity (i.e., Achilles). Additionally, discussions on onanism in the eighteenth and nineteenth centuries reveal anything but certainty in regard to the male body.

Even more than Thomas Laqueur's book, Judith Butler's study, *Gender Trouble*, is strongly inspired by Michel Foucault's genealogical work, *The History of Sexuality.*[49] Although, in contrast to Foucault, Butler foregoes a historical reconstruction of gender differences, her discursive-analytical approach is of particular interest to German literary studies. Predicating her work on symbolic forms of representation, which perform a *unifying* function, and which we have termed here "images of masculinity," she describes gender differences as discursive constellations, which in a Foucaultian sense are a biopolitical condition of the individual's constitution as subject. Thus, for example, in bourgeois society, a legal "subject" can only be one that is clearly either "man" or "woman."[50] Butler no longer inquires into the characteristics of authentic gender identity, as early feminism did and as contemporary authors such as Camille Paglia still try to do,[51] but rather she interprets the categories of identity strictly as the result of complex sociohistorical developments and power relations.[52] Among her central theses belongs the notion that biological differences are overdetermined by the respective discursive order of gender relationships. Gender identity is understood in a discursive-analytical sense as *meaning*, "which an (already) sexually differentiated body assumes."[53] Like Laqueur, the body is therefore "already, and always, a cultural sign."[54] Gender identities, which we in our language hold to be "natural" or "normal," are for Butler the result of social constructions of coherence.[55] Art and literature, however, have not greatly supported this conception of symbolic coherence and its historical continuity. To Butler's analysis it must be added that art and literature also have continually undermined these coherences.

Gender Trouble articulates itself in opposition to anthropological and identity-philosophical substantialisms predicated on a precultural (biological or ontological) gender identity. Antithetically, Butler proposes a "performative" model ("I baptize you . . .", "I declare myself . . ."), a "call to the subject" in an Althusserian sense, according to which the individual immerses himself in an already existing discourse, in order— apparently—to "find himself."[56] In contrast to Foucault, Butler suggests that the body, as well as its sex, is fully discursable. Thus a claim that Foucault never presumed to make is implicitly made here: that things such as human nature and, concomitantly, non-discursive practices (pain, suffering, contentment, lust, etc.) do not exist, at least not as a social element. This total obscuration of nature is the theoretical weakness of Butler's book and relativizes her studies of symbolic forms of representation.

"Man" As a Category of Literary Studies?

Literary studies of images of masculinity, which have until now mostly taken place in other thematic contexts, are based—implicitly or explicitly—upon one of these aforementioned four approaches. As such, only one or the other of these specific aspects emerges in our field of vision: the sex role (socialization), ego-identity/sexuality (individuation), rituals of masculinity (ethno-sociology), symbolic forms of representation (dispositive/discursive). Literary texts, however, whether synchronic or diachronic, are of enormous complexity. Not only does the author, with his or her ideologies, perceptions, obsessions, wish-phantasies, fears, repressions, irony, or seriousness, play a role; so does language itself, with its automatisms and rule-breaking; and so do writing style, intertextuality, plot, characters, images, symbols, and, not least, mimesis and the double historicity of creation and reception. The reduction to a single approach can hardly do justice to this complexity. For a literary analysis to be able to claim plausibility, the respective categories of knowledge about masculinity should not be universalized to form an explanatory model; rather, the various categories should be placed in relation to one another. First, literary texts provide access to the process in which social norms of masculinity arise, to the ways in which they determine familial and public power structures and the conflicts to which they lead. Second, literary texts illuminate the ambivalent, conscious/unconscious development of gender identities, their phases and mechanisms, their disruptions and contradictions, and finally their consequences for everyday life. Third, literature is an archive recording the historical continuity of cultural myths and rituals of masculinity, as well as their critique and destruction. Fourth, literary texts conceptually, playfully, or deconstructively organize knowledge about masculinity into symbolic forms of representation and poetically condense this knowledge into (self-)images of masculine subjects.

Literature's fourfold achievement does not raise it to a universal or privileged means for understanding and self-understanding about gender identities and gender relations, although when we think of love poems, it has often enjoyed this reputation. But at the very least, it allows us to comprehend the ways in which, and to what effect, that thing we have called "gender" creates "texts," "subjects," and "his/stories."

II. THE HISTORY OF "IMAGES OF MASCULINITY" IN GERMAN LITERATURE SINCE THE EIGHTEENTH CENTURY

The following remarks, still fragmentary, are not intended to take the place of a detailed analysis of the history of images of masculinity in German literature. However, since no attempt has yet been made to write such a history, some context and evolution may at least be outlined here. German literary images of masculinity, from the Enlightenment to the Romantic period, depict an impressive adaptation to the deep-seated economic, social, political, and cultural upheavals of this epoch. New demands arose out of the category of property, and consequently, men became increasingly responsible for securing and increasing assets through capitalization and inheritance. Male gender identity was constructed around and through the category of property; "real" men were identified as *producers-protectors-providers* for themselves, their families, and their communities. Literary images of masculinity must thus be viewed in the context of demands placed on men of the bourgeois classes. The body, which the heroes of antiquity and the Middle Ages were continually required to expose to deadly risks in order to be "manly," was now martyred in other ways. It was scientifically (rational-enlightened) grounded and thus disciplined as a goal-oriented and organic-economic (*lebensökonomisch*) construct. Certain heroic deeds now appeared as irrationally wasteful, while others, such as work, were perceived as appropriate and purposeful. The bourgeois man was still considered a fighting hero only when fighting for the fatherland:[57]

What an honor it is to be a German man,
Thank the Lord I am a German man!
How I would grieve if it were not so,
I would look enviously upon German men![58]

Consequently, bourgeois masculine identity became bound to the
ideal of the family man. While with bourgeois order the risk of violence
decreased for men, social obligation and physical proximity to the other
gender increased. There arose a growing social pressure on the individual
man, who reacted to it with new forms of behavior that had previously
been, in part, regarded as "unmanly." Baron von Knigge, a popular phi-
losopher of the late Enlightenment, had at hand the following suggestions as a remedy to the consequences engendered by this form of
demasculization:

> Be then simple in your clothing and your manners, honest gen-
> tleman; be earnest, modest, polite, quiet and truthful, do not
> speak too much and never of things about which you know
> nothing, nor in a language which you do not know. . . . Carry
> yourself with dignity and sincerity and without being coarse,
> without being uncouth."[59]

In a disintegrating feudal society, coherence was achieved by representing gender identity through an unambiguous system of signs and an
equally unmistakable codex of behavior. (Mozart's "Marriage of Figaro"
[1776] is a wonderful example of this, while Kleist's *Amphitryon* [1807]
displays its limits.) In the eighteenth century, the coherence of the masculine image was dependent upon an ever-increasing continuity between
biological sex, gender identity, and sexual practice. The binary opposition of gender—masculine versus feminine—was clearly and broadly
strengthened, as was the simultaneous differentiation of the two gender
positions in the education of children, to name just one example. The
family, or more precisely, the bourgeois small family, became the dominant form of living. Proximity or intimacy arising within the confines of
the small family threatened to reduce gender boundaries to an aspect
of the "natural" division of labor. Consequently, differentiation concerned itself with making the function of *producers-protectors-providers*
visible in daily life as a universally male position and with that, for
example, modes of behavior such as care and tenderness were codified as
masculine.

Images of the masculine, which until that point had been unrefined, and stories of men's lives, which had until then been unambiguously clear, now became part of a subtle system of differentiation that was previously grounded in an unprecedented coarseness of sexual anatomy. Out of a small biological difference arose a large social, political, and cultural difference that permeated every aspect of daily life. In the eighteenth century, this difference was constantly discussed. Like the giver of advice who recommends that "before, during and after relations or physical contact" one should "comport oneself so that one's health is not disadvantaged and so that the increase of the race is promoted by beautiful, healthy and strong children," numerous pedagogues, lawyers, and philosophers (such as Rousseau, in his *Emile*), as well as dramatists, novelists, and poets from Gottsched to Goethe, all had something to say regarding the difference between the sexes and how one may recognize them.[60] Here is just one example:

Whosoever has not had his neck bowed by wantonness
And had the marrow sucked from his health
May be described with a proud word
The heroic word: I am a man.

.　.　.　.　.　.　.　.　.　.

The most noble of the virgins bloom
They bloom and are fragrant just for him
O happy one, whom he chooses!
O blessed one, who enjoys his presence!

.　.　.　.　.　.　.　.　.　.

All of his life shimmers
Like wine, surrounded by a garland of roses.
His happy wife, pressed to his breast,
Is intoxicated by him into love and lust.

.　.　.　.　.　.　.　.　.　.

Rejoicing she looks around:
"Where are there any more men like him?"
Flee, weakling, flee! She is laughing at you.
Only he is admitted to both bed and breast.

.　.　.　.　.　.　.　.　.　.　.

Such is the glittering reward he enjoys,
So that the race which stems from him
Will never bend its neck from wantonness
And will never have the marrow sucked from its health.[61]

Gender difference not only permeated everyday practices, it also was legitimized scientifically and philosophically. In the process of differentiation, the position of the man was universalized to encompass all of humanity, as one can read in Fichte's *Grundriß des Familienrechts*: "The situation of the man is in this respect thus: he, who can admit within himself all that is in humankind, and thus finds the entire fullness of humanity within himself, can have an overview of the entire relations in a way that the woman will never be able to have."[62] Simultaneously, however, alternative or complementary possibilities were being tested in literature up until the Romantic period. Of these, I mention only two: the cult of friendship and the attempt to give men access to "the language of the heart"—the ability to articulate and communicate feelings—which culminated in Goethe's *Die Leiden des jungen Werthers* (1778).

By the nineteenth century, however, one could still hardly recognize differentiations in the masculine image. After the Romantic period, the man who was emotionally oriented or connected to nature simply became a marginal, antibourgeois figure who was mostly equated with an artistic lifestyle, as Joseph von Eichendorff's *Taugenichts* (1826), Novalis's *Heinrich von Ofterdingen* (1802), and Eduard Mörike's *Maler Nolten* (1832) clearly show. This type also included the "dandy" who played with gender boundaries, who placed his singularity and originality above a male image that conformed to roles and conventions.

From the beginning of the Romantic period and continuing through the period of Realism and up to the period of Naturalism, the dominant male image was strongly shaped by traditional patriarchal order and, like the order itself, it was represented as natural, eternal, and holy. Marriage and family were considered the "holiest, strongest foundation of human and civic virtue as well as happiness."[63] The universalization of the male image to encompass all of humanity (or, more precisely, the civilized, technological "man of culture," who was at the same time constructed in racial and class terms) finally became dominant. Against the background of familial, social, and state power structures, the polarity between the genders developed into a mutual mystification of the other sex. At the same time, a normative gender identity verging on the stereotypical was achieved. This is evidenced even in the literary figures of authors such as Kleist, Heine, Büchner, or Hauptmann, to whom at times a critique of the dominant male image has been wrongly imputed. No doubt existed about how men and women recognized each other and how they were to behave. What they (in the deepest possible sense) are, what their "nature" is, becomes a secret and with that the cause of the "war of the sexes." Traces of this ambivalence are to be found in most of the works of the nineteenth century, perhaps the clearest being Büchner's *Dantons Tod* (1835), Friedrich Hebbel's *Judith* (1840), and, programmatically, Gerhart Hauptmann's drama *Einsame Menschen* (1891).[64]

Beginning in the middle of the nineteenth century, a new model of masculinity appeared in the form of the *officer-entrepreneur-engineer*, who seemed most closely to approach the contemporary male ideal of *hard-cold-fast*.[65] In many of his stories, the French writer Guy de Maupassant subtly portrayed this image of masculinity in its social consequences and in its individual fragmentation:

> When Captain Epivent passed by on the street, all the women turned to watch him. He was the very image of an officer of the Hussars. Thus he paraded and strutted unceasingly and high-spiritedly, concerned mainly with his legs, his waist, his mustache. Naturally, they were of course magnificent, the mustache, the waist, and the legs. The first was blond, very thick, and fell martially over his lips, a wonderful little sausage of the color of ripe grain, but it was noble, carefully curled, and swung up in total impudence on both sides of his mouth in two mighty tufts of hair. The waist was as small as if he were wearing a corset, and over it swelled the wonderfully curved, strong male breast. His legs were admirable, the legs of a . . . dancer, and the close-fitting cloth of his trousers revealed every movement of the muscular flesh.[66]

An insurmountable discrepancy arose between the partly prebourgeois image of "real" masculinity and the everyday life of bourgeois and pe-tite-bourgeois men. This is thematized repeatedly in the genre of the novel, from Gustave Flaubert to Theodor Fontane, as steeling, competi-tive behavior and emotional impoverishment. Thus we read in Fontane's novel *Effi Briest* (1894–95), in a "men's conversation" about one of the male protagonists: "Naturally a man in his position must be cold. After all, what is it that trips one up in life? Isn't it always warm-heartedness?"[67] Only a very few socially critical or satirical texts, such as Heinrich Mann's novel *Der Untertan* (1916), attempted to deal with this discrep-ancy through the de-idealization of male characters. In contrast to the eighteenth century, the literature of the nineteenth century barely still played a role in the formation of the male image. Rather, it reacted apologetically—affirmatively or distantly critical—to models of mas-culinity that originated in other discourses. In the nineteenth century, before the age of mass media, men displayed themselves repeatedly in public in military procession, student parades, ceremonial appearances, and other pageants that demonstratively referred back to male domains of society such as the military, the economy, and technology.

The rapid modernization of society, having begun at the turn of the century, was experienced, among other things, as a threat to masculine identity. Arthur Schnitzler's *Leutnant Gustl* (1900) is a document symptomatic of this crisis in the image of masculinity, despite the fact that it thematizes the regressive, infantile inner world of the *hard-cold-fast* officer type.[68] Social contexts that had been stable until then, now broke apart and collapsed. As women were included in the industrial processes of production, the construction of gender identity and biological sex through the male-female dichotomy began to fragment. Modern avant-garde literature perceived this as a chance to test new gender identities in a playful fashion, even to the point of blurring gender difference, or gender-bending: this is symbolically excessive in Thomas Mann's *Tod in Venedig* (1913), provocative in the early works of Klaus Mann, such as *Der fromme Tanz* (1925) and *Treffpunkt im Unendlichen* (1932), and playful at the end of the Weimar Republic in Reinhold Schünzel's film *Viktor und Viktoria* (1933).[69] In contrast to the avant-garde, traditionalist and premodern currents from *Heimat* literature through the "Conservative Revolution" and the folkist writers attempted to win back coherence by violently imposing a new cult of masculinity, mostly through male group structures; among the most well known works, one must certainly include Ernst Jünger's war diary, *In Stahlgewittern* (1920). Moreover, in one of the most successful educational books of the time, aimed at the conservative middle class, we read:

> There are three strengths through which true, well-founded male honor is attained and maintained. First the strength to be brave and courageous, second the strength to work, third the strength of one's sexuality. . . . Every one of us who wishes to live as a real "contemporary" man must sense that he can only become one if he turns his strength and his will to the eradication of the personal, the egoistic. He who . . . no longer desires to bend his life to mechanical forces, but instead struggles to bring these forces under his control, can be called a contemporary man.[70]

The development of a cult of masculinity, through which the differentiation of the relations between the genders was once again reduced to a bipolar pattern, reached its high—or, more appropriately, low—point during fascism in the racist male image:

> True manhood includes strength, bravery, honest decisions (without cunning excuses), farsightedness, initiative, objectivity in regard to people and things (without avoiding reality), and readiness for the serious and dangerous situations in life. Dominant participation in public affairs and the struggle to fulfill the tasks of the community are the man's way. By being a warrior with the task of defending and securing the community body through the exercise of authority, assistance with education, and the assumption of leadership and governing roles, the man experiences his natural precedence. The man forges the state, the hardness of which corresponds to the hardness of his own being, bears historical conflicts and wages war.[71]

Although these attributes of masculinity were discredited because of their association with National Socialism and the war, the images of masculinity which grew out of them continued to be transmitted, not only in the everyday life of postwar society, but also in art and in literature.[72] The shadow of this past still exists, for example, in Lothar Günther Bucheim's extremely successful novel *Das Boot* (1973).

Neither the literary experimentation with gender identity nor the cult of masculinity, as we have seen with literature from the Enlightenment to the Romantic period, was—at least in West Germany—consciously handed down to post–1945 literature.[73] In his novel *Suchbild: Über meinen Vater* (1980), Christoph Meckel describes the return of the "defeated men": "A man came, unexpected, into his city. Emaciated, ruined and anonymously he orientated himself in the mountain of rubble. Past and future stood still, it was a personal zero hour and nothing. . . . The trained masculinity was suddenly at end. It stood there and cried."[74] Post–1945 literature yielded to a "bourgeoisification" similar to that aspired to in the bourgeois realism of the nineteenth century, which tended toward indifference; instructive in this context is Martin Walser's *Anselm-Kristlein-Trilogie* (1960, 1966, 1973). As such, "male fantasies" found their location in trivial literature (war stories such as the widely circulated *Landserhefte*, describing the war adventures of German soldiers, H. H. Krist's best-seller *08/15*, crime novels, etc.) and in the media. The masculine image in postwar literature from Heinrich Böll to Martin Walser is informed primarily by the father-son conflict, which advanced through the so-called father literature (*Väterliteratur*) of the

1970s (Bernward Vesper, Christoph Meckel, Peter Härtling) to become a central theme within German literature. The fathers in postwar literature are "weak" men who have collapsed under the pressure of the heroic masculine image and who retain only the function of provider; despite the Economic Miracle and rearmament, they can no longer regain their credibility as producers and protectors. In the above-quoted novel by Christoph Meckel, the narrator experiences the return of his father as the loss of a masculine role model:

> My joy at seeing my father was limitless. The memory of early childhood seemed to have gilded the picture of him. I flew to him as if into that gilded image. After a few months the sheen had disappeared. The disillusioning went deep, was confusing at first and then endlessly grey. The demi-god in whom the child believed was a nervous man, an instructor with a need to regain his authority. He worked on re-establishing his family, which meant: on his own controlling position in it. He examined clothes, fingernails and manners, supervised schoolwork and took each ink-blot as a reason to make a fundamental declaration about work, order, honesty and a child's duty. . . . Whilst still a child I stopped going to him. Nothing wanted of him and no questions to him.[75]

One can interpret the images of masculinity that emerged in the 1980s as antitheses to the image of the weak fathers and their eternally young, rebellious sons—the '68 generation—who did not want to become "real" men. Be that as it may, they signal a break, as in the case when, in a form of historical amnesia, the fascist male image is revived in advertising. Examples include the fashion corporation Joop and the cosmetic manufacturer Piz Buin. In addition to the current plurality of images of masculinity, ranging from the "gentle father" to the "tough boys" of the heavy metal scene, there are other differences from past images of masculinity.[76] Continuity between biological sex and gender identity is not only manufactured but rather a connection is established between sexual desire (passion/sensuality) and gender identity. References to biological sex alone in a time of propagated equal rights are neither able to evoke superiority nor guarantee gender identity. Consequently, one may observe within the transition from the 1970s to the 1980s, above all in advertisement (always a plurality that seems to allow for its opposite), a decline of phallic symbols and penetrating action for the sake of narcissistic self-portrayal or the presentation of social-communicative daily situations (as, for example, in ads for confections or beverages). The bodies shown, however, are still organized according to the ideal image of the Herculean man.

Unfortunately, the various constructions of the masculine in the media may only be briefly mentioned here. The enormous amount of material that I have collected over the past few years lies beyond the scope of this general overview. It is clear, however, that today's images of masculinity, despite myriad differences, also have their roots in the eighteenth century and, consequently, in the beginnings of the bourgeois era. We must ask, however, whether the proliferation of masculine signifiers today, which both men and women can view in the media to their hearts' content, does not blind us to the still unsolved problem of masculine identity in modern society.

A conspicuous difference between recent and past images of masculinity is that the "New Men" (and "New Women") in advertising and film no longer act in a way that is destructive toward nature (as, for example, the *Heart of Darkness*-paddling Camel-man still does), but rather they adapt themselves to it. Men dive into nature ("Cool Water" by Davidoff), they live out their passions without destruction and allow women to participate in them ("Café Noir"), or women simply function as objects of desire (Levi's jeans). Even if they adhere externally to the image of the heroic man, they are to a large extent freed from the function of *producer-protector-provider*, which constituted them in the eighteenth century—and simultaneously they are freed as well from the requirement to discipline their bodies and passions. More precisely, they are freed from the doctrine of discipline through work and from the concept of work as an end in itself, which shaped the men of the postwar generation. Of course, the Herculean bodies of the "New Men" represented in the media are themselves the result of discipline. But the work that goes into forming these bodies remains invisible. It is necessarily absent and silenced. This male type becomes an object of desire for women—and today, increasingly narcissistically, for men themselves—only with the denial of what one might define as work on masculine identity. What is portrayed in the media as a "relaxing" of gender relationships, presented as "soft-warm-slow" behavior (a wonderful example of this is seen in the advertising campaign for "Relax" and "Escape" by Calvin Klein) still in reality requires striving (in vain) toward the proven male pattern of *hard-cold-fast*.

These preliminary and still tentative observations bring me back to my initial thesis. The current plurality of images of masculinity in the present, from which successful German films such as *Allein unter Frauen*

(Alone among women, 1991) and *Der bewegte Mann* (The sensitive man, 1994) have pieced together their plots, can be interpreted from a present-day perspective as a postmodern "liberation" from a hegemonic image of masculinity. An examination of the history of literary images of masculinity, however, renders skepticism appropriate. Only when we are presented with proof that the (symbolic) construction of masculinity today corresponds to altered gender and power relations and obeys different discursive rules than those that emerged in the eighteenth century will we be able to speak of "New Men." For the moment, I see few reasons for doing so.

NOTES

1. Ulrich Beck, the influential cultural sociologist, interprets these alterations as a "liberation" from traditional gender requirements in the course of the modernizing trend in West German society after 1945. See Ulrich Beck, *Risikogesellschaft: Auf dem Weg in eine andere Moderne* (Frankfurt a.M.: Suhrkamp, 1986), 181 ff.

2. See Tyler Brûlée, "Mann macht an," *Stern* (June 1993); Christiane Winter and Christian Alvensleben (Photos), "Männer, Messer, Mythen," *Zeitmagazin* (November 26, 1993); Michael Rutschky, "Nichts als Helden," *Zeitmagazin* (March 4, 1994).

3. An allusion to a highly successful rock song, "Neue Männer braucht das Land" (The country needs new men), from the women's movement of the early '80s.

4. Ulf Preuss-Lausitz, "Der 'richtige Junge' stirbt aus: Von den Problemen, heute ein Mann zu werden," *Schüler 1996: Liebe und Sexualität*, Christine Biermann, et al, eds. (Velber: Friedrich Verlag, 1996), 61.

5. See Cornelia Helffrich, *Jugend, Körper und Geschlecht* (Opladen: Westdeutscher Verlag, 1994). See also Alfred Steffen, *Portait of a Generation: The Love Parade Family Book* (Cologne: Taschen, 1996).

6. See Susan Jeffords, *The Remasculinization of America* (Bloomington: Indiana University Press, 1989). See also Miriam Cooke and Angela Woollacott, eds., *Gendering War Talk* (Princeton, N.J.: Princeton University Press, 1993).

7. Friedrich Schiller, "Die Räuber," *Sämtliche Werke*, vol. 2 (Berlin: Aufbau Verlag, 1981), 315.

8. See Klaus-Michael Bogdal, ed., "Männerbilder," *Der Deutschunterricht* 47: 2 (1995); Maria Kublitz-Kramer and Eva Neuland, "Differenzen—Diesseits und Jenseits von Geschlechterfixierungen," *Der Deutschunterricht* 48: 1 (1996); Walter Erhart and Britta Herrmann, eds., *Wann ist der Mann ein Mann? Zur Geschichte der Männlichkeit* (Stuttgart: J. B. Metzler, 1997).

9. Space prevents me from discussing a third level of analysis here. German literary studies must include the examination of prebourgeois and premodern images of masculinity. One must determine whether, over an attenuated period of time, *archetypes* of

the masculine have arisen that continue to influence the modern era and thus (to express it cautiously) might suggest anthropological constants.

10. See Heinrich Popitz, *Der Begriff der sozialen Rolle als Element der soziologischen Theorie* (Tübingen: Mohr, 1967).

11. Max Horkheimer, "Authorität und Familie," *Kritische Theorie. Eine Dokumentation*, Alfred Schmidt, ed., vol. 1 (Frankfurt a.M.: Fischer, 1968).

12. See, among others, Friedhelm Neidhardt, *Die Familie in Deutschland. Gesellschaftliche Stellung, Struktur und Funktion*, 4th ed. (Opladen: Westdeutscher Verlag, 1975).

13. See Helge Pross, *Die Männer. Eine repräsentative Untersuchung über die Selbstbilder von Männern und ihre Bilder von Frauen* (Reinbek bei Hamburg: Rowohlt, 1978).

14. Ibid., 27. Helge Pross belonged to the small group of women who actually held a university position in sociology in those days. She influenced scientific research and contributed to influential journals and newspapers. One of the cofounders of the campaign against §218 (the punishable offense of abortion), she was very active in women's politics during the 1970s.

15. Ibid., 154.

16. It is important to note here that a critique of sex roles based upon sociological principles ("We weren't born girls, we were made into girls") became—beginning in the mid-1970s and continuing for ten years—an important subject in literary studies. Above all, it was an obligatory subject in every curriculum aspiring to be emancipatory. In the teaching of literature, there was a boom, for example, in the ideological critique of gender stereotypes in literary readers as well as in children's and young people's literature. One of the numerous examples of this is A. C. Wagner, H. Frasch, and E. Lambert, *Mann-Frau. Rollenklischees im Unterricht* (München: Urban und Schwarzenberg, 1978).

17. Compare Ulrich Beck, *Risikogesellschaft: Auf dem Weg in eine andere Moderne,* and Ulrich Beck, "Jenseits von Stand und Klasse? Soziale Ungeleichheiten, gesellschaftliche Individualisierungsprozesse und die Entstehung neuer sozialer Formationen und Identitäten," *Soziale Ungleichheiten*, Reinhard Kreckel, ed. (Göttingen: Schwartz, 1983).

18. Klaus Theweleit, *Männerphantasien*, vol. 2, *Männerkörper. Zur Psychoanalyse des weißen Terrors* (Frankfurt a.M.: Verlag Roter Stern, 1978).

19. Ibid., 248.

20. Ibid.

21. Volker Elis Pilgrim, *Muttersöhne* (Dusseldorf: claassen, 1986), 15.

22. Ibid., 8.

23. Hans-Jürgen Wirth, "Foreword," *Psychosozial* ("Helden") 10: 31 (1987): 6.

24. Theodor Adorno, quoted in Hans-Dieter König, "Rambo. Zur Sozialpsychologie eines den amerikanischen Pioniergeist wendenden Reagan-Films," *Psychosozial* ("Helden") 10: 31 (1987): 26.

25. Hans-Jürgen Wirth, "Die Sehnsucht nach Vollkomenheit. Zur Psychoanalyse der Heldenverehrung," *Psychosozial* ("Helden") 10: 31 (1987): 99.

26. Adorno, quoted in König, "Rambo," 27.

27. Horst-Eberhard Richter, "Heldenmythos und psychischer Militarismus," *Psychosozial* ("Helden") 10: 31 (1987): 12 ff.

28. Klaus E. Müller, *Die bessere und die schlechtere Hälfte. Zur Ethnologie des Geschlechterkonflikts* (1984; Frankfurt a.M.: Campus Verlag, 1989).

29. Ibid., 359.

30. Ibid., 68–100.

31. Ibid., 364.

32. Ibid., 365.

33. Ibid., 367.

34. In its German translation, Gilmore's book appeared under the unfortunate title *Mythos Mann. Rollen, Rituale, Leitbilder* (München: Artemis Verlag, 1991), or roughly translated, Man of Myth: Roles, Rituals and Models. Originally published in English as *Manhood in the Making: Cultural Concepts of Masculinity* (New Haven, Conn.: Yale University Press, 1990).

35. Ibid., 245.

36. Ibid., 11.

37. Ibid., 245.

38. See Ute Frevert, *Ehrenmänner. Das Duell in der bürgerliche Gesellschaft* (München: C. H. Beck, 1991).

39. Gisela Völger and Karin von Welck, eds., *Männerbande-Männerbünde. Zur Rolle des Mannes im Kulturvergleich,* 2 vols. (Köln: Rautenstrauch-Joest-Museum, 1990).

40. See Bernd Widdig, *Männerbünde und Masse. Zur Krise männlicher Identität in der Literatur der Moderne* (Opladen: Westdeutscher Verlag, 1992).

41. Völger and von Welck, xxi.

42. Ibid., xxii.

43. Ibid.

44. Since 1991, Suhrkamp Verlag has edited the series *Gender Studies. Vom Unterschied der Geschlechter,* with contributions from German and American scholars. However, the series is published only at irregular intervals, such that one cannot really speak of a continuous publication of research results. Although excellent studies are included in this series, only Judith Butler's work has found significant public resonance.

45. See Thomas Laqueur, *Auf dem Leib geschrieben. Die Inszenierung der Geschlechter von der Antike bis Freud* (Frankfurt a.M.: Campus Verlag, 1991).

46. Ibid., 20 f.

47. Ibid., 31.

48. Ibid., 36.

49. Judith Butler, *Das Unbehagen der Geschlechter* (Frankfurt a.M.: Suhrkamp, 1991). Originally published in English as *Gender Trouble: Feminism and the Subversion of Identity* (New York: Routledge, 1990); Michel Foucault, *Sexualität und Wahrheit,* vol. 1, *Der Wille zum Wissen* (Frankfurt a.M.: Suhrkamp, 1977).

50. In Germany, such absence of ambiguity is present even in first names. This continually leads to bizarre court cases, as when, for example, a boy in a multiethnic society is given a name that, according to the German ear, sounds "feminine." As early as the 1950s, the German Supreme Court decided that the Italian boy's name "Andrea" could only be used for girls in Germany. Italians in turn find this extremely comical: behind every German "Andrea" they suspect a transvestite.

51. See Camille Paglia, *Sexual Personae: Art and Decadence from Nefertiti to Emily Dickinson* (New Haven, Conn.: Yale University Press, 1990).

52. Butler, 9.

53. Ibid., 27.

54. Ibid., 60.

55. Ibid., 199.

56. Ibid., 49 ff.

57. See Hans Peter Herrmann, "Arminius und die Erfindung der Männlichkeit im 18. Jahrhundert," *Der Deutschunterricht* 47: 2 (1995): 32–37.

58. "Ein deutscher Mann zu sein ist Ehre/Gottlob ich bin ein deutscher Mann!/Ich grämte mich, wenn ich's nicht wäre/Säh neidisch deutsche Männer an." Johann Wilhelm Gleim, *Der Deutsche Mann* (1779), quoted in Hans Peter Herrmann et al., *Machtphantasie Deutschland* (Frankfurt a.M.: Suhrkamp, 1996), 173.

59. Freiherr Adolph von Knigge, "Über den Umgang mit Menschen" (1788, 1790), quoted in Gräfin Sybil von Schönfeldt, *Kulturgeschichte des Herrn* (Hamburg: Marion von Schröder Verlag, 1965), 253.

60. This text can now be found in the wonderful anthology, *"Ob die Weiber Menschen sind?" Geschlechterdebatten um 1800*, Sigrid Lange, ed. (Leipzig: Reclam Verlag, 1992), 51 ff.

61. Gottfried August Bürger, "Männerkeuschheit," *Gedichte. Erster Theil. Sämmtliche Werke*, Karl Reinhard, ed., vol. 1 (Wien: I. Klang, 1844), 230 ff.

62. Johann Gottlieb Fichte, *Grundriß des Familienrechts*, quoted in Sigrid Lange, ed., *"Ob die Weiber Menschen sind?"* 371.

63. Carl Welcker, *Geschlechtsverhältnisse* (1838), quoted in Ute Frevert, *"Mann und Weib, und Weib und Mann." Geschlechter-Differenzen in der Moderne* (München: C. H. Beck Verlag, 1995), 111.

64. Here we read of a dialogue between the "Russian student" Anna Mahr and the "solitary man" Johannes Vockerath: [A.M.] "You have often said to me that you could foresee a new, more elevated condition of community between man and woman." [J.V.] "Yes, I can sense it. It will come, perhaps one day. Then the animal will not take first place, rather the human will. The animal will no longer honor the animal, rather the human will honor Man." Gerhart Hauptmann, "Einsame Menschen," *Ausgewählte Werke*, Hans Mayer, ed. (Berlin: Aufbau Verlag, 1959), 267–268.

65. I am thinking here of the character of the Drum Major in Büchner's *Woyzeck* (1878).

66. Guy de Maupassant, *Bett 29* (Bed 29), Maupassant, *Novellen*, vol. 4 (1884; Berlin: Aufbau Verlag, 1986), 338.

67. See Theodor Fontane, *Effi Briest*, chapter 5 of the novel.

68. Reprinted in W. Lutz, *MannsBilder. Von Männern* (München: dtv, 1993), 128 ff.

69. Erich Kästner also runs through the new constellations with a melancholy undertone in his novel *Fabian: Die Geschichte eines Moralisten* (1931).

70. Hans Wegener, *Wir jungen Männer. Das sexuelle Problem des gebildeten jungen Mannes vor der Ehe* (Königstein im Taunus und Leipzig: Langewiesche Verlag, 1917), 9, 11 f.

71. "Mann, Mannestum" *Der Große Herder* [Dictionary], quoted in Frevert, *Geschlechter-Differenzen in der Moderne*, 33.

72. Gunter Otto and Maria Otto, *Auslegen. Ästhetische Erziehung als Praxis des Auslegens in Bildern und des Auslegens von Bildern* (Seelze: Friedrich Verlag, 1987), 120 ff.

73. GDR literature must be examined separately. In the 1950s, the hero type lived on, uninterrupted, in the factory novels and plays. On the other hand, texts such as Franz Fühmann's *Drei nackte Männer* (Three naked men, 1977), which problematized masculine identity, were also written in early postwar society.

74. Christoph Meckel, *Suchbild: Über meinen Vater* (Frankfurt a.M.: Fischer, 1983), 71.

75. Ibid., 74. English translation here by M. S. Jones, Christoph Meckel, *Image for Investigation: About My Father* (London: Hutton Press, 1987), 64–65.

76. Unfortunately, space prevents me from devoting much attention to the important subject of the culture of "really hard men," who, due to their archaic behavior, exercise a not inconsiderable fascination. Thus the American band "Manowar" views itself as being a successor to Richard Wagner and chooses as its male image the material of the legend of the Niebelungen. Bits and pieces of the Siegfried legend are even used in their videos. The proximity to fascist images of masculinity cannot be overlooked. In one song, the message is "the strong will survive." Sharp distinctions are drawn in regard to the soft, "unmanly," so-called hippie culture. In the video "Secrets of Steel," sexual masochism is used to demonstrate that women are only good for "one thing." A "masculine" solution to conflict without loss of honor—an obsessive subject of their songs—can only be imagined in a violent form: "Now people keep asking if we're going to change. I look them in the eye, tell them: No way! Stripes on a tiger don't wash away, Manowar is made of steel not clay!" (I owe this view into the world of "real" men to the extensive knowledge of one of my students at Freiburg, Burkhard Richter.)

Part II

Theoretical Considerations to the
Problematic of Postwar German
Masculine Identity

An Interview with Tilmann Moser on Trauma, Therapeutic Technique, and the Constitution of Masculinity in the Sons of the National Socialist Generation

Roy Jerome

Tilmann Moser is a psychoanalyst and writer living in Freiburg, Germany. His work in the field of *Körpertherapie* (psychomotor therapy) has had a tremendous impact on psychoanalysis. Since 1989, he has devoted much time to developing theories on the psychic legacies of National Socialism in those Germans born shortly before, during, and after the Third Reich. His work has led to therapeutic techniques that enable therapists to expose and treat psychopathologies arising from the Third Reich. On August 28, 1996, I met with him to discuss his view on the relationship between the psychic effects of National Socialism on the children born to the "National Socialist" generation and the constitution of masculine identity in postwar German society.

I. NATIONAL SOCIALISM, BORDERLINE DISORDER, AND THE SUPEREGO

RJ: Doctor Moser, your text, *Demonic Figures: The Return of the Third Reich in Psychotherapy*, may be understood in its broadest sense as a psychological investigation into the effects of a National Socialist ideology which produced fear, trauma, and corruption, and which led to the traumatization of a second generation of Germans. In order to better understand the psychic legacies of the Third Reich, you suggest expanding the classical psychoanalytic family model through an analysis of the political processes of National Socialism and the psychic effects of these processes. These pathologies are, according to you, politically produced cases of borderline experiences. I would like to ask you to explain more

fully the relationship between National Socialist ideology, with its terror
and persecution, and the experience of borderline disorder.

TM: By "borderline disorder," we mean psychic problems characterized
by an individual's high fragility and discontinuity, problems such as high
affect fragility, diminished control of reality, oscillating feelings of self-
esteem, unpredictable ego states, and unpredictable social control. Until
recently, psychoanalysis recognized direct connections between these
conditions and pronounced oscillations in relationships with the parents,
with the family whose psychic life was not often placed in relation to
societal tensions or radical changes. In the twentieth century, however,
there have been political catastrophes that have massively disturbed or
destroyed the function of the family. Thus, we could speak of the borderline state of entire societies, in which an enormous pressure to conform mixes with rapid social change. In the era of National Socialism—
that is, the war and the persecution—and in the postwar period it
means this: the fathers'—or both parents'—sudden shift from enthusiasm, fanaticism, fear, terror, and subservience to distancing, untruthfulness, and silence, inhibited cohesive ego and superego constitution in
their children. Later, fractures stemming from occupation, fleeing, struggle for survival, interment in camps, and so on, compounded this. The
ego cannot process so many psychic or real fractures and discontinuities.
It remains fragmented.

RJ: In *Demonic Figures*, you begin your analysis of the psychic legacies of
National Socialism by refuting the classical psychoanalytic acceptance
that the German fathers themselves functioned both during National
Socialism and then after the war as autonomous containers of societal
and familial prohibitions. In addition, you extend the psychoanalytic
term "paternal superego" to include the term "demonic figures," demonic figures being not completely internalized introjects in the psyches
of the adults and children. Why have you replaced the Freudian term
"superego," as an instance of prohibition and as a structural concept,
with that of introjected representations of demonic figures?

TM: Naturally, the "paternal superego" also functioned during National
Socialism and afterwards as a personal instance mediated through identification with the father, that is, as a source of familial, social, and cultural demands, prohibitive functions, norms and ideals. It would be in-
accurate, however, to localize the entire proportion of societal terror
stemming from commandments and prohibitions exclusively in the indi-

vidual superegos of the fathers. The German fathers had already been exposed to enormous societal pressure to represent those in power during the Wilhelmenian era, through the Kaiser and religion. The pressure was further intensified during National Socialism, which wanted to totally revolutionize this entire model. One could say that politically organized instances formed behind the paternal superego during National Socialism, and that these instances constantly exerted pressure on the parents and children to feel enthusiastic about Hitler as an idol, about their master race, and about anti-Semitism. The demand to be enthusiastic about Hitler constituted an ideal for the fathers, but at the same time it required that the fathers partially relinquish their authority to the National Socialist power. As an obedient and performing instrument of the state, one is allowed to and should let new superego contents—specifically, the National Socialist ideology of a German master race and anti-Semitism—go through one virtually like a loudspeaker, so that one can indoctrinate subordinates, fellow men, and children.

These requirements for National Socialist ideals and norms were implanted through seduction, threat, exclusion, or punishment, that is, through fear and terror. Societal pressure to display inner conformity to those in power was so intensified through fear and terror, as well as through consent, enthusiasm, and ideology, that the fathers functioned virtually as containers or transmission wires for National Socialist norms. Thus, the center of the father's superego contents existed outside his person. The fathers reproduced something that was in part indoctrinated. For this reason, we should speak of a shift in emphasis. The superego should not be replaced entirely as a structural concept. Rather, we should speak of a change through a "societal superego" that originated from the outside.

RJ: In what way may we understand these revolutionary, politically organized contents as demonic figures?

TM: The term "demonic figures" refers not only to terroristic or fascistic instances in an individual's psyche, but also to their sources. Take the internal image of Hitler as an example. When I ask therapists in a group to look at a large, dark board on the wall and imagine that this is a picture of Hitler, and when I ask them to further close their eyes and think about what their parents might still have to settle with Hitler, then astonishing changes take place in these people. They identify with their fathers and mothers and stand before Hitler as before a fallen, negative god. This negative god Hitler—or Goebbels, Göring, the Gestapo, and

so on—has embedded itself in them as a demonic instance. This instance occupies the same function that the devil, the dear Lord, or an
evil or good angel did earlier. Only now it is Hitler, Stalin, or the
Gauleiter.

With "demonic figures," I refer to persons, institutions, or entities,
from whose internalized image fear and terror emanate. Next to figures
like Hitler, Stalin, or the *Gauleiter,* demonic figures can be institutions
like the Gestapo, the SS, the concentration camps, Auschwitz, the Final
Solution, expulsion, the Nazis, the Russians, the English or American
bombing squadrons, the act of fleeing, and so on. The term does not
refer to real persons and institutions, but rather to their representations
in the psyches, which are connected to childhood fears.

RJ: How may we understand demonic instances in the second generation, that is, in those who were not alive during the war, but rather were
born after the war? The psychoanalyst Dan Bar-On, for example, distinguishes between the psychological mechanisms that enabled the perpetrators and accomplices to spread terror and to be enthusiastic about National Socialism, and the psychic legacies of repression or de-realization
of National Socialism in German postwar society.

TM: I believe that the psychological legacies of National Socialism in
the second generation have not yet been adequately researched. Children
who grow up with parents who fade out and deny an entire period of
their lives will sense a void filled with phantasies of what is wrong in the
parents' psyches. For example, when the father cries out at night, or
when the mother tells the child to be good and not to upset the father,
or else the father will have a heart attack, or when the mother prohibits
the child from reminding the father of his war years or his actions in the
family, the child senses that the father carries in him ideals or figures he
cannot cope with. They are either pushed down, or to the side, or they
are silenced to death, or different still, the child senses that these forces
place the parents in a state of agitation.

Thus, unconscious processes take place in these children, whereby
the children identify with these instances, which they perceive to be
stronger than the parents, or they identify with the parents' secret heroic
phantasies as victors or avengers. The parents are now defeated and broken. They must now be ashamed of themselves, yet they preserve secret
heroic phantasies. Either the children identify with this or they revolt
and take radical positions of opposition as victims. They then demonize
their parents by phantasizing that the parents are real or potential mur-

derers. They react to these phantasies by saying, "I am an absolute pacifist, or I am a friend of the Jews, a philo-Semite, or I will go into social
work or to the Third World." This means, "I have a type of biography
of reparation." Yet all of this ensues, for the most part, unconsciously.

These are two ideal types, mind you. It is more common to see the
mixed forms in which children of the National Socialist generation carry
within them fragmented selves. In the interviews of Dan Bar-On, many
speak of their ideals: to be peaceful, sociable, successful—European ideals. But suddenly, fragments appear in their conversations when they
think about Jews, blacks, and foreigners: "Piss Off! What do you think
you are doing here?!" Such racist thoughts often appear only in a subtle,
disguised form through remarks and comments. But they show that the
self is not cohesive. At one moment, a pacifist ideal dominates; at another, a terroristic or racist thought. These fragments come from entirely
different psychic strata, from hidden repositories.

RJ: What inhibits the integration process of these two split parent-
imagines, or better still, these split-off fragments of the self?

TM: First of all, they do not fit with each other. They arise out of
different psychic phases or spheres of identification. I would like to clar-
ify this with a short example. A ten-year-old boy admires how his father
speaks about the French or the Russians and he thinks, "My Dad is a
great guy. He is so smart and talented. He knows that the French are
soft, the English are wrong, the Russians are underhanded." He hears
this and admires his father. Or maybe he admires him when he speaks
about a few war scenes. But then he sees, for example, how his father
lays into a worker at his business. Suddenly, he realizes, "This could
happen to me. My father is a tyrant. I would rather identify with the
weak because I don't want to become so tyrannical or evil." These antagonistic modes of reaction can only be integrated when one speaks with
the child, or in this case, with the son, and explains to him that differing
feelings can exist in one person. The same would be possible if he were
allowed to speak with the father. Then the father could say, "Yes, suddenly I saw this worker, who was missing work, as a Polish saboteur in a
camp or a forced laborer in a factory." Even in 1955, the father will still
react to his worker as he reacted to a forced laborer or a Russian captive
in his agricultural business when in the service of National Socialism.

The youth of the second generation had no one to talk to about
this. They were forced to divide their psyches/emotions into many separate spheres; a phenomenon that psychiatry terms "splitting" took place

on a mass level during the war and in its aftermath. Let me give you an example. A colleague in a seminar told me that he had at one time identified with the heroic acts of his father in Russia. The son was at *Gymnasium* for ten or eleven years. One year, he had a new teacher, a leftist "'68er" who instructed the class that the war in Russia had been a criminal act. When he went home to his father to speak about his confusion, the father said that the teacher was a "leftist asshole." The teacher responded to this by telling him his father was a fascist. When he went to his mother, she told him, as she always did, that she got heart palpitations when he spoke about this topic. Thus, my colleague had to internally split his identifications with the heroic father and the despised father and was always uncertain as to which side was the "right" side. As a result, he was in fact ashamed, because he sensed that he was not a unified person. This is an example of a politically induced borderline typology; he is ashamed that his ego or self is so dependent upon the mood or climate that dominates in a social situation or in a person.

II. TRAUMA AND THE STAGING OF THE NATIONAL SOCIALIST PAST

RJ: In *Demonic Figures*, you make a case for treating the children of the National Socialist generation with therapeutic techniques that include a mutual staging or scripting of a personal experience of German history. This is meant to replace the classical position, in which the analyst is the object of the transference. When delving into a patient's experiences of the National Socialist past, why is it helpful or even necessary to replace the classical stance of the analyst in the transference/countertransference scenario with a mutual staging of this past?

TM: As I said before, these terroristic instances or demonic figures are such powerful societal forces that the analyst would have to be able, in the dyadic relationship, to be Hitler, racial teachings, the Russians, the English bomber squadrons, a part of the SS terror, Stalin, and so on. The analyst would virtually have to take inside himself an immense condensation of the societal terror of a dictatorial epoch while simultaneously maintaining a good interpersonal working relationship with the patient. This is an excessive demand. First of all, these demonic figures are housed in a different psychic location than, for example, the memory of a strict father at the lunch table. These terroristic instances are stored in a deeper psychic stratum. Even though they are buried, they remain radioactive. One could say that the therapeutic relationship would be in danger of becoming contaminated by radiation. For this reason, it is more meaningful when both patient and therapist open up the dyadic relationship, in which everything good and evil is viewed in the therapist, and instead become partners in a staging. This means, we open up the personally experienced history of National Socialism as contemporaries, perhaps also as siblings, in view of a third phenomenon, namely the psychic effects of the National Socialist or Stalinist dictatorship.

In staging the time of National Socialism, the analyst functions as a companion experienced in putting scenes together, someone who knows the patient's, family's, or social group's fears of confrontation with these demonic instances and understands how to thematize them in doses, with appropriate support. Through role-playing, having conversations with persons from childhood who are imagined to be sitting on an empty chair in the room, and so on, we look at the patient's feelings for the father who was in the war or perhaps worked in a concentration camp. When these feelings come up, the patient speaks with the father just as he saw him as a child in SS or SA uniform. In such situations, the therapist does not have to take on phantasized SS or SA qualities. Rather, the therapist can simultaneously offer explanations, give direction and encouragement, provide a measuring out of fear, and perhaps provide historical knowledge. Above all, the therapist can offer the patient protection. When one looks at an enemy who is evil to the point of inhumanity, like the SS, or as in Goldhagen's book, in which the Germans possessed a national character which led to eliminatory anti-Semitism, then the patient needs protection so that these instances can even be confronted. When I look at this enemy together with the patient, I even offer to build a wall around the patient so that there is less fear that Hitler or the soldier-father could directly attack. Fear, splitting, and disorientation in the face of demonic figures and demonized political-psychic instances are so great that if the patient had to see me as Hitler, Göring, Goebbels, or an SS man, the fundamental relationship would shatter.

In all the cases I've known, I have seen an unusual burden placed on both patient and therapist, or I see the relationship breaking down. In *Generations of the Holocaust*, Bergmann, Jucovy, and Kestenberg speak again and again of their treatment of and interviews with Holocaust survivors and children of survivors who have had one or two analyses with Jewish analysts, and have never spoken of their Holocaust memories. These traumatic experiences can be so terrible that they are not spoken about in therapy. Thus, it can happen that these traumatic experiences do not even appear in the transference. Alfred Drees maintains in *Folter: Opfer, Täter, Therapeuten* (Torture: Victims, perpetrators, therapists) that the relationship between victim and torturer cannot be brought into the transference at all without damaging the relationship. Drees starts from the belief that it is more meaningful when the therapist builds up a relationship in which he or she helps the patient to look at these experiences virtually as pictures so that they both may endure the horror together. Similar defense mechanisms can even be seen in the children of the perpetrators. This must not lead, however, to the blending of perpetrator and victim in the first generation.

In my experience with children of National Socialist perpetrators and accomplices, it is more fruitful when therapist and patient sit down together and look at such pictorial, scenic portrayals of the past as if they were standing in front of Picasso's "La Guernica." They can then attempt to decipher it together: What is happening to this figure? What is happening with this bellowing horse? What is happening with the contorted face of the woman? Why is a dead bull lying here in the street? This communality not only helps the patient, but it also helps the therapist, who in the classical transference situation stands alone with the psychohygenic problem of how much horror he or she can endure in the transference without losing orientation or placing a kind of preserving solidarity with the patient at risk.

RJ: How are these traumatic memories and their resulting split-off parental dispositions integrated into the totality of the person through a staging of the National Socialist past?

TM: Let me give you an example. You see three beanbag cushions here (TM points to three large, light brown cushions lying next to the wall). A colleague of mine who had had traumatic childhood experiences stemming from the time of National Socialism took part in a therapeutic group meeting. The colleague was born in 1948. She knows only the depressed father with a head injury who returns from a Russian prison and perpetually complains that his life is ruined. But she also knows a tender infant father who plays out an idyll—a new beginning—for her. Thus, she discovers in the memory of a photo of her father in uniform that he was a blond follower of Hitler with hopes for the future, who, after being married for two years, had to go to war. The mother and father had developed the following plan for their lives: "We will become farmers in Greater Germany in the *Lebensraum* Poland," or "I will become an engineer and a bridge architect for the freeways." Their mutual belief was, "It's getting better. We are getting stronger. We are a strong people with a strong Führer. We can be proud of ourselves." After the war begins, the father is a hero for two years in France and Poland. Then, in Russia, the front comes to a stop near Stalingrad and the war is lost.

This colleague speaks to four fragments of the paternal-imagines, one after the other, on entirely different age levels. Heinz Kohut spoke of "vertical splitting," and classical psychoanalysis speaks of "horizontal splitting." According to Kohutian Self Psychology, fragments of the paternal-imagines exist simultaneously: the idyllic, the depressed, the father with head injuries, and the father who as a result of frostbite on his feet is no longer able to pursue his career as an engineer. In addition to this, four fragmented paternal-imagines on the side of her mother arose: the fragment of the mother's fiancé—full of hope—the soldier during the time of victory, the soldier during the time of defeat, and the soldier who spent three years in a Russian prison. All of these paternal-imagines had different effects on the child, and through repeated conversations with the fragments she came to the understanding that her father consisted of four or five persons and that she was allowed to have a relationship with all of them. Furthermore, it became clear to her that in the course of therapy she could lose her feelings of guilt and have a relationship with the heroic father and with the depressed father who had misused her for his own support.

In the staging of the time of National Socialism, one could allow her to speak with the mother—with the mother who was married to the hero-father and with the mother who was horrified at the condition in which the father returned in 1948. These four or five paternal-imagines are so confusing that it overtaxes the therapist's ability to find an orientation; in the paternal-transference alone, the therapist must portray five or six people. Once we have clearly illustrated this in a scene, then the transference may become clearer and with that become analyzable. In my experience, confusion returns again and again. The patient is confused and thinks, "Who was my father really? Who am I, if I am his daughter?" But when the patient is able to look at the individual fragments like a pictorial broadside again, and is able to speak to the individual fragments, then they gradually order themselves and the confused feelings become clearer.

RJ: From American theories on trauma, we understand that these demonic instances, terroristic experiences of totalitarianism—here, experiences of war, the collapse of National Socialist ideals, and so on—can be so overwhelming that they cannot be integrated into the totality of the person as an aspect of their larger biography. How does the patient deal with this fact when confronting an evil object, whether it's the National Socialist father or Hitler as a symbol of traumatization, and finding it impossible to integrate that object?

TM: This is similar to victims of torture. Many victims of torture refuse to allow the memories of the torture to come up, because the torturer is as threatening to them as Hitler is for my patients. Because of this, the question arises as to whether there are possibilities of walking around the experience of torture, and only looking at it with a sidelong glance: "Yes, that was it, but over there is again a good landscape," as if one were allowing a hedge to grow over and cover the disaster. I would call this a good-natured, voluntary, disciplined repression, a disciplined forgetting that is reached through the rediscovery of positive images anterior to the traumatization. There is also a culture or therapy of forgetting for the traumatic National Socialist histories of certain individuals. Even the surviving Jewish people have various solutions: total silence, speaking about it in a small group or with like-minded people, a ritual remembering and a ritual forgetting in which the trauma is still only carefully intimated. That is, they let the experience be and protect themselves from situations in which traumatic memories come up again.

There is a difference, however, between a public, political forgetting, which is in reality only a politically organized repression or de-realization, and a therapeutic forgetting, which is obtained by a slow working through. One could characterize the therapeutic processing of traumatic experience as a therapy of "being able to forget."

RJ: What specific self-conflicts do males of the second generation present during the staging of their experiences? Can we speak of a typology of conflict that has affected masculine identity in the sons born to the National Socialist generation?

TM: It is difficult to speak of a typology, because these self-conflicts often concern themselves with a continuous shifting from one extreme to the other. A child of war can take a determined pacifistic position as an adult, even as National Socialist tendencies continue to exist in his unconscious, which he must constantly combat. These tendencies are covered up by shame, yet they remain effective in the unconscious. It requires a great deal of courage to look at these National Socialist tendencies and ideals and to gradually take leave of them. Conversely, there are hardened, successful men who cannot admit to their soft sides because they are reproached by National Socialist paternal judgments; they fear being seen as feminine or incompetent. Here, conscious or unconscious shame plays a role. Often, such a man never emerges from this constant tension.

III. *KÖRPERTHERAPIE* AND TRAUMATIC EXPERIENCE

RJ: I would like to shift the discussion of the psychic legacies of National Socialism to the theme of therapeutic techniques, those you have termed *Körpertherapie*. You employ *Körpertherapie* to treat psychopathologies arising from a National Socialist past. In the classical setting, physical contact between therapist and patient constitutes a transgression. I would like to press you a little bit both to explain the theories that underpin *Körpertherapie*, and to give the reasons you have developed therapeutic techniques that, among other things, employ physical contact with the patient.

TM: Since Freud, trauma has come to mean that the ego's processing capabilities do not yet or no longer exist, because the ego itself is petrified or fragmented by the traumatization. When abused children, women who have been raped, people who have been tortured or persecuted, attempt to approach the traumatic experience in classical analysis, the psychic space exists only as a container. The patients fear, however, that the trauma will tear them to pieces, make them explode, or petrify them. Thus, the body of the therapist can offer a support rather like the arm of the mother. A child who drops a hammer on his foot panics, believing that the pain will kill or overwhelm him. If the mother conveys the following message with her body: "I will hold you together. I know that it hurts like crazy. You hear my voice and I know that it will get better," then the mother's body functions like an embracing helping ego and the child can release some of his panic to the mother.

This is precisely how it is in approaching traumatic situations in psychotherapy. When I sit down on the floor, for example, and allow the patient to lie against my lap or my chest, then my legs and arms offer support. The patient has the feeling of being surrounded by a protective receptacle. In this way, much more of the trauma may be viewed. The therapist is simultaneously a witness who says, "I sense, I can feel how terrible that was." Most traumatized people are alone with their experiences of trauma. *Körpertherapie* concerns itself with finding forms in which the therapist can serve as a witness to traumatic experiences.

Bodily contact allows the therapist, above all, to reach affects that exist outside of the linguistic form. Besides, lying on the couch without eye contact or touching constitutes a repetition of earlier trauma or a repetition of the absolute aloneness during a later traumatization.

RJ: One could also argue that physical contact during therapy violates societal prohibitions against physical contact between men. What specific male conflicts are released and treated during *Körpertherapie*? What role does *Körpertherapie* play when the therapist delves into the traumatic experiences of the time of National Socialism in males of the second generation?

TM: As a general rule, men do not touch each other in Germany. It was only through the '68ers or the "Softie movement" of the 1970s that men started to hug each other. Yet, it was also the prohibition against identifying with the National Socialist father that led to the Softie movement, which was extremely pronounced with us. The movement stressed that one no longer had to appear "masculine-aggressive," that one could wear long hair, very soft, flowing robes, and so on. Above all, it allowed us to touch one another. In *Male Fantasies*, Theweleit wonderfully portrays how, in the National Socialist or soldier body, a specific form of aggressive masculinity is laid down that makes the body into an instrument through training; this is not an expressive body, but rather a fighting body. When someone is fifty years old and has hardly received any tenderness, then a conflict permanently plays itself out in his body between an enormous longing for maternal or paternal tenderness and a defense against this tenderness for fear of being feminine or "soft." Moreover, he fears that when he is touched during holding, he will become a homosexual.

In males between the ages of forty and fifty who came from potential National Socialist parental homes, very unhealthy body feelings exist: a mixture of the repressed need for holding and tenderness, an athletic body that wants high performance in many forms, a petrified fighting body, an expressive body, and a sensual body (*Berührungskörper*). If I do not touch a patient between the age of forty and fifty and he lies there relatively rigid on the couch, then he can only rid himself of his longing for tenderness and the integration of these various bodies through phantasies. His longing for tenderness and the integration of these different bodies are never really resolved, and he will never be a free person in his dealings with his body. It is only when he is touched that it becomes possible for his sorrow at not having a father who touched him to come up. Then the tears come. When a man lies on the couch on his side with his face to the wall and I sit myself down with my back against his, then he feels what it means to receive paternal protection and backing. Then he can let go and become "soft." During *Körpertherapie*, the therapist says, "No matter how soft you are, I will not abuse you." This counters earlier messages that men are not allowed to touch one another.

My experience is that, through touching, this permanent condition of tension in the sons of authoritarian fathers—that is, Wilhelminian fathers, National Socialist fathers, or church fathers who were also "antibody"—dissolves. The ten-year-old boy in the patient, who heard from his National Socialist father that boys are not supposed to cry or that he has to pull himself together, notices that he becomes stronger when he is allowed to cry with the father's touching. This makes him stronger than he is when the father says, "Pull yourself together!" because he is only able to pull himself together with the muscular part of his body. The vegetative part remains uncomforted and must be split off. All splittings require psychic energy. When he is allowed to cry while touching the body of the father, the pain dissolves. The patient experiences that the father allows him to be strong sometimes and weak sometimes. This makes him more tolerant and perhaps less susceptible to ideology.

RJ: How does *Körpertherapie*, or better still, the therapist's messages through bodily contact, protect the patient against the societal pressure of different ideologies?

TM: The danger of ideology is that an undelivered, conflict-ridden psyche expects healing from without—either a strengthening of one's backbone with the chest out and a "Heil Hitler," or a collective consolation for inferiority conflicts, a statement like, "We are the greatest." Mass ideology serves in this form as a type of false healing or a medicine for inferiority complexes.

Seventeen-year-old right-wing radicals, for example, feel strong when they stand in a row and make a "Heil Hitler" or wave a flag. If they had had fathers against whom they could lean their bodies in their weakness, they would not need an emblem, a staff, or a Heil. Rather they would know that they are sometimes strong, sometimes weak. They wouldn't need to imagine that they came from a superior race. They wouldn't need contempt for the weak in order to feel strong. They could accept the weaker side of themselves while being pleased about their strengths, and without using their bodies as instruments of threat. Everything in fascism is about the power of threat. When the need for paternal bodily contact, specifically, for a partaking in paternal omnipotence, and the need for comforting stemming from psychic and bodily weaknesses can be balanced out through the therapist, I believe that ideology has less of a chance. Then the images of the father and the mother are not opposed in such a polarized form.

RJ: Is there a typology of physical contact with the therapist that proves particularly useful in treating males of the second generation?

TM: More important than a typology of contact are the messages that are sent into the patient's body through touching. When I, for example, lay my hand on the chest of the patient, then he receives the message that he is allowed to borrow a portion of my protection and energy so that he can better cope with overwhelming feelings. One could describe this type of bodily contact as a filling with or giving of energy. When I sit down with my back against the patient's back, I give support or even set boundaries for him. For the children of the National Socialist generation, exercises that set boundaries are very important in countering feelings of omnipotence that arose from parentification—an earlier assumption of care—eroticization, or sexualization of the mother-son relationship during the war. Many sons functioned during wartime as replacement partners for the mothers, whose husbands were away at war. In addition, the fathers who returned home from the war were often broken, weak, disabled, and depressed. They could no longer set clear boundaries—except for authoritarian ones—for the young boys. When I invite a patient to place his head in my hands while standing and to show me whether he can push me through the room, as in a bull fight, then he notices that he can receive affectionate contact from me, on the one hand, and on the other, he can show me his energy unhindered. This reduces his omnipotent phantasies or his fear that he could want to kill the therapist. After this, I say to the patient, "That was well fought. This isn't about winning or humiliation. This is about you being able to show full power in my presence and seeing that I can affectionately delimit it."

If I have a father who has high SS or racial ideals and I can never touch him, then the only possibilities that remain for me are to identify with him and his ideals or to fully devalue them. When I, as a therapist, allow a patient to lay his head on my lap or in my hands, or to lean his back against my back, it is as if a three-year-old or five-year-old child were leaning against the father and letting out his entire sadness. The voice of the father's body in the therapist says, "When you are weak, it is also okay. I know that you will become strong again. When you are weak and need protection, then I will protect you. And when you want to go again and try your energies, then that is also okay."

Being able to lean against me means, for the weak, needy child in the patient, that there is someone who can help carry his weakness, who doesn't judge him and who doesn't send splitting messages like "pull yourself together" into his body. Staging messages such as "I'll protect you when it is necessary," or "You can lean on me, when it is necessary," or "You can fight with me when it is necessary" offer the patient the opportunity to gain a bodily contour.

IV. THE TRANSCRIBED SESSIONS

RJ: In your transcribed sessions with the son of an SS officer in *Demonic Figures*, you establish a scenario with the son in which he speaks to you as if you are his "ideal father." The son speaks to the "ideal father" about the real father's inability to express himself and give praise. What role does this idealization of the father play in the therapeutic scenario?

TM: Idealization plays a large role in therapy. Heinz Kohut spoke of phase-appropriate idealization, as when the child observes the behaviors of the parents and wants to imitate them. The child sees how the father speaks without fear to the teacher at school, or sees how he performs a work by hand and then idealizes him. The child's motive is, "I want to learn that, too." In this case, idealization leads to the child's strengthening. In contrast, the National Socialist fathers demanded, in general, an exaggerated idealization: "We were in Russia. We fought." As a result, the sons defend against this idealization for various reasons. Firstly, they defend against this idealization because of an official societal prohibition against idealizing the National Socialist father. Secondly, they sense that the fathers need the idealization, they need it because they are weakened and defeated: "We lost all our ideals. We lost Hitler and the war."

Therapy concerns itself with understanding why the father wants to be so idealized, why he demands iron obedience. It is because disobedience signifies to him the loss of his self-worth as a father. Earlier in the German family, one was not allowed to look the parents in the eyes. That was a sacrilege. One was not allowed to observe the parents at all, because perceiving their characteristics already constituted a diminishment of obedience—a seeing through. It is not without reason that Alice Miller titled her book *Thou Shalt Not Be Aware.*

Idealization is important, but in the work of staging, the patient is allowed to look at all aspects of the father, even if contempt is also present. For this reason, one must allow many patients to despise a part of their fathers. One sees this particularly clearly in Christoph Meckel's *Suchbild: Über meinen Vater (Image for Investigation: About My Father)*, as the father returns from being a prisoner of war and wants to be the same person of authority that he was eight years before. He wants to begin again where he left off. The son, however, is already thirteen years old and thinks that the father is crazy.

Contempt within the German family seems to be the aspect of the therapeutic endeavor most difficult to overcome. To despise the parents is subject to both a Christian and fascist prohibition. For this reason, it is also important for the integration of the paternal-imagines to allow the patients to express those aspects that they despise. Then the patients wither and need weeks or months before they can say, "I despised this in you," because this is the place where they have feared the parents' revenge the longest, their withdrawal of love, or that they could fatally injure them.

RJ: Can we not speak of a public contempt for the National Socialist fathers during the '68 movement?

TM: That was, so to speak, a contempt organized on a societal level. Naturally, in many families, the students went and swore at the father because of his past, or reproached him. Then the mother started crying, the father pounded on the table and with that the scene was ended for another year. This contempt concerned itself in all actuality with a provocation and not an interaction. This is why it must be recovered in therapy. It must come to a dialogue, where the father stays and the son can say, "It hurts me, but I despised you in this respect." But at the same time, there is an image of the father who did homework with him, who taught him how to ski, whom he loves and even admires. Both of these parts must be brought together.

The contempt of the '68ers constituted a breaking off in contact. Therapy endeavors to keep it within an interaction. Interaction concerns itself with integrating contempt as a legitimate quality of perception, as a form of distancing—perhaps even to correct a false Oedipal triumph. The sons would thus not need to be the arrogant judges of their own fathers, as if they would have acted on a higher ethical level in those days.

RJ: In your therapeutic sessions with the son of the SS officer, you encounter a family constellation in which the mother uses the son as an emotional substitute for her husband who was absent during the war, and who was imprisoned after the war for his involvement in the SS. After the father's return from prison, he suffers from impotence, and so the mother continues to use the son—in a complaining manner—as a witness to her suffering. You state that paternal absence, eroticization of mother-son relations, and also the dissemination of information about intimate marital relations were a mass fate during and after the war. How do eroticization and parentification of the mother-son relationship affect the constitution of masculine identity?

TM: The feeling of masculinity is unstable. On the one hand, it is excessively increased when the task of projecting the father is unconsciously or consciously taken on; this results in secret phantasies of omnipotence. On the other hand, the child or young boy cannot really fulfill the role offered to him. This leaves behind a latent feeling of failure, the tendency to overburden the self, and fear that women could abuse them, giving rise to a mistrust in women. In the most favorable case, this situation releases great psychic/emotional energies as well as a pronounced ability to produce, if the parentification does not lead to an excessive increase in performance or to illusory phantasies of omnipotence.

RJ: In addition, in the therapeutic sessions with the son of the SS officer, we read of a father and mother who never allowed themselves to appear sick or in need. Moreover, the parents never even spoke of their illnesses. This image of a strong mother and a stoic father stands in stark contrast to the image of an impotent father and a mother who uses her sons as replacements for a "lost" husband. What effects do the polarization of parental-imagines have on the children?

TM: This situation impedes separation from the parents: the son cannot develop an appropriate sense of caring in which feelings of strength and weakness are simultaneously integrated. Unconscious images of the parent remain all-powerful. The "stoic" father is experienced as powerful and inaccessible; he remains a puzzle and is only later, against great resistance, perceived for how weak and helpless he was behind his mask.

The result is a great personal insecurity that is often compensated for through emphatic accomplishment. The longing for an understanding, emotionally recognizable father remains preserved and must be strongly defended against out of fear of homosexuality.

BIBLIOGRAPHY

Bar-On, Dan. *Legacy of Silence: Encounters with Children of the Third Reich*. Cambridge: Harvard University Press, 1989.

Bergmann, Martin, Milton Jucovy, and Judith Kestenberg. *Generations of the Holocaust*. New York: Basic Books, 1982.

Drees, Alfred. *Folter: Opfer, Täter, Therapeuten: Neue Konzepte der psychotherapeutischen Behandlung von Gewaltopfern*. Gießen: Psychosozial-Verlag, 1996.

Goldhagen, Daniel. *Hitler's Willing Executioners: Ordinary Germans and the Holocaust*. New York: Knopf, 1996.

Meckel, Christoph. *Suchbild: Über meinen Vater*. Düsseldorf: claassen, 1980.

Miller, Alice. *Thou Shalt Not Be Aware: Society's Betrayal of the Child*. Hildegarde and Hunter Hannum, trans. New York: Farrar, Straus & Giroux, 1984.

Moser, Tilmann. *Dämonische Figuren: Die Wiederkehr des Dritten Reiches in der Psychotherapie*. Frankfurt a.M.: Suhrkamp, 1996.

———. *Körpertherapeutische Phantasien: Psychoanalytische Fallstudien neu betrachtet*. Frankfurt a.M.: Suhrkamp, 1991.

———. *Ödipus im Panik und Triumph: Eine Körperpsychotherapie*. Frankfurt a.M.: Suhrkamp, 1994.

———. *Vorsicht Berührung: Über Sexualisierung, Spaltung, NS-Erbe und Stasi-Angst*. Frankfurt a.M.: Suhrkamp, 1992.

Theweleit, Klaus. *Male Fantasies. Vol. 1: Women, Floods, Bodies, History*. Minneapolis: University of Minnesota Press, 1977, 1987.

———. *Male Fantasies. Vol. 2: Male Bodies: Psychoanalyzing the White Terror*. Minneapolis: University of Minnesota Press, 1978, 1989.

Paralysis, Silence, and the Unknown SS-Father: A Therapeutic Case Study on the Return of the Third Reich in Psychotherapy

Tilmann Moser

The patient, F., born in 1942, is both a psychologist and a psychotherapist. After an earlier period of therapy in which no relationship to the time of National Socialism was ever established, the patient approached the issue of National Socialism in his training-analysis with an established colleague who had confronted this issue himself.

As such, the patient had finally found a warm-hearted, encouraging father who took an interest in him. For this reason, it was particularly difficult to bring the NS-father, or the Aryan or the Jew, or the SS, or Hitler or Himmler, into the transference. The analyst was the "ideal opposite image" of the father about whom they spoke, but who was never encountered on the level of affect. He begins treatment once again after having had two long periods of therapy because, while wanting to learn *Körpertherapie* in a seminar with me (during this time he also addressed me in the "Du-Form"), issues associated with National Socialism surfaced to an extreme in several patients and were subsequently confronted through role-playing. Because he is on the road much of the time, we conduct double sessions now and then. This transcribed hour takes place approximately six months after the beginning of our work. He accepted

This chapter was originally published in Tilmann Moser, *Dämonische Figuren. Die Wiederkehr des Dritten Reiches in der Psychotherapie* (Frankfurt a.M.: Suhrkamp, 1996). The utmost care has been taken in this translation to mirror the original German. Consequently, ellipses appear here in English as they appeared in the German and represent both Dr. Moser's editing and the patient's structure of expression. As in the original German, italicized comments represent the inserted thoughts of Dr. Moser's assistant who was asked to listen to the therapeutic sessions and insert her reactions and observations within the transcribed sessions. Dr. Moser's own comments on his and the patient's assertions were inserted in roman type and set off in parentheses.

my suggestion from the very beginning to record these sessions on tape—initially with brief skepticism, then with full determination. He now listens to these hours regularly during pauses in his therapy.

The following transcription is taken from the second hour of a double session, the first hour of which centered on his memories of the SS-father. He has now placed around him a number of beanbag cushions that represent members of his family. Now and again, he questions whether issues associated with National Socialism lie dormant within him, near the surface, or whether he occupies himself with these issues merely out of sympathy for me and out of conformity. Most of all, he would like to rid himself of these issues and would sometimes be relieved if these were only my suggestions, he himself having sufficiently worked through them. Laboriously, he recognizes many indications that his family's NS history still greatly troubles him. He is not the first patient whose defense takes the form: "So, you have a new research project!"

I always like to admit this, express the hope that I am not imposing my research on my patients, speak briefly about my family history and my recent realization of its importance for me, and say with conviction that: this has helped me become more sensitive to signs during the sessions.

The patient sits in the same place as before, that is, relatively near me among a landscape of cushions and pillows that represent the members of his family of origin. I turn on the microphone a few seconds too late. . . . I believe he has just asked, as he often does:

Patient: Well, where do we go from here? (As if he were entirely willing to allow himself to be led.)

Therapist: The question emerges once again—because you so often say, "I am easily willing to conform"—how great a part in you knows that I am interested in this subject. What else has occupied you this week? (I want to examine again where his own "authentic" materials lie, and whether the subject of "conformity" has broken into our own casting of themes.)

Pause.

(An astonishing change takes place in him—one that is still visible after a ten-minute break, during which I have brought him tea; he appears entirely rested.)

The patient now moans, breathes loudly, swallows; suppressed crying. He seems weary and extremely in need of protection.

P: (crying) And then . . . I had . . . (He can hardly speak. I wait and then, breaking his struggle for expression, say to him:)

T: I would like to briefly describe to you the images that appear before me as I look at you. There are two images. In one, you are lying on the couch, where you are resting or building a wall (a protective wall of cushions). In the other, I see all that is unknown of your father in the closet over there—the one at which you are staring spellbound. *Suppressed crying of the patient. The therapist also breathes with difficulty, unclear whether he is sighing or simply congested.*

T: One could imagine that in this bright and exceedingly orderly room . . . (The patient's desire to speak comes in waves, yet is repeatedly interrupted, so that it becomes unclear when exactly he wants to speak.) But you also really wanted to say something?

P: I wanted to say . . . It occurred to me . . . *He seems confused, overtaxed. Listening, one senses an atmosphere full of suppressed rage and irritation.* . . . over and over again with my mother and father and so on . . . (he is furious that at the age of fifty, and after so many hours of therapy, he still must be confronted with his parents and the effects of National Socialist history), but on the other hand, I realize that I react most strongly then. Because of this, I feel that these are really inner themes. One realizes it by my tears as well. Outside of your therapy, I do not cry! (A curious formulation, which occurs to me now and has occurred to me on numerous occasions: "your therapy," not "our" or "my." This formulation reveals his passive disposition, perhaps also a distancing, and almost an appropriation of guilt.)

I sometimes get tears in my eyes from the wind, but beyond that, I never cry. Astonishingly, not even in my own therapies. Because of this, I realize that I am working on very personal issues here.

He coughs. It sounds more like he is choking, though.

In reference to the closet with my father's things, which you mentioned before, I had this image that the door opens up and my father comes out in black leather clothes (the memories of SS colors; particularly evident are the emphasis on and the retention of the color). I will bring you a photo of him so that you can see what type of person he was. On the one hand, there was something very serious about him . . .

Choked voice, patient swallows loudly and convulsively. Transcribing this tape, one senses the revulsion that he is forced to swallow. It is clear that the next statement about his father will touch upon something unpleasant or will be embarrassing to him.

What disturbed me about him was the black leather pants that he once bought for himself. I always had the feeling that they were perverse and didn't suit him. Everything else he wore was gray. Because of this, I cannot wear anything of his. I don't want to, either! Recently, as my mother and I were at the cemetery, she wore an ochre brown vest of my father's. My initial fantasy was that she was now arming herself with my father's things. Then, there was a side where . . . *he breaks off, breathes deeply, one senses feelings which are overwhelming* . . . such a dark . . . which came up out of my father, and which one could not speak about. I had this fantasy of saying that I thought the vest was ugly and that it reminded me of the Nazis or the SS . . . but even that would have been too much!

(Long pause . . . then he begins to answer my question:)

What else has occupied me this week? Work was very draining. I worked ten hours a day, as if I had to earn my vacation. As of today, I have two weeks of vacation. At the moment, I am much occupied with my own differing reactions to my patients. I am currently working with a very lively, impulsive, and highly affected woman. She wants to test out the boundaries and these sessions here have helped me with this. I think this is good and realize that through her own character, she is also reviving me! Then, I have another patient who cries a great deal and who also speaks much about her crying attacks. In those moments, I notice clearly that there is rage hiding behind this. I fall into a state of paralysis with this patient. . . . (He looks at me as if searching for advice.)

T: Do you not know what you should say? Is the empathy diminishing?

P: I notice sometimes that I become very tired. Also, she often speaks in a very confused manner, so that I don't know where she is at the moment with her affect (very much like himself and other patients in sessions burdened by National Socialism). Naturally, it weighs on my conscience when I wander off in my own thoughts. She is right when she gets the feeling that I am not with her. (I think involuntarily of Ralf Zwiebel's book, *Der Schlaf der Psychoanalyse* (The sleep of psychoanalysis), not only because of the therapist's tiredness, "running away," and desires for merging, but perhaps also because of the unfathomable subject of National Socialism, which can paralyze patient and therapist equally.)

T: I'm still missing the central theme. Is this now a short supervision?

P: No, no! What occupy me are my reactions to such experiences. In this context, my wife also comes to mind. When we first met each other, she cried a great deal and I was certainly more impulsive then when something ran contrary to my expectations. . . . Then she would start crying! (This contains the overtone: She relieved me of crying or cried for me.)

I have many patients who have a compulsive-depressive side, as I do, one that is walled off by depression. . . . My first patient had a psychotic father, a mother sick with cancer, and he was the strong, silent type! I have many patients who have such a hardened, reticent, and silent side. I am one of those types who attempts to revive them and who attempts to dissolve their petrification through empathy. (This accumulation is astonishing—for him as well. A vague idea is developing in him that he is "collecting" patients who depict the silence and the numbness of his parents, so that he, as the therapist, is finally able to do something to counter this.) I certainly embody the type of therapist toward whom it is difficult to become aggressive, because I am so understanding. This has been occupying me lately. Especially with the patient I mentioned before, I notice that I feel better subjectively when I am not so withdrawn. (A few months later, we will practice "exercises," or more specifically, stage scenes, in which this feared aggression is allowed to come out with secure support from me: impulses to fight and murder instead of the false self of a "good guy.")

T: I have the feeling that speaking develops in this patient on an entirely different level than that of affect. I would ask her, is it possible that we can have another type of contact, something other than speech?

Summary of the next sequence: Discussion about the female patient. In the meantime, the voice of the therapist grows noticeably weaker because of a cold. He appears extremely tired. He explains this to the patient, and lies down on his own couch. The patient does not feel irritated by the change in the situation but rather responds to the therapist's question as to whether he may lie down on the couch or on the floor.

P: I don't find this disturbing because, for me, our game is still very present. . . . *choked voice, he swallows, strong surging feelings.* This even feels pleasant. I never saw my father lying on the floor (soft voice).

T: Yes, perhaps this has something to do with a lot of things: he always maintained his composure.

P: For me, this is an atmosphere of playful encounter. It makes the son more aware of all that is possible. *He laughs in fact, but this has the effect of resignation, pain.*
   Very long pause.
   Stifling, tormenting atmosphere, strain, underground sorrow, the longer the pause lasts, the more difficult it is to bear.
   He also never said that he was tired or exhausted (softly, reproachfully). I can't . . . (breaks off, moans) . . . I notice how deeply this is internalized in me, this "inability to allow myself to be helped." My parents were very alike in this respect: appallingly upright, disciplined, clean. I believe that I, my children . . . *He breaks off, one senses his suppressed crying . . .* although friends always say that we are relatively generous parents. I would never make myself out to be someone who believes that he must make his children toe the line at any cost. Quite the contrary!
   Pause.
   Something else occurs to me with respect to this issue of "closeness":
   Low tone of voice, hearing this tape, I suddenly experience shame in the expectation of the patient's next statements.
   I recently threw my sweater at G. (a female therapist with whom he was participating in a seminar on *Körpertherapie*) and said, "Get lost!!" as she came up to me in a friendly manner. I was in a panic.
   Pause.
   If you were to come toward me now, it would also be too close for me. I'm quite happy that you are staying over there. (He laughs. My lying down naturally arouses both desires and fears. Because I have changed the setting immensely by lying down, fears also arise that I could approach him in an "uncontrolled" manner, as his father had done. A few weeks later, he reports that his father always wanted to kiss him on the mouth when greeting him or leaving him, while he himself turned away in disgust.)

T: It would be conceivable that a coming closer together could take place through a reversal of roles. I could imagine that I lie over there as sick as I feel right now and you sit next to me. In this way, you can measure out a closeness in doses. . . . You mentioned before that you never saw your father lying tired on the floor. When one extends this situation in a fantasy, where your father is exhausted or has a fever, then it would be imaginable that a guarded closeness or a reversal of care could take place. Were your parents ever sick? (He takes in the image of caring for a sick father with a sense of longing and for a long time.)

P: I never saw my father in bed!

T: Then you can never do anything for him and never experience him as weak or in need of help.

P: My mother was in the hospital once, but beyond that, she has always been a get-up-and-go type of person. . . . If I would like to have more contact with her, I would have to chase after her, because she is constantly on the move. I felt more of a desire to care for my father. I noticed that he reacted to attacks very sensitively and then withdrew inside himself.

T: Verbal attacks from you?

P: Yes, though only during puberty. I let it go later; my attitude was quite gentle after that. After that, I had more sympathy for him.
   Pause.
   Right now, I have two images of him that confuse me and are muddled together. On the one hand, my father was never sick, never lying on the floor as you are doing now. There was a friendly, benevolent atmosphere that functioned according to the motto, "I won't do anything to you if you don't do anything to me." Even when I came home at five o'clock in the morning, he never asked where I was. He only asked, "Was it nice?" But I felt this question to be more "inharmonious." (It sounds more like "forced.") This is one image. In the other one, I see my father dressed entirely in black—like a Rocker—coming out of the closet. (Pause, full of thoughts, or more specifically, full of images. It is possible that the patient is returning to a question I asked earlier: What was your parents' blueprint for their lives directly before or in the first five years of National Socialism?)
   I think he was the first in his area to drive a BMW 500 before the war. Later, he always carried around a picture of this motorcycle in his vest pocket just as he would to remember another person (or a lost identity, I add to myself). In such a situation, another type of power is at work (he means, presumably, a controlled, athletic power). On one level, he was certainly not violent, but I also told you that he ruptured my brother's eardrum in anger while trying to slap his face. (Violent fantasies appear again and again in him. No wonder! He is often uncertain how much violence is in him, or how much violence the father perpetuated or experienced during his unknown, silenced years in the SS.)

T: It occurs to me here that through National Socialism and the war, the normal athletic violence of late adolescence was released into a collective psychopathic violence. If the war hadn't come, your father might have developed into an athletically inclined person with a thirst for adventure and traveling, and might have worked his way up a little in his profession. But then all standards were lost: one was allowed to trap, torment, deport, torture, shoot, colonize, enslave, hunt, spy upon, monitor other people. . . . Looking back at this, the picture of the BMW suddenly becomes suspicious. Looking back at this, the broken eardrum of your brother becomes a symptom. Who knows whether your father would ever have done these things without Hitler.

P: I don't think so. Before then, he also played trombone in the YMCA. My father was more a mother's boy. His brother, whose funeral my father didn't attend, was a deceitful person and also stole my father's motorcycle once. He had an illegitimate child my father didn't know about. My father would never have done such a thing. He is correct through and through and possesses fundamental Prussian virtues (!), which also have their positive sides.

Pause.

Someone once supposed that my first therapist had an NS history of her own. If this had been a matter of concern in those days, the problem would have been thematized much more in my first therapy, because she knew that my father was in the SS. But she never brought this up on her own.

T: I cannot imagine that this person had addressed or worked through this issue in her own analysis. Otherwise, she would have passed this on to you. My supposition is, many analysts internally conjoin with Freud via a transgression into a persecutory thought structure.

P: Your main thesis is that the fathers could not mourn or speak about their memories because they never had an object that could hold this?

T: Yes!

P: I am convinced that my father in fact never had anyone who understood him. Had he been able to speak about it . . .

(The thought he began dies out again here. . . . I look at the clock. We have only a few minutes left. A few months earlier, I read that it is important in specific forms of family therapy training to transfer insights gained through the sculpting of one's own family back onto one's family of origin and to ask at which points they might have needed therapy, as well as how therapy, with today's opportunities, could have affected them.)

I convey this to him. He appears to think about when therapy could have begun for his parents.

Long pause.

T: Can you briefly, before the end of the hour, tell what was important for you today? Or can you perhaps listen in on yourself and say what is still missing?

P: Perhaps it was really good that I didn't somehow . . . because the last sessions were concerned with my parents, with the diary . . . *strained, exhausted; listening to the tape evokes an atmosphere of heavy tiredness, as if the patient were about to fall asleep* . . . with my mother . . . (moans) . . . I liked this other scene where I wasn't under such pressure to work something out for myself.

Pause.

I would like to work once again on what sort of patients come to me or what sort I search out spontaneously. It has even occurred to me that they are in part depressed, silent persons or compulsive patients who have difficulties associated with shame. I probably have special capabilities in this area: my father was silent, my mother was silent. (quietly:) From early on, I had to adapt myself to such situations! But to see this: at which point I actually . . . (breaks off, moans) . . . assume such a liveliness . . . for others . . . it is simply too exhausting . . . it was too difficult. . . . This is certainly the issue that has occupied me this week. Because I worked so much, I noticed this especially. This is naturally always a difficult profession, but that it . . . *very low voice, breaks off, strained atmosphere* . . . comes through so much! I don't play enough; inside myself as well. Sometimes I probably identify too much with some patients. (He senses how much his professional attitude is determined by the shadows of National Socialism.)

T: It has helped me a great deal when I have provided patients who are somewhat awkward with stage directions in the beginning or when I have helped organize a "stage" with them. I cannot do it differently today. This is an important subject: when do I work with the transference, when do I enter once again into a scene through role-playing? I cannot continuously endure a tortuous transference. One can use both to avoid something. One can use both as a defense.

End of the hour.

ADDITIONAL COMMENTS

The above is a much shortened account of a "pedagogical" explanation with the goal of making it easier for him to shape a transition to a "staging" with some patients, from which he can carefully begin to experiment. For, when he collects such patients, it must be tremendously exhausting to sense the "demonic" instances and persons only in the transference, or to sense them only as a paralysis that is itself a last protection against a threatening transference or countertransference. The end of the hour (after the therapeutic work of a double session) was sustained by me adding to our solidarity through research practices, as well as by collegial support.

His exhaustion is also connected to his role as "someone who revives" partially numb patients. In either of these roles—through reparation to the parents or through the attempt to successfully continue their failed endeavors—one can slave away until one is exhausted. The patients' slow progress, or their thankfulness, confirms a charted course and gives them the unconscious signal: You can still do it! To do this, one works in part in the present; one works in part with parentified children's roles, especially when sorrow, worry, numbness, or resigned silence—which also burdened the parents—play a role.

THE TRIP TO SACHSENHAUSEN

A few weeks after the previous session, the same patient, F.

P: I was in Halle at my cousin's. She has cancer. There is nothing more they can do, because she went to the doctor much too late. Her husband didn't know anything about this. This is also an example of how unconnected my family is. She is the daughter of my father's brother, whose funeral my father didn't attend. You remember: the brother doesn't attend his own brother's funeral! So much fear of feelings. It suddenly occurred to me how reticent, how unconnected, how sunken in silence, this whole clan is. Just like my father and his brother.

In addition, I absolutely wanted to go to Sachsenhausen because there was an exhibition at the time about the camp. I wanted to go to Sachsenhausen because I knew that my father was there in the orderly room of the sick bay from 1939 to 1941, as a member of the SS. I wanted to see it for myself and . . . *Patient suddenly breaks off, sobs convulsively, voice dies away.*

I don't know why I have to cry right now (cries spasmodically). I have been in such a good mood over the last few days.

T: This is not a contradiction. A tunnel into your past suddenly opens up when you come here.

P: I was more disappointed (in a crying voice, sobs, breathes deeply).

It was pouring down rain as I was traveling there. I went there with my cousin's husband.

Voice is now somewhat steadier, but the patient still seems very fragile.

I was actually more distanced and interested there, just as in a museum. I naturally thought that many more buildings would be standing. There was an information center, coal-burning stoves, yellowed display books . . . *During this description, the patient seems to calm down a little, his voice takes on an almost normal tone.* I wanted to buy a book about the history of the concentration camp and was stunned that there weren't any. My brother-in-law's son had told me that they used to perform ceremonies initiating young people into adulthood at one time in the concentration camp. This was also a special place for antifascist fighting for the GDR. I was stunned, anyway, and I don't know where these tears are coming from now. (He cries.) I thought to myself, something like this can't be. If I were the director of such an exhibit, I would have first of all published a book of everything that happened there. Just the facts, nothing else. I simply cannot imagine that this hasn't happened. At least reports from inmates . . . but there isn't any documentation at all.

Patient seems to be calm at this moment.

There is a historian in Göttingen. I have to ask him where this archive is. I would like to visit the archive sometime in order to trace what my father actually did in the camp. . . .

When I was at the camp, I spoke to the gatewoman. She maintained that only two rows of the original barracks were still standing. One can hardly believe how shabby and small the rooms were where these terrible things happened. Mind you, Sachsenhausen was not an actual extermination camp. The gatewoman told me that the former sick bay was in these barracks. The section in which my father must have worked is still standing and . . . (Suddenly and unexpectedly the patient begins to cry again, silently.)

I wanted . . .

(He doesn't continue speaking, but sobs again convulsively and briefly.)

During the trip there, almost an hour away from his home, I thought, what could have gone through my father's head as he took this way in the morning?

(The patient attempts during the train journey to transport himself "into the head" and experiences of his father, to take in the same sensory impressions, because he knows absolutely nothing about his father from this time. His voice sounds calm and collected.)

T: Where is the concentration camp located?

P: North of Berlin. Thirty kilometers away from the city center. My father commuted from Halle then.

Long pause.

We have to have something to do with this (unclear whether he means "both he and I" in our work together, or his family, or the members of the second generation), because I am crying here. The visit with my terminally ill cousin at the clinic in Halle had already affected me a great deal. The prognosis is bad. She is going to die. I only learned about it fourteen days ago.

(The visit to the clinic resonates with an atmosphere of cancer, death, and extermination, because they are silenced, underground, uncanny processes as well.)

In 1970, I traveled to Halle especially to meet my cousins. For my mother, my father's relations were always a taboo. I didn't notice this earlier, though. The wife of my uncle apparently stole something from my mother long ago—some small offense or other that was then carried on for decades. I went to Halle at that time in order to meet them. I like my cousins, too. As I was with my sick cousin, I thought, this just cannot be true, that she feels symptoms and doesn't ask me, a doctor, for advice. This probably shook me a great deal because I suspect that my father and mother could have done the very same thing: keep silent about something deadly! My cousin has already had a half-year of chemotherapy and she never told me about this. Three quarters of a year ago she discovered a lump in her breast. I first heard of all this fourteen days ago from the nurse.

*Atmospherically, a shudder from so much disguise and hide-and-seek—
from his close relatives as well as from himself.*

T: Let's go back to the feelings of pain and sorrow; they are valuable and
important. You seem, sometimes, so indignant when these come over
you. (*P. laughs, half relieved and half pained.*)

You said that you traveled his route. I'm wondering how you felt
there.

Long, quiet pause.

P: It was as if (cries suddenly) I could read in the trees what he did. (A
profound attempt at merging; as with a lover along whose path one
walks in order to feel something from her soul.)

*With a crying voice, swallows, is interrupted again and again by crying,
breathes heavily, sobs.*

I need a tissue. (Goes out of the room to get a tissue out of his
rucksack, even though there are some lying next to my chair.)

I wanted to find some sort of trace and this is . . . (begins to cry
silently again, sighs.)

Somehow it is really . . .

Coughs, sounds as if he needs to throw up.

It is as if he never returned again after '45, although he was still
there till a year and a half ago and I gave speeches on his birthdays. (He
senses the extent to which there exists an unknown, lost part of his
father.) I was just reading your book, *Der Erlöser* (The savior). And you
ask this patient what you would have to say in order for you to be, for a
moment, an ideal father for him. I apparently had a momentary debilitation with this sentence (laughs a little) and had to read it about five
times. The sentence is perhaps a little complex, but this is no reason
why I should be slow in catching on. I thought then of what I would
really want from my ideal father.

There is somehow . . .

*He pauses, breathes very deeply, sobs once, then a loud scream appears to
want to come out, which he suppresses however.*

T: Allow a sound to come out, too. These are almost sounds of panic, or
cries of pain, that I believe I hear. Screams perhaps, or a type of high-
pitched crying.

(Patient sobs loudly and convulsively, breathing and crying mix together. Yells, full of despairing rage:)

P: That you would talk to me for once!

(He cries again, but no longer silently as in the beginning; he shudders from crying. Though it seems he wants to calm himself as quickly as possible, he cries for a long time.) I don't want to hear anything about your past! (He wants to say: Don't be afraid. I won't dig up your guilt!) But you should talk to me for once: what affects you, what you think about me, what makes you happy. I never heard anything that came from inside of you.

He no longer sounds enraged now, rather resigned and sad.

I always had to guess what you . . .

He sighs, it sounds as if he feels sick, one senses suppressed crying in his voice.

Such simple things, that you were happy that I found my wife, that you thought she was nice. I heard nothing from you. . . . No wonder you also never kept a diary. . . . It also just occurred to me that my mother still hasn't given me her diary. She kept one. Keeps it in a safe (another "radioactive" archive) and wanted to give it to me. First she says yes, then she says no, like bait. I go back and forth and think, just kiss my ass and keep what you wrote. If I have to work so much in order to get something, then she should just forget it. I notice that there is also anger there, whereby I am, or rather was, able to express this more easily to my mother. Meanwhile, she has gotten old.

He breathes very hard. Speaking seems to tire him out.

But he never really said anything. You will ask me, "Why didn't he talk then?" That is exactly how these fathers were! He would sometimes say what the weather would be like, that there could be black ice. In any case, technical stuff or careful sentences. He was always very stubborn and didn't want to let me drive the car later on. But when my mother said that he should let me drive, because he himself could no longer drive so well. . . . (He breaks off. His voice becomes hoarser, sounding more strained, sad.)

Something just occurred to me. I wanted to say that I am a good driver. I have never injured anyone driving. People feel safe with me because I don't race (he says this as if advertising or swearing an oath to me, to the ideal father who is supposed to believe or acknowledge this). As I was driving for the second time with my parents, a tire blew out on me. We were lucky, however, and nothing happened to anyone. . . .

But I actually wanted to say something about this speechlessness: I'm driving and suddenly my father goes, "Brrr," as if I were a horse! I am speechless, but I should have said, tell me, are you crazy? Talk to me.

Secondly, it makes me angry that he doesn't seem to trust me, to trust that I can know without him when I am supposed to brake.
The voice of the patient sounds animated and excited.

T: A suggestion: you might tell him about your trip to Sachsenhausen and say: I searched for you in Sachsenhausen and on the trip there.
Long pause.
He takes a deep breath and moves the beanbag cushions audibly.

P: As I sat down on one of the comfortable cushions on the floor today, I thought that I wanted something soft instead of a chair. Sometimes, there is such a stiff side in me and I don't necessarily want to sit on my thinking throne today (this is what I call the chair across from me; the one which he has for a long time routinely used, the one in which his brooding, emotionally distant side more easily emerges).

I always experienced my father as being so stiff. My first emotion with respect to the old horse was that I could wring his neck or shake him so that something would fall out as from a machine, or from an "iron case" (of which Helen Eppstein speaks in *The Children of the Holocaust*). To my father: I think that I had to tie you down so that you would stay seated. You never really remain seated when someone wants to talk to you.
Pause.

I don't want to tie you down, but when I don't block your escape route, you run away immediately. *The voice of the patient sounds hoarse, his throat rattles.* One word and you were already gone. You have always done this (yells unexpectedly:) Do you hear me? You always ran out when I wanted to talk about something. As if you were deaf. No, you weren't deaf at all. You ran out immediately because you wanted to be deaf.
Pause.

(voice is calm again:) I see your face as it becomes totally moved and distraught. This paralyzes me. I can't look at you at all, or I will be silent. (He experiences how his screaming produces an effect on the imagined face of his father, senses immediately a reaction to take it easy on him, and senses his own looking away or the paralysis of all curiosity because it could cause injury.) *Voice becomes quieter, sounds extremely sad.*

Now I would have to give you your escape route, otherwise . . . Yeah, what would happen otherwise? I can already hear how mother screams, "Your father will have a heart attack. Leave him alone!" I always left you alone. My brother argued with you. I was always the good son, whom you also left two things in your will (breathes deeply, swallows).

You liked me more, but you liked me more because I . . . (breaks off, takes a loud breath, one senses suppressed crying). . . because I was good!

Pause.

(still to his father:) Your eyes just appeared to me now, how you look at me. So imploring, but sometimes I don't know at all where you are. (The reality of his imagining is astonishing: he really sees the face of his father for the first time, because earlier, in reality, he was not allowed to look his father in the face for very long.)

T: I'm wondering whether this sentence fits: "Now I was there where you were."

P: Yes, I was looking for traces. I was in Sachsenhausen and looked around for where you were. I notice that such a confusion is coming up in me now. When you were alive, you never said this to me at all. This would have been grasping at nothingness, and now, when I look for you in this place, you are dead. I am not saying that I couldn't go there because it was in the GDR. I also traveled to Halle to your family, but there as well you never said whether that made you happy. I always had to carry it around inside me, that I really wanted to travel with you one time to Halle, and that I wanted you to show me everything. I always wandered around lost in confusion. I asked myself, what did Dad do here?

(voice changes, sounds cracked)

Pause.

(yelling:) You never said you were happy, that you thought it was nice that I traveled to Halle, that I followed your footsteps. (This generation often could not experience its children's searches for it as love, but rather as a search for or a digging up of the repository of a threatening past. The parents did not want to be "found" or recognized at all.) The first thing I did after my exams was to travel to Halle. It was an entirely conscious decision. I also told you, "I want to go to where you come from. I want to learn about it." (This love frightens the father, but naturally he cannot say this.) I still see you exactly as you were when you returned from the war and prison. I always had sympathy for you because you seemed to me so lost in this maternal family. Everything was completely strange to you. You seemed to me so lost. Drenched in sweat, you stood at the kitchen table and mother said that this was water soup from Russia. I didn't know what water soup was at all, but you were so quiet and distraught.

The voice of the patient is full of sorrow and sympathy.

Pause.

I just thought that this closeness that I have with you now never would have been possible in reality. You had already had one heart attack. You could never bear to hear me speaking so intimately with you. That would have been unthinkable. What would have happened?

(After a very long pause, the patient breathes deeply, as if he wants to shake off an overwhelming burden.)

I look at this chair and know that I never could have spoken to you like this. You would leave. Closeness and talking would be unbearable.

Suddenly, he begins to cry again. Initially it is not recognizable as crying. It sounds very suppressed and "interior."

I really have to sit down now.

End of the first hour.

ADDITIONAL COMMENTS

After fifty years, "archives" become the guarantors of reality. They are silent witnesses. What can no longer personally be obtained still holds a place in reality in the archive. Double meaning: archive of the unconscious and archive as a collection of records. In the unconscious: lost or burnt archives, taboo zones. The parents' psychic-emotional archives were sealed. Thus, the real archives take on an excessive meaning and force of attraction.

It is as if F. would like to dig into the unknown identity of his father. To first calm him, he assures his father that this does not concern his "past." From the consciousness of the adult son, who is trained to take it easy on his father, comes another message. This message is different from the son's longing—now becoming a conscious longing—for his father's stories. Different still is the longing for "vision" that arises out of the deep unconscious. Sorrow, longing, and the feeling of emptiness are so strong that the question of guilt seems for the moment to remain in the background.

THE DEMONIC NATURE OF
SILENCE AND SPEAKING

This session follows the previous one after a ten-minute pause. Right from the beginning, I notice an especially sad expression, one which I cannot immediately name, yet which I soon address.

T: One could call what I see in your face grief. (The patient feels acknowledged, as well as slightly embarrassed—it occurs to him that earlier I often said his face could "fall apart" from one moment to the next. He makes a movement toward me, perhaps through a gesture of encouragement on my side, or, better still, through an invitation on my part.)

P: I also needed to come closer to you. Now, I am throwing the cushion (on which he is sitting) at your feet so that I can at least hug you a little. (He lies down on the floor, wraps his arms around the cushion as if it were my chest, and speaks:) I still have to look away (so that merging and emotion do not become too great). *He breathes spasmodically. It sounds almost like sobbing.*

T: Your ideal father would have spoken with you again and again, saying something like, we would have thought over together how much of the past I could endure and how much of the past you could endure. We would have tried to find that out together.

P: That would have been so nice. . . . *low voice, sounds extremely resigned and melancholy.*
    I didn't want to know everything, but I could have learned where your dignity is and how I should respect it, and what you have the right not to tell me much about. I understand it, too, when Mom says that you were impotent. (A typical example of the son being drawn in by the mother to make him her partner in sorrow, even in very intimate questions, a fate of many especially during and after the war.) Then I realize that I really don't want to know about this at all. Because then this doesn't concern closeness either, rather it is more a come-on from her. I think that I have difficulty with boundaries . . .

T: I hear this sentence becoming discernible in me as you could have spoken it to your father: I will never know the largest part of you. . . . *Patient breathes with difficulty, sometimes a sob breaks through, silent crying again, very long pause in the conversation.*

P: This probably makes me so sad because I was still a child and wasn't able to feel that at all in those days. *The patient suppresses crying with difficulty; he becomes somewhat stronger with the next sentence.*
    My brother spoke only with my mother after he fractured the base of his skull (a fall down the stairs). She also studied with him then—he was a replacement for her husband—and said, "We belong together."

(speaks to me again while holding the beanbag cushion:) My tears show that I did long for that (for a supportive closeness to his father). He was very speechless. (directed toward his father:) You have become for me the embodiment of someone who creates crossword puzzles. I can't do crossword puzzles!

I noticed right now that I just spontaneously did something, which my handicapped younger brother always did. Whenever he is sitting somewhere, he always does this (the patient demonstrates the movement: a kind of self-stimulation of his face, caressing at first, then appearing more like he is causing himself pain). As if he would have felt something. *The patient's voice begins to tremble; suppressed crying becomes perceptible.*

He never does this . . . (again a movement: reaching out for a touch from the person sitting across).

T: I have a strange thought. It is meant symbolically: whether he (the father) might have implanted evil in your handicapped brother. Now you can sense for yourself whether this thought changes anything in you and how. . . . Can I say something else about myself? I once wrote a fictitious letter to my father, in which I said, "Perhaps you were only potent with Adolf Hitler behind you." And the thought, "I am making children for him," had allowed my father to cross the threshold of his sexuality. It is in this manner that I now have fantasies about your father, that there are energies, good and demonic, which are moved back and forth.

The patient stutters, makes an expression of being somewhat overtaxed.

P: I notice that I become confused when I think a little further. (directed toward his father:) It was a strong feeling, that . . . (begins to cry, screams) to really be able to tell you, that I also have difficulty with my (handicapped) brother, not only with him (he suddenly begins to narrate; the father's confrontation with direct rage, because of K., still seems too threatening. To his father again, however:) That it is also terrible . . . (he cries, sobs, coughs break out of him in an almost explosive manner) never to be able to speak with my brother. For him, my father, it was also so terrible that he was around. (A National Socialist and SS man, and a child, or better still, a piece of "life unworthy of living in the family," one who would have belonged in a euthanasia program, a disgrace, one who must absolutely be hidden, as his mother hid him from the outside her entire life.) This ideology . . . that mother didn't take K. to the funeral, . . . didn't even mention his name on the obituary announcement . . . *The patient seems confused, distraught, flooded with memories; parts of his sentence are almost incomprehensible; he speaks in a very high, tear-swollen voice.*

Evil may appear as good, when everyone believes it, as in the Third Reich. But everything disabled was evil. I told you (he means the therapist) my mother travels to see my brother at the home, yet she says, "It would be so terrible if my husband were paralyzed like that. For heaven's sake, I wouldn't want to have that." I then think that this simply cannot be true! This also shows how damaged she must feel, that she cannot accept this at all and instead travels to South America for vacation just like that, for four weeks!

The patient sobs.

Pause.

I don't want to caress myself like my brother in his world so devoid of relationships. I would rather hold onto you. (Clings tighter to the cushion.) It is all so dead. . . . What makes me so sad now is the fact that, from the outside, we were such an ideal family and she was such a good mother. This mother with her ideology: "I only buy butter, even if we only have a little money, because my son shouldn't eat margarine." (Laughs.) But with everything I received emotionally, I always had the feeling that I had to pay it back. It occurs to me again now, as an example, that to this day my brother still doesn't talk. My father doesn't talk. My mother talks a great deal, a hideous amount, yet basically she doesn't say anything, either. At least she kept a diary. But there as well, I was the one who bought beautifully bound books at the Christmas market and then wrote both parents at Christmas telling them how I experienced them, what I valued in them, what was difficult, and so on. I tried to bring words into the family! Both were happy. It also became quite clear to me that if I didn't do this, then my mother wouldn't do it either, despite her talk. She would rather lie in the sun and think about nothing. Well, she did in fact write a diary about the war years, and even wanted to give it to me, yet she doesn't give it to me. I am slowly getting tired of asking again and again. . . .

Pause.

T: I am wondering whether your wife couldn't do this. The next time, when she calls your mother, she could simply say, "You promised then to give your son your diary. I think it would be nice for him if you would do this." You can ask her whether she could imagine doing this.

P: I could really imagine that she would do this.

T: And you say, "Kiss my ass." (P. laughs.)

P: Before I say kiss my ass, it would be better to actually be able to read it (laughs).

T: Certainly. And when your wife asks, then it will become clear whether she is going to give it to you or not. Only, so that you don't feel the insult as such. It really isn't as insulting for your wife when she asks and then doesn't receive it. That's how I imagined it, anyway.
   Pause.

P: I notice right now that I am still stunned about what is coming up today, although I feel quite . . .

T: *friendly, ironically:* Even though you were just in the camp at Sachsenhausen! (Both laugh.)

P: Subjectively, I have the feeling that I feel quite good and am not so needy. This is really the craziest: that they are really two different worlds. If I were outside right now, I probably would have talked quite normally about everything.
   Pause, which feels like he is resting.
   It occurs to me that I also had such a strange feeling after the last hour. I could have almost cried a little.
   Voice becomes quieter. The patient doesn't cry, yet seems to be deeply stirred by the memory.
   I just thought how nice it actually is when it isn't so hectic. I notice in myself how thin the line is between where I start to investigate and where I start to fight. At the same time, there is this side of me that has no desire to fight at all. As I was leaving the last time, I only thought, "Oh God, how lethargic and paralyzed I was." You had said it had appeared to you as balanced, but I seemed to myself a passive, regressive infant who had said very little. As if I had to sink into the ground and apologize that I had leaned against you with closed eyes and wasn't working hard. It was somehow a strange feeling, very mixed. And today it isn't quite like that. Last time, there were still blocked feelings. I sensed this very clearly. As if it were still somehow too close. It is difficult to describe.
   (I had invited him in the session two weeks before to lay his head on me, which he gladly did, in spite of an equally noticeable hesitation, as if this action were either "too much" or not allowed.)

T: After today's session, one could imagine that there were still bound-aries associated with loyalties impeding this closeness with me: a longing for your father and an unthematized bond or hope which still excludes closeness with me. This is naturally evoked by the offer of closeness here. Now you have recovered a piece of a "search-for-nearness" to him. I mean that your inhibition against bodily closeness to me should not only be seen as a defense, but also as a measure of loyalty to the person who could not give it to you. A part of you is still bound to the longing for him and experiences this as a betrayal when you recover it from me.

P: I understand your train of thought, only it could also have been exactly the opposite. During the last time, I didn't know that I was traveling to Sachsenhausen. I wasn't in such a conflict of loyalty like today, because I really only tried to get close to you.

Pause.

After today's session though, I would say that it has something to do with my talking to him. So, both are there. Perhaps this was connected to your provocation in the last hour. You said, "You are not here for therapy anyway!" (I meant, the breaking through of a longing for close-ness belonged exactly here, even though he defended against this.) Per-haps because of your provocation, I skipped over a feeling, even though I still initially hesitated. After that, the desire was also naturally present.

I imagine that I must first have encountered him—my father—through speech as well, before I allowed myself a physical closeness to you; that the circumstances in my family will become even clearer, in spite of the fact that we were a family outrageously bound together. . . . Especially as far as any overt sexuality was concerned, a considerable strictness dominated. I was always afraid when I masturbated that my mother would look to see if spots were visible. On a fantasy level, my mother was certainly very present. This latent sexualization often occurs in families when nothing is going on anymore between the parents. I think that this experience, this fear of sexualization, often played a role when I said, "Not too close." The last hour contained precisely these overtones as well. Naturally there is closeness when I sleep with my wife. One doesn't want to talk a lot then. (His father and his mother had sexualized closeness to him.)

What is becoming clear to me is my longing for symbiosis, for a profound closeness, where words are no longer necessary. (Contains the overtones: with this, sexuality is almost disturbing or is only a bridge to symbiosis, is considerably confusing, yet still hides the desire for merging, which is threatening without sexuality, because it is extremely regressive.)

This is basically an extension of an ideal fantasy: at home, no one had talked, but you had this dream: "bodily very close and very profound." With this, it is clear to me that talking was neglected in the family. (By speaking so much about closeness, he now seems to lose the closeness again. Because of this, I ask:)

T: Would it be all right if you came a little nearer? Or is it okay like it is? From my side, my hand could reach out to you. In any case, it is already moving. (I sense he longs to touch my hand, which is becoming warm.) This doesn't mean that it has to be today. But it is a next step that may be prepared for.

Pause.

P: This is good enough for the moment.

Pause.

I'm asking myself whether that is true—"this is good enough"—or whether I am being too modest. I spontaneously said just now that it was enough for me, because I was still involved in my fantasies. Everything that you said earlier—"talk about the past and see at the same time what you want to say"—is a dialogue, and this is exactly what I never experienced with my father. (This unexpected linguistic closeness activates a longing for touch as well as a defense.)

I told you that he played trombone, piano, and violin. But I first learned about this only ten years before his death. Through my entire youth, I didn't know this at all. It wasn't until I bought a violin after a concert that my father mentioned it for the first time.

(So much shame probably arises in the father about himself that he cannot even once effect or allow himself an identification with his son through the pleasure of an instrument.) But I'm telling this to you now in order to illustrate how little my father talked. I talk about him as if he were actually a handicapped person! At the same time, he wasn't externally handicapped at all.

Pause.

(He is moved by his father's muteness as well as by its preserved and silenced contents; he then looks at me:)

I am still thinking about the offer of your hand.

The patient breathes deeply, it is as if he has to muster his courage. While listening, an impression arises, through the particular way in which he takes a breath, that something long held secret or uncomfortable for the patient will be brought out.

What comes to me right now is the thought that I have to have a clean hand when I give you my hand. Just like the saying, "Wash your hands first." In my mind, I know that this is nonsense. I also feel the desire not to want to be so grabby and pushy. Perhaps all this is connected. The first spontaneous idea that occurs to me is a thought about the institution in which my brother was placed and where he still is. On the one hand, I did have sympathy for him, but on the other, there were other patients who perpetually grabbed on to you, greedy, grabby. (In other sessions, he expressed again and again that he felt both pestered and fascinated by the inhabitants' distanceless searches for closeness. In his unconscious, closeness, handicap, and impurity seem to mix, an NS thought that is not extended here but rather simply triggers a bit of shame. It is possible, however, that the mother's mania for cleanliness is not only shaped by anal, instinctual conflicts but also by the racial-biological "impurity" of one of her children.)

Then, my parents occur to me again. For example, my mother used to soap me down when I was young. I think that this holding onto me plays a large role here. (Here, cleanliness coincides with Oedipal bonds and eroticization.) *Patient takes a deep breath, seems relieved to have discovered and articulated this connection.*

(The topic of improper eroticization has already played a role in this session, in the mother's remarks about the father's impotency and in her interest in the sexuality of the pubescent boy. Also, with the following description of the father, the collapsing of closeness and sexuality becomes noticeable once again.)

When I think about it, it becomes clear to me how much I identify with my parents, or rather how much I think that I could be like them. I was always afraid when greeting my father; he never let go of me. Besides this, he always wanted to kiss me on the mouth and laughed when I turned my head away. Even if I were dying, I wouldn't have managed to say that I didn't want a kiss on the mouth. Such a simple sentence! (From his father as well as his mother emanates an open or latent overstimulation. The father is not conscious of this excessive intimacy, this search for comfort through kissing. Not even through the son's repeated turning away does he sense its impropriety; he repeats the attempt again and again.)

T: Therefore, one can say that he also suffered from this distance and that you would have used this, in order to make him talk to you and see you, and touch you. But he eroticized this. It is as if one were seeking a false bridge, a false intimacy.

Pause.

This is perhaps a strange sentence, but you could say to him: My mouth is sealed, but . . . also from longing. (With this extremely condensed sentence, I attempt an explanation that the son could give his father: through the son's desire to be seen in his longing for the father, which in turn makes the mouth "thin-lipped, his turning away is made understandable to the father." The real father appears like a fool who, through his coarse eroticization, exterminates, extinguishes, and makes unanswerable undreamed-of longings.)

P: A journal entry from 1967 just spontaneously occurred to me. In one place, I wrote that I long for a longing. (An almost poetically condensed sentence: longing is already a clear feeling that he seldom has in connection to his father, and so it remains a longing for longing; real feelings are unrecognizable, yet may be enjoyed in the form of a diffuse *Weltschmerz.*) In addition, I mention omnipotent fantasies in which I stretch to the horizon and want to grasp for him. I am shaken when I read this today (the omnipotence of a longing that stretches to the horizon). On the one hand, it is becoming clear to me how torn I was internally, while from the outside, I was the beloved F. I had many friends, both male and female. Even in my feelings about life, I felt quite happy. I never would have had the idea to go to therapy. I first noticed this through my work in the drug clinic, that one can use something like this. (Laughs.) To me, only others were sick and in need.

I have to think about it right now—because I had to cry earlier— that in my very first therapy, I hardly ever cried. You see in fact how thick the armor was that I had to train myself to have with my family. And how this longing is connected to the sealed mouths in our family.

T: Something just occurred to me with respect to your mother's perpetual talking, which is intended to obscure (laughs): Her bill overflows. There are really such things as animals with bills you know—duckbilled platypuses. (Patient laughs as well. Then, after a pause, he returns from his memory to the actual situation. Later, it becomes clear that the mother's continuous talking is meant to drown out the past.)

P: This here is an atmosphere that I really enjoy: we sit together and talk. Now and then, there is a pause. I never had anything like this at home. When my mother comes, she opens up the door and begins talking. You can't imagine this at all. (Laughs.) It is like she is wound up. The children laugh and say, "Grandma, take a breath now." She stops briefly, but almost immediately it continues. Through this, you see how much this incredible fear of emptiness has engulfed her. I could never manage this myself, to ramble on about something.

(In spite of this actually serious subject, the patient now seems to have cheered up. We tacitly remember a scene in which he repeatedly spoke about his mother's "deafening" stream of words. I suggested to him that he demonstrate this to me once. He entangles himself in her grammar and cannot connect this continuous babble with his own grammatical needs. For this reason, I suggest that he imitate only her "music," without words. He hesitates, shy, almost fearful, full of shame. But then he lets go, like a gobbling turkey, unbroken, for minutes at a time, cracked; it is like the regurgitation of a bad feeding of sound, taken in through the ears for years. As he calms down, he is exhausted and emptied out in a positive way.)

If someone were to ask her at what point she actually began a sentence, she wouldn't know herself. She always complained that my father didn't say anything, but he could never get a word in anyway. . . . (in a changed voice:) I have determined that this fits together: her perpetual talking and his silence.

In the last half of the hour, the patient seemed substantially calmer and collected again. Even subjects that were a burden to him did not lead to such intense reactions (crying, screaming) as in the previous hour. Perhaps, however, this ostensible stabilization is an expression of his exhaustion or his fear of new and possibly even more stirring feelings.

Listening to this tape, it gradually becomes clear that the patient shows, in moments when he does not appear to be excited, clear signs of an affected impression; for example, the occurrence of almost exhibitionistic coughs and a sudden plugging up of his nose. In this hour, the strong desire for touch— which in the previous hour did not appear at all—is striking.

ADDITIONAL COMMENTS

There is presumably a connection between the amount of child abuse— extending from after the war to today—and National Socialism, the war, captivity, delayed returning home from the war, and destroyed marriages. A possible objection: The subject of abuse comes from America. After all, there was World War II, the Korean War, the Vietnam War; three massive wars with fathers distant for years and destroyed by war. Important is: the persistent silence of the fathers (like the mothers in other families) leads to an unconscious magnification of them, an actual demonization of their person. The unsaid, the unknown, and the silenced awake unconscious mythic fantasies. This also seems to be the place for the unconscious appropriation of characteristics that were never a subject of conversation. The subject of violence is not gone when it is kept silent; it merely goes underground, becomes cryptic, gets covered up, perhaps, as in F.'s case, by a pronounced cultivation of "niceness." From there, there is perhaps even a parallel to Springer's "be nice to each other" as a German postwar motto.

The German-Jewish Hyphen:
Conjunct, Disjunct or Adjunct?

Harry Brod

In the 1946 film *The Stranger* Edward G. Robinson plays a federal agent on the trail of a fugitive Nazi war criminal in hiding.[1] He tracks the criminal, played by Orson Welles, to a small New England town. There, Welles eventually reveals himself to be the Nazi by a remark he makes over the dinner table at the home of the family of his new bride, played by Loretta Young. When Welles's new brother-in-law mentions Karl Marx in order to make a point about the German character, Welles argues against the point, saying: "Marx wasn't a German. Marx was a Jew." Only when he recalls the conversation later does it occur to Robinson that only a Nazi would deny that someone was German simply because he was Jewish.

"Ay, there's the rub," as Hamlet says. One wishes that Robinson's deduction were entirely accurate. The Holocaust has left scars on all of us, however, and one of those scars is the partial victory attained by the Nazis in their effect on our collective consciousness of the relationships between German and Jewish identities. For in our post-Holocaust world it does produce an ever so slight hesitation, a questioning pause, when one claims both a German and a Jewish identity. The two designations are now on opposite sides of a great divide, isolated from each other by the seemingly unbridgeable gap that separates the perpetrators from the victims.

There has, therefore, never really been a German-Jewish identity in the sense in which we now understand hyphenated identities, as in, for example, Italian-American or African-American identities. In part, this is because the phenomena of hyphenated identities are products of postwar consciousness. This is also because, as I have argued above, the Holocaust places "German" and "Jewish" on opposing sides of a disjunction, and thus prevents the hyphen in "German-Jewish" from signaling the kind of conjunction one would otherwise intend by such a hyphenated phrase. I am certainly aware that other hyphenated identities are also problematic. The facts of American slavery and racism render an "African-American" identity problematic in some ways similar to the problems created by the Holocaust and anti-Semitism for a "German-Jewish" identity. But in the disjunction between "German" and "Jewish" there exists more than a failure of two cultures to conjoin. Rather, one faces two cultures torn asunder, two cultures that were once conjoined in significant symbiosis. The failure of the hyphen to connect the two sides signals tragedy from within in addition to catastrophe from without.[2]

Because the Holocaust marks a temporal divide in any consideration of German and Jewish identities, the German-Jewish hyphen thus necessarily invokes the wartime hyphen, the one we use to mark off pre- from post-Holocaust consciousness. The hyphen thus signals a temporal as well as a cultural gap. I recall how I was hyperconscious of this divide when I spent the academic year 1976–1977 in Germany as a graduate student on a grant to study at the Hegel archives in Bochum. I immediately categorized the people I saw in reference to their age. The question in my mind was always: "Are you someone about whom I need to wonder, 'Where were you then?'" I always wanted to know, needed to know, as if my personal safety still depended on it. Indeed, my emotional safety did. I acutely remember how self-conscious I was when, as Passover approached, I was walking back to my apartment in Köln carrying under my arm a box of matzoh, a good-sized box with prominent Hebrew lettering. I would alternately search the faces of everyone I passed for any reaction from them, and then avoid looking at or being seen by anyone as much as I could.

I suppose I should at this point situate myself in this discussion. I am a child of temporary Holocaust survivors. By "temporary" I mean that though my parents both survived the war years, they died earlier than I believe they would have had they not had to endure those horrors. My mother died at age 49, and my father at 59, both of heart attacks. Thus, they survived the Holocaust, but only temporarily. In my view, the gruesome tally of Holocaust victims is not yet complete, for these events are still in living memory. Only when the last of those who survived those years has died, and we have made a judgment as to whether or not his or her life was shortened by the ordeal, will we know how many victims there were. For now, the ledger is still open.

I am also a Berliner. I was born in 1951 in what was the British sector of occupied Berlin, to stateless parents. My mother was a German Jew who survived the war in Berlin as a nurse at the Jewish hospital that functioned there throughout the war.[3] The hospital served those non-Aryans who, for one reason or another, were allowed to remain. It was also the headquarters for the "Reichsvereinigung der Juden in Deutschland," the official state Jewish organization under the Nazis. My father was a Polish Jew who made his way to Berlin with the advancing Soviet Army.[4] He met my mother in that hospital while recovering there from the amputation of his leg, and I was born in that same hospital. Both of them lost most of their families in the Holocaust. The depth of my mother's rejection of her German identity can be measured by her response when the presiding magistrate at her marriage to my father asked her whether she realized that by this act she was giving up her German citizenship. "Mit Vergnügen," she said. "With pleasure."

My parents and I emigrated to the U.S. when I was two years old. Perhaps not surprisingly, my relationship to the German language has always been ambiguous. I grew up bilingual in German and English, and was told I spoke English with a German accent that I lost only after I started school. German was the preferred language of the household, and when I knew two words for certain foods, one German and one English, it seemed to me as a child that the food's "real" name was the German word we used at home, and the English version was only a sort of front for public consumption. But despite my feeling "at home" in German, I also inherited my parents' antipathy for things German, so that I am never entirely comfortable using the language. And when I do use it I also have a sort of split linguistic ability—at the level of everyday use I function like a native speaker, but in any kind of intellectual discussion I lack necessary vocabulary and stumble over sentence structure.

My father and I returned to Berlin for the first time since our emigration when he came to visit me while I was studying in Germany in 1977. It was while watching my father's reactions to his surroundings during this visit that one aspect of the specifically gendered nature of Holocaust remembrance was vividly brought home to me. I watched him take notice of the militarized security guards at the airport, young men in German uniforms carrying machine guns, men of roughly the same age my father and the soldiers he faced had been during the war. As I have written elsewhere:

My father's discomfort at being unarmed was so strong I could almost see his fingers twitching, so strong that I felt it too, feeling disarmed for the first time in my life. Though I have never carried a gun, I can still remember the world of difference between simply not having a gun, and being unarmed.[5]

I also made a gendered categorization of persons of a certain age when I was in Germany. While I wanted to know where everyone had been and what they had been doing, I experienced this need to know especially acutely whenever I saw men of that certain age. I pictured them in uniforms. I looked at their hands and wanted to know if they had held weapons and, if so, at whom they had pointed them. I fantasized about wearing a yellow star, so I could see their reactions, and respond to them. I found welling up within me a desire to refute, by my own aggressive and even violent (re)actions, the slander that we went "like lambs to the slaughter." I certainly experienced that slander as against "us," not just against "them," i.e., this is a calumny not just against the generation of the Holocaust but against subsequent generations as well. The text of the Hagadah, the book of the service for Passover, instructs Jews to tell the story of the liberation from Egypt (the Hebrew word for Egypt is "Mitzrayim," literally "a narrow place," and Jewish practice has traditionally interpreted this as referring not just to a specific land but also metaphorically to any place or condition of constriction or oppression) as a story of how "I" was liberated; thus, we are to see ourselves as members of that generation. For children of Holocaust survivors the admonition is unnecessary; the projective identification is bred in the bone.

I was made aware of this generational divide among German men in a different way in the 1980s when two men from the Berlin Men's Center came to one of the annual Men and Masculinity Conferences in the U.S., the principal annual gathering of the American profeminist men's movement. What struck them most about the gathering, they told me towards its end, was the presence of significant numbers of older men. In Germany, they said, such gatherings were almost exclusively made up of baby boomers. When I wondered what might account for the difference, they had a ready explanation. Those in the older generation who might have been sympathetic to these values had been systematically killed by the Nazis: leftists or progressives of all kinds, gays, Jews. That generation of men who would have now made up the older constituency of the movement was simply not there. In the U.S. profeminist men's movement, as in other progressive political movements, Jews make up a significant percentage of the membership, a percentage far beyond their proportionate presence in the general population. And at that time approximately half the membership of the profeminist men's movement would have identified themselves as gay or bisexual. As for the progressive ideological component of adherence to this movement, without reducing politics to psychology, it is nonetheless safe to say that for many men a rebellion against the perceived militarist values of their mainstream fathers played a significant role here in the United States as well as in Germany.

From a postwar perspective, the absence of that generation of men has for obvious reasons been experienced and theorized as the absence of the fathers. Of course, on the side of the victims the literal obliteration of that generation has meant a literal absence of children, of future Jewish generations that might have been. On the side of the perpetrators, we are speaking of a figurative rather than a literal absence, of a generation that grew up with a void of silence about crucial aspects of their fathers' lives.[6] This figurative absence is also present, but for different reasons, in the lives of the victims who survived. This is a silence, an absence, with which I grew up as well.

Since in patriarchal societies most parenting is mothering, fathers who are absent or silent because of particular circumstances in their lives are in one sense thereby compounding an already present father absence that is characteristic of patriarchal culture. In this sense their silence may make them even more imposing figures if it appears to be the silence of the brooding patriarch. Since patriarchal authority is typically exercised and communicated from on high and from afar, father absence in the sense of paternal physical or emotional distance from children does not necessarily diminish patriarchal authority. Indeed, such absence is often how this authority is maintained. But the Holocaust-induced silence of my father and others like him is not the silence of those who silence others, but the silence of those who have been silenced by others. It is a dictated rather than a dictatorial silence, one rooted not in power but in pain, and while the two silences may intertwine in complex and perhaps sometimes even inseparable and indistinguishable ways, they are nonetheless different. While the silence of the silencers translates into a voice of authority, the silence of the silenced leaves the next generation with a void rather than a voice. This vacuum is felt especially acutely by young men striving to inherit their fathers' patrimony.

My father's silence ran deep. In the eulogy I delivered at his funeral on September 15, 1981 (Elul 16, 5741 by the Jewish calendar), I said:

> Perhaps one reason I feel the need to speak is that my father left
> so much of his life unspoken of. Those of us who knew him
> best learned to measure the depth of the loss he felt for my

mother by how difficult he found it to speak of her these last ten years, and we learned to gauge the hardships he went through in his life by how rarely he spoke of them. But what is left undone in one life is left for others to complete, and the mitzvah [meritorious act] of speaking of my father's life should begin today.

Speaking of him even now raises the paradox faced by those who wish to connect to their fathers through these silences. The poet Adrienne Rich expressed the problem eloquently in her "Split at the Root: An Essay on Jewish Identity":

> It comes to me that in order to write this I have to be willing to do two things: I have to claim my father . . . and I have to break his silence, his taboos; in order to claim him I have in a sense to expose him.[7]

Many men as well as women have experienced this same sense of their fathers' silences as taboos of this kind, taboos felt all the more strongly for never having been expressly articulated, for in cases such as this silence speaks much more loudly than any words could possibly do. These taboos, in the tormenting double bind in which they leave the next generation suspended, cast filial loyalty as betrayal. The child's search for intimacy and connection is experienced by these fathers as trespass and intrusive encroachment. What the children intend as restorative acts of resuscitation and revitalization of the fathers appear to the fathers, tragically, as acts of parricide. That many of the works in which postwar children come to terms with their fathers are published so many years after the events discussed in them is at least partly explained by this phenomenon. In many cases only the deaths of the fathers, or at least their passing into an age in which they no longer appear so threatening to their children, have enabled the children to speak. Indeed, for some, the act of caring for an aging father marked a crucial turning point, as recorded in these lines, the first and last stanzas of Ted Hirschfield's poem "Aftermath" in his *German Requiem: Poems of the War and the Atonement of a Third Reich Child*:

> The aftermath was our beginning,
> The sons of disowned fathers —
> Our very language in disgrace.
>
> .   .   .   .

The aftermath was our beginning,
Until we learned to father
Fathers, and laid the sons to rest.[8]

I gained a new way of understanding my father's silence during my training session to be an interviewer for the Shoah Visual History Foundation, the project initiated by Steven Spielberg to videotape and archivally preserve oral testimonies of Holocaust survivors. During the training session the trainers played for prospective interviewers an interview with a survivor in Sydney, Australia. When asked whether all of these experiences still affect him on a daily basis, he responded, "I don't live here in Sydney. I live back there." While I would have expected to have felt saddened by someone's statement that he was psychologically absent from his own life in this way, I was surprised to find that I instead experienced this as an empowering statement. This was because when I had felt my parents' absences I had assumed that parts of them were simply gone. To hear now that these parts had not vanished into thin air and been obliterated but were really present elsewhere, "back there," gave me a more hopeful perspective. One is better able to recover and heal lost parts of oneself when one is dealing with the repression or erosion of memory rather than with its erasure, with the flight of parts of the self rather than with their death.

Studies on memory, and especially on the return of the repressed, have played a highly significant role in recent theorizings of German and other masculinities.[9] Psychoanalytic theory has been of particular use in understanding how memories are repressed rather than lost, and how they may return at unexpected moments and in unforeseen ways. Perhaps this helps to account for the influence of psychoanalysis in recent work on German masculinities, as is evident in several of the chapters in this volume. The recent German work on masculinity that has had the greatest impact on Anglo-American discourse on the subject has been Klaus Theweleit's *Male Fantasies*, a work thoroughly grounded in psychoanalysis, even though as a work of historical analysis it is not specifically in the psychoanalytic strain of memory work.[10] Given the long-term interplay of ideas across the Atlantic it is highly significant that the classic work in this vein by Alexander Mitscherlich, *Society without the Father*, was brought back into print in the U.S., after being out of print for a significant period, in an edition with a foreword by Robert Bly, who is probably the single most influential popular commentator on the masculine condition in the U.S.[11] Mitscherlich's investigation greatly influenced Bly's follow-up to his successful *Iron John*; *The Sibling Society* expounds the theme of a society suffering from the loss of the father.[12] And of course, a foundational text dealing with collective memory and responsibility specifically in the postwar German context but also more broadly, though it has come under criticism in more recent years, is Alexander and Margarete Mitscherlich's *The Inability to Mourn*.[13]

In English, to remember is literally to "re-member," to make that which is remembered be again part of something from which its membership had been lost, to reunite lost parts. We speak of the "members" of a culture or the body politic, or even the "members" of one's physical body. In German, memory is "Erinnerung," literally "internalization." To remember is to take back into oneself that which has been cast away from one, to reunite that which was rent asunder. In this sense, to re-member and recapture a German-Jewish identity is a foremost task of postwar consciousness.[14]

For theoretical tools to aid in this task we may look not just to psychoanalysis but also to certain elements of feminist thought.[15] Bridging the gap between the Jewish and the German aspects of German-Jewish identity requires a more nuanced and fluid understanding of both, indeed a more fluid understanding of the nature of identities in general than the absolutely polarized view I presented at the beginning of this chapter, in which the two sides of the hyphen are separated by an unbridgeable chasm. For much of contemporary feminism, identities are not fixed essences but rather mutable statuses, performances in flux. From this perspective, there is no need to define and hypostasize fixed essences of Germanness or Jewishness that then must be somehow brought together. Rather, German-Jewish identity, or identities, can be reforged and redefined as circumstances, in this case postwar circumstances, require. At any given moment we carry multiple identities, choosing from time to time to highlight or perform only a certain subset of them. Thus, to return to the problematic posed by the subtitle of this chapter, the way to decide whether "German" and "Jewish" should be essentially conjoined or essentially disjoined is to dissolve the essentialism assumed by the question, and to assert instead that Germanness and Jewishness are two identities among many others, identities perhaps rooted in gender or age or class or in other dimensions of our lives, that may be added to or subtracted from our personae at various times and in various circumstances. This would open the way to, among other things, more gender-nuanced conceptions of German-Jewish identity than we now have.

We should note, however, that not all forms of feminism are equally suitable for this reconstructive task. Some indeed share the essentialism or reductionism that continue to be the problem. For example, Jewish feminist scholar and pioneer Susannah Heschel has reported in "Configurations of Patriarchy, Judaism, and Nazism in German Feminist Thought" on a particular strain of German feminist thought that is very troubling from a Jewish perspective.[16] This perspective produces an argument that consists of a number of steps which, when considered individually may appear non-problematic, but when conjointly asserted end up blaming the victims for the Holocaust. One begins with the idea that Nazism is best understood as being simply an extreme version of patriarchy. This sort of monolithic reductionism is occasionally found in some versions of radical feminism, analogously to the way in which fascism was understood as being simply an extreme form of capitalism in some reductionist versions of Marxism. The problem with these theories is that they are overly simplistic. While it is true that Nazism is patriarchal and that fascism is capitalist, they are also more and other than that. They cannot be completely or even adequately explained by mono-causal theories. But taking as their starting point the analysis of Nazism as patriarchy, the theories Heschel examines then go on to see patriarchy as fundamentally having its origins in the overthrow of ancient Goddess worship and its replacement by masculine monotheism, a change that they and others erroneously regard as the fault of the Hebrew Bible. At this point one need only add one and one to come to the conclusion that since patriarchy is responsible for Nazism, which is responsible for the Holocaust, and since the Jews are responsible for patriarchy, the Jews are therefore responsible for the Holocaust. It is hard to think of a more paradigmatic case of blaming the victim. Such are the perils of oversimplified monolithic theories.

More adequate forms of feminist theory, especially in their influence on the profeminist men's movement, may also be useful in overcoming another conundrum.[17] The question of collective guilt or responsibility hangs heavily over German memory. The profeminist men's movement has had to come to terms with questions of collective responsibility for crimes against women. Theoretical and practical strategies have been developed for coming to terms with being a member of a group that has wronged another group. These strategies articulate how one may retain a sense of pride in those aspects of one's personal identity that stem from this group membership, without feeling inappropriate guilt or shame, while at the same time becoming effective in acknowledging the wrongdoing and taking remediating and preventive action with others of this group against that wrongdoing.[18]

We should be aware that, in addition to the guilt of the perpetrators there is what has in the psychological literature come to be called "survivor's guilt." This is sometimes felt as a sense of having undeservedly survived while others perished, or as a sense of shame that one did not do enough to resist. Given traditionally gendered expectations that men will be the protectors of and fighters for their families, these burdens often rest particularly heavily on the shoulders of Jewish men. One response among some Jewish men of the postwar generation has been to identify vicariously with and concomitantly overvalorize the heroism of the soldiers of the Israeli army, or to themselves adopt an overly aggressive or militaristic stand on such issues as Israeli policy toward the Palestinians. In any diasporic community, such as the American Jewish community, the temptation to attempt to create or validate one's own identity through vicarious identification with others who are perceived as more authentic representatives of one's history is particularly strong.[19] American Jewish identity tends to vacillate between the twin poles of what are seen as the tragedy of the Holocaust and redemption through the state of Israel. In one of the most perceptive visual representations of the Holocaust and Holocaust survivors, Art Spiegelman's *MAUS*, a novel in comic book form in which a son tells the story of his father's experiences during and after the Holocaust, the Jews of the Holocaust are drawn as mice, with the Germans as cats, and postwar American Jews are drawn with masks of mice on their faces.[20] The latter is a striking and scathing portrait of ersatz identity. In the United States, what has come to call itself a Jewish Renewal movement sees as one of its prime tasks the development of a more internally self-generated contemporary Jewish consciousness and practice.[21]

Nuanced discussions of how one can analyze moral agency under conditions of oppression that have emerged within feminist theory may serve as useful models for coming to terms with analogous German and Jewish issues. There are underexplored gendered dimensions of issues here ranging from interpersonal family dynamics to the complex international politics between Germany and Israel and even to the adoption of a revived modern Hebrew as a national Jewish language in place of Yiddish, now commonly associated both with the German persecutors and with the status of the persecuted as victims, experienced as a feminized position.[22]

Perhaps I should close by returning to the autobiographical writing in which I engaged earlier, but this time with an emphasis on the intellectual rather than emotional aspects. I alluded to my study of Hegel when discussing my time in Germany in 1977. This was part of writing my doctoral dissertation (and a subsequent book) on Hegel's political philosophy.[23] One of the results of having studied Hegel is my having developed an aversion to gratuitously describing something as "dialectical," an appellation I often find too loosely applied. But I find now that my consideration of the topic of German-Jewish postwar masculinity imposes the term on me. To work dialectically is to engage in both analysis and synthesis, to break something into its component parts and then reconstitute it so that the re-engaged parts yield a new organic whole that is not reducible to the sum of those parts. A consideration of hyphenated identity is to me necessarily a dialectical analysis, as the hyphen by its very nature both unites and separates what it simultaneously conjoins and disjoins. I have attempted here to follow some of the threads of the complex phenomenon of German-Jewish postwar masculinity, culling different aspects for analysis at different times while simultaneously paying attention to their ultimate inseparability. I wrote this essay in response to Roy Jerome's solicitation of my reflections on postwar German-Jewish masculinity. My thoughts inevitably led me to situate the question of German-Jewish postwar masculinity within larger questions regarding the Holocaust, German-Jewish identities in general, and some broader issues of masculinities, especially issues relating to fathers and sons. I hope these personal and theoretical reflections may help us to re-member that which was rent asunder.[24]

NOTES

1. *The Stranger*, International Pictures, Inc., 1946, dir. Orson Welles.

2. On the split consciousness of contemporary German Jews see *Strangers in Their Own Land: Young Jews in Germany and Austria Today*, Peter Sichrovsky, trans. Jean Steinberg (New York: Basic Books, 1986), originally published as *Wir wissen nicht was morgen wird, wir wissen wohl was gestern war: Junge Juden in Deutschland und Österreich* (We don't know what tomorrow will be, we know well what yesterday was: Young Jews in Germany and Austria) (Köln: Kiepenheuer & Witsch, 1985); *Jewish Voices, German Words: Growing Up Jewish in Post-war Germany and Austria*, ed. Elena Lappin, trans. Krishna Winston (New Haven, Conn.: Catbird Press, 1994); *Speaking Out: Jewish Voices From United Germany*, ed. Susan Stern (Chicago: edition q, 1995); *Jews in Germany after the Holocaust: Memory, Identity, and Jewish-German Relations*, Lynn Rapaport (Cambridge, Mass.: Cambridge University Press, 1997); *Jews in Today's German Culture*, Sander L. Gilman (Bloomington: Indiana University Press, 1995), *Germans and Jews Since the Holocaust: The Changing Situation in West Germany*, ed. Anson Rabinbach and Jack Zipes (New York: Holmes & Meier, 1986); *After the Holocaust: Rebuilding Jewish Lives in Post-war Germany*, Michael Brenner (Princeton, N.J.: Princeton University Press, 1997); and *Post-Mortem: The Jews in Germany Today*, Leo Katcher (New York: Delacorte

Press, 1968). For a recent brief treatment of the pre-war history of German Jews see *German Jews: A Dual Identity*, Paul Mendes-Flohr (New Haven, Conn.: Yale University Press, 1999).

3. See *Zerstörte Fortschritte: Das Jüdische Krankenhaus in Berlin 1756–1861–1914–1989*, Dagmar Hartung-von Doetinchem and Rolf Winau, eds. (Berlin: Edition Hentrich Berlin, 1989) and *Das Jüdische Krankenhaus in Berlin zwischen 1938 und 1945*, Rivka Elkin (Berlin: Edition Hentrich, 1993).

4. I have written of their stories elsewhere. On my mother see "The Lasting Legacy of Temporary Survival" in Wanda Teays, ed., *Second Thoughts: Critical Thinking from a Multicultural Perspective* (Mountain View, Calif.: Mayfield, 1996), 336–340. On my father see my Introduction to *A Mensch among Men: Explorations in Jewish Masculinity* (Freedom, Calif.: Crossing Press, 1988), 1–15.

5. *A Mensch among Men*, 10.

6. On the legacy of silence on the perpetrators' side see Dan Bar-On, *Legacy of Silence: Encounters with Children of the Third Reich* (Cambridge, Mass.: Harvard University Press, 1989) and Ursula Hegi, *Tearing the Silence: On Being German in America* (New York: Simon & Schuster, 1997).

7. Adrienne Rich, "Split at the Root: An Essay on Jewish Identity" in *Nice Jewish Girls: A Lesbian Anthology* (Freedom, Calif.: The Crossing Press, 1984), 67, reprinted in Adrienne Rich, *Blood, Bread, and Poetry: Selected Prose 1979–1985* (New York: W. W. Norton, 1986), 100.

8. Ted Hirschfield, "Aftermath," *German Requiem: Poems of the War and the Atonement of a Third Reich Child* (St. Louis, Mo.: Time Being Books, 1993), Part Four: Fathers, 69–70.

9. See Tamar Fox, *Inherited Memories: Israeli Children of Holocaust Survivors* (New York: Cassell, 1999).

10. Klaus Theweleit, *Male Fantasies*, Volumes I and II, trans. Stephen Conway, Erica Carter and Chris Turner (Minneapolis: University of Minnesota Press, 1987 and 1989), originally published as *Männerphantasien* (Frankfurt a.M.: Verlag Roter Stern, 1977).

11. Alexander Mitscherlich, *Society without the Father: A Contribution to Social Psychology*, trans. Eric Mosbacher (New York: Harcourt, Brace & World, 1969), originally published as *Auf dem Veg zur vaterlosen Gesellschaft* (Munich: R. Piper & Co. Verlag, 1963).

12. Robert Bly, *The Sibling Society* (Reading, Mass.: Addison-Wesley, 1996).

13. Alexander and Margarete Mitscherlich, *The Inability to Mourn: Principles of Collective Behavior*, trans. Beverly R. Placzek (New York: Grove Press, 1975), originally published as *Die Unfähigkeit zu trauern, Grundlagen kollektiven Verhaltens* (Munich: R. Piper & Co. Verlag, 1967).

14. For me personally, the philosophical and political heritage of the German-Jewish intellectual tradition was personified in the work and person of Herbert Marcuse, whom I had the great privilege of knowing first as a teacher and then also as a friend when I was a graduate student in the Department of Philosophy at the University of California at San Diego. I dedicate this chapter to his memory.

15. See for example Judith Butler, *Gender Trouble: Feminism and the Subversion of Identity* (New York: Routledge, 1990) and Rebecca Walker, ed., *To Be Real: Telling the Truth and Changing the Face of Feminism* (New York: Anchor Books, 1995).

16. Susannah Heschel, "Configurations of Patriarchy, Judaism, and Nazism in German Feminist Thought" in *Gender and Judaism: The Transformation of Tradition*, ed. Tamar M. Rudavsky (New York: New York University Press, 1995), 135–154.

17. I attempt to articulate the ideology of this movement in "To Be a Man, or Not To Be a Man—That Is the Feminist Question" in *Men Doing Feminism*, ed. Tom Digby (New York: Routledge, 1998), 197–212, and "The Profeminist Men's Movement: Fraternity, Equality, Liberty" in *Feminist Philosophies: Problems, Theories and Applications*, Second Edition, eds. Janet A. Kourany, James P. Sterba and Rosemarie Tong (Upper Saddle River, N.J.: Prentice Hall, 1999), 504–510.

18. See my "To Be a Man . . .", op. cit.

19. See Naomi Seidman, "Fag-Hags and Bu-Jews: Toward a (Jewish) Politics of Vicarious Identity" in *Insider/Outsider: American Jews and Multiculturalism*, eds. David Biale, Michael Galchinsky and Susannah Heschel (Berkeley: University of California Press, 1998).

20. Art Spiegelman, *Maus: A Survivor's Tale*, Volumes I and II (New York: Pantheon Books, 1986 and 1991).

21. See Michael Lerner, *Jewish Renewal: A Path to Healing and Transformation* (New York: Grosset/Putnam, 1994) and Arthur Waskow, *These Holy Sparks: The Rebirth of the Jewish People* (New York: Harper & Row, 1983).

22. I analyze some of these dynamics in "Of Mice and Supermen: Images of Jewish Masculinity" in *Gender and Judaism*, ed. Rudavsky, 279–293.

23. Harry Brod, *Hegel's Philosophy of Politics: Idealism, Identity, and Modernity* (Boulder, Colo.: Westview, 1992).

24. I wish to thank Richard Brod, Roy Jerome, and Karen Mitchell for their assistance in the writing of this chapter.

Masculinity and Sexual Abuse in Postwar German Society

Klaus-Jürgen Bruder

I. INTRODUCTION

Sexual abuse, or rather the discussion of it, affects our image of masculinity. In 94.7 percent of all cases of sexual abuse, the sexually abused interviewee names a man as the violator.[1] This is a fact that males must confront. How do they do this?

Discussion of sexual abuse in the public media invites men over and over again to negotiate this confrontation through the defense mechanism of splitting: the violator is excluded from male society by being declared a "monster." The media reports instances of sexual abuse almost every day, and in these reports, the violating man appears almost invariably as a stranger, someone unknown to the victim whom he treacherously attacks, a "sex gangster," a "beast." This propensity toward splitting is likewise expressed by demands voiced in the media for the castration of the perpetrator, if not for the death penalty itself.

The defense mechanism of splitting is becoming less convincing, however. More and more often, the press must report cases of child sexual abuse by fathers or other family members: the extensive trials of Flachslanden and Worms, Germany, in which entire family clans (including the grandmother!) have been accused, are examples. At the trial of Worms, which began on November 24, 1994, in the district court of Mainz, the parents of five children and a sixty-four-year-old grandmother were accused of orally, anally, and vaginally raping their children and two more children not their own, over a period of eight months. The children ranged in age from six months to eight years. The parents were further accused of lending their children to strangers for a fee. Trials against other alleged violators, including uncles and aunts, were held separately. At Worms, in June 1997, the accused were acquitted. (In the charge of child abuse, the prosecutors had focused on the "sex ring" that could never be proved, while the actual abuse within the family never became a subject of the charge). At Flachslanden, in October 1994, the ten accused—mother, father, uncle, and friends of the family—were sentenced from three and a half to ten years for the abuse of nine children, the youngest two years old, over a period of more than one and a half years. In both cases, the accused were part of the lower middle class.

Ascribing sexual abuse to the lower classes, a popular way of splitting societal outrages, flagrantly denies its actual occurrence in all social classes. In the above case, however, the media's splitting of the violator from the violation was attempted by questioning the status of the father: "Can he still be called a father?" asked *Bild*, one of Germany's most popular boulevard newspapers.[2] Thus sexual abuse by the father was vehemently presented to the public, while sexual abuse by other family members, above all, by the mothers, sisters, aunts, and other adults outside of the extended family, remained underexposed.

The feminist answer to the question of whether the abuser can still be called a father is that he can. *Väter als Täter* (Fathers as perpetrators) is the title of a book by Barbara Kavemann and Ingrid Lohstöter, two who have considerably influenced the discussion of sexual abuse in the Federal Republic of Germany.[3] Kavemann and Lohstöter take as their point of departure the belief that in the majority of cases it is the father who sexually abuses his children, and consequently, being a father and being an abuser do not rule each other out.

In Peter Wetzel's first representative interviews with victims in Germany, the image of the father or stranger as sole perpetrator is substantially corrected, however. In only 27 percent of all cases were family members identified as the violators. Sixty-nine percent of the offenders were known to the child. In addition to the 27 percent of violators who were family members, 42 percent were acquaintances from outside the immediate family circle. The number of offenders unknown to the victim, that is, strangers, was around 25 percent. It can be concluded, therefore, that the two images most often invoked in public discussion—the unknown monster and the father as violator—are untenable, the invention of fantasies. What is true is the fact that in an overwhelming majority of cases, the violator can be found among the child's acquaintances, and almost all of the violators are men. But if the questions are addressed differently, that is, not in the form of questionnaires intended for representative sections of the population, but if the actual victims themselves are asked, and if, furthermore, the most severely injured and/or traumatized victims are selected, then we find a significantly higher percentage of victims sexually abused by family members, a higher percentage of women as violators, and a higher percentage of male victims.[4]

What is the reason for this discrepancy? Wetzels, coauthor of the questionnaire, notes that in order to properly evaluate such representative questionnaires, the following must be taken into consideration: (1) specific groups often appear underrepresented in a representative sample survey, especially those in which a certain prevalence of victims may be assumed, such as drug addicts, prostitutes, prison inmates, and institutionalized individuals; and (2) incidents occurring before the victim has reached age three are vulnerable to childhood amnesia and consequently do not appear on retrospective questionnaires. Furthermore, it is essential to add that representative questionnaires do not take into consideration those processes that specifically aid the victim in assimilating the experience of abuse, which in turn lead the victim to stop talking about experienced violations: these processes are first and foremost repression and splitting. As a result, studies relying upon questionnaires have only limited validity with respect to their representation of the actual extent of sexual abuse, as well as to the percentages of family and other groups as violators. Moreover, it can be assumed that the actual extent of sexual abuse, the percentage of violators from the immediate family, the percentage of abused men, and the percentage of female violators are higher than representative questionnaire studies suggest. This has consequences for the discussion of (1) sexual abuse as an expression of masculine violence and (2) the relationship between sexual abuse and masculinity.

When we are compelled to realize that boys also are the victims of sexual abuse and that women also are capable of sexually abusing children, we will no longer be able to characterize sexual abuse as an expression of masculine violence against females. We will instead be obliged to admit that children of both sexes are sexually abused by adults of both sexes; that sexual abuse is, as such, a behavior not exclusive to men, and not directed solely toward girls; and that sexual abuse is an expression of violence emanating from adults (or adolescents) and directed toward children. We have only recently recognized the existence of the sexual abuse of boys, and only very lately realized that women—mothers, aunts, sisters, and female educators—may also sexually abuse (their) children. These facts are slowly entering the public consciousness, which shows that these well-kept secrets contradict socially acceptable ideas and images of motherhood and challenge images of the father, who, as a "man," is more readily placed in the category of "violator."

II. SEXUALIZATION OF THE
MOTHER-SON RELATIONSHIP

We know nothing of the actual statistical extent of sexual abuse by women in Germany. Published figures speak only for the extent to which we are aware of the abuse, and here, the numbers are on the rise. In a study conducted by the psychologist Craig Allen, two interesting results were found, however. Generally, women—whether they are abusive or not—have a higher threshold of perception concerning abuse than men. That is, there are things women do not recognize as abuse, but men do. In addition, women who have sexually abused their children are much less likely than men to admit to their abusive actions (30 percent of abusive women, compared to 47 percent of abusive men).[5] Could it be that the preponderance of male sexual offenders is an artifact of the greater denial of women?

A study by Gerhard Amendt sheds light on this very question.[6] In the spring of 1992, Amendt surveyed 903 women on their attitudes toward both their sons' bodily hygiene and their sons' sexuality in relation to shame and abuse. Amendt did not pose questions about sexual abuse as such, but rather about possible boundary violations that could immediately precede the actual abuse. The question of why sexual abuse by women of their sons is rarely spoken about was answered by 4.1 percent of those surveyed with, "Mothers do not abuse their sons," whereas 64.5 percent said, "They do it much less often," and 35 percent stated that, "Mothers do it differently." "When women are asked to describe the difference between paternal and maternal boundary violations," he writes, "they give violence and pain great importance."[7] This understanding, however, does not take into consideration "the emotional effect that sexual stimulation has on the child, who is unable to cope with it."[8] In the mother's imagination, the absence of violence "becomes proof of mutual desire."[9] Males, on the other hand, cannot reconcile the experience of being seduced with their sense of self-worth. They therefore deny such experiences. Feelings of shame, awakened within them by women who violated boundaries with them, "make it difficult for them to remember."[10] They would much rather "believe they provoked the mother's desire themselves."[11]

Further, when the boy is too "small" for his mother's wishes, he will be continually wounded. Shame results from his desire to be "big" when he is in fact too "small." He senses that he is too small for the mother's expectations and desires, yet he is unable to see that this skewed perspective comes from the mother. How do women perceive the son's smallness and his attempts to be bigger than he can? First, women underestimate the son's abilities and overlook the son's desire for independence. Second, women overestimate the son's capabilities, and they burden the son with expectations and wishes that the son would like to fulfill, but by which he is overwhelmed.[12]

Amendt has concluded that, "Women make their sons ashamed; and they are unable to recognize it."[13] It is a very painful experience for the son to have his feelings of shame overlooked. He experiences this as powerlessness and as an inability to exist independently from his mother. How often do women overlook the son's expressed feelings of shame? To the question, "When your son is ashamed, do you overlook it?" 26.1 percent answered with "quite possibly." If this number is compared to the mere 14.5 percent who answered affirmatively the question, "Do you think it is possible that your son will at some point regard as seduction what you only did in meaning well?" then the discrepancy between the mother's self-perception and her perception of the son's feelings becomes obvious. Amendt interprets this disparity as an indication of the mother's self-deception; the mother idealizes the relationship with the son:

> What causes shame in the son creates closeness in the mother, one that she has the power to determine. By denying her son's shame, the woman allows herself a vast array of well-meant care. She creates for herself the opportunity to practice sexual incursions "shamelessly." She can assert her own needs under the cover of nurture without being aware of the sexual content of her actions.[14]

He continues, "Most inappropriate relationships with children exist under the veil of modern parenting as (nonviolent) encroachments on the children's intimacy."[15] There exists a "wide range of 'inappropriate' care, training in cleanliness, as well as moments of playing and cuddling."[16] Through this, the mother views the son's penis as an "early object of endless motherly care."[17] Amendt learned that many of the mothers were still washing the genitals of twelve-year-old sons.[18]

Compared to 58.9 percent of the mothers who are so concerned with the son's penis, the interest mothers have in the daughter's genitals seems strikingly smaller (21.8 percent). One of the mothers' preoccupations with the penis is the "narrowing of the foreskin," the normal state in which a boy is born.[19] In spite of this, more than a few mothers resort to preventative measures (against the feared medical operation, circumcision); in some cases, these measures, which Amendt compares to the widening of the girl's labia, persist until the son is twelve years old.[20] In addition, only 57.3 percent of the women who were concerned had actually consulted a doctor.[21] "If one further considers that only 20.3 percent of the women consult their male partners, it becomes clear that women are concerned with the fantasy world of the son's penis as well as their own possibly exclusive occupation with it."[22] Moreover, "The 'disease' phimosis permits certain actions to become acceptable; ones which women could otherwise not justify."[23] That is, the manipulation of the penis through this conduct (phimosis) is explained as an action of careful nursing.

"There are mothers who have difficulties with touching the son's penis," the survey continued. "What are or were your experiences concerning this?" "Touching his penis is feeling-neutral," answered 62.2 percent of the women. In the process of neutralizing feelings through playfulness, however, repressed feelings become barely perceivable. As Amendt observes: "In the group that insisted on the normality of touching the penis, some of the violence that women do to themselves and their sons when they deny their feelings becomes evident."[24] The mothers maintain that touching the son's penis is "feeling-neutral." By doing so, they commit violence toward themselves through the denial of feelings and perpetrate in the same moment violence toward the son, for whom touching is just as unlikely to be neutral. One can assume that the son perceives such treatment as sexual stimulation. Likewise, there is just as little ground for saying that women also would be unaffected by such sexual stimulation. When feelings are subjugated, there exists a likelihood that the relationship itself will be sexualized. What appears as genuine concern is, in essence, an inappropriate relationship, one that leads to the sexualization of the relationship between the woman and the son in small, barely perceptible steps. On the level of emotion, this is an action of secret mutual arousal and at the same time an external, rigid denial of this arousal.[25] As such, an incestuous element can gradually be introduced into the relationship. This is not a sudden injection of the incestuous into the mother-son relationship but rather a slow and gradual insertion. There is no line at which one action suddenly takes on a different emotional quality.[26] The denial of the double-sidedness of feelings, as well as the fiction of being able to dissolve those feelings through neutrality, offers no security against seductive actions. Splitting offers no protection for the woman or the son; it merely makes the explosive element invisible.[27] Further, the longer the stimulation of the genitals occurs, the more the son will become an actively participating partner, which will in turn lead to feelings of shame and guilt.[28]

The mother's actions toward the son, camouflaged as motherly care, may manifest themselves in the adult male as a disturbance in male sexual identity and may eventually lead to an inability to enter into relationships.[29] Cultural disinterest in the inappropriate actions of the mother must be paralyzing for the boy. The boy finds no understanding for his situation, no recognition, and no language in which he may express himself and be understood. An "inability to cry and to show feelings" may have its basis in this.[30]

III. MALE BOUNDARY VIOLATIONS AND DENIAL OF CONTROL AND RESPONSIBILITY

Men do not possess the same self-understood contact with the child that women do. For this reason, men often cannot integrate their abuse into their care for the child. Rather, they must justify their care for the child, as they must likewise justify their unmediated access to the child. Men must make excuses for what remains open to women without question: unmediated access to the child, physical contact, caring for intimate parts of the child's body, and so on. Consequently, men transgress a boundary with the child before each abuse. They approach the child from without; this is their unique situation, and the conspicuousness of the abusive element is grounded in this distinction.

Women are able to integrate and conceal their sexual abuse in their actions of care; for men, this is not as easily accomplished. Physical closeness to the child is not as self-evident for men, and they are therefore threatened with appearing to have committed a boundary violation, which they then must justify. Male (abusive) boundary violation is much more obvious, which explains the special precautions men take to preserve secrecy and, as a consequence, the justifications themselves. Through their excuses, one sees the specifically male element of sexual abuse: men justify their abuse with arguments that fall back upon masculine possibilities grounded in the division of roles within the family, and for this reason their arguments even emphasize that which is not self-evident. Men justify their abuse: (1) as "sex education," as an aspect of fatherly care; (2) as a special "love" relationship; (3) with the fact that their partner rejected them; and (4) by stating that they were so intoxicated that they no longer knew what they were doing.

Men deny too—women have always known this. It is not through denial, however, that they distinguish themselves from women, but rather through the difference in their denial. As a first step, both men and women deny the boundary violation and the abuse. But men deny it by playing down abuse as an expression of their special relationship with the child, whereas women see "nothing special" in the fact that they disregard the son's (shame) boundaries. Men deny the deed, while women deny its sexual character. In addition to the denial of the fact, "the denial of responsibility" also plays a central role in sexual abuse.[31] We are inclined to view this denial of responsibility as a typical male behavior. Yet the demand to take responsibility, the need to be the author—even of events that he did not cause—and the need to be in control of the situation, are all central to the image of the male in our society, and therefore also central to male socialization. Control belongs to the concept of "masculinity." To have lost control contradicts our image of masculinity. Denying this injurious loss of control—unacceptable to the man and to patriarchal society—is the most important strategy for protecting a threatened masculinity. Further, arguments denying responsibility for the abuse of a child (one's own) contain different metaphors of masculinity and show that the attempt to preserve masculinity simultaneously places this very masculinity in question. The enigmatic task of (upholding) masculinity—"Loss of control through alcohol" as a socially acceptable expression of masculinity; "sex education" as an affirmation of the male's monopoly on violence in patriarchal society; the "partner's fault," though it reveals an ambivalence of subjectivity. On the one hand, it confirms the patriarch's right to choose as he desires among "his" women. On the other hand, his power to have his partner at his disposal is at once placed in question, revealing the defeat of not being desired. The metaphor of the "love relationship" with the abused child also affirms the masculinity of the "lover"; it is at the same time the "truest" argument and the most remote from reality because it interprets the search for love as actually fulfilled.

It is striking that three of these arguments (the alcohol, the partner, and a love relationship) deny and negate the barrier between generations more than they do sexuality itself. That is, these arguments affirm characteristics of "masculinity" that collapse upon themselves only when we bring the difference in generations into play—the question of power (of parents over children), the question of power abused by the parents, by elders, all stronger individuals in comparison to younger and weaker children. It is only by bringing the differences in generations into focus that a failure in masculinity—a disgrace—emerges. It is a debatable affirmation of power to use this power over dependents; it is ridiculous to conquer the child (one's own) as an object of love. Behind male denial hides not only the disgrace of having been caught doing what was forbidden—like a caught sinner who is not worthy of love and is dirty—but the disgrace to one's masculinity as well.[32] This is why denying the difference in generations is so important. The rejection of responsibility, like the denial of the act itself, concerns itself with rejecting the shame, the disgrace of having been caught. Yet the denial of responsibility is the denial of the subject-character: I prefer to be the object of the other's influence rather than to be responsible. This again contradicts the male role, the need to be the subject. If all that is left to me is the denial of responsibility, then I have already been substantially driven back in the defense of my masculinity. This is most evident in the love metaphor that enables me to say, "I did nothing that she did not want. I did not use force." This is certainly not the little girl's view. It is an attempt by the abusive male to claim and maintain his masculinity by contesting that which is held up for and to him as a man: the image of the violent one (*Gewalttäter*). He knows that he does not become a man by employing violence but rather through the possibility of employing violence and his control of this possibility. The concept of (self-)control belongs to the (self-)image of the man, and, with that, responsibility. His doubt in his ability to control himself, to remain in control of the situation, places his masculinity in question.

The decisive factor in the sexual abuse of children is not whether or not the man used force, however—as we have seen with Amendt, women also differentiate between violent and nonviolent acts—but rather that he disregarded and crossed the barrier between the generations. He denies this fact when he makes his daughter his lover, when he fantasizes his daughter to be his lover. (The same is true for pedophiliac abuse of boys; here, as well, the abused boy is stylized as a friend or a lover.) Negating the barrier between the generations simultaneously means making the child an adult, construing oneself as a child—creating a level of equality, an equality of means and possibilities. This also may be interpreted as a deficit in the perception of reality and of (self-)criticism. The attempt to claim and maintain the doubted masculinity is the result of an inability to initiate and form relationships with actual equals, with male and female partners, and, of course, with children. This inability is denied during the abusive act itself, and not only in the subsequent justification. In an abusive relationship that lasts several years (as is most likely the case within the family), each single abusive act is denied immediately after it occurs.

During the process of boundary violation—which is denied every time—the boundary itself is simultaneously displaced. It is an invisible process to which the abusive adult surrenders. The abuser's perception adjusts to the newly created boundary. If originally the boundary of affection was marked by the taboo of touching the genitals, then this boundary will be continually pushed further during the process of abuse, until the genitals are included within the boundary for the first time. The *quality* of the touch itself will now mark the new boundary, and will be considered the point where the realm of what is forbidden begins. The touch will be short and timid at first, but as soon as this newly defined boundary has been assimilated, more arousing stroking and so on will mark the new boundary. Through a series of small steps, the boundary will again and again be pushed further. Here, too, we find the "sexualization of the relationship in small steps," the "slow appearance of the incestuous element in the relationship" that Amendt encountered with the mothers.

The boundary displacement is not only accompanied by an adjustment of perception to the newly acquired boundary line—through which it is made invisible—but rather is at the same time protected through the construction of systems of rationalization. The abusive adult male takes these rationalizations from a variety of spheres: (1) from the pedagogical: he tells himself that he shows the child something important for the child's development; he tells himself that he introduces the child to sexuality; (2) from the area of health and hygiene: he tells himself that he sees to the child's cleanliness and looks after the child's physical development; (3) from discursive elements on "free" sexuality: he gives the reason that today everyone runs around naked in the house, that there are no boundaries of shame within the family, that one is unable to turn off the television when one watches pornographic films even if children come into the room, that one can show and explain to children everything about sexuality, not through picture books, but rather with one's own body and with the bodies of the children, even with touch that arouses the genitals, and so on. Naturally, he simultaneously protests against the contention that he is doing this for his "own arousal and satisfaction." He maintains that this is all "self-understood" and that to assert the opposite would be outmoded, prudish, dishonest, and hypocritical. It is in this way that the male violator reinterprets the abuse. He is involved in a steady, continuous process of reinterpreting his abusive behavior by adapting it to the ideal image he maintains in regard to his behavior: the image of the "good father," the image of the one person who really loves the children, the only one who understands them.

As with men, we also have seen the mothers' rationalizations of boundary violation, if not of overt abusive behavior: their concern about the development of the son's penis, combined with a denial of his sexuality, a denial of arousal. These strategies of denying the reality of sexual abuse function at the same time to protect the self-image (of the loving father, of the caring mother), as well as to keep fears and feelings of guilt at a distance.[33] In contrast to women, however, men are not concerned with denying the other's embarrassment; they instead deny their own embarrassment, defend against threatening, shameful memories of their own experiences (of humiliation), deny their own history of abuse, and the reasons for this abuse. The career of the abusive man is most often a career of denials: denials of deficits, of humiliation, and of injuries to his masculinity. Denying such humiliation offers him the possibility of rescuing the (self-)image of masculinity. This is because humiliation is an experience that cannot be integrated with the self-image of masculinity. The denial of humiliation makes it possible for him to conquer the experience of humiliation—which would otherwise be very difficult to integrate—and to preserve a feeling of control. His aim here is to deny the experience of victimization.[34]

IV. THE REPETITION OF DENIAL AND ABUSE

Denial also can be seen in the abused boy, as Amendt has pointed out. It is well recognized that boys deny the experience of having been beaten.[35] Further, boys appear more inclined to employ compensation strategies that enable them to deny their victimization—for instance, hypermasculine and aggressive behaviors toward others. Boys who attribute the cause of their sexual assaults to their own female or supposedly homosexual characteristics most often employ compensation strategies. The adaptive function of these modes of behavior is grounded in the experience of renewed feelings of control and security, which in turn condition a reorganization of cognitive constructs (self- and object-images) with respect to a positive self-image and a relative invulnerability.

Further, the experience of victimization changes the cognitive and emotional orientation of the child and has a traumatic effect by destroying the child's fundamental cognitive constructs of himself and the world. It obliterates his perception of his own invulnerability, as well as the meaning (*Sinnhaftigkeit*) of his world and his self-worth. This is accompanied by intense feelings of fear and helplessness. The affected boy no longer feels safe and secure in his world. His self-image, or more specifically, his self-concept, is placed in question by his experience of victimization. Above all, his perception of powerlessness and helplessness caused by his experienced loss of control leads to a reevaluation of the self in the sense of a loss of self-worth and self-respect.

The most important opportunity to overcome the experience of victimization lies in reevaluating the events in a way that assimilates them with previous schemes without fundamentally changing those schemes. In this way, the threat to cognitive constructs (images of self and the world, object-images) and the ensuing consequences are reduced to a minimum. Thus one may explain the positive valuation of the experience of sexual abuse by boys and men: they reorganize their experiences in accordance with traditional sex roles that do not accommodate the role of the victim. The abused boy's desire to regain the feeling of being in control during a situation of utter helplessness also could be a decisive motive for appropriating the role of the violator. The role of the violator seems to be a genuine "processing form" of the role of the victim.[36] Gail Ryan, Sandy Lane, and others speak of processes of "cyclical victimization" that lead to abusive sexual behavior by adolescents.[37] Further, the classic masculine role demands that the boy/man be able to protect and defend himself (gender-specific socialization). In accordance with this demand, the boy interprets victimization as a sign of his own weakness or failure, or as a consequence of his own behavior. It is unlikely that he will seek help. Instead, he introjects the guilt for the abuse and cannot process his feelings of helplessness and rage. During puberty, with its ongoing development of masculine identity, a sexually abused boy runs the risk of attempting to conquer his feelings of confusion and helplessness by creating extreme experiences of control. He may even, under certain conditions, repeat his own victimization—this time in the role of the violator. Through this, he assures himself of his power as a man. As tension is repeatedly built up and then discharged, sexual behaviors have the tendency to reinforce themselves. The same is true for abusive behaviors. Here reinforcement arises from the thrill of secrecy, the thrill of what is forbidden: while anticipating the abusive action in fantasies during the planning phase, while approaching the victim, during "habituation" and its resulting need to look for newer and more intense experiences. On a behavioral, or more specifically, a physiological level, reinforcement comes through sexual arousal and ejaculation, both during anticipatory fantasies and during the abuse itself. The experienced feelings of power and control combine with physical satisfaction and outweigh all possible negative consequences. A cycle of abuse thus comes into existence, which has a course comparable to addiction. One must add that "only" approximately 20 percent of abusive boys were themselves the victims of sexual abuse. Conversely, only an insignificantly larger percentage of abused boys become abusers themselves. This

indicates that other causes in the development of the male into an of-
fender, as well as a wide spectrum of alternative methods for processing
the experience of sexual abuse, must be taken into consideration.[38] In
spite of this, the experience of sexual abuse remains the most common
cause.

The following excerpts are taken from a therapy session with M., a
twenty-eight-year-old man who abused his four-year-old daughter by
pressing himself against her and masturbating in front of her.

M. would like to talk about his "compulsion" to "stare" at women's
breasts. The more he fights it, the stronger this compulsion becomes. It
arises whenever he meets a woman superior to him, such as his boss, or a
woman toward whom he feels aggression. He forces himself to look into
her eyes, but—"pow"—his glance abruptly slips downward! He interprets his behavior as an expression of his desire to devalue women, of his
wish to humiliate them. As an adolescent, he thought the way other
boys glanced at girls was dirty; he did not do it himself. His mother
described all men as "pigs," even his father: "Don't become like him!"
and "Thank God, you're not like him!" The young M. assimilated this.
By doing so, he could please his mother, cut out his hated father, and
take over his father's place in his mother's heart. Now he is forced,
through his compulsion, to "realize" that he is nothing more than a
"pig" himself.

It is, however, through his mother's evil expression that he sees himself. He takes this in when he perceives his glance slipping "downward."
This glance is not initially lustful, but rather a look of humility, a lower-
ing of his eyes before the eyes of his mother. Thus the poor boy finds
himself looking at her breasts, which was precisely where he was not
allowed to look. "Look me in the eyes," she had demanded.

In M.'s case, we see how he reinterprets his gesture of humility as an
aggressive, "misogynist" one. By doing this, he denies his humiliation.
This denial of humiliation also forms the nucleus of the denial of the
abusive man; it is a fight for his doubted masculinity. In his eyes, humiliation negates his "masculinity." In order to maintain his masculinity, he
must negate humiliation. I do not contend that the denial of humiliation compulsively leads to abuse, but rather the opposite: through depre-
cation, the damaged masculinity—a masculinity called into question—
may be affirmed. Abuse and the denial of humiliation are aimed at the
same objective, that of rewinning a lost masculinity. The abusive man
does not want to face the fact that he abuses his child because of his
incapability, his weakness. Not only is the deed denied, but so is the
deficit itself, the nucleus of masculinity—to maintain control over the

situation. This deficit points to a deficient socialization. In general, one could say he had a failed, destructive history (socialization)—one that destroyed his feelings of self-worth—during which the resources and educational requirements necessary for his successful personality formation were withheld from him. His was a childhood in which he was not allowed to develop independently. In turn, he now inhibits his child from developing on her own. This may be fully interpreted as a compulsion to repeat, a repetition compulsion. He was not allowed to accept his needs and to fight for their gratification. His needs were poisoned as insubordinate, impertinent, "dirty." To his shame, the possibility of fighting to satisfy his needs was taken from him. Nonetheless, those needs did not simply disappear. He was forced to make himself small, to look for his satisfactions behind other people's backs. He accustomed himself to obtaining gratification in secret, against social norms and in avoidance of the public. A life in a forbidden realm.

And herein lies the reason for the secrecy with which the adult man veils his abuse. Secrecy, which binds both violator and victim, occupies an important place in acts of abuse—in their maintenance and in their screening from the environment. It occupies an important place in the psychodynamics of the violator and the victim as well. The abused children guard the secret: consider the reluctance of abused children to speak about what they have experienced. Reviving the memory and the affect associated with the memory are resisted, above all, because children do not like to be reminded of the unbearable relationship with the bad object. Fairbairn emphasizes the importance of the shame that is connected to the experience of the relationship with a bad object. Because identification plays an important role with respect to children's feelings about themselves, children believe themselves evil when they experience the parents as evil or humiliating. Hence children must repress both the parents and the bad relationship with them in order to protect their egos from being persecuted by them.[39]

V. THE CORE OF SEXUAL TRAUMATIZATION: SEXUALIZATION AND ITS DENIAL

The sexualization of (power) relations and the simultaneous denial of sexualization, more specifically, of power itself, or even more precisely, the denial of the abuse of this power—this is the core of a child's traumatization through sexual abuse. The possibility of traumatization is immensely greater *within* a close, (life-)sustaining, emotional *relationship* between the child and adults—one that the child cannot or does not want to do without, a relationship that the child depends upon, a relationship of dependence that the child cannot leave behind—than outside of such a relationship, with a stranger. In studies conducted by Peters, Rosenfeld, Landis and Rosenfeld, and others, sexual assault by a *stranger* also appears less traumatic for the child than assault by someone within the family because: (1) an assault by a stranger is often a singular event; (2) the relationship between the child and the family is more often such that the child is better able to obtain help; and (3) the child does not have the feeling of having been betrayed in trust.[40]

Thus it is not the sexual assault alone that is traumatizing but also its embeddedness within a relationship that is important for the child. The pathogenic effects have their etiology not only in overstimulation and fear but also in a confusion of perception and in a weakening of reality proofing and primary trust. Abuse from within the *family* cannot be isolated from existing relationships: "The climate within the family in which the incest happens is traumatic even before the event itself occurs."[41] Still, it remains relevant whether the "actual" incest occurs. Even within the family, the consequences differ depending on how much the nonabusive parent is able to protect the child, to get help from outside, to leave the abusive partner. Additionally, the *duration* of sexual abuse within such a relationship is of importance. Sexual abuse within the family is almost never a singular or an "accidental" event. It often takes place over a period of years. Each day is filled with fear, and each time it occurs, the abuse goes qualitatively (and quantitatively) further; it is not uncommon for the abuse to reach a stage where penetration occurs. Moreover, incest is more harmful the earlier it begins.[42] Incest develops over many years through a series of boundary violations, denials, compulsions to secrecy, repetitions, and ritualizations, during which the "consequences" of sexual abuse are produced daily and gradually.

The family, or in more general terms, the emotionally important relationship (between the child and the adult), would therefore be the decisive precondition for the destructive consequences of sexual abuse: the incestuous relationship within the family, the sexualization of this relationship, and the simultaneous denial of this sexualization.

We have seen that denial plays a role for both the male and the female violator, as well as for the victim. Both types of denial, as well as the possibilities for sexualizing the (power) relationship, are gender-specific. Both sexes return concurrently to images of masculinity and femininity that are related to each other in a polarized form. These images make denial easier or, for their part, more difficult as they contribute to whether or not the abuse will be perceived. Consequently, denial is the destructive element for abused children. Before Amendt's study, Sandor Ferenczi greatly emphasized the denial of the abuse on the part of the adult.[43] It is because of this that the children are left alone with the unbearable contradiction that the trauma comes from those individuals who are most important to them. Abused children must deal with extreme pain, fear, humiliation, and not least of all, anger; the only people these children can turn to for help are the torturers themselves, if they are the parents. Therefore, the only possibility left to the children is to deny the abuse itself, that is, to split off the experience; this comes at the price of ego splitting, however.

VI. MASCULINITY, SEXUALIZATION, AND DENIAL THROUGH THE PERSPECTIVE OF MODERNITY

If we believe the traumatizing element of child sexual abuse to be the sexualization of the relationship and the simultaneous denial of this sexualization, then we can immediately see that this is not specifically male, not simply the expression of masculine sexual violence, but rather that it is a possibility for both sexes. Both men and women can sexualize the relationship with (their) children, albeit in different ways. Amendt sees this sexualization as a result of the denial of feelings, as well as the inability to communicate feelings and desires to others in a different manner. This structure already determines the relationship between the partners before the child even appears as a substitute partner. The partners bring the propensity to create such a structure into the relationship: both enter the relationship with desires that they simultaneously deny, or more specifically, that they project onto the child. Both the father and the mother transfer onto their daughter those needs that are intended for the mother.[44] Thus they overwhelm their relationship, and they overwhelm the child. Both parents have fled into this relationship and need it "in order to create for themselves a certain sense of security that they are unable to get anywhere else," as Anthony Giddens makes clear.[45] With this indication, sexual abuse may be situated within the overall relationship structure of "co-dependency." I am not only interested, however, in how one may order sexual abuse, but more importantly, I am drawn to Giddens's observations of how "co-dependency"—boundaries, boundary violations, and the acceptance of boundaries—is thematized in therapeutic work itself. The boundaries damaged through sexual abuse are, at first sight, those of the other as subject. Yet in the violation of these boundaries, the abusive adult simultaneously negates his or her own boundedness, negates the impossibility of making the other into an "object."[46]

Giddens has examined many therapeutic case studies and has found that the first goal of many therapy programs is a reflexive one: the creation of a reflexive attentiveness. Reflexive attentiveness encourages the understanding that one has a choice, which in turn implies an acceptance of boundaries and compulsions to which one is subject. This is seen as a path toward learning to gauge possibilities.[47] One could say that the project of the "reflexive self"—the prerequisite for acceptance of one's own boundaries—is required for respecting the boundaries of the other. With this, sexual abuse would be ordered within a broader cultural frame as an answer to the deficiency of a "reflexive self." Some term this reflexive element a "talk with the self," or a direct reflection on the nature of the self.[48] Choice not only implies external or marginal aspects of individual attitudes but also defines who the individual "is." The project of the "reflexive self," the reflexive history of the self; the idea of an individual life story that can and must be constantly (re)written; and the development of a narrative self referred to as "biographical accounting" in which the self feels emotionally well.[49]

The project of the reflexive self is a historical one. Giddens views its creation as bound to the fact that "in a society in which traditions have been erased more thoroughly than ever before, and in which many parts of personal life are no longer determined by preset patterns and customs, the individual must try to find security within the self, through the individual's own 'style of living.'"[50] The opportunity to choose a style of living is, however, constitutive for the reflexive history of the self.[51] The individual is constantly compelled to renegotiate the possibilities of a style of living, to work through the history of the self, and to make those applied styles of living commensurate with the self if the individual wants to harmonize personal autonomy with feelings of ontological security.[52] The project of the reflexive self is part of a set of new ideas, interpretation models, and orientations that appeared in the second half of the eighteenth century. Klaus Wahl calls these the "promises of modernity": (1) the promise of a new image of humanity, tending toward the universal (an autonomous, self-conscious, humane subject possessing human dignity); (2) the promise of universal progress in science, technology, economy, law, and society; and (3) the promise of a new family model (individualized marriage based on love, familial happiness, and autonomy).[53]

It soon became clear, after these promises had grown to be an aspect of social reality, that social changes that simultaneously began with these cultural innovations by no means happened without conflict. Dissonance appeared between the promises of modernity and the experience of daily social reality, which led to disappointment, subjective suffering, and "private" unhappiness. Above all, the triangular relationship between individual, family, and society proved to be the source of momentous conflicts. For instance, the individual interests of women, men, and children in autonomous play within the family are hardly a priori congruent, but rather are laid down through possible conflicts. The same can be seen with the orientation toward family and with individualism, which have spread parallel to each other since the eighteenth century. In addition, the family did not appear as a universal instance that compensated for missing self-affirmation and recognition.

If self-consciousness, as a focusing on one's own person and worth, belongs to the nucleus of the modern image of man, if individuals have adopted the education and demands of their own self-consciousness and self-esteem—even if only unconsciously—as a maxim, then this claim suggests much danger.[54] The danger lies in the fact that the individual no longer, or now only in a limited fashion, holds the right of disposal over the cultural and societal conditions governing the fulfillment or realization of this project of self-consciousness. Certainly there are many paths leading to an individual's self-respect, which is necessary for survival.[55] However, "where there is no longer the guarantee of minimal economic success, . . . self-consciousness, self-respect, and individuality will be undermined because they are firmly based on the success of such material criteria."[56] Individuals then run the risk of becoming trapped between internalized promises of self-conscious autonomy, family happiness, and social progress on the one hand, and their real experiences of denied respect, disregarded human dignity, and damaged self-confidence on the other hand. This trap—between the triangle of promises and the discovery that they cannot be carried out in the reality of modernity—is subjectively experienced as suffering. The individual suffers from not being what or as he should, from not being able to be what he should. He experiences this as a failure, a not-getting-enough (Zu-kurz (ge)kommen-Sein), a being discriminated against, an inferiority. He experiences this inability, this not-(being)-right, as shaming. The individual takes the promises seriously and ascribes their nonfulfillment to his own fault, to his failure, to the failure of his parents; he does not place the promises themselves in question, however. The trap between the myth and the reality of modernity is not without consequences for individual behavior.[57]

Some long for recognition in the form of different demonstrations of power toward weaker individuals; others are bound by neurotic strategies that compensate for the defects of their own self-images. Disappointment leads to aggression.[58]

Feelings of guilt are replaced by mechanisms of shame, the feeling of being worthless, the feeling that life is empty and that the body is not an adequate vessel of the self—all results of the diffusion of the self-referential systems of modernity.[59] In this situation, sexuality takes on the task of filling the "emptiness." Sexual activity tends to be drawn to this emptiness, this search for fulfillment so difficult to obtain, which influences each gender differently.[60]

In his extensive project on sex and how it is made discursive, Michel Foucault characterizes the historical development of sexualization as thus: "In the space of a few centuries, a certain inclination has led us to direct the question of what we are, to sex."[61] Moreover, "between each of us and our sex, the West has placed a never-ending demand for truth: it is up to us to extract the truth of sex, since this truth is beyond its grasp; it is up to sex to tell us our truth, since sex is what holds it in darkness."[62] Sex is a history that, according to Foucault, began in the eighteenth century with the establishment of the hegemony of the bourgeois class.

> And this was far from being a matter of the class which in the eighteenth century became hegemonic believing itself obliged to amputate from its body a sex that was useless, expensive, and dangerous as soon as it was no longer given over exclusively to reproduction; we can assert on the contrary that it provided itself with a body to be cared for, protected, cultivated, and preserved from the many dangers and contacts, to be isolated from others.[63]

As far as the bourgeois classes were concerned, sex had nothing to do with "asceticism, in any case not a renunciation of pleasure or a disqualification of the flesh, but on the contrary an intensification of the body, a problematization of health and its operational terms."[64] Moreover,

> [t]he bourgeoisie made this element identical with its body, or at least subordinated the latter to the former by attributing to it a mysterious and undefined power; it staked its life and its death on sex by making it responsible for its future welfare; it placed its hopes for the future in sex by imagining it to have ineluct-

able effects on generations to come; it subordinated its soul to
sex by conceiving of it as what constituted the soul's most secret
and determinant part.[65]

All of these strategies "went by way of a family which must be viewed,
not as a powerful agency of prohibition, but as a major factor of sexualization."[66] Further, the discourse of sexuality was masculine, was conducted by men who turned their masculine gaze toward women, making
women the object of masculine sexuality.

For women today, however, sexuality contains the promise of intimacy.[67] It is a "means of establishing relationships with others based on
intimacy."[68] Masculine sexuality, on the other hand, remains untouched
by this; it remains "episodic." Giddens characterizes masculine sexuality
as often compulsive and interprets it as an "obsessive acting out of rou-
tines devoid of their former context," precisely because it denies the
emotional dependence that it arouses.[69] Its compulsive character becomes
more pronounced the more women insist on an ethic of love based on
partnership. This in turn places pressure on masculine sexuality, "which
fluctuates between self-confident sexual dominance that includes violence and constant fears about one's potency."[70] Masculine sexual violence in modern societies results more from insecurity or inadequacy
than from a smooth continuity of patriarchal dominance. It is a "destructive reaction to the decay of female complicity."[71]

The more the life of the individual concentrates on itself, and the
more "identity" is understood as a reflexively organized project, the more
sexuality becomes the property of the individual.[72] Sexuality was split off
or privatized as part of that process in which motherhood was invented
and declared to be a fundamental component of the female realm; it is
the result of social rather than psychological repression. What was involved was the restriction or denial of an expressly feminine sexuality
and an acceptance of the general assumption that masculine sexuality
was unproblematic. These developments renewed the emphasis on the
difference between the sexes.[73]

Women were burdened with the changes in intimacy that modernity
had effected. For women, the problem of having to constitute love as a
medium of communication and development of the self emerged, both
in relationship to children and in relationship to men. The demand for
female sexual desire made up a major part of the reconstitution of intimacy, and this emancipation was as important as all others fought for in
the public arena.

For men, sexual activity remained compulsive to the extent that it remained untouched by these concealed changes.

> The man connects primary trust with domination and control—including self-control—which stem from his suppressed emotional dependence on women. The need to neutralize these suppressed desires or to destroy their object collides with the desire for love. What men seek to suppress is not the ability to love, but the emotional autonomy necessary to endure intimacy. Intimacy is more dependent on communication than on the need to express emotions as such (communicative competence as compared to instrumental competence of the boys).[74]

"Above all," Giddens writes, "intimacy is a question of emotional communication with others, with the self, and thus, within the context of interpersonal equality."[75] This presupposes that "the other is understood as an independent being, that personal boundaries are defined and maintained, that the boundaries of the other are accepted."[76] Such boundaries are disregarded whenever one person uses another to implement old psychological formations.[77] Sexual abuse belongs to this category. Men and women differ in how they use (their) children by such means. These differences reflect the differences in the meaning of sexuality for both sexes, as well as the construction of the history of the self.

VII. CONCLUSION: FASCISM AND SEXUAL ABUSE

Fascism as a specifically German phenomenon cannot be purged from history. Consequently, we must consider, along with the question of sexual abuse, the effects of fascism on sexual abuse in Germany. I take as my point of departure the family as the place of sexual abuse and concentrate on the meaning that sexual abuse occupies within the family. I also take as my starting point the destruction of relationships between the abusive adults and the abused children, as well as within the family as a whole. Fascism itself brought about a destruction of families and pressured families to open up intimate spheres—above all, through children and youth—to the controlling organs of the fascist state. Youth were exposed to a tension of loyalty that forced them out of the family and instilled mistrust in them, mistrust that was subsequently brought back into the family. Silence and concealment became a "principle of survival," even within the family itself. Foremost was the parents' silence; they were forced to conceal their differences with the fascistic system. They did not speak about what they saw outside, what they experienced, what they went along with or took part in, the reasons they were compelled, or the ways in which they bowed to pressure. Likewise, they remained silent about the discrepancies between their actions and their ideas of a moral and just life, ideas that they perpetually had to violate. They remained silent about the horrors and atrocities that they knew, half-knew, or suspected. To escape unscathed, they tried to look away. These attempts created a mental climate of untruthfulness, concealment, and secrecy that ripped deep wounds in their self-consciousness. With this damaged self-consciousness, with strategies of conformity such as looking away and concealing, the Germans experienced the defeat of fascism and stood intimidated, laden with feelings of guilt, vulnerable to what would come at them. Only a few experienced this period as a liberation. One spoke of "collapse," yielded oneself to "reconstruction," desired most of all to erase history.

We must place lying at the center of the relationship between National Socialism and sexual abuse. Lying is the specific aspect of National Socialism that intrudes into the intimate relationships between people. Inside the lie, the murder of Jews—which distinguishes National Socialism from other dictatorships—was brought into the family. Lying was the people's "survival strategy" in the face of horror. No one "knew" of the murder of the Jews—although everyone could see how the Jews "disappeared" from their field of vision, from their midst. The looking away, the concealment, the lying, became endemic in National Socialism; it colored everyday life, thought, speech, and the actions of the Germans (even those who were outside of the sphere of influence of National Socialism). Never was there so much lying.[78]

The lying that poisoned relationships between people did not stop at those intimate relationships. Lying, the concealment of knowledge, is at the center of sexual abuse. Lying, the opportunity for the subject to say something different from what he thinks or knows—to be different from that which he is (Lacan)—is certainly a "weapon of the weak." It destroys, however, the most important and fragile instrument of human coexistence: speech, the breath of the soul.

Lying did not stop with the defeat of National Socialism. On the contrary, one could in fact say that it actually began to flourish for the first time and on a large scale, as if in a hothouse. The millions of members of the National Socialist Workers Party (NSDAP), who swore they had had nothing to do with the Nazi system ("denazification"), that they knew nothing, continued and informed the nascent phase of the Federal Republic—always severely shaken by the discovery, the unmasking, that extended into the ranks of the political classes.

The fathers concealed from the children what they knew, what they had known before, what they had experienced, what they had seen. They lied to the children, while the mothers remained silent. This climate of concealment—"Silence is reactionary" (Sartre)—determined the developmental period of the postwar Federal Republic. In this silence, relationships atrophied. Diversion lay in an ecstasy of consuming. Silence, speechlessness, lying—all are part of the climate in which sexual abuse also prospers. Putting an end to the silence is certainly the first step in the liberation of the destructive imprisonment of the victim, and in the liberation of the perpetrator from the relationship of abuse.

NOTES

1. See Peter Wetzels, *Gewalterfahrungen in der Kindheit. Sexueller Mißbrauch, körperliche Mißhandlung und deren langfristige Konsequenzen. Interdisziplinäre Beiträge zur kriminologischen Forschung*, vol. 8 (Baden-Baden: Nomos, 1997).

2. "Daughter raped two thousand times. Can he still be called a father? The word 'father' implies protection, kindness, love. This man, however, was a torturer, cold and boundlessly cruel" (*Bild*). In this excerpt, *Bild* attempts to reconstruct the image of the undamaged family in which sexual abuse does not take place.

3. Barbara Kavemann and Ingrid Lohstöter, *Väter als Täter* (Reinbek bei Hamburg: Rowohlt, 1984).

4. M. Metcalfe, R. Oppenheimer, A. Dignon, and R. L. Palmer, "Childhood Sexual Experiences Reported by Male Psychiatric Patients," *Psychological Medicine* 20 (1990): 925–929; R. L. Palmer, D. A. Chaloner, and R. Oppenheimer, "Childhood Sexual Experiences with Adults Reported by Female Psychiatric Patients," *British Journal of Psychiatry* 160 (1992): 261–265; A. Jacobson and C. Herald, "The Relevance of Childhood Sexual Abuse to Adult Psychiatric Inpatient Care," *Hospital Community Psychiatry* 41 (1990): 154–158; J. Kinzl, W. Biebl, and H. Hinterhuber, "Die Bedeutung von Inzesterlebnissen für die Entstehung psychiatrischer und psychosomatischer Erkrankungen," *Nervenarzt* 62 (1991): 565–569; J. Surrey, C. Swett, Jr., A. Michaels, and S. Levin, "Reported History of Physical and Sexual Abuse and Severity of Symptomatology in Women Psychiatric Outpatients," *American Journal of Orthopsychiatry* 60 (1990): 412–417; G. M. Margo and E. M. McLees, "Further Evidence for the Significance of Childhood Abuse History in Psychiatric Inpatients," *Comparative Psychiatry* 32 (1991): 362–366.

5. Craig Allen, "Socio-Demographics, Family Satisfaction, and Child Sexual Abuse Experiences of Women and Men Who Sexually Abuse Children," Address, Ninth International Congress on Child Abuse and Neglect, Chicago, September 1992.

6. See Gerhard Amendt, *Wie Mütter ihre Söhne sehen* (Bremen: Ikaru, 1993).

7. Ibid., 41.

8. Ibid., 43.

9. Ibid., 45.

10. Ibid., 38.

11. Ibid., 26.

12. Ibid., 49–50.

13. Ibid., 48.

14. Ibid., 50.

15. Ibid., 13.

16. Ibid., 35.

17. Ibid., 59.

18. Ibid., 55.

19. Ibid., 72.

20. Ibid., 63, 72. These precautions obviously do not reach their goal of preventing circumcision: more circumcisions have been reported in the new *Bundesländer* (17.1 percent compared to a previous 10 percent), although the number and duration of preventative measures is higher there than in the old *Bundesländer*: D5, D6, D7.

21. Ibid., 68–69.

22. Ibid., 63.

23. Ibid., 77. Here Amendt also compares these motherly measures of prevention to the roughness of doctors toward female patients.

24. Ibid.

25. Ibid.

26. Ibid., 63.

27. Ibid., 70.

28. Ibid., 83.

29. Ibid., 63.

30. Ibid., 74.

31. T. S. Trepper and M. J. Barret, *Inzest und Therapie: Ein (system)therapeutisches Handbuch* (Dortmund: Verlag modernes Lernen, 1989), 152.

32. Compare Klaus-Jürgen Bruder, "Die Scham des Mißbrauchers und die Probleme der Therapie," *Psychoanalytische Blätter* 4 (1996): 104–119.

33. C. Marquit, "Der Täter, Persönlichkeitsstruktur und Behandlung," *Sexueller Mißbrauch von Kindern in Familien*, L. Backe and N. Leick, eds. (Kölm: Deutscher Ärzte Verlag, 1983), 128.

34. See Ronnie Janoff-Bulman, "The Aftermath of Victimization: Rebuilding Shattered Assumptions," *Trauma and Its Wake: The Study and Treatment of Post-Traumatic Stress Disorder*, Charles R. Figley, ed. (New York: Brunner Mazel, 1985).

35. See H. Petri, *Erziehungsgewalt* (Frankfurt a.M.: Fischer, 1989).

36. W. R. D. Fairbairn, "The Repression and the Return of Bad Objects," *Psychoanalytic Studies of the Personality* (London: Routledge and Kegan Paul, 1952), 19.

37. G. Ryan, S. Lane, J. Davis, and C. Isaac, "Juvenile Sex Offenders: Development and Correction," *Child Abuse and Neglect* 11 (1987): 385–395.

38. C. Cooper, W. Murphy, and M. Haynes, "Characteristics of Abused and Nonabused Adolescent Sexual Offenders," *Sexual Abuse: A Journal of Research and Treatment* 8 (1996): 105–119.

39. Fairbairn, 65. The children's symptoms are predominantly attributed to a failure of defense mechanisms through which bad objects would be kept repressed.

40. J. J. Peters, "Children Who Are Victims of Sexual Assault and the Psychology of Offenders," *American Journal of Psychotherapy* 30 (1976): 398–421; A. Rosenfeld, "Incidence of a History of Incest among Eighteen Female Psychiatric Patients," *American Journal of Psychiatry* (1979) 136: 791–795; A. Rosenfeld et al., "Incest and Sexual Abuse of Children," *Journal of American Academic Child Psychiatry* 16 (1977): 327–339; J. T. Landis, "Experiences of Five Hundred Children with Adult Sexual Deviation," *Psychiatric Quarterly* (Supplement) 30 (1956): 91–109.

41. B. F. Steele and H. Alexander, "Long-Term Effects of Sexual Abuse in Childhood," *Sexually Abused Children and Their Families*, P. B. Mrazek and C. H. Kempe, eds. (New York: Pergamon, 1981), 224.

42. See R. S. Kempe and C. H. Kempe, *Kindesmißhandlung* (Stuttgart: Klett, 1980); L. L. Shengold, "Child Abuse and Deprivation: Soul Murder," *Journal of the American Psychoanalytical Association* 27 (1979): 533–559. See also B. F. Steele and H. Alexander, "Long-Term Effects of Sexual Abuse in Childhood," op. cit.

43. Sandor Ferenczi, "Die Leidenschaften der Erwachsenen und deren Einfluß auf Charakter und Sexualentwicklung des Kindes: Sprachverwirrung zwischen den Erwachsenen und dem Kind," *Schriften zur Psychoanalyse*, vol. 2 (1932): 303–313.

44. See M. Hirsch, *Realer Inzest. Psychodynamik des sexuellen Mißbrauchs in der Familie* (Berlin: Springer, 1978), 126 ff.

45. Anthony Giddens, *Wandel der Intimität. Sexualität, Liebe und Erotik in modernen Gesellschaften* (Frankfurt a.M.: Fischer Zeitschriften, 1993), 100. Published in English as *The Transformation of Intimacy: Sexuality, Love and Eroticism in Modern Societies* (Stanford, Calif.: Stanford University Press, 1992).

46. Ibid.

47. Ibid., 103.

48. Ibid., 103, 105.

49. Ibid., 87.

50. Ibid.

51. Ibid.

52. Ibid., 87 f.

53. Klaus Wahl, *Die Modernisierungsfalle* (Frankfurt a.M.: Suhrkamp, 1989), 181 f.

54. Ibid., 162.

55. Ibid., 79.

56. Ibid., 97.

57. Ibid., 161.

58. Ibid., 163.

59. Ibid., 190.

60. Ibid., 46.

61. Michel Foucault, *The History of Sexuality: An Introduction, Volume 1*, Robert Hurley, trans. (New York: Vintage, 1978), 97. This and subsequent citations are from Robert Hurley's translation.

62. Ibid.

63. Ibid., 147.

64. Ibid.

65. Ibid., 149.

66. Ibid., 137.

67. Giddens, 91.

68. Ibid., 190.

69. Ibid., 144.

70. Ibid., 132.

71. Ibid., 137.

72. Ibid., 189 f.

73. Ibid., 192 f.

74. Ibid., 168 f.

75. Ibid., 145.

76. Ibid., 106.

77. Ibid., 204.

78. Alexander Koyre, "Betrachtungen über die Lüge (1943)," *Freibeuter*, vol. 72 (Berlin: Wagenbach, 1997).

Part III

Reading Masculinity in Postwar
German Literature

The Motif of the Man, Who, Although He Loves, Goes to War: On the History of the Construction of Masculinity in the European Tradition

Carl Pietzcker

This chapter outlines the history of a motif as it has been depicted in European literature for more than two millennia. Against the background of this tradition, contemporary constructions of masculine identity have become increasingly easier to understand. Historically, various adaptations of this motif can be read as short anecdotes, each of which manifests a cultural context: the production of masculine identity through love for a woman, but also through aversion to her. At issue is a phantasy that has contributed to the formation of European culture and has even influenced male behavior today, as it has also influenced literature that avoids the contradictions of social reality in favor of escapist entertainment. Since the turn of the century, however, this phantasy has been disappearing from texts that confront reality. Men who seek to extract themselves from patriarchal determinations of gender roles must also liberate themselves from this phantasy.

I will begin with an early example: the Omphale saga reported by Apollodorus (book II, lines 6 and 3 ff.)[1] and Diodorus (book IV, line 31),[2] which experienced various adaptations in antiquity.[3] Heracles, stricken with illness as a punishment for murder, questions the oracle and discovers that he will be freed from his suffering, provided that he sell himself for three years as an indentured servant and give the money to the father of the man he has killed. Heracles has himself sold as a slave to Omphale, Queen of Lydia, recovers from his sickness, and spends three years in her service. He establishes order, vanquishes thieves

This chapter was originally published in German in Carl Pietzcker, *Einheit, Trennung und Wiedervereinigung. Psychoanalytische Untersuchungen eines religiösen, philosophischen, politischen und literarischen Musters* (Würzburg: Königshausen und Neumann, 1996).

and monsters, and wins her love; she bears him a son named Lamus. In his opulent living, he forgets his masculine virtues and loses himself in feminine work. Omphale, whom he obeys, carries his club, dresses herself in his lion's skin, and commands him to wear women's robes. She brings him to the point where he spins wool at her feet; he fears her reproach. When the three years pass, however, he awakens from his confusion and discards his women's robes. It takes but a moment and suddenly he is Zeus's powerful son again, who sets out to take revenge upon his enemies. This demi-god, the epitome of heroic masculinity, has escaped the danger of impending emasculation as it threatens blind lovers in phantasy. Such a love means the loss of masculine-phallic activities that profoundly shape the civilizing of the world. Emasculation is abhorrent, and men are only saved from it by coming to their senses.

Recognizable here is a mythically shaped phantasy that twentieth-century psychoanalysis has studied, not only in boys, but also in men.

THE CHILD BECOMES A BOY

We read in psychoanalytic literature that the little boy takes a significant step toward masculine identity when he turns away from the overly powerful mother and looks to the father as a redeeming third factor; "triangulated" by the father, he gains distance from the mother. Since birth, he has experienced himself as dependent upon her; his survival depended upon her, her power was absolute. She nurtured and cared for him, and also necessarily frustrated him. Thus he developed images of an all-powerful "good" mother who nurtured and protected him, yet who was simultaneously all powerful and threateningly "evil." Through identification, these two images permeated his self-images as well as his resulting identity. As Janine Chasseguet-Smirgel describes it, the image of a castrated mother originates during the phase in which the boy extracts himself from his identification with the mother and begins to define himself as a man: "Analysts have mainly stressed the horror (the 'Abscheu') the little boy feels when he realizes that his mother has no penis, since it means to him that she has been castrated, thus confirming his idea that such a terrifying possibility exists."[4] This "horror" is connected with a "triumph at last, over the omnipotent mother"; the boy, who had previously submitted to her omnipotence, now possesses an organ that she lacks, which in patriarchal societies means power for him. This seems to be especially important for the boy's narcissism, Chasseguet-Smirgel points out.[5] He who had felt powerless is now, as the possessor of a penis, superior to his mother, and can vent his rage about his dependence. He distances himself from his mother and loathes her in fear-driven "horror"; she embodies the threat of losing that with which he now triumphs. Often she seeks to hold onto him, above all through feelings: "Mother cries so much,/She has lost her little Hans." He seeks new security through identification with the penis-carrying father. Yet this also means relinquishing a closeness to his mother, one that had provided security and the gratification of his desires.

As long as the adult man remains bound to the image of an omnipotent, yet also castrated, mother, he will seek triumph over women as successors to the mother. He must always prove his phallicity anew, narcissistically overcompensate for the threat, and devalue women whom he experiences as threatening.

> The little boy's triumph over the omnipotent mother has many effects on his future relations with women. Bergler [an analyst] points out that men attempt to reverse the infantile situation experienced with the mother and live out actively what they have endured passively, thus turning her into the dependent child they had been.[6]

Filled with fear, he will devalue and distance himself from women as soon as he experiences them as active, controlling, or even devouring, often to escape Oedipal threat as well. He will phallically go out into the hostile world and convert his aggression, which springs from his rage at the all-powerful mother and her successors, into heroic and cultural deeds. He will experience this as masculine. Yet this drama does not necessarily have to take place in such an acute manner.

> If the little boy has not been traumatized by the omnipotent mother, if her attitude has been neither too restraining, nor too invasive, he will be sufficiently reassured by the possession of his penis to dispense with constant reiteration of the triumphant feeling he once experienced.[7]

The adolescent man also possesses the ability to extract himself in significant ways from the image of the omnipotent mother. Masculine identity, on the other hand, will remain threatened, precisely because it is grounded in dis-identification with the mother. "Greenson holds the opinion 'that men are far more uncertain about their maleness than women about their femaleness. I believe women's certainty about their gender identity and men's insecurity about theirs are rooted in early identification with the mother.'"[8] Consequently, the father gains particular importance as a third factor that helps the boy detach himself from the symbiotic duality, that is, the father gains significance as a triangulating authority.

> Abelin assumes that the object representation of the father (or of a father-substitute) must take shape as a contrast-representation in addition to a self-representation and object representation of the mother in order to enable a child to experience a conception of its separation outside of the self-object unity with the mother.[9]

If the small boy is successful in identifying with the triangulating father, he can, under optimal conditions, give up the symbiotic relationship with his mother and identify with characteristics of the mother as well as the father.[10] However:

> In many men for whom the identification with the father was insufficiently successful, one observes a forced masculinity later in life (such as a disgust for anything female or feminine feelings, an affinity for super-masculine sports, reckless driving, a high regard for intellect and reason, etc.). Behind the fractured masculine gender identity, a residual identification with the mother and the jealousy for her must be fended off, so that this forced masculinity can be regarded as a reaction formation.[11]

Jealousy for the mother stems from dis-identification. After all, the boy cannot be like her any longer. He has lost a part of himself: he has had an experience of devaluation. He answers with jealousy and rage toward the mother who represents or perhaps possesses what he lacks, such as the ability to nurture and to connect directly with others. He now differentiates between feminine and masculine with a sharp dualism, devaluing the feminine and exalting the masculine. This naturally leads to a situation in which he is now forced, and perhaps later as an adult as well, to stress his masculinity and to avoid closeness to everything feminine; nearness could, after all, threaten the clear border between woman and man, push the man toward the woman, and perhaps even emasculate him. In longing for what he lacks, he would be lured out from the cold battlement of the fortress he built out of fear, into the dangerously warm swamps of vile femininity. More secure are mistrust, distance, barriers, clear masculine realms, hierarchies, avoidance of feelings, especially empathy, and, without fail, a rationality clearly separated from and placed far above emotions.

Phantasies of separation from the mother leave their marks on the construction of masculine identity and also influence the behavior of men. These phantasies are awakened when a man loves a woman. Love brings him back to his dearly beloved, but also feared, mother. Early mother-images resurface: the omnipotent "good" mother, the "evil" mother, and also the "castrated" mother. With them also surface fear, desire, rage, envy, and the old drama of separation—a longing for symbiosis and a fear of it. This is generally observed when the man defines himself through the negation of the woman as the Other and then projects onto her parts of himself that he negates; especially when he excludes her, as "nature," from the culture he sees as an essentially masculine realm. Masculinity thus creates itself through images of women in which early mother-images reappear, and through separation.

THE INTENTION

The psychoanalytic reconstruction of this phase of masculine identity construction and its consequences runs the risk of ahistorically generalizing the results of contemporary analyses. The question remains whether, and to what extent, such ahistorical generalizations can be sustained. It is my opinion that we must expect a phase of dis-identification, at least in those cases where the boy is raised by women within a patriarchal society, even if it perhaps takes various courses and is worked through differently. In fact, in more than 3,000 years of European history, scenarios of this separation drama have found their way into the literary texts of male authors; this is certainly demonstrated by the motif of the man who loves a woman, arises, leaves her, and goes off to battle. It seems that boys in patriarchal societies continually reshape their fear-driven phantasy of separation, their accentuation of phallic aggression, and therefore, their tendency toward phallic domination. It also seems that adult men incorporate these elements into historically different literary conceptions of reality, such as the rivalry of empires or the threat to confessional or social order, and also the conflict between duty and desire. Here we can study an aspect of the history of a mentality as a history of the imaginary.

I would like to extract from its textual coherence the scene in which a man who, though he has just loved, now departs, as a literary motif, in order to retrace its history. It is not my intention to interpret the texts in their entireties, nor even to determine the location of the scene within the functional coherence of the text itself, but rather to pursue exclusively the formation and history of this motif and thus to examine the extent to which it has changed over the course of literary history. Only then shall I begin to probe the reason for this change. I must necessarily work with analogies, especially with the analogy between the relationship of the boy to his mother and the relationship of the adult man to mother-images—that is, to his lover—but also the analogy between these relationships and the relationship of the fictionalized man to the fictionalized woman.[12] I see myself compelled to work with analogies through psychoanalytic theory, which holds that early scenes return in later behavior. However, this also obliges me not to overlook the variances between early scenes and their later manifestations.

I am thus expanding the traditional research of a literary motif to include the psychological processes to which the motif owes its respective adaptations. The history of a motif becomes the history of a phantasy, and, indirectly, that of the psychological progenitors of that phantasy. I cannot, however, reconstruct the history of these psychological progenitors in its entirety here, if for no other reason than because I am exploring a single motif without examining those related to it. Essential desires and fears of this one phantasy can transfer themselves onto other motifs, in our case, the motifs of the man who returns (for example, according to the motto "The child comes to its senses,/Comes home quickly") or never leaves in the first place, or even frees himself from a given order through love. Thus I will not arrive at a psychohistorical literary history but perhaps at perspectives on paths that lead to one. These selected examples are, I hope, representative of the adaptations of the motif; they need not prove representative of the literature of their respective eras.

HERACLES AND ACHILLES

The Omphale episode allows male producers and recipients to stage phantasies of separation from the mother anew—as if in a psychodrama with Heracles as their surrogate—and to assure themselves of their masculinity after temptation, threat, and separation. The scene plays out not in the interior of a figure, but rather, between figures—between Heracles and Omphale—who are not psychologized. Yet with the affectionate Omphale, the image of the loving, nurturing, and protective "good mother" whom men frequently long for in love, also converges with that of the active, devouring mother who summons first the son and then the man away from his endeavors in the world back into her hermetic space and into passivity. This arouses the image of the "castrating mother" who robs the man of his laurels. Even identification with the mother resurfaces in gender transformation; masculine gender identity threatens to dissolve. The mother-images appear in mythological apparel; Omphale is understood as both the "Earth-Goddess" and the "Death-Goddess" at the same time, and Heracles, as a hero, is persecuted by mother-deities, that is, by mother-images translated into the mythological:

> Hera, who persecutes the hero, O., who robs him of his masculine strength and honor, Deianeira, who kills him, are all essentially one and the same mythical personality: the personification of the mighty Earth- and Death-Goddess; the gynecocratic element finds its mythical explanation here.[13]

In the case of Heracles's love for Omphale, fear of this mother-image is controlled supernaturally three times over. First, the hero does not succumb to love of his own free will, but rather love appears as part of his punishment. Love is thus externalized, so as to not threaten or overwhelm those who adopt this phantasy from the inside. Second, this love conquers Heracles, and yet as the masculine hero par excellence, he will certainly escape it again. Third, fear of the mother-images, and thus fear of women, remains concealed and only reappears behind the mask of contempt for the feminine, perhaps along the lines, "We're not afraid; on the contrary, we despise the feminine from the higher standpoint of the masculine!" In this scenario, flight is not necessary; contemplation of one's own masculinity suffices and is highly valued for the sake of despising the feminine. Passivity now turns into activity; the static becomes dynamic. Rage at the menacing mother-images becomes externalized; from there it does not assert itself in haphazard phallic aggressiveness but rather is channeled and sublimated through cultural tasks. Masculine identity defines itself through such a transition to a highly valued active cultivation of the world. Here, however, we have a pregenital identity that is grounded in the exclusively dualistic opposition of man and woman and not upon mutual exchange. The woman remains forgotten; Heracles does not return to Omphale.

If we keep in mind that Omphale stood as an allegory for the Orient and its supposedly lavish, even orgiastic lifestyle, then we see in Heracles an early image of the culture-producing European: he remained bound to the image of the omnipotent mother, dis-identified himself through a clear division, and thus sought to subdue the "effemination" (*effeminatio*), the softness, the "Orient" within himself. He achieved masculine identity, autonomy, and opportunities for self-determined action, the likes of which were denied to women because they had far greater difficulty extracting themselves from the pull of early unity; when successful, then not with such a clear division—thus not driven by fear either. The motif of the man who loves and then goes to war demonstrates one of the manners in which masculinity was determined in the process of history; with it, one can observe what European men saw as a threat and what values they employed against the threat posed by the loving woman. Here we can observe specific instances, where various eras made one into a man, where men saw their strengths, their weaknesses, and the contradictions in which they moved and in which they had to maintain themselves as men. What space was open to them? What did they forfeit with the woman, how did they treat themselves, and how did they treat what they had lost?

Consider this further example from Greek antiquity: Thetis has hidden her young son Achilles—dressed in girl's clothing—on Scyros at the court of Lycomedes. She wishes to save him from an early death; according to an oracle, death is to befall him before the walls of Troy. He is raised with the daughters of Lycomedes performing women's chores. He wins the love of Lycomedes's daughter Deidamia and secretly becomes her consort; she will bear him his son Neoptolemos. The Greeks, however, need Achilles for victory over Troy, so Odysseus is sent to find him. Odysseus cannot, however, recognize him among the girls, so he cleverly commands that jewelry and dresses be brought as presents, and among them a shield and a spear. He then has a trumpet sound suddenly. The girls flee, but Achilles seizes the weapons. Revealing his identity, he must return to Troy and leave Deidamia. Thus here is the birth of the hero out of effeminating love.[14] Disguised as a woman by his mother and kept away from men's battles, he arises phallically, changes clothing, and sets out to kill. This requires even less justification than in the case of Heracles, who, unlike Achilles, does not manage to detach himself under his own power but rather by the intervention of a third factor. Like the boy in psychoanalytic theory who gains his masculine identity through dis-identification and with the support of a masculine third, so here does the boy become a hero. Fear of the threatening mother is not felt, while masculine heroism, on the other hand, is naturally recognized. He who would succumb to the woman would make himself a comic figure in the heroic scenario; it is better to kill and die before Troy.

VIRGIL: *THE AENEID*

Aeneas leaves Dido for the sake of his descendants and the future Roman state; his principles are more important to him than his love.[15] He has come ashore on the African coast with his fleet, and a passionate love ignites there between him and Queen Dido. He sets to work to build a city until Mercury speaks to him under orders from Jupiter. He tells Aeneas that he is building Carthage like a woman's servant, forgetting his fate and his future empire. He should remember his son Ascanius and his rule over Italy. Aeneas immediately prepares for departure. Dido pleads with him to stay, yet he shows no reaction and forces his grief back into his heart. Aeneas tells her that he shall not forget her, but departs nonetheless for Italy, saying the gods have ordered it. His love is one thing, his fatherland another. He says he cannot rob his son of the empire promised to him. His great love for the queen moves him, but she is unable to make him waver. He then flees, just in time before she kills herself.[16]

Here the heroic man obeys a divine injunction and sacrifices his love to the future state. He still knows feelings of love, even expresses them, yet he does not allow himself to be determined by them and thus conquers his grief. The father now enters into the drama of separation from the mother, a scenario we encounter in this text as well. As a third factor, the commandment pronounced by the father-god raises itself between the mother- and son-figures and separates them. It functions just as in the father's childhood separation drama. There it assumes special importance as a third and thus triangulating factor that helps the boy extract himself from the symbiotic dyad.[17] In the Heracles myth, the father-instance Zeus had barely managed to help the son-figure against the threatening mother-figure; in the Omphale episode, the father-figure did not intervene at all. Apparently, when the Heracles myth was conjured, patriarchal order had not yet become completely dominant. Here in *The Aeneid*, Jupiter's commandment and Aeneas's obedience suffice to immediately break the woman's power over the man in love. From this point on, the triangulating moment will be further depersonalized: from the father to the father-god, to his commandment, to the norms of society, to the voice of conscience, and finally to the structured text, which provides an assuring distance for writer and reader alike. The more this third factor fades with increasing abstraction into the interior of the individual, and finally into the form of a literary text, the more it risks losing its triangulating power. For men who love, it can barely continue to provide them with a refuge from dangerous mother-images outside of

themselves and the work of art. Only the individualism of the eighteenth century, and even more clearly the form-conscious literature of
the twentieth century, will venture so far. Here in *The Aeneid*, Jupiter's
commandment rationalizes the son-figure's flight, does not allow it to be
recognized as a fleeing, and renders it morally unassailable. It also creates
the reassuring distance from the threatening mother-image that allows
one to partially dispense with the devaluation of the woman, as well as
to empathetically perceive the suffering of the one left behind. The loss
of gender identity is barely perceptible anymore, and aggression is more
clearly directed into sublimating channels. The epic presents the history
of domination; the power struggle between Rome and Carthage is justified by a love story that follows early phantasy scenes. Men who possess,
attain, or secure power must guard themselves against womanly love, for
womanly love threatens power.

Aeneas's abandonment of Dido marks the historical moment when
the obedient man enters the field of literature as an identification figure
for the reader. At this point, the commandment he follows is not yet
fully internalized as duty, since it still reaches him from the outside
through Jupiter's messenger, yet it serves to form the construction of a
masculine-dominant ego by dividing the man from the woman. Consequently, it immediately demands the sacrifice of one's own happiness in
love. The text shows the suffering to which it leads and reflects at least
indirectly the hero's guilt.

This view of *The Aeneid* shows us that we can read in our motif
those feelings that are permissible for the man, what they mean to him,
and how he contends with them. We can read how each separation is
justified as masculine behavior, under which circumstances the man ar-
rives at the separation, and under which circumstances he can overcome
it. We would be oversimplifying if we regarded this as an exclusively
male problematic. Separation from early unity and from scenes in which
this unity returns are, for men and women alike, the unavoidable necessities of becoming an adult, and ultimately, of the subject's constitution.
Only those who conquer the disparity between staying and leaving and
then move on can take their lives into their own hands, gain a measure
of autonomy, and experience the world. Women who were denied this
by patriarchal structures and who were not forced to flee early unity had
a more difficult time constituting themselves as autonomous subjects
who actively explore or shape the world. To this extent, "effemination"
was a catastrophe for women as well as for men. Women often could not
escape it, and to this degree could not constitute themselves as subjects.
In contrast, men fled from effemination through splitting, devaluation

of the feminine, and overvaluation of the masculine—the constitution of the subject, but at the cost of aspects of the self and the other gender. A free exchange between autonomy and submission, between experiences or phantasies of unity and those of separation, was rarely possible for either men or women. In the literature of recent decades, with the disruption of patriarchal structures, women such as Nora, who separate themselves and assume control over their lives, and men who free themselves from the old pattern, appear with increasing frequency. The motif loses its capacity to construct masculine identity. In today's reality, just as in literature, stronger, more self-assured women are taking up the search and are themselves walking the path through separation and guilt. Thus they also are becoming more interesting as literary heroines; there is little earth shattering to tell about a woman who sits at home, even if she is being courted, and lures, keeps, loses, or has lost a man. After a separation, however, readers could follow her throughout the world.

HARTMANN VON AUE: *EREC*

At the end of the twelfth century, Hartmann von Aue adapts the motif of the man who loves and then leaves in his *Erec*, so that it leads to the dissolution from a devouring love, but not to the ultimate separation from his beloved wife. King Erec "lies around" (*verligt sich*) with his wife Enite until he loses his "honor" (*êre*) at court.[18] Enite discovers this, holds herself responsible, and laments while she believes he is sleeping. He overhears everything, however, and makes her explain to him about his loss of "honor." He immediately rises from his bed and leaves on an *aventiure*.[19] In a maneuver that is otherwise foreign to the motif, Enite must accompany him and perform a maid's services. Blame is placed on her, and she sets out with him. This offers her, at least potentially, the possibility of becoming a subject who behaves responsibly; moreover, it aggrandizes her. They both then prove themselves during the *aventiure*. Erec internalizes chivalrous norms to such a degree that he is able to save and instruct Mabonagrin, a knight who had allowed himself to be detained in the paradise of love:

> [T]hough no manner of good thing so gladdens the heart as when two lovers lie side by side—as is so with you and your wife—nonetheless, one ought, in truth, to escape upon occasion from the women. I have secretly heard from the lips of a woman that they do not object to our coming and going.[20]

"Honor" is finally restored; Erec and Enite assume the role of an ideal ruling couple in their kingdom. He can turn to her without "lying around."

Almost as in antiquity, we still find no hero who falls into an inner psychological crisis, no essential conflict within the figure itself, but rather, one between figures. Norms have not yet been internalized; neither Erec nor Enite have first-hand knowledge of what they are doing wrong. Only the court knows. It is only from the court, that is, from outside, that the impetus comes; it also is the court that restores their "honor." Erec and Enite have already become individualized, however, giving rise to at least a rudimentary inner psychological crisis and the internalization of norms. The courtly epic plays out a confrontation with the danger of "lying around" and exhibits to the audience a path of self-discipline. The aim is to avoid exposing oneself to the draw toward merging, not to selfishly "lie around" in love but rather to consider the common interest, in this case, royal obligations. To this end, the text employs the phantasy of a man who still loves yet accordingly goes off to battle.

In contrast to other adaptations of this motif, the identity of the ruler who proves himself "masculine" but nevertheless loving is successful. Erec redeems himself from the disgrace of "lying around" through chivalrous deeds and proves himself a man. He does not, however, come to his senses through a man, but rather through a woman. She had to accompany him, thus he never divorces himself from her fully. Consequently, the text does not completely split off the hate that is directed at the mother-image from the beloved woman and carry it out into the world, but rather, the hate is directed toward the wife as well: Erec humiliates her. Because she is always with him, he can sense her love in the end. Since hate and devaluation remain connected to the woman herself, producers and recipients can identify with the hero and imagine scenes in which the woman, in her aggressive treatment of others, re-emerges from behind archaic images—scenes in which the man gains the capacity for ambivalence and empathy.

Like a third factor, the norms of the court separate the lovers; they disengage the two from a love that devours, providing them with a distance between one another. Erec can refer to these norms as an authority, because they provide him with the free space in which he can manage the separation. In this manner, affinity without fear is possible and successful because, although a male author places a male hero in the spotlight here, the text is still more concerned with the behavior of both, and thus includes the woman's behavior. Erec and Enite have both failed to live up to their duties as rulers; both learn to combine love with a conduct suitable for courtly society. On the *aventiure*, Enite learns the proper times to speak or to be silent, and if necessary, to transgress one norm for the sake of a more important one. Erec, whose aggressive-phallic characteristics become milder and more sublime in the service of others, learns to have the correct relationship to love and to battle. The courtly order triangulates and pulls both away from the attraction of "lying around"; thus the third factor does not exclusively serve in the procurement of masculine identity but rather helps both man and woman achieve distance and love at the same time. This double perspective, aimed at both of them, can be understood if we keep in mind the patron noble audience, which consisted of mostly educated literary women and predominantly illiterate men, to whom the text was sometimes read even during the writing process.[21] In contrast to the present, the poet knew for whom he wrote. Since he also had to offer models of identification to the women, the male perspective could not exert itself uncensored: from the perspective of developmental psychology, the early phantasy scene unfolded on a more mature level of phantasizing. Subsequently, however, the motif could no longer assert itself in a form that simultaneously cultivated love and distance between lovers. Masculinity was openly directed toward the woman, then it disappeared again. The enticement of devouring love, redemptive separation, and phallic-aggressive masculine self-empowerment further stimulated manifestations of the motif: in developmental psychology, this is an archaic pattern of behavior and phantasy.

TORQUATO TASSO: *JERUSALEM DELIVERED*

In the sixteenth century, the tradition of this more archaic pattern surfaces in a condensed and intensified form in Torquato Tasso's *Jerusalem Delivered*.[22] In this story, Rinaldo leaves Armida. Prince Höllenfürst seeks to prevent Godfrey of Bouillon's siege upon Jerusalem, and for this reason he sends the sorceress Armida to the Christian encampment. She diverts Christian knights from their duties and takes them prisoner. Rinaldo manages to free them, however. There Armida tries to charm him; when she fails, she attempts to kill him but instead falls in love with him and whisks him away to a distant island. Godfrey dispatches two knights to retrieve him. They reach Armida's palace garden—a lover's paradise—where she and Rinaldo enjoy their love. Steadfast, the knights harden their hearts against the temptations of desire and take advantage of the moment when Armida leaves Rinaldo alone. They show him the magnificence of their weapons.

> Even as the fierce war-horse that has been retired unbeaten from the hard-won honor of arms and wanders loose among the herds and through the pastures a wanton husband in a vile re-pose, if sound of trumpet or glint of steel awaken him, at once he is turned to it whinnying: he longs for the lists and (bearing his master on his back) to answer shock for shock in full career;
>   So the youth responded when the glitter of weapons sud-denly struck his eyes. That spirit of his so warlike, that spirit so burning fierce, by that gleaming was wholly awakened, though it had been languishing among soft delights and drunk and drowsy among pleasures. (28–29)

They hold their shields up to him, and he sees in his reflection what has become of himself: "How much adorned with delicate elegance: he breathes forth all perfumed, his hair and mantle wanton; and his sword . . . made effeminate at his side by too much luxury; it is so trimmed that it seems a useless ornament, not the fierce instrument of war" (30). "As a man by deep and heavy sleep oppressed returns to himself after long delirious raving, so he returned by gazing upon himself" (31). He is ashamed. They urge him: "'Up! up! The army is calling you, and God-frey calls . . . Come, soldier of destiny, and let . . . the wicked sect . . . fall to earth perished beneath your inevitable sword'" (33). He then tears off his dishonorable trim and rushes off. One last time he hears Armida's lamentations and her attempts to seduce him; however, "Love does not enter to kindle the old flame anew in his breast" (52). He only feels sympathy and advises her to free herself from this terribly enflamed passion: "Stay here in peace; I am going; you are not allowed to come with me; he who is guiding me forbids it" (56). She accuses him of an inhuman lack of compassion, but fails to see the bitter suffering in his eyes. Compassion torments him; "harsh necessity drags him along with her" (62). He rides away. Filled with rage, she wishes to avenge herself against him and the Christians.

Like Heracles and Achilles, so too does Rinaldo—awakened from his "effemination"—rush to his weapons. Like Aeneas, he leaves for the sake of a higher purpose: he is to liberate Jerusalem. He too is saved by men from the tempting unity of love, where warlike phallicity risks its own destruction. Masculine third factors dissolve the dyad and compel the heroic man to recognize his own disgrace in reflection. Triangulated in this manner, he can tear himself free. In addition, the Christian knight's duty, as a secure third factor that grounds him religiously in society and therefore also psychologically, provides him with a sure footing. Since his security has increased, the enticing danger also can be heightened: the seductive powers of the woman who, in succession to Circe, becomes a sorceress, the rapture in the garden of love with its emasculating lure, as well as the sympathy for the one left behind. The inner struggle between "passion" and "reason" can now be more clearly developed. With confidence, the hero can separate himself from his beloved while maintaining a compassionate but nonetheless superior position, and can even ask that she restrain herself; he is an exemplary knight whose Christianity and masculinity are restored through the act of separation. Only much later will he save Armida from suicide and convert her. Tasso wrote this at the time of the Counter-Reformation; the sensuality that the Renaissance had previously displayed can now, under the threat of blazing funeral pyres, only be enjoyed at the price that it is attributed to a diabolically devious woman. Christian duty also demands escape from her magic. It demands, after one's own sexuality has been devalued and repressed, the struggle with the Other, the heathens; after self-repression, it demands the repression of others. This is well served by the phantasy of the man who loves and then goes off to battle.

THE EIGHTEENTH CENTURY: GOETHE

With the rise of bourgeois lifestyles in the eighteenth century, the image of masculine love changes, and so too does the motif of the man who loves, then leaves. With the continued advancement of individualization and subjectification, which is easily observed in Goethe's writings, the man's feelings become the center of attention. His love for a woman and the separation from her become occasions for him to perceive himself as a feeling person. The man now no longer escapes from love through aggression, but rather as a sensitive Narcissus, a genius, just as Faust abandons Gretchen; or as an artist who finds himself again after the chaos of passion. He seeks to protect his autonomous subjectivity from the woman by leaving her. In this manner, he extends his subjectivity in order to find stability in her, as well as in a third factor. It seems that what should triangulate him is thus only "in" him or created by him. In the adaptation of this motif, even the aggression against the image of the evil mother hardly directs itself as a projection outward against evil ene-

mies. At best it flows sublimated into cultural work. More often, however, it turns against the lover himself and leads to images of his guilt,
weakness, or divided nature. Neither triangulating men nor duty to the
common good rescue him from the arms of a loving woman. On the
other hand, when duty does call, it is in the form of fidelity toward
the beloved, thus producing feelings of guilt. Since it is hardly possible
any longer for the man to flee a union in the name of a socially recognized third factor, authors have him passively suffer through the separation, rather than consciously and willfully carry it out. Such a farewell
forces him to retreat to the only thing to which he knows he is bound:
to himself and his genius, to art.

In the second version of Goethe's "Willkommen und Abschied"
("Welcome and Farewell"), we read:

> Yet alas, already with the morning sun
> Departing pains my heart:
> In your kisses, what delight!
> In your eyes, what pain!
> I went, you stood and gazed at the earth
> And watched me with tear-filled eyes:
> And yet, what joy to be loved!
> And to love, gods, what a joy![23]

The stifling farewell takes place without the lover being called away by
duty. Alone now—without her, and only externally triangulated by
imaginary "gods"—he can ecstatically enjoy the feelings of happiness in
love by himself. The woman occasions a heightened sense of feeling in
which the man joyfully experiences himself, and through which he escapes from her by triangulating himself through feelings and lyric
creativity.

In Goethe's cantata "Rinaldo," from 1811, one can study the dawn-
ing of a new male image.[24] Whereas Tasso, adhering fully to the tradition, had his Rinaldo escape from effeminating feelings of love and into
noble masculinity, and moreover, as he transferred his and his reader's
feelings of love onto the woman, staging them only as a phase to be
overcome in the man, so now does Goethe have his Rinaldo recall Armida with wistful sadness after the separation and succumb completely
to his emotions:

> My only joy, here have I lost it.
> Return to me the golden days

The paradises once again,
Dear heart, yes beat, beat!
Spirit true, bring them back![25]

The subjectivity of the reminiscing, loving man who leaves is now capable of becoming literary material. Rinaldo again relives his feelings of love; the once exterior, yet now interior, world created in his own memory out of emotion lures him back into the dangerous union of love but at the same time estranges him from the beloved outside through triangulation. At this point the two knights show him the diamond shield for the second time. Thus he must leave Armida for a second time. Not until after the completion of the mourning process does the hero gather enough courage to adhere to the old triangulating norm, the "ancestral virtues": "Yes, let it be so! I will pull myself together": grow up, construe myself a subject and so out, onto the waves of the sea

[t]hat refreshes
And blears
The bygone.
The blessedly
Begun
Awaits you.[26]

In the harmony of inner and outer nature, which "blears" the "bygone," he can set off with his eyes on the army commander, on Jerusalem, which must be liberated, on his duty and his goal:

Our glorious destination is here!
Ring out to the holy strand
A motto to the promised land:
Godofred and Solyma![27]

Before he summons the courage to redemptive duty, as was usual until this point, he gives himself over to the memory of feelings of love and separation; in doing this, he recuperates.

In this courtly cantata, Goethe seems able to combine an old model in which the man, triangulated by duty, flees to combat, with a new one: the difficult attempt to escape to one's own subjectivity.[28] He begins to destroy the old model, however, in the bourgeois genre of the novel: *Die Wahlvewandtschaften* has Eduard flee from his chaotic love life into war, but to no avail. He believes it necessary to avoid Ottilie, whom he loves, and when his wife Charlotte writes that she is pregnant by him—"Let us revere this strange accident as ordained by heaven, to create a new bond for our relationship"—he proceeds to seek refuge in combat.[29] Contrary to the tradition, the narrator portrays this as an escape and even names its social and psychological foundations:

> What took place in Eduard's soul from now on would be hard to describe. In such a predicament old habits and inclinations finally reappear to while away time and give life meaning. Hunting and war are always ready ways out for the nobleman. Eduard longed for external danger to preserve his internal balance. He longed for death, since life threatened to become unbearable; . . . Now it was a glorious feeling to set out under a general of whom he could say to himself: under his leadership death is probable and victory certain.[30]

The social-historical and psychological gaze of the bourgeois male is now turned directly upon the man who sets out for battle. This is the beginning of the intraliterary analysis of heroism and of the measure of a man who leaves his wife and goes off to war. From this point on, the man's heroism, social importance, and psychological motivation will be called into question until it becomes clear at the end of the nineteenth century that the motif is no longer useful for drafting literary masculine identity.

In *Faust*, Goethe shapes a bourgeois path. At the beginning of Part Two, Faust, like Rinaldo, is recuperating after having left Gretchen in prison.[31] In *Faust*, we also find intense feelings on the part of the man after the separation from his beloved. The redeeming commandment and the saving third factor are, however, missing. Feelings of abandonment, guilt, and love, as well as the staging of one's own identity and one's own path, have taken the place of commandments and duty that had previously aided in leaving one's lover:

> I am the fugitive, all houseless roaming,
> The monster without air or rest,
> That like a cataract, down rocks and gorges foaming,
> Leaps, maddened, into the abyss's breast!
> And side-wards she, with young unwakened senses,
> Within her cabin on the Alpine field
> Her simple, homely life commences
> Her little world therein concealed.
> And I, god's hat flung o'er me,

Had not enough, to thrust
The stubborn rocks before me
And strike them into dust!
She and her peace I yet must undermine:
Thou, Hell, hast claimed this sacrifice thine![32]

The masculine genius separates himself under the sign of the law along his own path, and under the sign of the demonic from the devalued woman with her "young unwakened senses," and thus intensifies his own emotions. The man cannot escape the woman who threatens to hold him captive in her "little world," neither in aggressive phallicity, nor in duty; thus he flees into himself, to his subjectivity, which he thereby unfolds and at the same time seeks to preserve. This subjectivity, for the sake of whose autonomy he has left the woman, is supposed to deliver him from her through triangulation: he must pull himself out of the swamp of devouring femininity by his own hair—a difficult, if not impossible, undertaking. Yet in his anxiety he imagines a colossal pony-tail for himself, intensifies his emotions and their contradictions, and raises himself into the mythical. Faust does not do it as a "monster," a creature with "god's hat flung o'er" or as an earth-shaking "cataract"— "How it simmers again, how it glows again!" Terrified of the woman and uncertain of his masculine identity, he stylizes himself as a natural event and his flight as an act between Heaven and Hell: "Thou, Hell, hast claimed this sacrifice thine!" The poor wretch makes himself important and becomes the epitome of German masculinity for more than a century.

THE MIDDLE OF THE NINETEENTH CENTURY

Texts from the nineteenth century sought to oppose such individualism with a socially constructed common interest: the man leaves the beloved, and in so doing, he assumes his duty as a universal category with which he can save himself; he internalizes it. Bourgeois authors portrayed this in the dominating feudal man, who, for the sake of his obligations as a civil architect, sacrifices the woman he loves. She must be killed so he can mature into a ruler conscientious of his duties.

In Friedrich Hebbel's tragic play *Agnes Bernauer* (1852),[33] which he regarded as a "strange portrayal of the tragic,"[34] Albrecht, the Bavarian heir to the crown, weds Agnes Bernauer, the daughter of a barber-surgeon, and abdicates the throne for her sake. When the line of inheritance is thus disrupted and civil war threatens, his father, Duke Ernst, has her condemned and executed; she has "disturbed the order of the world, divided father and son, and estranged a people from their prince."[35] Seeking vengeance, the son goes to war against the father. For his part, the father voluntarily hands the ducal scepter over to him, wanting to conduct "a ceremonious death service for Agnes, such that the purest sacrifice made to necessity in all the centuries never fades from the memory of the people."[36] The father then goes to a monastery. Albrecht bows to the "power of justice" and becomes the new ruler. After all, it was not he who killed his beloved woman, nor did he leave her. He accepts, however, the sign of masculine rule from her murderer and thus accepts the relationship between the individual and the state and society: he internalizes it as infallible necessity. The message is, therefore, that with the sacrifice of a woman, the man matures into a virtuous, conscientious ruler who knows "that the individual, as . . . noble and beautiful [as] he may be, must under all circumstances bow to society, because in it and . . . the state . . . all of humanity lives, yet in the former only a single facet of humanity is ever revealed."[37] After the failed revolution of 1848, the social bourgeois conflict between the liberation and the obligation of individuals, as well as the political bourgeois conflict between liberalism and constitutional monarchy, achieve, displaced onto the social and political past, literary expression in the motif of the man who leaves:

> I have long felt the desire to arrange a memorial for the old German Empire; the last four years, perhaps the most terrible in our entire history, have heightened it frantically, and the death of Agnes Bernauer, in whom common human interests and the highest social interests coalesce most definitively into an inextricable knot, provided for my work the focal point I had long sought in vain.[38]

The real social-historical conflicts are displaced onto irreconcilable tragic ones, where they are condensed and ontologically stylized in such a way that they demand the sacrifice of the individual: political-liberal freedom, the beloved woman, and love. This "new play . . . as politically and socially harmless as it is throughout," could entirely, Hebbel hoped, "be welcome" in post-revolutionary Vienna.[39]

Bourgeois literature seeks here the triangulating common factor in a feudal past, which is as far removed from the bourgeois man as it is from bourgeois society. A recognized bourgeois commonality, which could make it easier for the individualized citizen to gain masculine identity through separation from the woman, is nowhere to be found. With displacement onto a feudal commonality, the threat to the loving man from the woman also is displaced; it is now directed more toward the state than toward the man himself. This has been inherent in the motif since *The Aeneid*. Since then, the tendency also was for the fear-driven separation of one man from one woman to become a tragic conflict in the male individual himself. This development has reached its pinnacle here. The woman is not only abandoned now, but rather executed; she threatens commonality, thus she must be destroyed. The man must tragically affirm this. The aggression of the self-constructing man hides behind the stone mask of the tragic.

Similarly, in Franz Grillparzer's tragedy *Die Jüdin von Toledo* (*The Jewess of Toledo*), which was completed after 1850, Alfons, King of Castile, succumbs to the love of the young Jewess Rachel and neglects his duties toward his empire and his wife.[40] The Moors are threatening; Alfons's grandees have Rachel murdered. He recognizes from her corpse that "she was not beautiful. . . . An evil look around the cheeks, chin and mouth,/An insidious something in her fiery gaze/Poisoned, disfigured her beauty."[41] After he has devalued her, thereby devaluing himself as a sensual person, he acquiesces as a good Christian to the common demands, and within these constraints directs his aggression outward:

I am only my son's field commander.
For as the pilgrims distinguished by the cross
Leave for penance to Jerusalem,
So would I, conscious of my faults,
Lead you against those non-believers
Who at the border, from Africa afar
Threaten my people and this my peaceful land

. . . .

Onward! Forward! If it please God: toward victory.[42]

Matured into a Christian ruler, he raises himself out of the entanglements of soulless sensual love and into battle against the others; in battle, he does penance for his imperfections. Once again, literature resurrects the norm- and guilt-conscious, antisensual, aggressive Christian man; following Spanish-Catholic material taken from the twelfth century, which had been reworked many times since, Grillparzer reworks the themes of the enchanting woman (like Circe and then Armida), the disenchantment of a king, and his participation in the crusade. Yet, while in these cases the king's blindness is resolved by a triangulating angel or by the actual breaking of a spell, or had never been motivated in the first place, Grillparzer has the king separate himself from Rachel through an internal process.[43] In this, too, he is close to Hebbel, where the external denigration and demonification of the sensually appealing woman also are missing. Moreover, in Grillparzer's adaptation of the motif, aggression directs itself inward and generates a moral consciousness; then, however, it directs itself outward without obstruction. With the phrase, "To dust with all the enemies of the Habsburgs!" one can hear the conservative Austrians after the Danube Monarchy had nearly collapsed in 1848–1849.

THE END OF THE NINETEENTH CENTURY

Whereas bourgeois authors in the middle of the nineteenth century had transposed the bourgeois man's contradiction between individual need and common demands onto the feudal dominating man, Theodor Fontane undermines such historically distant, grand constructions and as early as 1887 adapts this contradiction in the figure of a contemporary, insignificant nobleman in *Irrungen, Wirrungen (Delusions, Confusions)*.[44] In so doing, he alters the traditional pattern. The ruling order does, in fact, demand the separation from love, yet with this separation the man now secures for himself a comfortable existence. Indeed, the character Botho von Rienäcker preserves a love of humanity and a skeptical eye on himself, yet he, who gives up his love for the sake of fulfilling the Prussian nobility's code of honor and also to bring the family estate out of debt through marriage, is in the end a weakling surviving in a vacuous day-to-day existence. From now on, the man who abandons love proves increasingly to be a weakling who diminishes himself even further; one has little sense of an open aggression directed outward. Commonality, for the sake of which he leaves, increasingly loses its legitimacy; the power of commonality to save one from the woman through triangulation when she appears in the image of the "evil" mother is disappearing. More often it is now domineering mothers who demand responsibility instead of love from their sons. Even Botho was prompted by a letter from his mother to separate himself from his beloved seamstress and to marry the rich heiress. Further development of the motif shows that the sacrifice of love is no longer capable of saving or indeed constituting traditional masculinity. For the man, the woman is becoming unimportant as a representation of the other gender, against which he defines himself in order to gain masculine identity. Correspondingly, masculinity created by severing itself from the woman is beginning to disappear. Since there appear increasing numbers of female characters who leave the man (Nora, Lulu), the motif of the man who loves, then leaves, loses its power to draft masculine identity.

In *Frau Jenny Treibel* (1892), Fontane had already had Corinna end the secret engagement with Leopold Treibel after he, while under pressure from his mother, was unable to definitively stand at the side of the woman he thought he loved.[45] He who lacks the energy and courage will be married off to a woman of his mother's choosing, one who befits his status. However, Corinna finds her way back to the man she loves. The feudal milieu has disappeared; we find ourselves in the bourgeoisie. This continues in Thomas Mann's *Buddenbrooks* (1901), in which Thomas leaves his beloved flower girl Anna: "If I am still living, I'll take over the business, I'll make a go of it."[46] Thomas Buddenbrook must earn his bourgeois status in the face of internal and external difficulties, as well as in the face of his need for love. Renunciating his love, he represents for Mann the modern-heroic life and lifestyle of the overburdened, overdisciplined master ethicist working to the brink of exhaustion: achievement versus love. He leaves Anna and goes off to battle in the bourgeois business world, where he must learn to recognize harshness, even ruthlessness, as the norm. Under the banner of the firm, under the banner of bourgeois order and attitude, he submits to duty, separates himself from love, estranges himself from his wife and child, and finally collapses, having become a withered, worn-out man, "who held up his body with effort and skill, elegantly, correctly and straight."[47] Taking the place of military conflict are the battle for the preservation of the business, which is at least a private common interest, and the battle for self-preservation. In Thomas's case, the novel depicts the desertion of love for the sake of the business only as an episode. The novel elaborates on the motif, however, to a much greater extent with the example of his sister Tony. She feels connected to Morten, the student, yet her father wants to marry her to a businessman. He writes to her, "We are, my dear daughter, not born for that which we regard with short-sighted eyes to be our own small, personal happiness, for we are not loose, independent single beings who live for themselves, but rather links in a chain."[48] She protests briefly, but then too she regards herself as a "link in a chain" and agrees to the engagement.[49] There follows a series of unhappy marriages, along with the decline of her family. The woman's separation in the service of commonality can now also be found in texts by men; it no longer fosters clearly masculine identity.

Near the end of the nineteenth century, we can certainly still observe final attempts to find a socially legitimate triangulating common factor, which allows the man to leave the woman and maintain his masculine identity, in the form of scientifically recognized laws and political activism in the service of humanity. Both can be studied in Gerhart Hauptmann's naturalistic social drama *Vor Sonnenaufgang* (*Before Sunrise*), which premiered in 1889.[50] Social revolutionary Loth promises lifelong love to Helene.[51] He sees himself in a "battle for the interests of progress": "My struggle is the struggle for the happiness of all; if I am to be happy, so must everyone around me first be."[52] Helene wishes to follow him as his wife and thus leave her terrible surroundings. He soon discovers that she comes from a family of alcoholics and that the son of her sister "at the age of three was already destroyed by alcoholism."[53] For Loth, who is convinced that alcoholism is hereditary, "the bodily and mental health of his bride" is "conditio sine qua non,"[54] and so he leaves Helene, even though he just admitted that he can "not even think without her any more."[55] In his desperation, he departs; he would otherwise become a "traitor to myself,"[56] to his principles: "live! fight!—forward, ever forward!"[57] We know the pattern. Helene kills herself. At the end of the nineteenth century, the loving man fleeing a woman searches one last time in scientifically recognized laws and in the social-revolutionary struggle for human happiness, for an accepted commonality that could triangulate him. Yet the drama already indicates how fragile this legitimization is; the man who fights here for a humane society fails precisely at the point where he could have lovingly helped.

THE TWENTIETH CENTURY

The number of instances of triangulation, which often enough also rationalize separation, tends to decrease in the twentieth century; an early example is a song in Rilke's *Die Aufzeichnungen des Malte Laurids Brigge*, from 1910, in which order is no longer internalized; not to mention that the man does not flee to outward phallic aggression. He no longer exists as one who, after a dangerous effemination, identifies himself as a club-swinging Heracles or a dutiful ruler. Further, the fear of the image of the dangerous woman is so great that the man will no longer dare return to it at all in love. He does not merge and thus has no need to separate himself. He is *always already* separated; only in his imagination is a union created. To this extent, he is also separated and united at the same time. In the simultaneity of love and separation, there is, in the process of their dissolution, a meeting between the triadic configurative pattern and the motif of the man who loves, but now goes:

'You, whom I do not tell that in the night
I lie weeping,
whose being makes me weary
like a cradle,
you, who do not tell me when you lie wakeful
for my sake:
how if we should endure
this glory in us
without assuaging?'
.   .   .   .   .   .
Look at those who are lovers,
when avowal has once begun
how soon they lie.
.   .   .   .   .   .
You make me alone. Only you can I interchange.
A while it is you, then again it is a murmuring,
or it is a fragrance with no trace.
Alas, in my arms I have lost them all,
only you, you are born always again:
because I never held you close, I hold you forever.[59]

This is a poetic path that has been recognizable at least since Goethe's "Willkommen und Abschied." The man who speaks is searching for the "splendor" of love, but not the beloved. In intransitive love, which is no longer directed at the woman, he has already separated himself from her before he comes to her. Thus he does not have to escape from her in a redeeming battle. He knows no triangulating duty and gains no phallic-aggressive masculine identity. Rather a new identity—one that no longer required the destruction of the woman or the battle against others— could thus dawn, at least in literature.

The drama of separation from the images of a powerful nurturing-protective "good" mother and a demanding "evil" one can be sensed in the need for both distance and closeness, in the longing for love and in the fear of commitment. The opposing tendencies of loving merging and dis-identification, the movement toward a woman and away from her, are laid to rest in a vibrating tension between closeness and distance, togetherness and loneliness, being cradled but not nurtured, dissolving in a "murmuring" or "fragrance" on the one hand and conversing with a "you" on the other hand, even holding it tight. The loving masculine ego can be driven back to images of intimate understanding between mother and infant, who lies "weeping," while she lies "wakeful" on his account, whom she could nurse—suckle? pacify? ("without assuaging")—and rock to sleep ("makes me weary/like a cradle"). Yet the tension remains; the mother lies "wakeful" somewhere else and does not nurture. It is a scene before the development of the child into a boy. Through it, the infant who has not yet been defeminized can phantasize itself into the position of the mother where it then nurses the mother ("how if *we* should endure/this glory in us/without assuaging?"); later, the image of the lover approaches that of a mother even more clearly: "you are born always again." Now the beloved is the child who, at least indirectly, is borne by him.

In this early stage, the narrating "I" is not yet masculine, let alone adult. Yet insofar as it speaks, it is no longer infantile; it has left the preverbal space of being nursed and cradled and invokes those early scenes as an adult. This "I" fashions that which the infant cannot: union ("whom I do *not* tell," "*without* assuaging"). In this sense, the narrator interrupts the phantasy of intimate symbiosis into which it is venturing. This allows the ideal image of the intransitive love among adults, who, as adults, withhold their sexual and possessive desires and protect one another's solitude. Such early scenes between the mother and child shine through, even though they are now rephantasized as if both were capable of union. Adult and infant, autonomy and the pull of symbiosis, necessarily divisive language and preverbal unity, converge here in lyric speech. Clear and thus divisive speech, however, would betray preverbal love; it would become a lie: "Look at those who are lovers,/when avowal has once begun,/how soon they lie." This "I" speaks to the "you" and yet does not speak to it ("You, whom I do not tell that in the night/I lie weeping"); it holds on to the "you" and nevertheless allows it to disappear in transitions ("A while it is you, then again it is a murmuring"). The "I" preserves this "you" as an autonomous one, yet still dissolves its identity. Likewise, it even relinquishes itself to the disintegration of clearly defined identity, but nevertheless preserves itself. It preserves itself as a crying, negating, suggesting ("if we should"), pointing ("Look at"), lamenting ("Alas, in my arms"), and praising ("only you") "I." Attending completely to the beloved, it governs speech and attempts to assign a role to the beloved, thus attempting to govern her as well. In the obliteration of identity, there does in fact remain a residual of patriarchal-dominating identity. As in tradition, even this residual is occasioned by scenes of separation from the mother that are then transferred to the beloved.

In fact, masculine love now retreats to the space preceding genital masculinity: in the pre-Oedipal stage of being nursed and cradled, when there was still no defined sexual woman, but certainly a hazy, indeterminate, asexual motherly being; no man jumps too quickly into bed with a "cradle." The pre-Oedipal fear of being trapped by the mother-image leads in this case to the wish for neither the "I" nor the "you" to commit; and the Oedipal fear of sexually uniting with the mother leads to his own desexualization, as well as to that of the woman. It also leads to sexual abstinence. What remains is the path back to the pre-Oedipal stage. Cradled by the pre-Oedipal mother and protected from her through negation and dominating speech, the "I" can give up the need to dominate the woman, which stems from early helplessness, and hazard a balance of power: "You make me alone. Only you can I interchange." and "You whom I do not tell. . . . You, who do not tell me." This masculine, loving "I" plays through the scene of the loving man who goes anew and departs from the traditional phallic-aggressive and socially accepted masculine identity; it has, however, not yet attained a new masculine identity.

As far as I can see, in German literature of the twentieth century, the motif of the loving man who departs no longer serves to fashion phallic-aggressive masculine identity, except in texts that propagate clear norms and duties, as with the military, for example; texts by women even utilize the motif in order to devalue it. In texts by men in the last decades, the motif has reversed itself: the man is left by the woman and exposed in his dependency and desertedness. The poor soul hardly puts on airs anymore. He whimpers.

In *Der gute Gott von Manhattan* (*The Good God of Manhattan*), from 1958, Ingeborg Bachmann depicts the man who leaves his lover as one who flees from absolute love into a banal daily routine:

He had suffered a relapse, and for a moment, order stretched out its arms toward him. He was normal, healthy and honest, like a man who quietly drinks a glass before dinner, and who has driven his lover's whisperings from his ears and her captivating scent from his nostrils—a man whose eyes light up again at printer's ink and whose hands must get dirty on a bar.[59]

He has sacrificed his love and himself not to a higher principle but to order and banality; from a female perspective, his masculine identity is determined by such a separation. Contempt resonates—the higher ideal would be the absoluteness of love. This can be found in the woman, but not in the man who leaves her. The motif of abandonment now fosters a devalued masculine identity, whereas that of being abandoned contributes to the highly valued feminine identity. The male phantasy of the man who loves and now goes is reevaluated. But does Bachmann not merely conform here again to a male phantasy—that of passion, of the absolute love of a woman, which is intensified to the point of self-annihilation? And does she not also adhere to the image of the weakness of the man who leaves, as we know it at least since Fontane?

In the following decades, the motif fully reverses itself in texts by men as well. In Peter Handke's *Die Stunde der wahren Empfindung* (*A Moment of True Feeling*) and *Die linkshändige Frau* (*The Left-Handed Woman*) or Botho Strauß' *Rumor*, for example, the man no longer leaves the woman; rather, she leaves him.[60] Presumably, the male author thus fulfills his wish that the woman keep her distance from a man who is uncertain about himself, and that she no longer threaten him; that she therefore spare him the trouble of tearing himself away, as well as the feelings of guilt that accompany it. A subplot in *Die linkshändige Frau* provides an indication of this, as the man explains:

> Not long ago I broke with a girl I loved. . . . We were riding in a taxi at night. I had my arm around her, and we were both looking out the same side. Everything was fine. Oh yes, you have to know that she was very young—no more than twenty—and I was very fond of her. For the barest moment, just in passing, I saw a man on the sidewalk. . . . I only saw that he was rather young. And suddenly it flashed through my mind that the sight of that man outside would force the girl beside me to realize what an old wreck was holding her close, and that she must be filled with revulsion. The thought came as such a shock that I took my arm away. I saw her home, but at the door of her house I told her I never wanted to see her again. I bellowed at her. I said I was sick of her, it was all over between us, she should get out of my sight. And I walked off. I'm certain she still doesn't know why I left her.[61]

At the center of this novel by a male author stands a woman who leaves her husband, yet in the subplot above a man leaves a woman. In my opinion, the hidden impetus of the text reveals itself here: the man's disgust at himself and his own body, which he experiences as too old, and thus no longer soundly masculine. Such disgust and sexual angst lead here to the need to liberate oneself from the body, from one's own and from the woman's, to gain autonomy from the body, and for this reason, to leave the woman. In the service of this desire, fear arises that the woman will leave the man, and in order to escape this fear, as the inserted subplot shows, the man leaves her. A male author spares his weak hero such a remnant of activity when he has the woman leave: "Finally she leaves me!" Yet the man gains nothing in such novels, especially not his old phallic identity. It is shattered. The man's many-tiered ambivalence toward the woman is becoming visible: his oscillation between love, even enchantment, fear, hate, and flight. Such a tortured oscillation had previously been prevented by the succession of love, escape, and battle, or with Rilke, at least by an oscillating simultaneity of distance and intimacy. Now, however, the man appears wracked with the fever of ambivalence. It is the end of old phallic-dominating identity.

This end also is an opportunity. Were a man to subject himself to his ambivalences and still remain close to a woman, a concrete woman could emerge from behind the mother-images. Perhaps a new masculine identity would become possible, which no longer binds itself to the early drama of dis-identification and no longer requires forced, fearful, phallic activity or triangulating duty. Could empathy, recognition of the woman as an Other, and reciprocity increase?

HERCULES REDIVIVUS: HERACLES IN THE TWENTIETH CENTURY

Generally, the more reflective and theoretical texts and manifestos of the men's movement, with which men seek to escape their patriarchal identities, make allusions toward altering the masculine image, and thus also the phantasies that support it.[62] New literary adaptations of traditional forms of the motif also attest that the distance from the old masculine image is increasing, as, for example, in the reworkings of the Omphale episode. In this case, writers can treat a given material from a safe distance and transform it to correspond to their conscious intentions, perhaps even to platforms propounded by political groups; thus they must hardly subject themselves to their unconscious phantasies.

At the beginning of the twentieth century, Frank Wedekind had still depicted his Heracles in deep "disgrace" with Omphale:

>   Heracles: For your amusement with a disguised soul,
>   To mock a man dressed as a girl—
>   No disgrace more abysmal will my heart endure.[63]

He can no longer fulfill his redeeming triangulating duties:

>   Heracles: Who has mercy upon the yammering race of man,
>   When Prometheus chained to the Caucasus moans,
>   When enfeebled by women Heracles cowers!
>   Who shall deliver and protect Deianeira![64]

Omphale humiliates him and thus wins his love:

>   Omphale: Shall I spew contempt in your face?
>   Heracles: Oh, Omphale, you are the most glorious,
>   The most beautiful woman, so deeply do you humiliate me.
>   . . . .
>   Now, Omphale—lay waste to Calydon
>   Who will—now I remain a slave to your beauty.
>   Omphale (falls to her knees):
>   Now I believe what I feel. Heracles,
>   Invincible, tames Omphale.[65]

The old motif, the humiliation of the loving man by the woman: Danger! However, this is only one of many pearls of sexual escapades tied together on the colorful necklace of triumph for Heracles's feats of vitality. Humiliation—masochism?—is also a pearl; danger allows masculine potency to shine in the rays of victory. Wedekind ventures phallic-narcissistically into the phantasy of the dangerous woman, discards his redeeming duty ("Calydon"), and allows both the man and the woman to win, but only through a masculine decision:

>   Heracles (embracing Omphale):
>   You sink to the earth, that I raise you
>   To the battlefield of your victory with a burning kiss.[66]

Now the ambivalences should flare up; but a few lines later, Heracles is with the next woman, Deianeira. It does not seem worth showing how or why he leaves. This clearly phallic-narcissistic adaptation manages without triangulating moments, brings the phantasy of the overpowering woman, which had long operated covertly and was thus inaccessible, into the spotlight (a prerequisite for overcoming it), and at least alludes to a notion of equality between men and women.

Adaptations of the Omphale episode have appeared in the GDR since the late 1960s. In comic opera and in novels written for youth, this material, which is so far from the reality of men today that it hardly affects them directly, was adapted to stage new images of the loving man who must no longer gain his identity by alienating himself from his "feminine" side. In these genres, it was possible for male authors to playfully pursue their dreams of a more humane masculinity. For the most part, they could keep them free of distressing situations and phantasies of their own love; they also were protected by the political will to emancipate the sexes.

Peter Hacks wrote the libretto to the comic opera "Omphale" (1969), a fantastically unreal play in which, for example, the son of Heracles is born and begins to speak the same night that he is conceived.[67] Omphale returns from the hunt with a lion's skin and a club; Heracles enters wearing her dress and putting on makeup. For the sake of a more humane identity, he seeks to discard his old phallic one:

Loving women, I emulate them.

.   .   .   .

A hero, that simply can't be everything.

.   .   .   .

Hereafter I shall not show myself as a man,
With each blow of the club strike dead my ego.
How strained: a man. How little his own.
What I am not, I would dare to become.

.   .   .   .

A person would I be in a man's stead.
Oh these supermen, these heroes,
I am sick to death of them.[68]

Not without a comic turn, his transformation from a "hero" into a "person" launches him into clichés of femininity:

Heracles: Sit down next to me in distant nearness
And speak to me of love and not of lust.
Omphale: What do you separate thus?
Heracles: What must first be together.

> Omphale: Would you rebuke lust as loveless, love lustless?
> Heracles: Scarcely shall lust swell in me without love.
> Omphale: In me scarcely love without lust. Quickly, quickly
>
> . . . .
>
> Heracles: Oh, you do not understand me.
> Oh, you do not love me.[69]

In the protected space of the comic play, Hacks ventures a shift toward nonphallic masculine behavior. However, his Heracles is then overtaken by the need to aid others against the "monster" Lityerses: "I am of a mind to fight because I must."[70] Although they both depart for battle, he in Omphale's dress and she in his lion's skin, they go their separate ways again, once there. *Heracles gives a cry of victory, Lityerses a cry of death, Omphale that of those surrounding.*[71] "Chained to her natural womanliness" she bears him triplets.[72] He is equally chained to his manliness, however, he plants his club in the ground where it grows into an olive tree:

> The merry game, so gentle, so full of hope,
> Has fulfilled nothing and yet meant everything.
> What was long since accomplished, is overpowering.
> Vanquished, alas, we stand before the vanquished enemy.[73]

Only briefly did the comic opera provide space for the interplay of a different gender relationship; but this remains a utopia in the face of social and political reality:

> Omphale and Heracles: As long as humanity's open wound festers,
> How should love endure unscathed?[74]

There we have it again, external necessity and duty; one must fight until the "wound" closes. At least in this manner the man within the man may be helped.

Youth novels also provide authors with a significant distance from the ambivalences in their own unconsciously repressed phantasies of love and masculinity. This makes it simple to readapt a given material according to conscious, sometimes even politically motivated, conceptions. Rolf Schneider has Heracles, who has become fat and lazy with Omphale, who puts on makeup and ointment and plays with dolls, go to the market to buy fish.[75] A fisherwoman speaks to him there:

Heracles, you are a repulsive sight. Heracles shrugged his shoulders. . . . Heracles, the fisherwoman continued, the strongest and most famous hero of Greece looks like a woman and acts like a woman. What is objectionable about that? replied Heracles. Lydia has no more enemies . . . so she also doesn't need any more heroes. . . . Is a woman any worse than a man? The customs of this world claim so. But I dispute it. Since deeds still count more than words, I am declaring by my visible example, that I find women equal to men. . . . Originally I wanted, since I am only a half-god, to become a whole god. I was destined to fail because I have a powerful enemy, that is Hera. . . . Thus I decided, where I could not become a whole god, I would at least be a whole human. . . . I am by birth a man, and now I want to be a woman as well. A more inclusive human than I is simply not thinkable.[76]

The fisherwoman claims that his mother Alkmene would have expected that, "He would certainly now become a helper and world-reformer by design, an especially humane human."[77] Finally she reveals herself as Alkmene and hands him a mirror:

He saw himself. . . . He sighed. He lowered the mirror. He lowered his eyes as well. . . . He passed through the gate of the capital city and did so for the last time. He would never again enter the capital city.[78]

The effemination of the man is not only impossible in today's situation, as with Hacks, but if we wish to believe Rolf Schneider's Alkmene and the behavior of Heracles, it is a "disgrace."[79] It is necessary to be a "whole man," a "helper and world-reformer."[80] In the youth novels, the realist-socialist triangulation at least still functions. But as an opportunity to become a "more inclusive person," that is, to overcome alienation, the text continues to play out "effemination."

ON THE RELATIONSHIP BETWEEN PHANTASY AND LITERATURE

In its therapies, psychoanalysis in the twentieth century finds a phantasy scenario which, in the literature of the time, only forms the background to other scenes, or at best, surfaces in adaptations of earlier versions.

Ages ago, on the other hand, this motif was fashioned far more clearly in myths such as that of Heracles, and then in literary texts. How can this be understood? In my opinion, we have to consider the status of phantasies. Phantasies that the child once created need not necessarily determine the behavior of the adult; adults can free themselves from phantasies to some degree, or bring them into other scenarios. After all, phantasies only gain literary importance when they help to dramatically · or emotionally condense experiences of reality and the corresponding desires and fears of adults. Therefore, they must adapt themselves to the psychological structure, the experiences and the modes of interpretation of producers and recipients alike. They, in turn, are subject to historical transformation. In ancient martial societies, for example, physical strength was assigned importance as a quality that shaped and secured empires; correspondingly, men could find their identities in aggressive physicality and in myths that almost openly staged the early drama of separation to the point of phallic aggression. Yet in complex, highly technological societies, physical strength is no longer assigned such weight as essential for survival; phallic corporeality loses its power to form identities. Thus "the man" loses the chance to seek his identity by absolutely dissociating himself from "the woman" through physical strength and aggression. This is particularly true of sophisticated literature that measures itself against carefully reflected current experience and against possibilities of interpreting them. Subject to historical change in such a case is likewise whatever could function as a third factor: norms and socially accepted activities, religions, political structures and ideas, duties, cultural demands, and reason of any sort. With their transformation comes a change in literary treatments of masculine separation phantasies as well.

When instances disintegrate, which until then had triangulated, and when women increasingly assume leadership roles and other socially recognized roles, and thus potentially triangulating activities, it becomes more difficult for men to reassure themselves of their gender identities through such factors. This is happening in Europe now. In this situation, if early mother-son scenes arise in the man who loves, or writes of love, then he is at the mercy of his ambivalences with even less protection—in life as in literature. The behavior of adults can now no longer be shaped in sophisticated literature through the drama of the boy's childhood separation from the mother. This does not rule out that this drama continues to determine the behavior of adolescent men today, that it endures in the entertainingly reassuring clichés of the mass media (for example, in Western movies), and that it is revived in the phantasies of adult analysands. It is disappearing, however, from those texts that attempt to confront today's reality.

NOTES

1. Apollodorus, *Apollodorus: The Library. With an English Translation by James George Frazer*, vol. 1 (Cambridge, Mass.: Harvard University Press, 1976), 240 ff.

2. *Diodorus of Sicily in Twelve Volumes*, Charles Henry Oldfather, trans., vol. 2 (Cambridge, Mass.: Harvard University Press: 1935–67), 440 ff.

3. Cf. August Friedrich von Pauly, "Omphale," *Paulys Realenzyklopädie der klassischen Altertumswissenschaft*, Georg Wissowa, ed., vol. XVIII/1 (Stuttgart: J. B. Metzler, 1939), columns 385–396; Frank Brommer, *Herakles II: Die unkanonischen Taten des Helden* (Darmstadt: Wissenschaftliche Buchgesellschaft, 1984), 126–128.

4. Janine Chasseguet-Smirgel, "Feminine Guilt and the Oedipus Complex," *Female Sexuality: New Psychoanalytic Views* (Ann Arbor: University of Michigan Press, 1970), 113. Originally published as *Recherches psychanalytiques nouvelles sur la sexualité féminine* (Paris: Payot, 1964).

5. Ibid.

6. Ibid., 114.

7. Ibid.

8. Wolfgang Mertens, *Psychoanalyse* (Stuttgart: Kohlhammer, 1992), 59. Here Mertens quotes Ralph Greenson, "Dis-Identification," *International Journal of Psycho-Analysis* 49 (1968): 370. [Translator's note: Unless otherwise cited, all German quotes are my translations —G.H.]

9. Ibid., 65. Mertens is referring here to Ernst Abelin, "The Role of the Father in the Separation-Individuation Process," *Separation-Individuation: Essays in Honor of Margaret S. Mahler*, John McDevitt and Calvin Settlage, eds. (New York: International University Press, 1971), 229–253.

10. Ibid., 61.

11. Ibid., 60.

12. Cf. Arnold van Gennep, *Übergangszeiten* (Frankfurt: n.p., 1986). Originally published as *Les rites de passage* (Paris: É. Nourry, 1909). For a comprehensive interpretation, see Carl Pietzcker, *Einheit, Trennung und Wiedervereinigung* (Würzburg: Königshausen und Neumann, 1996), 57–196.

13. von Pauly, "Omphale," column 394.

14. August Friedrich von Pauly, "Achilleus," *Paulys Realenzyklopädie der klassischen Altertumswissenschaft*, vol. I/1 (Stuttgart: J. B. Metzler, 1893), 226.

15. Virgil, "Aeneis" liber XII, *Virgil: With an English Translation by Henry Rushton Fairclough*, vol. 2 (Cambridge, Mass.: Harvard University Press, 1969), 298–365.

16. Virgil, "Aeneis" IV, 259–705.

17. Mertens, 61.

18. Hartmann von Aue, *Erec*, Albert Leitzmann, ed. (Tübingen: Niemeyer, 1957), 2968–2998.

19. Ibid., 3007–3060. [Translator's note: The term *aventiure*, from the Middle High German, is generally not translated into modern German by contemporary scholars. In English, it encompasses both "quest" and "adventure."]

20. Ibid., 9420–9428.

21. Joachim Bumke, *Höfische Kultur*, vol. 2 (München: Deutscher Taschenbuch Verlag, 1992), 704–709.

22. Torquato Tasso, "Gerusalemme Liberata. Canto Sedicesimo," *Opere di Torquato Tasso: A cura di Giorgio Petrocchi* (Milano: n.p., 1969), 356–369. Published in English as *Jerusalem Delivered: An English Prose Version*, Ralph Nash, trans. (Detroit, Mich.: Wayne State University Press, 1987), canto sixteen. Subsequent references to this canto will be taken from this edition and cited parenthetically by line number.

23. Johann Wolfgang von Goethe, "Wilkommen und Abschied," *Sämtliche Werke nach Epochen seines Schaffens*, Karl Richeter et al., eds., vol. III/2 (München: C. Hanser, 1990), 15 f. A detailed interpretation can be found in chapter 5 of Carl Pietzcker, *Einheit, Trennung und Wiedervereinigung* (Würzburg: Königshausen und Neumann, 1996), 116–142.

24. Johann Wolfgang von Goethe, "Rinaldo," *Goethe Gedichte 1800–1832*, Karl Eibl, ed. (Frankfurt a.M.: Deutscher Klassiker Verlag, 1988), 270–278. For an interpretation, cf. Carl Pietzcker, "Goethes 'Rinaldo,'" *Torquato Tasso in Deutschland: Seine Wirkung in Literatur, Kunst und Musik seit Mitte des 18. Jahrhunderts*, Achim Aurnhammer, ed. (Berlin: Walter de Gruyter, 1995), 661–681.

25. Ibid., 270–278.

26. Ibid.

27. Ibid.

28. Carl Pietzcker, "Goethes 'Rinaldo,'" 672, 676.

29. Johann Wolfgang von Goethe, "Die Wahlverwandtschaften," *Johann Wolfgang von Goethe: Hamburger Ausgabe*, vol. 6 (München: Deutscher Taschenbuch Verlag, 1977), 358 f. Published in its English translation by Victor Lange and Judith Ryan as *Elective Affinities*, David Wellbery, ed. (New York: Suhrkamp, 1988).

30. Ibid., 359.

31. Johann Wolfgang von Goethe, "Faust," *Johann Wolfgang von Goethe: Hamburger Ausgabe*, vol. 3, 10th rev. ed. (München: Deutscher Taschenbuch Verlag, 1976).

32. Goethe, *Faust*, 107. "Wald und Höhle" scene translation by Bayard Taylor (1871).

33. Friedrich Hebbel, *Werke*, Gerhard Fricke, Werner Keller et al., eds., vol. 1 (Darmstadt: Wissenschaftliche Buchgesellschaft, 1963), 679–765.

34. Ibid., 810.

35. Ibid., 751.

36. Ibid., 764.

37. Cf. Hebbel, Letter to Werner (1852), *Werke*, 807.

38. Hebbel, Letter to Gervinus (1852), *Werke*, 808.

39. Hebbel, Letter to Dingelstedt (1851), *Werke*, vol. 5 (Darmstadt: Wissenschaftliche Buchgesellschaft, 1967), 707.

40. Franz Grillparzer, *Die Jüdin von Toledo*: *Werke in 6 Bänden*, Helmut Bachmaier, ed., vol. 3 (Frankfurt a.m.: Deutscher Klassiker Verlag, 1987), 483–555.

41. Ibid., 551 ff.

42. Ibid., 533 f.

43. Cf. Elisabeth Frenzel, "Die Jüdin von Toledo," *Stoffe der Weltliteratur* (Stuttgart: A. Kroner, 1992).

44. Theodor Fontane, *Sämtliche Werke*, Wilhelm Keitel, ed., vol. 2 (Darmstadt: Wissenschaftliche Buchgesellschaft, 1962), 319 ff.

45. Ibid., vol. 4, 297 ff.

46. Thomas Mann, *Gesammelte Werke in 13 Bänden*, vol. 1 (Frankfurt a.m.: Fischer, 1960), 170.

47. Ibid., 660.

48. Ibid., 148.

49. Ibid., 160 f.

50. Gerhart Hauptmann, *Werke*, Hans-Egon Hass, ed., vol. 1 (Berlin: Propylaen, 1966).

51. Ibid., 78.

52. Ibid., 47.

53. Ibid., 93.

54. Ibid., 63.

55. Ibid., 91.

56. Ibid., 80.

57. Ibid., 95.

58. Rainer Maria Rilke, *Sämtliche Werke*, Rilke Archiv, ed., vol. 6 (Frankfurt a.m.: Insel, 1966), 936. Published in English as *The Notebooks of Malte Laurids Brigge*, Herter Norten, trans. (New York: Norton, 1949).

59. Ingeborg Bachmann, *Der gute Gott von Manhattan* (Frankfurt a.m.: n.p., 1963), 81.

60. See Peter Handke, *Die Stunde der wahren Empfindung* (Frankfurt a.m.: Suhrkamp, 1975); Peter Handke, *Die linkshändige Frau* (Frankfurt a.m.: Suhrkamp, 1976). Published in English as *The Left-Handed Woman*, Ralph Mannheim, trans. (New York: Farrar, Straus, and Giroux, 1977). See also Botho Strauß, *Rumor* (München: Hanser, 1980).

61. Handke, *Die linkshändige Frau*, 53 f.

62. See, for example, Volker Elis Pilgrim, *Manifest für den freien Mann* (Reinbek bei Hamburg: Rowohlt, 1983).

63. Frank Wedekind, "Herakles: Dramatisches Gedicht in drei Akten," *Gesammelte Werke*, vol. 7 (München: Georg Muller, 1920), 207.

64. Ibid., 207 f.

65. Ibid., 210 f.

66. Ibid., 211.

67. Peter Hacks, *Oper* (Berlin: Aufbau-Verlag, 1975), 109–153.

68. Ibid., 131.

69. Ibid., 135 ff.

70. Ibid., 147.

71. Ibid., 131.

72. Ibid., 151.

73. Ibid.

74. Ibid.

75. See Rolf Schneider, *Die Abenteuer des Herakles: Nach alten Sagen neu erzählt von Rolf Schneider* (Berlin: Verlag Neues Leben, 1978).

76. Ibid., 171–173.

77. Ibid., 173.

78. Ibid., 174.

79. Ibid.

80. Ibid., 175.

"I have only you, Cassandra":
Antifeminism and the Reconstruction of Patriarchy in the Early Postwar Works of Hans Erich Nossack

Inge Stephan

I

The year 1945 was by no means the "zero hour" touted as the starting point for a new periodization of time and an unimpeded reconstruction in a devastated country, as research on the early postwar period has brought to light with welcome clarity. The question of responsibility for the "German catastrophe" (Friedrich Meinecke) divided not only exile authors and those of the "Inner Emigration," as demonstrated by the (in)famous controversy between Thomas Mann (as representative of the exile writers) on one side and Walter von Molo and Frank Thiess (representing the "Inner Emigration") on the other over Germany's so-called collective guilt, it also called into question the political, moral, and artistic identities of those authors who had remained in fascist Germany.[1] Even when authors such as Elisabeth Langgässer, Marie Luise Kaschnitz, Ilse Langner, Marie Luise Fleisser, and Hans Erich Nossack could not be counted among the party supporters of the fascist regime, they nevertheless experienced the "German catastrophe" as a threat and a personal defeat. This strong personal identification with the "German catastrophe" was inextricably bound up with the shameful memories that these writers had of their own complicity, of their helpless attempts to conform, and of their humiliating powerlessness.

The debate over German guilt carried on by intellectuals between 1945 and 1948 has yet to be subjected to a systematic, scholarly investigation. This debate, as a perusal of the relevant texts from this period reveals, diverted attention away from the traumatic experiences of National Socialism and further served to repress the memory of the Holocaust in a breathtakingly rapid and cynical manner. We know today that the effects of this diversion from and repression of the catastrophe during the early postwar years have had repercussions that continue to influence the political and intellectual climate of present-day Germany: the *Historikerstreit* (1986–1987), the German–German literary debate (1990–), the Goldhagen debate (1994–), and the controversy and critique surrounding the German *Wehrmacht*'s role in World War II (1996–). To outline an initial thesis in brief, the discourse of guilt and the "apologetic literature" (*Bewältigungsliteratur*) that arose in response to it in the early postwar period both served to exculpate and construct a new identity, which, mediated through literature, was intended to extinguish memories of the traumatic experiences of the war. It was not until 1968 that the patriarchal complacency of this approach to the past was disrupted by the questions and demands from the postwar generation of daughters and sons. Building from the initial thesis, a second thesis proposes that the process of repression and forgetting was bound up with a revival of conventional sex roles and, in yet a third thesis, with a return to images from ancient mythology. Archaic and burdened images of the sexes predating fascism, with its cult of motherhood and heroization of soldierly masculinity, were reactivated with gender imagery taken from ancient mythology—as much a fixture in fascist ideology as in the iconography of Teutonic mythology—in order to detract from personal responsibility for the crimes of National Socialism, as well as to legitimate a national discourse of regeneration and renewal.

The early postwar texts by Hans Erich Nossack (1901–1977) exemplify the connection between the apocalyptic imagery of antiquity, the myth of national rejuvenation (*Grundungsmythos*), and the return to regressive gender models. In his postwar writings, Nossack achieved a belated literary breakthrough denied him during the Third Reich, when he had been banned from writing. Nossack had studied law and philosophy in Jena, and in the early 1920s had been enthusiastic about the Russian Revolution, breaking away from his wealthy bourgeois family to become a factory worker and a German Communist Party member. After the Nazis came to power, however, Nossack returned to the protective environment that his family provided, assumed the helm of his father's business, and wrote secretly in his free time. Nossack belongs to the class of writers that cultivated the image of the critical protester and radical nonconformist and enjoyed tremendous popularity in the West Germany of the 1960s and 1970s. Nossack's popularity and stance are evidenced by the awards bestowed upon him: the Büchner prize, the Pourlemérite award, and the German Grand Cross of Merit.

The damage to masculine identity as a result of the "German catastrophe" is a theme that runs through Nossack's writings. In the texts to be discussed here, Nossack's depictions of masculinity reveal him to be neither the proud individualist nor the radical outsider he professed to be in public. Rather, his texts show him to be an author who both ideologically and aesthetically bore close resemblance to those writers whose works are representative of the repression and forgetting that characterized much of early postwar literature. Nossack's early postwar writings do not contain anything remotely rebellious or transgressive but are rather the notes of someone debilitated by trauma, someone who experienced Germany's political breakdown as the breakdown of masculine identity. Nossack reacted to this perceived collapse of masculine identity with arguments combining Otto Weininger's antifeminism in *Geschlecht und Charakter* (*Sex and Character*, 1903) and Johann Jakob Bachofen's plea for the restoration of patriarchy in *Das Mutterrecht* (*Mother Right*, 1927). In this context, the story of the Trojan War served as the background against which personal traumatic experiences could be played out, glorified, and mythologized. Nossack's texts can be read as representative of a category of early postwar literature (by authors such as Langgässer, Kaschnitz, Jünger, and others), in which mythological references also served to distract from questions of guilt and responsibility through flight into conservative sex/gender typologies.[2] All of these texts both anticipated and laid the groundwork for subsequent political restoration. At the same time, these works grew precariously out of the mythological reception prevalent during the Third Reich and, in an equally problematic fashion, linked the discourse of nationalism with a reactionary discourse on the sexes.

II

In his 1948 narrative "Kassandra," Nossack used the Trojan War as a point of reference in order to stage both German history and his own. Nossack posed the question, "Of what relevance is Cassandra to us?" appropriating a doomsday vision for his own purposes at a time when the seer had become a controversial figure (after a checkered and contradictory reception history spanning more than 2,000 years) for various political camps in their evaluations of fascism, the Holocaust, World War II, and the postwar period. Thomas Epple and Solvejg Müller[3] brought together a wealth of examples in their Cassandra studies, *Der Aufstieg der Untergangsseherin Kassandra* (The rise of the doomsday seer Cassandra, 1993) and *Kein Brautfest zwischen Menschen und Göttern.*

Kassandra-Mythologie im Lichte von Sexualität und Wahrheit (No bridal feast between men and gods: Cassandra mythology in the context of sexuality and truth, 1994) respectively, demonstrating that Cassandra, as seer, protester, and admonisher, had become a symbolic character,[4] functionalized either as a figure of resistance or as a cipher of legitimation[5] by authors of all political stripes.

An overview of the reception of Cassandra texts in the 1930s and 1940s reveals the figure of the seer and protester—so engaging and powerful in Karl Hofer's painting of 1936—to be politically dubious, aesthetically bankrupt, without unique profile, and susceptible to arbitrary appropriation.[6] The prerequisites for a progressive, emancipatory conceptualization of the Cassandra figure, as for example Christa Wolf's rendering in her 1983 novel, *Kassandra,* nearly a half-century later, seemed to be completely lacking in fascist Germany. I consider it no coincidence that Ernst Bloch, in *Das Prinzip Hoffnung* (*The Principle of Hope*), a work of the 1940s, not only portrays Cassandra in a negative light but also dismisses her as an anti-utopian figure. In a segment entitled "Unavoidable and Avoidable Fate," Bloch polemicizes against the concept of destiny derived from antiquity:

> Moira is that which is unavoidable . . . such that not only reason is paralyzed, but also the blood runs cold. It is senseless to try to act under such conditions, even if the first step is without obstacle. . . . Neither Oedipus nor Cassandra can do anything, let alone change anything.[7]

Here Bloch explicitly distances himself from the chthonic-demonic cult of fate favored by fascist Germany (illustrated, for example, in Gerhart Hauptmann's *Atrides-Tetralogy*) and attempts to create a space for a transformative, engaged mode of thinking that unfortunately found no support in the dominant discourse of the 1940s and 1950s. It was not until the 1960s that Bloch's work received any notable reception and the Cassandra image promoted by fascist writers began to change.

Against the background of the Cassandra reception of the 1930s and 1940s, the opening statement in Nossack's "Kassandra," "Of what relevance is Cassandra to us?" attains a deeper meaning than the casually stated question would seem to suggest.[8] It is a rhetorical question that appears and reappears in multiple variations throughout the text. Obviously Cassandra is of some relevance to "us"—but who is in fact this "us"? For Nossack, at least, Cassandra is important enough that he names his story after her and returns to her frequently in other texts.

This "us" in the opening question reveals itself at first to be of a familial nature. Odysseus, the veteran who returned home late from the Trojan War, uses this question to deflect the question his son Telemachus asks about Cassandra. Telemachus acts on behalf of his mother, Penelope, who was hoping that the question would provoke Odysseus—disturbed and silent as the result of his experiences—into speaking. That Penelope was not only acting out of the therapeutic intentions her son attributed to her ("she thought it would be better, if we could get him to speak more about his experiences") becomes clear during the conversation that ensues.[9] The question posed by the son and instigated by the mother sets off a laborious and hesitating conversation further complicated by narrative interjections of Telemachus's recollections and enormous temporal leaps. The domestic scene in which the conversation about Cassandra is embedded is recalled more than fifty years later by the now aging son.

Before the narrator returns to the son's question and the father's counterquestion, two recollections of Telemachus are interjected. First, Telemachus recalls an encounter with a nameless youth from Asia Minor, who compares Cassandra to a "slim, bluish gray column of smoke" rising from the plain and merging with the brilliant sky.[10] This image is so strongly imprinted upon Telemachus's memory that it is still present more than fifty years later when he recalls the event. In company with this poetic image there also are numerous details from the Trojan War that do not relate directly to Cassandra but that Telemachus has gathered from Orestes's friend Pylades. Through Telemachus's recollections of Pylades's stories, the transmitted myth undergoes three interesting alterations. First, it was not Clytemnestra who murdered Agamemnon, but rather her lover Aegisthus. Second, it was not Orestes who murdered his mother, Clytemnestra; rather she was "regrettably" killed in a skirmish.[11] And third, Orestes was not driven from the country and pursued by the Erinyes for matricide, but rather he decided for unknown reasons to embark on a journey, leaving his friend Pylades in charge of the kingdom in his absence.

What do these images, recollections, and alterations in the mythological narrative have to do with the initial question, and why are they presented by the narrator in such an elaborate manner? In my opinion, the hesitating narrative flow indicates that the recollections revolve around taboos. The association of Cassandra with a column of smoke swimming into the ether can be read as an erotic image, while the recollection of the relationship between Agamemnon and Clytemnestra reveals a marriage in which the partners have become strangers to each other. Unfaithful husbands, unchaste wives, and murderous lovers cast shadows over monogamy as the ideal for relationships between the sexes.

These wish fantasies and, above all, horror fantasies, form the narrative background for the conversation about Cassandra that finally evolves between father, mother, and son—a conversation that develops more and more into an argument between the estranged couple, Odysseus and Penelope. Telemachus is confused and embarrassed by his father's counterquestion, and his mother comes to his aid with an odd and unexpected question: "She can't possibly have been that young anymore. Why wasn't she married?"[12] It is this question that points to the actual theme of the story, a theme for which Telemachus's recollections served as a prelude: the "riddle" of attraction and repulsion between the sexes.[13]

If Nossack makes the question of the relationship between the sexes and the role of sexuality the center of his Cassandra portrayal, then he does so at a point in history when one would be more likely to expect a political reinterpretation of the figure. The discursive connection between sexuality and truth that forms the basis for Solvejg Müller's reading of Cassandra has been apparent at least since Schiller's poem by the same name and has led, depending on the political climate, to either the sexualization or desexualization of the figure. In Nossack's rendering, Cassandra's political potential is sacrificed by reducing the connection between sexuality and truth to the question of why Cassandra resisted the affections of the god Phoebus. This is a question that appears strange even to Telemachus and seems as out of joint with his image of his father as does the interpretation of Odysseus in the myth and the scholarship that followed. If one follows Herfried Münkler's argument in his study *Odysseus und Kassandra* (1990), Odysseus—already portrayed by Homer as the wily politician par excellence—and Cassandra together represent the "politics in myth":

> Cassandra is the prototype of the intellectual. Yet Odysseus is no less of an intellectual than she, and both together mark the end-points of a spectrum of positions that intellectuals have moved through since Odysseus and Cassandra. Cassandra, the extreme of powerlessness, reduced to the role of the ignored and unheard warner, is a subversive subject whose proclamations no one wants to hear and whose knowledge no one wants to use, even when it could be useful. Odysseus, in contrast, is the intellectual in complete possession of power, his commands are always followed, the heros dance to his drum. He is the man behind the scenes, the great director. Odysseus can be silent,

Cassandra must speak: power and powerlessness. It is hardly a coincidence that both stepped onto the stage of world history together.[14]

It is certainly also no coincidence that Odysseus and Cassandra are brought into close connection with each other in Nossack's story. Of course Nossack activates very different aspects of the constellation than Münkler brings to light in his political reading of the two figures, and of course the concept of the political is multivalent. We have accustomed ourselves at least since 1968 to conceive of the private as political, while Foucault's work on the politics of the body has made us sensitive to the relationship between sexuality and politics. With a bit of effort, but not without justification, the question of sexual refusal that Nossack makes the focus of his story can here be interpreted politically.

A look at Horkheimer and Adorno's discussion of *The Odyssey* makes clear, however, that in their civilization's critical interpretation of Odysseus the two authors of *Dialectic of Enlightenment* (1944) were situating the concept of the political in an explicitly antifascist context, precisely at the time when Nossack was at work on his Cassandra–Odysseus configuration. Once again, such comparisons make apparent both how great the divide was that separated the exile authors from those of the "Inner Emigration" and how different the meaning of myth's appeal was to them. Nossack's Cassandra–Odysseus configuration, with its pointed question concerning the origins of sexual refusal, appears even stranger against this background than it does to the son of Odysseus in the story: "What surprised me the most was that my father of all people seemed especially interested in the story of Phoebus."[15]

For Odysseus, in any case, this question seems so important that he not only poses it to his wife but also formulates it in a series of insistent queries during a conversation with Cassandra, which he reports to his wife and son in detail. Despite protestations to the contrary, Cassandra's response that she had been "afraid" does not completely satisfy him, as the subsequent return to the question in his conversation with his wife reveals.[16] Cassandra's refusal of the affections of a god remains in the end just as inexplicable as Agamemnon's attraction to Cassandra, who compared to Helena was plain: "For what reason did Agamemnon seek out this Cassandra? Her hips are much too slim."[17]

This question is posed in ever-changing formulations by various figures in the text. The shy, fine-boned Cassandra becomes the foil to Helena's voluptuous, seductive femininity. In contrast to Helena, sexuality appears as repellent to Cassandra as the company of other women.

By her own admission, she can "no longer stand the smell of other women," and for her, the worst are "the huge, shimmering flies that . . . engage in their games in the sun."[18]

If one contemporizes the story Odysseus tells surrounded by his family with Pylades's report, from which the aging Telemachus attempts to glean a retrospective impression of Cassandra, an image arises of a woman trying to escape the sexual advances coming from her environment, whether out of fear, disgust, or the elitist consciousness that is the sign of the chosen. A passage from the text offers support for this last thesis. Agamemnon, whom Odysseus respects as the "most human"[19] of all of the Trojan warriors, recognizes a kindred spirit in Cassandra:

> But for us the usual division into friend and foe does not apply. We have to engage with each other in a different manner. I always believe that it is necessary for those select few of us to interact outside of the accepted mores when we encounter each other, and that we openly reveal to each other those things that we keep secret from others. Because if one of us errs, then it is much worse than the minor damage that results from the errors of others. Perhaps I too have once met a god.[20]

This passage lays the groundwork for the later fusion of the two figures in which, however, the gender-specific pattern remains inscribed: Cassandra becomes the "shadow" of Agamemnon.[21] The elitist camaraderie between Agamemnon and Cassandra rests on a kind of asceticism that normal people do not understand and find suspect because of their own false assumptions. In contrast to the "blessed pair," Menelaus and Helena, who remain behind as victors in the war and of whom Odysseus speaks only with contempt, Agamemnon and Cassandra form the "other pair" who go to their death together.[22] The third pair, Odysseus and Penelope, never find their way back to each other over the course of the narrative and finally separate from each other permanently. The next generation gives rise to no couples at all: Telemachus remains unmarried, as does Pylades and the wandering Orestes, for whom, according to Pylades, only Cassandra would have made a suitable partner, "not as man and wife, she was older, but rather . . . hmm, how should I say it? They would have understood each other immediately."[23] Here Orestes and Cassandra are made into a dream couple—a constellation that I will return to later. The friendship between the surviving sons was limited to a kind of placeholdership in the case of Orestes and Pylades, and in the case of Telemachus and Pylades to the exchange of greetings and small gifts passed on by "mutual hosts."[24] It is here that the solitary masculine position of the narrative "I" manifests itself, a position that Nossack retroactively raised to the level of an aesthetic program in his Büchner prize acceptance speech of 1961, and one that he would return to again and again until the end of his life. Cassandra, because she is an exception to the conventional norms in a number of ways, is the only figure who comes under consideration as a possible partner for the solitary heroes. She does not conform to the traditional images of women. As the "younger brother,"[25] she is simultaneously "the untouchable one" who remains "pure" in every aspect, and she is a visionary, who sees the "gift" bestowed upon her by Phoebus not as a reward but as a "punishment."[26] In this perception of her task, Cassandra converges with Nossack, for whom writing always represented a burden, the cross he must bear, as the gift of clairvoyance was for Cassandra.

In the text "Ich habe nur dich, Kassandra" (I have only you, Cassandra) of 1952, Nossack takes a humorous approach to this connection between the masculine authorial "I" and Cassandra, a connection Christa Wolf later imagined as one between the feminine authorial "I" and Cassandra. After a reading, an author is confronted, as on so many previous occasions, with the ignorance of his audience. In this particular instance, it is a "commanding lady," a woman from Hamburg who irritates him with her query of whether he actually experienced what he writes about. The writer is only able to save himself from the attack of "sadness" that befalls him by retreating into his hotel room, where Cassandra is already waiting for him:

> As the elevator door closed behind me, I saw immediately that Cassandra was waiting for me. The same Cassandra who was murdered with me some three thousand years ago. The one with hips that were "too slim," an attribute that arose out of some remark the beautiful Helena made. There is only one Cassandra and I have experienced her.
>
> She crouched in one of the armchairs that were standing in the hallway in front of the elevators; next to her was a round table with a vase of white tulips. Hanging on the wall was an old etching. A bunch of people in old-fashioned clothes looking at the sea.
>
> I kneeled in front of Cassandra—yes, excuse me, because now I am describing the real and not just how one conducts oneself down below in the dining room. I did it because I wanted to see her eyes. You see, I thought that she was crying,

but naturally a girl who has turned down the love of a god does
not cry so easily. "I thought you were lost," she said.

"It almost came to that. For three hours I tried to deny you.
It was terrible."

"Did you have to drink a lot?"

"Oh, come on, it was okay. Will it ever be different with us?
Again and again there is a Clytemnestra standing there with an
ax in her hand waiting to murder us. Will we always only be
allowed to die together?"

"If we resist that, we will lose each other completely."

"I have only you, Cassandra."

"I know," she said, and smiled. "But now go to your room,
do you hear. The elevator is humming again. Otherwise they'll
think you are drunk again."

I went down the darkened corridor to the rooms, past all
the shoes that were standing in front of the doors. Was Cassandra following me? But why would she! We have each other,
in order to die together, again and again.[27]

In this passage, the author and Cassandra merge into one, albeit one
inscribed with pessimism and melancholy. Both are loners, forsaken ad-
monishers, voices crying in the wilderness, who remain unrewarded by
any hoped-for resonance from the public. It is here that the identification between the author and Cassandra occurs, an identification that
Wolfgang Koeppen, in his Büchner prize acceptance speech of 1962,
although with a very different purpose than Nossack, raised to the level
of a credo for a whole generation of authors refusing to conform to the
"tenor of the times": "The author is no party member and he does not
celebrate with the victors. He is a man, alone, frequently in the same
situation as Cassandra among the Trojans."[28]

III

Let us now return to the 1946 version of the "Kassandra" story, which,
in contrast to the ironic sketch of 1952, is still very much bound up
with the meaning of the original myth. The "us" we identified as a
familial one in the first interpretive reading not only refers back to a
mythical "primordial situation" but simultaneously refers to the present
shared by the author and the reader, who have been brought together
through the figure of Cassandra. Cassandra, the author's alter ego, be-

comes a provocation to the reader as well as a clarification of her significance for him and his time.

In another story published along with "Kassandra" in the 1948 volume, "Interview mit dem Tode" (Interview with death), Nossack makes the connection between the mythical figure of Cassandra and the present explicitly obvious. The story "Dorothea," written between 1946 and 1947, is not set during the Trojan War but rather in the bombed-out city of Hamburg in 1943 and during the "hunger winter" of 1946–1947. A fictive first-person narrator attempts in vain to tell a comrade of his experiences in the form of a Cassandra story:

> I will simply begin as follows: "Once upon a time there was a young girl named Cassandra."
> "Why Cassandra?" he will ask in astonishment.
> "She was a Trojan princess. Her hips were too small."
> "How do you know that?"
> "Helena, I mean the famous Helena, made fun of her."
> "Were you there?"
> Then I will simply continue the story, with what I know.
> One has to fill in the gaps with figures. There is enough room there.
> But if he now gets angry and shouts: "Of what relevance is Cassandra to me? I thought her name was Dorothea?"
> What do I do then?[29]

Dorothea, the "gift from God," is thus only a cover for Cassandra.[30] The experiences in the Hamburg firestorm and the encounters that follow are nevertheless so traumatic and so unusual that they cannot be pressed into the old, mythical Cassandra narrative: "Yes, of what relevance is Cassandra to me? It would be a twisted lie to speak of her. I will tell my comrade the story of Dorothea."[31] Dorothea's separation from the mythical parallelism succeeds only to be bound up immediately in a new relationship: Dorothea appears as the reincarnation of a woman whom the narrator has seen in a painting by Karl Hofer. Even if the detailed description of the painting reveals that it is not Hofer's Cassandra painting, the connection to Hofer, a persona non grata in fascist Germany, still remains noteworthy.[32]

More decisive than the question of which Hofer painting the narrator was actually referring to is the fact that Nossack as narrator cannot keep himself from having his characters meet without mystifications. Dorothea seems to have sprung from a painting by Hofer and is banished back to the painting in the narrator's memory, while the narrator is seen by Dorothea as the alter ego of the man who had rescued her during the Hamburg firestorm. As in "Kassandra," the coming together of man and woman as a couple also fails in "Dorothea." Both texts tell of unsuccessful relationships between the sexes and, in the process and in very different ways, both make references to the figure of Cassandra.

Cassandra is here neither "arbitrary," as Epple implies,[33] nor is she the "harmless" figure that Müller suggests.[34] While in the context of studies that, because of the volume of material they present, treat individual works only briefly, and in light of the unsatisfactory state of Nossack scholarship such evaluations are understandable and even excusable, they nevertheless underestimate the figure in Nossack's postwar writings in a most striking manner.[35] Worse still they distort the perception of the problematic connection between Nossack's interpretation of Cassandra and the controversial interpretive patterns developed simultaneously by exile writers, authors of the "Inner Emigration," and National Socialist writers. In my opinion, Nossack's Cassandra texts show that he did instrumentalize Cassandra offensively as an "apologetic figure."[36] The parallels between the Trojan War and the Hamburg firestorm may well be subjectively plausible, but from a political perspective they are extremely dubious, because the question of responsibility for the horrors of the war disappears behind such parallels.

The sex/gender discourse in which Nossack situates his figuration of Cassandra is no less problematic than the political discourse. Nossack outlines the image of an ascetic heroine who is like a brother to Agamemnon and who can therefore be admitted to the circle of heroic loners. Apart from the latent *Männerbund*-like orientation present in such a portrayal, the massive discrimination against women, and the denial of female sexuality and corporeality it conceals, such a Cassandra fantasy paralyzes exactly those manifestations of the political that Christa Wolf later foregrounds in her Cassandra project. Moreover, political paralysis as a contemporary phenomenon is the real scandal at a time when the confrontation of the crimes of National Socialism would have been expected.

From this perspective, the image of the bluish gray, slender column of smoke read as a representation of Cassandra in the first interpretative analysis becomes readable as a compulsory recollection of the columns of smoke that rose from Germany's crematoria under fascism. Cassandra's "ashes" provoke the memory of those whose ashes are not commemorated in the text.[37] The turn to myth is a flight from the confrontation with the crimes of one's own country. In the process, Cassandra becomes a problematic accomplice to repression. Through this appropriation of the myth, Nossack does not find himself in good company but rather situated within a larger society of authors who sought and sometimes found consolation and sanctuary in Greek mythology, both under fascism and during the early postwar years. One has only to recall the *Griechischen Mythen* (Greek myths) of Kaschnitz and Jünger, Langgässer's *Märkische Argonautenfahrt* (Voyage of the Argonauts in the Mark Brandenburg), and the Iphigenia dramas by Rutenborn, Langner, Schwarz, and Vietta, all of which avail themselves of a more or less ahistorical discourse of fate and seek to flee from a confrontation with personal complicity in fascist politics by escaping into myth. With his mythic texts written during the early postwar period—including in addition to "Kassandra" the stories "Orpheus und . . . ," "Daedalus," and, above all, *Nekyia: Bericht eines Überlebenden* (*An Offering for the Dead*) and "Der Untergang" (The apocalypse)—Nossack belongs to the circle of these post-fascist writers who were more strongly marked by fascism than they themselves were aware and than we as subsequent critics may find appealing.

IV

A brief look at the stories "Der Untergang" (1943) and *Nekyia* (1946) should once again suffice to illustrate Nossack's problematic appropriation of the Cassandra figure from another perspective. "Der Untergang" and *Nekyia* are not Cassandra texts in the sense that "Kassandra," "Dorothea," or even "I have only you, Cassandra" are. These two stories are not about Cassandra, but rather Nossack assumes Cassandra's role as the "clairvoyant of catastrophe."

Both works belong to the context of modern apocalypses.[38] They reflect the traumatic experiences of the "Hamburg catastrophe," the term Nossack used in a letter of September 18, 1946, to Hermann Kasack to describe the destruction of Hamburg.[39] "Der Untergang," which Nossack introduced to his correspondent as a "very intimate report" about "the time from July 24th until approximately August 15th" 1943, and then referred to in the same breath as a confession, is inscribed with a mythologizing perspective on historical events.[40] The image of the dead city that is conjured in both texts reactivates mythical and magical memories.

In "Der Untergang," it is above all the fantasy of matricide that binds the text to archaic contexts. The guilt for the destruction of the city, at least this is *one* reading that the text offers, is assumed by the authorial "I" who, like a murderer, must return again and again to the "murder site."[41] The mythic parallels to the mother-killer Orestes—whom Nossack will absolve from guilt in his "Kassandra" story and bid farewell to as a "model"[42] in his later sketch "Orestes" (1971) in order to have him resurrected as an "older brother"[43]—serve as the archaizing background for the story. The author's Cassandra vision is, however, not directed at a distant future with an air of prophetic warning but rather looks backward fatalistically at a "primordial situation" doomed to repeat itself as an endless cycle of "dying and becoming" in the history of both individuals and peoples.

The "dream couple" Orestes and Cassandra, already familiar to us from the "Kassandra" story, reappears as a phantasmatic configuration in "Der Untergang." As a mother killer, Orestes fulfills a destiny that Nossack as Cassandra can only prove retroactively. On different levels, Orestes and Cassandra function as the author's mythic alter egos. From this perspective, it is not surprising that Nossack originally toyed with the idea of entitling his "Kassandra" story "Orestes." The choice of one figure over the other is not based on principle but is rather aesthetic and strategic. In "Der Untergang," Nossack dispenses with an introduction to the mythic figures in the narrative plot but reclaims them as "apologetic figures" with no less intensity than in the texts where, as title characters, they are portrayed as identificatory figures in a heavy-handed fashion. Nossack takes a more subtle approach in "Der Untergang" and keeps the mythic references concealed, if for no other reason than that he was convinced that only a chosen few would be able to comprehend the "truth." In the letter to Hermann Kasack already mentioned above, Nossack emphasized that, in comparison to other people who had the same experiences, he had "more sensitive ears,"[44] above all, because his "will to consciousness"[45] set him apart from the rest: "I hear exactly how cautiously people speak of those things that lie behind them, and one must respect this caution. One cannot force anyone to turn around; not yet, the danger is too great."[46] Without examining all of the text's complexities and contradictions, it is nevertheless possible—in relation to our topic—to say that in this story, Nossack shifts the question of guilt to one of the existential meaning of horror, stylizes himself as one of the elite endowed with greater powers of perception, and contributes through his appropriation of the Cassandra position to the mythification of history.

The connection to myth also is significant for the interpretation of *Nekyia*.[47] By choosing the title *Nekyia*, which means "death sacrifice,"

Nossack is making a direct allusion to Greek myth. At first glance, however, it is not the mythic moments that stand out but rather the multiple references to the tradition of the fairy tale and science fiction. Nossack's subtitle, *Bericht eines Überlebenden* (*Report of a Survivor*), explicitly relates it to the tradition of apocalyptic visionary literature, as represented, for example, in Mary Shelley's *The Last Man* (1826). With the motto "Post amorem omne animal triste," Nossack also introduces a dream of association that is well known to us from the "Kassandra" story. The motto signals that there is a relationship between political collapse and private catastrophe. The relationship between the sexes is here also the secret point of connection from which the problem of guilt can be unfurled.

The text outlines a disconsolate scenario that is recollective of the fairy tale that the grandmother relates in Büchner's *Woyzeck*. The people, the cities, and the trees have all died. There are not even stars anymore. The moon has become a "blind mirror" and hangs in the sky like a "mushy pear."[48] The narrative "I" in the text has neither name nor reflection.[49] The world seems to be in the state of chaos that preceded Genesis. The world is a "loamy sea,"[50] and the people are "like lumps of clay"[51] awaiting their maker. Only the narrative "I" and the friend he meets in a clay crater appear to be alive. In one scene that leaves no element of the grotesque to the imagination, both men form a woman out of clay and end up in a fatal argument over the result of their work:

> "You didn't give her any navel," he shrieked and jumped up. And before I could stop him, he ran over to her. "How can she have a navel, when she was not born to any mother," I called and ran after him. But he was faster, and it was already too late. I had only made it halfway and then something terrible happened. He stood across from her and bored a navel into her belly with his extended index finger. "Get away!" I screamed, but he was not listening anymore. The woman made a step in his direction. It looked as if he were pulling her toward him by his index finger. Then she bent over him, first as if with affection and then as if unconscious. The last that I saw of my friend was how he raised his hands to protect himself from her. But the body fell on top of him and pulled the entire wall, which it was still attached to, after it.[52]

The narrative "I" of the story remains behind as the "survivor." In dream and nightmare sequences, the narrative "I" wanders aimlessly through a deserted and empty world, searching for the mothers and a solution to the question of who bears the "guilt"[53] for the condition of the world:

> "Mother, did something awful happen," I asked her from her shoulder. "I acted the whole time as if I didn't care and as if one could simply continue living thus. But that is a lie and now it has reached the point that I want to scream. And perhaps it is too late. And perhaps I am guilty of everything. There were children playing with dolls in the sand. The girls looked happily into the morning when they shook their bedclothes out at the window.
>
> And youths, ringed by the blue of evening, rode their horses gracefully to the watering hole and dreamt of heroic deeds. And then the old people sitting before their house doors between the flower bushes of their front gardens. All that, mother, is no more. It went under because I had no real part in it. The people will point accusing fingers at me. And the name, that they have been only whispering secretly up to now—and I acted as if I didn't hear it—now they will call it out loud: There he is, Death! O mother, make me nameless.[54]

In response, the mother tells the son an encoded version of the story of the Trojan War. Through this long narrative, which apart from a few small differences resembles the mythic original, she gives her son his lost identity back. As in "Der Untergang," the narrative "I" in *Nekyia* is revealed to be Orestes, who is simultaneously the victim of the war and of his familial situation. As in Nossack's "Kassandra" story, here too Orestes is not a mother killer, but his mother Clytemnestra is still the murderer of his father.

Where is Cassandra in this constellation? As in "Der Untergang," she functions here as the alter ego of the author, a seer and a knower like Cassandra, whom no one believes, and who bears the weight of his knowledge heavily:

> There is no savior, except for one alone and that one is oneself. O what a burden for him, to live from one day to the next! If he can take that, then in truth he has been tested. If one would only tell it to the people, then it would have the result—assuming, of course, that they would believe it, which is unlikely—

that the flood would begin to rise today already. Therefore one must be silent, even though that is the most difficult.[55]

Nossack definitely did not remain silent. On the contrary, in ever-new variations he attempted through his early postwar texts to offer clarification, interpretation, and meaning. In the process, the myth of the Trojan War, along with its cast of characters, above all Orestes and Cassandra, served as the precarious reference point, precarious because it transcended into a metatemporal sphere where the question of guilt and responsibility could no longer be posed in concrete political terms.

NOTES

1. For more on Friedrich Meinecke and the "old" historians' debate of 1945, see Winfried Schulz, *Deutsche Geschichtswissenschaft nach 1945* (Munich: Oldenburg Verlag, 1989). On the "new" historians' debate, see Dan Diner, *Ist der Nationalsozialismus Geschichte?* (Frankfurt a.M.: Fischer, 1987).

2. Cf. Inge Stephan, *Musen & Medusen. Mythos und Geschlechterdiskurs in der Moderne* (Cologne: Böhlau, 1997).

3. Thomas Epple, *Der Aufstieg der Untergangsseherin Kassandra: Zum Wandel Ihrer Interpretation vom 18. Jahrhundert bis zur Gegenwart* (Würzburg: Königshausen und Neuman, 1993); Solvejg Müller, *Kein Brautfest zwischen Menschen und Göttern. Kassandra-Mythologie im Lichte von Sexualität und Wahrheit* (Cologne: Böhlau, 1994).

4. Epple, 227.

5. Müller, 194.

6. For a reproduction of Hofer's painting, see the exhibition catalogue: *Karl Hofer. Sammlung Rolf Deyhle III*, Thomas Gädecke, ed. (Neumünster: Schleswig-Holsteinisches Landesmuseum, 1996). There are astonishing thematic parallels between Hofer's paintings and Nossack's writings.

7. Ernst Bloch, *Das Prinzip Hoffnung*, 6th printing (Frankfurt a.M.: Suhrkamp, 1979), 1313.

8. Hans Erich Nossack, "Kassandra," *Die Erzählungen*, Christof Schmid, ed. (Frankfurt a.M.: Suhrkamp, 1987), 93–118.

9. Ibid., 94.

10. Ibid., 95.

11. Ibid., 96.

12. Ibid.

13. Ibid., 97.

14. Herfried Münkler, *Odysseus und Kassandra* (Frankfurt a.M.: Fischer, 1990), 88.

15. Nossack, "Kassandra," 98.

16. Ibid., 113.

17. Ibid., 101.

18. Ibid., 102.

19. Ibid., 104.

20. Ibid., 112.

21. Ibid., 117.

22. Ibid., 118.

23. Ibid., 106.

24. Ibid., 96.

25. Hans Erich Nossack, *Der jüngere Bruder* (Frankfurt a.M.: Suhrkamp, 1958).

26. Nossack, "Kassandra," 111.

27. Hans Erich Nossack, "Ich habe nur dich, Kassandra," *Aus den Akten der Kanzlei Seiner Exzellenz des Herrn Premierministers Tod. Glossen und Miniaturen* (Frankfurt a.M.: Suhrkamp, 1987), 160 f.

28. Wolfgang Koeppen, "Rede zur Verleihung des Georg-Büchner-Preises 1962," *Gesammelte Werke*, vol. 5 (Frankfurt a.M.: Suhrkamp, 1986), 259.

29. Hans Erich Nossack, "Dorothea," *Die Erzählungen*, 231.

30. Ibid., 224.

31. Ibid., 232.

32. In January 1947, Ingeborg and Gottfried Sello held an exhibition of Hofer's paintings in the Hamburg Gallery of Youth, where for the first time since the war thirty-six paintings and twenty other works by Hofer were exhibited. In 1953, another exhibition followed in the Hamburg Museum of Art. Cf. the Hofer exhibition catalogue (note 6), 99 f.

33. Epple, 217.

34. Müller, 196.

35. It was not until the most recent studies by Buhr and Söhling that Nossack scholarship has become more professional. See Wolfgang Michael Buhr, *Hans Erich Nossack. Die Grenzsituation als Schlüssel zum Verständnis seines Werkes* (Frankfurt a.M.: Peter Lang, 1994); Gabriele Söhling, *Das Schweigen zum Klingen bringen. Denkstruktur, Literaturbegriff und Schreibweisen bei Hans Erich Nossack* (Mainz: Hase und Koehler, 1995). It must be noted, however, that neither of these studies addresses *Cassandra*.

36. A stronger "apologetic figure" than Cassandra under fascism as well as during the early postwar period was the figure of Antigone, who was upheld as the icon of resistance. Cf. George Steiner, *Die Antigonen. Geschichte und Gegenwart eines Mythos* (Munich: n.p., 1988); Johanna Bossinade, *Das Beispiel Antigone. Textsemiotische Untersuchungen zur Präsentation der Frauenfigur von Sophokles bis Ingeborg Bachmann* (Cologne: Bohlau, 1990).

37. Nossack, "Kassandra," 106.

38. Klaus Vondung, *Die Apokalypse in Deutschland vom 18. Jahrhundert bis zur Postmoderne* (Munich: Deutscher Taschenbuch Verlag, 1988).

39. Cited in Nossack, *Die Erzählungen*, 862.

40. On the mythologizing tendencies in Nossack's work, cf. also Inge Stephan, "'Hamburg ist für alles Künstlerische immer lähmend gewesen.' Formen der Mythologisierung Hamburgs bei Hans Erich Nossack," *Liebe, die im Abgrund Anker wirft. Autoren und literarisches Feld im Hamburg des 20. Jahrhunderts*, Inge Stephan and Hans-Gerd Winter, eds. (Hamburg: Argument, 1989), 294–316.

41. Cited in Nossack, *Die Erzählungen*, 858.

42. Hans Erich Nossack, "Orest," *Aus den Akten der Kanzlei Seiner Exzellenz des Herrn Premierministers Tod. Glossen und Miniaturen*, 26.

43. Ibid., 27.

44. Cited in Nossack, *Die Erzählungen*, 858.

45. Ibid.

46. Ibid.

47. Hans Erich Nossack, *Nekyia: Bericht eines Überlebenden, Die Erzählungen*, 119–217.

48. Ibid., 207.

49. Ibid., 145.

50. Ibid., 177.

51. Ibid., 119.

52. Ibid., 187.

53. Ibid., 178.

54. Ibid., 201.

55. Ibid., 148.

Brutal Heroes, Human Marionettes, and Men with Bitter Knowledge: On the New Formulation of Masculinity in the Literature of the "Young Generation" after 1945 (W. Borchert, H. Böll, and A. Andersch)

Hans-Gerd Winter

On May 8, 1945, the weapons are silenced in Germany. The country is in ruins, state power has collapsed, and the National Socialist war ideology and its representatives are completely delegitimized. The war has created unimaginable sacrifices of human life for the Germans as well. Four hundred million cubic meters of rubble cover the destroyed cities, and over 40 percent of all housing is destroyed; in urban areas, the number exceeds 50 percent. Millions of people stream through the ravaged country—those rendered homeless because their homes were destroyed, the first returning soldiers, the first prisoners released from the Allied camps, (ethnic) German exiles and refugees, foreign "displaced persons," and foreigners who were forcibly relocated to Germany by Hitler's authorities. The economy has collapsed, and the black market and bartering are the order of the day.[1]

In May 1946, one year after the end of the war, the young Max Frisch makes the following note in his diary about a visit to the destroyed city of Frankfurt:

> A plaque indicates where Goethe's house once stood. That one is no longer walking on the former street level is decided by the impression: the ruins are not standing, but are sinking into their own debris. . . . What still stands are the bizarre towers of a weathered roof ridge; there a toilet pipe juts into the sky, three connections indicate where the floors had been. So one plods around . . . not really knowing where to look. . . . Sometimes one is astonished that there is no further awakening. Things remain as they are: the grass that grows inside the houses, the dandelions in the churches, and suddenly one can imagine how

it continues to grow, until a primeval forest takes over our cities, slowly, inexorably . . . an earth without a history.[2]

This description of stillness, this "zero point," or apocalypse, is followed and opposed shortly thereafter by a depiction of crowds of homeless people and wanderers at the train station. Here also, Frisch perceives an apocalyptic atmosphere:

Refugees are lying on all the stairways, and one has the impression that they would not look up even if a miracle were to happen in the middle of the square, so certain are they that none will occur. . . . Their life is apparently a waiting without expectation. They no longer hang onto life, yet life still hangs on them, phantomlike, an invisible animal that is hungry and carries them through bombed-out train stations.[3]

Wolfgang Langhoff, an actor, director, and theater manager returning from Swiss exile in 1946 to Düsseldorf and then to East Berlin, remarks in a "Germany Letter" on February 18, 1946:

Transfer this image of external decay and the habituation to it onto the psychological-moral condition of the majority of the population, then you have an approximate understanding of the tasks that are bound up with the words "reconstruction," "renewal," "spiritual recuperation" and so forth.[4]

The "zero point" years, as one may describe the period from 1945 to the currency reform in 1948, are a time of utmost desperation and spiritual paralysis, but also a time in which an attempt is made to fill the apparent ideological vacuum left by the collapse of Hitler's fascism with new positions. A new and active cultural atmosphere quickly develops in the destroyed cities; one attempts to compensate for the lack of food with intellectual nourishment arising out of a dire need for orientation as an aid to survival.

It is in this situation that the so-called young generation began slowly to find its voice. Alfred Andersch describes this in his first article in the journal *Der Ruf* (The call) in 1947 as "not coming out of the stillness of study rooms" but rather "immediately out of the armed battle over Europe, out of action," yet "distinct from the older generation through its lack of responsibility for Hitler, from the younger generation through its front and prison experiences, through its 'deployed' life as it were."[5] Andersch writes of those who are between eighteen and thirty, or at most thirty-five years old, in 1945. Dieter Wellershoff, twenty-two years old in 1947, later describes the evening of February 13, 1947, as "the initiation date of German postwar literature." At issue is the broadcast of Wolfgang Borchert's *Draußen vor der Tür* (*The Man Outside*) by the Northwest Radio:

> [*Draußen vor der Tür*] spoke in an as yet unheard of, passionate fashion of the ravages of war, of the desolation of the survivors, and of homeless homecoming. It portrays the nightmare of a returning soldier who does not escape his memories and stands before closed doors everywhere, and who, at the end when he awakes, cries out the question that echoes into the nothingness, why then should he continue living?[6]

For Wellershoff, it is clear from the outset that "the impulse, with which Borchert spoke, electrified me. . . . The overwhelming experiences of the war had buried everything. Here, someone had worked his way out of the rubble and in the process had also dug free the consciousness of others."

Wolfgang Borchert is recognized as the first writer to successfully find language again and at the same time be able to claim for himself the right to speak for his generation. Borchert becomes the reference point for writers such as Andersch, Wolfdietrich Schnurre, and Heinrich Böll. The first two of these writers were among the founders of Group 47, which awarded its literary prize to Böll in 1951. All three writers claim to speak for the younger generation. Andersch admits in 1948 that, "Borchert has already asked for all of us, conclusively and radically. We achieve nothing by repeating his question. We must find a solution."[7] However, as Joseph Brockington recently pointed out, the texts of the young authors are less a demonstration of solutions characteristic of utopian blueprints than they are of a fundamental negativity.[8] Although this negativity stems from the theaters of the war and rubble period, it performs simultaneously the more important function of encouraging a process of spiritual and social renewal. It does this through the negation of behaviors and values that have been transmitted and internalized, in the very same sense that Borchert himself formulated them in "Das ist unser Manifest" ("This Is Our Manifesto"): "For we are nay-sayers. But we do not say 'no' out of desperation. . . . For we must build a 'yes' again into the nothingness."[9]

We know today that the emphatic declaration of the "zero point" and the "clear cutting" (*Kahlschlag*) that is characteristic of the authors who entered the literary field also contained ideological continuities that we view critically. In the following, I discuss how these authors attempt to balance this "nothingness" while simultaneously building a "yes" into it in relationship to images of masculinity and the representation of gender roles. In what ways are preceding models of behaviors and mentalities negated and new ones postulated through critical reappraisal? How successful were these authors in taking stock of existing behaviors and in their development of new roles and images? At issue is the masculine gender as a social and psychological mode of conduct as well as a discursive product.[10] It is understandable that the collapse of the National Socialist empire delegitimized the image of masculinity that supported it and delegitimized patriarchal, fascist ideology as a whole. A completely different question, however, is the extent to which this could possibly be recognized and comprehended so quickly by the conquered Germans. In the following discussion, I primarily examine Borchert's work, but I supplement my analysis with texts from Andersch and Böll.

"HOT, WILD FEELING" AND FEAR OF DEATH

"Helmets off, helmets off: We've lost!" Thus begins Borchert's text "Das ist unser Manifest," which came to be read as the manifesto of a generation of young men:

> The companies have dispersed. The companies, battalions, armies. Only the hordes of the dead, they are still standing. . . . We will never again assemble in response to a whistle and say "yessir" in response to a bellow. The cannons and the field sergeants don't bellow any more. We will cry, shit, and sing, when we want. But we won't ever sing the song of the thundering tanks and the song of the edelweiss again. Because the tanks and the field sergeants don't thunder anymore and the edelweiss— that has rotted under the bloody sing-song. And no general says "hey buddy" to us anymore before the battle. Before the terrible battle.
>
> We will no longer have sand in our teeth from fear. . . . And never again the hot, wild feeling in brains and bowels before the battle.
>
> Never again will we be so happy that someone is next to us. . . . Because we will never again march together, because

from now on each marches alone. That's beautiful. That's hard.
(308 f.)

Borchert takes the defeat of the German army as a point of departure to
characterize the contradictory feelings present in the young, defeated
soldiers. For perhaps the first time in his life, the young male is now on
his own and can no longer define himself in relation to the soldier
collective. He experiences this at once as liberation and loss. The proximity to another, to a comrade in the army, was reluctantly endured and
yet also experienced as relief and "luck/happiness." Here Borchert cap-
tures the perspective of the lower ranks, the common soldiers. What
they share is the "deployed life," as Andersch formulates it.[11] What they
have in common is a sense of being equal to their fellow soldiers, which
in turn intensifies their sense of community in the face of death. Borchert's description of the soldiers' contradictory feelings before the battle
is striking. Before the battle, even the general seeks intimacy with his
lowest subordinates. The relativization and formation of the individual
in the enclosed mass of the army unit also provide the individual with a
solid definition, namely, as the smallest unit in the battle-machine army.
Formation for combat involves the preparation for a collective movement as well as the directional goal of the killing-machine army, which
is shared by all of its members and subordinates. It conveys, as Elias
Canetti notes in *Masse und Macht* (*Mass and Power*), a feeling of equality, independent of rank and personal individuality, despite the extreme
hierarchy of the military.[12] (Naturally this feeling is delusive, in that the
level to which one is affected during battle varies.)

    Among the subordinates, according to Borchert, fear of death or
injury merges, both before and during battle, with the "hot, wild feeling
in brains and bowels," precisely because one has become part of an
efficient killing machine. Feelings of aggression intensified to the level of
euphoria are produced by a fear of death, and temporarily are even able
to anesthetize that fear, yet cannot fully extinguish it. Ernst Jünger en-
thusiastically describes these contradictory feelings—which Klaus Theweleit has subjected to thorough analysis—directly after the First World
War in "Der Kampf als inneres Erlebnis" (The battle as inner experience).[13] This feeling of ecstasy is at its height during a troop advance,
which successfully and determinedly routs or destroys the enemy. Elias
Canetti has characterized this condition as the discharge of the warring
mass: "In the act of discharge, differences are shed, and all feel the
same. . . . The feeling of relief in response to this is enormous."[14] The
"remarkable and unmistakable tension" that can accompany acts of war

has, as Canetti describes in *Masse und Macht,* two other deep-seated causes: "One wants to conquer death and one acts *en masse.*" The point of war is to kill: "One wants to be among the larger mass of the living. Yet, on the opposing side should be the greater heap of the dead. In this contest lies an essential, or perhaps, the deepest, reason for warfare."[15] Additionally, individuals do not stand opposed to each other in war. Masses do. The de-individualization and surrendering of responsibility connected with the binding of the selves to the enclosed army mass provide the means for the soldier to anesthetize his fear of the loss of his own existence. Simultaneously, the opposing soldier is not imagined as an individual but rather only as part of the opposing mass, which is to be transformed into the "greater heap of the dead." The masculine act of forming into a constructed mass extends, in fact, beyond death. Even the dead are imagined as a formed mass. Accordingly, in Borchert's "Manifest," the "hordes of the dead" are still "standing," even after defeat. In *Draußen vor der Tür,* "millions of hollowly grinning skeletons" (124) appear in military formation in a dream Beckmann relates to the character of the Colonel.

During retreat or flight, however, the mixture of desire and fear transforms into bare existential fear as the formation of the mass dissolves and the individual is more or less on his own: "Just yesterday in unholy flight we escaped the battle and the maw of death. Our hearts are still pounding from that terrible flight from one grenade hole to another—those motherly hollows—and from fear" (311).

In his acclaimed short story "Die Kegelbahn" ("The Skittle Alley"), Borchert succinctly describes the ambivalence of emotions and behaviors that arise from fighting and killing. The epigraph that precedes the story reads as follows:

> We are the bowlers.
> And we ourselves are the balls.
> But we are also the pins,
> that fall.
> The bowling alley, where it thunders,
> is our heart. (169)

War visualized as a game that, in reality, serves as a happy leisure-time activity? The inappropriateness of this image in comparison to the technical, highly perfected destruction of human life in the Second World War is immediately obvious. As childlike as this perspective of the warring, mass destruction may be, the image of bowling still proves to be extremely meaningful in view of the previous discussion. That is, it makes concrete the ultimate formation of the individual within an overarching machine, the rules of which dictate how he is to function: in effect as a perpetrator ("we are the bowlers"), as a victim ("we are also the pins,/that fall"), as a weapon ("we ourselves are the balls"), and as a place, a site ("the bowling alley, where it thunders,/is our heart"). This last line of the epigraph preceding "Die Kegelbahn" convincingly demonstrates the absolute internalization of the game and the disappearance of the individual in the formed warring mass.

The story itself concerns two men sitting in a trench, shooting a machine gun at men of the opposing formed mass—men "whom they did not even know," "who had done nothing to them and whom they did not even understand." In the pauses between the shooting, both marksmen find time to reflect on their actions. They are acting according to orders, as one emphasizes, but also out of voluntary submission to the task, to killing, as the other notes. Statements stand opposed to each other: "But it was terrible," and "But sometimes it was fun." A sense of personal responsibility for one's own deeds is thus formulated. God as the absolute creator of meaning, even for senseless butchery, does not exist; "But we—we exist." "Indeed, now we're stuck with it" (170). Neither man resists his task, however. They are already so much a part of the machinery of mutual killing that they have fun performing the task. Still, that the heads of those they have shot sound to the marksmen like "soft thunder" in the night signifies a residue of personhood, of individuality. Responsibility for one's own actions cannot be delegated to anyone, not even to the one who gave the order to attack. Consequently, this reflection remains a momentary one. The men take up their weapons again and continue shooting. What else can they do, remaining within the imagery of the game, if they do not want to be shot themselves, to become falling pins? According to Canetti, their "death deflector is the enemy, and all that they have to do is forestall him."[16] Deflecting death means forestalling the enemy, who also desires the same, by deflecting one's own potential death onto him.

Using the image of the marionette, Borchert portrays the absolute reduction of the individual man in the battle of the masses. After the war ends, the former soldiers are torn from the strings that had controlled them, giving rise to the paralyzing experience of sudden functionlessness and uselessness. The individual soldier returning home from war has not learned to develop an identity for himself. "Who among us can stand the mute cries of the marionettes when they, torn from their strings, lie around so stupidly twisted on the stage?" asks the male narra-

tor in "Mein bleicher Bruder" ("My Paleface Brother") (176). In "Preußens Gloria" (Prussia's glory), set after the war, a night watchman falls
immediately into a flawless parade step when the march "Preußens Gloria" is played for him. He again becomes the soldierly marionette to
such a degree that he does not even notice the thieves clearing out the
warehouse in the meantime. Here a man is fundamentally incapable of
coming to terms with the demands of civilian life and instead falls back
into the old, prescribed attitude of making himself into a marionette.
This disposition is obsolete now that independent thinking and critical
attention are required.

As clearly as the image of the marionette expresses the formation of
the individual in the German army, it is apparent that war and killing
are experienced here as externally determined events. Certainly Borchert's texts do not appeal to ideological legitimations of the war and
political goals.

THE "NOT-YET-FULLY-BORN" SONS AND
THE "BETRAYAL" OF THE MOTHERS

The justifications that the older generation, as well as the military and
state leadership, found for the war are clearly foreign to Borchert's men.
The appeal to "childlike" models in the depiction of war is one means of
avoiding ideological connotations yet may be simultaneously viewed in
part as an expression of the desire to see one's actions from the perspective of the child.

In "Das ist unser Manifest," Borchert recalls how "masculine male
song" and "soldier song" were employed in order to incorporate the
individual into a mass. At the same time, however, he asks, "Did no one
hear the children screaming away their fear of the purplish mouths of
the cannons?" (309). This soldierly man is, to appropriate a formulation
used by Klaus Theweleit in *Male Fantasies*, "the not-yet-fully-born" man,
meaning that the man who has not yet fully separated himself from his
mother is fixated at an infantile stage or regresses to this stage when in
the soldierly mass.[17] "Did no one hear the cry for the mother? The last
cry of the adventurer's man?" (309) Borchert asks. The un-worked-
through separation from the mother is a central theme in the hallucina-
tions of Lieutenant Fischer, the hungry man returning home in "Die
lange lange Straße lang" ("Along the Long Long Road"). His mother has
pushed him into isolation and has sacrificed him to the military ma-

chine. He laments, "You should never have left me alone, Mother. Now we will not find each other again. Never again. You should never have done that. . . . Why did you leave me alone, why?" (245). Now the son has returned from the war. On his own, he is forced to recognize himself as an individual and suffers from the need to suddenly become responsible for his own actions in the warring mass, and to make decisions in the present that define him as an individual: "And on the right they scream 'BARABBAS.' And on the left they scream 'FOOL.' And I stand in the middle alone without Mother. On the rocking wave world alone without Mother" (259). The "rocking wave world" that tosses the individual back and forth constitutes an experience exactly opposite to that of the military formation.

The mother figures in Borchert's stories are given notably little individualization. They are defined through their function for the young man. In exemplary fashion, the protagonist in "Die Küchenuhr" ("The Kitchen Clock")—who has lost his parents during a bomb attack—remembers the mother in terms of her care and deeds for him. She got up at night and made food for him when he came home late, to cite an instance. "And I thought that this could never end," he remembers, "It was so self-understood." Now that he has lost his mother, he knows "that it was paradise. The true paradise" (203). "I want to go to my mother!" Beckmann also decides in *Draußen vor der Tür*. Borchert's young males define life at home as an everyday existence in which every action has its prescribed meaning, orientation is simple, and the son is cared for.

The mother motif in Borchert's narratives is closely bound to the motif of *Heimat*. That is, it concerns itself with a condition of safety and security. The German-Jewish author Jean Améry reflects on what *Heimat* means from the perspective of someone who was forced into exile. He defines *Heimat* as a "land of childhood and youth," in which we have learned and control the "dialectic of knowing and perceiving, of trust and confidence." For Améry as well as for Borchert, the experience of *Heimat* forms the basis of one's own identity: "If one has no *Heimat*, one deteriorates into disorder, disturbance, distraction."[18] Améry was forced to have this bitter experience—unlike Borchert's men—because he was compelled, as a consequence of his exile, to destroy his internalized image of *Heimat*. The child's first experience of *Heimat* is with the mother. Borchert's men are not forced into exile; neither do they experience being excluded from *Heimat*. They are, however, torn from their mothers and *Heimat* much too early. Contrary to National Socialist propaganda, which contended that the soldiers defended *Heimat* in foreign lands with their aggression, Borchert's soldiers experience the war primarily as the loss of *Heimat* and mother.

The war that follows the separation from the mothers is experienced by the sons as a "betrayal," a betrayal in the form "of metal, phosphorus, hunger and ice storm and desert sand" (240). *Heimat* and security are lost in favor of an existential exposure to the death threat of acts of war. In the face of the horrors of war, possibilities for individual perception fail; in the end, these experiences cannot be formulated after the return to a *Heimat* that has most often become alien. This is due in part to the fact that self-sacrifice to the warring mass leaves behind a sense of extreme devaluation. The lack of personal substance, as a result of the abrupt and externally determined separation from mother and home in favor of a marionette-like existence in the army, leads to the depressing realization that, "No one can recognize us anymore" (241).

The experience of identity loss after the war also results from the fact that joining into the warring mass had conveyed a kind of feeling of *Heimat*. As the two soldiers in "Die Kegelbahn" demonstrate, functioning as a marionette was absolutely welcomed by the individual because it relieved him of the burden of questioning the meaning of war, as well as his own part in it. By binding into the encapsulated, warring mass, elements of the experience of maternal protection also may be transferred onto the men's organization army. The army as an ersatz *Heimat* protects the individual at least from the danger of "disorder" and disturbance.

In the act of retreat, where the formed warring mass partially disperses, Borchert's men also experience the earth as Mother. "Motherly hollows" (311) protect the fugitives from the guns of the advancing enemy mass: "And when fear made us swallow the mud and threw us into the torn-up womb of the maternal earth . . ." (240). The reversal of direction of one's own mass is already experienced as its partial devaluation. This increases the fear of no longer being able to beat the "death deflector" enemy. As the sentence quoted above continues: "[T]hen we cursed into the heavens, into the deaf-mute heavens: And lead us not into desertion and forgive us our machine guns, forgive us that no one was there who forgave us, there was no one there" (240). As self-ironic as this particular sentence is, it is clear that the eighteen-year-old man in the story "Im Mai, im Mai schrie der Kuckuck" ("In May, in May Cried the Cuckoo") is searching for an authority capable of granting forgiveness, for an absolution for his own role in the killing. God, as Borchert never ceases to emphasize, cannot be this authority. Who, however, earlier forgave all the youth's exploits and misdeeds and continued to care for him? The mother.

The young man, who has not yet been fully born, remains bound to the search for maternal nurture and care—to "paradise"—after the war as well, as Beckmann's behavior in *Draußen vor der Tür* clearly demonstrates. In the first scene in which the homecomer Beckmann appears, the figure of the Elbe River already bears maternal qualities. Yet this "mother" refuses to allow the "little one" to "crawl under her skirt." She causes the "baby" to be thrown back again "onto the sand" (107). The only character Beckmann begins to trust to the point that he even temporarily takes off his gas mask is the Girl, though she too is characterized largely by maternal qualities. She cares for Beckmann, wet and freezing after his walk into the Elbe, and offers him clothing and food as well as a warm room. That Beckmann later allows himself to be driven off by the phantasmal figure of the one-legged man has been interpreted by Peter Rühmkorf correctly as an inability to hold his own in male competition over the woman.[19] This is because the attachment to the mother hinders Beckmann from a radical affection that asserts its own claim.

Parting from and losing maternal protection, which are carried out for the first time when the young male enters the military, prefigure for Beckmann—as well as for Borchert's other youthful characters—everrecurring farewells to the opposite sex. Consequently, it is no surprise that the young man and woman do not get together in Borchert's now famous text "Generation ohne Abschied" ("Generation without Farewell"). In *Draußen vor der Tür*, one finds only fleeting contact: "We meet each other in the world and are human being with human being— and then we steal away because we are without attachment, without permanence, and without farewell" (60). The attachment to the mother and to war experiences, interpreted as a loss of security and existential abandonment, hinders the development of any real encounters with the opposite sex. Borchert has gone down in literary history as the writer of being "on the road," as one who has accurately captured the existential situation of homelessness, flight, and the aimless wandering of masses of people streaming back and forth that characterized the years 1945 and 1946. The compulsion to be on the move also stems from the young men's inability to enter into relationships. Borchert asks:

> Or shall we commit our hearts for one night that of course has a farewell in the morning? Would we endure the farewell? And if we wanted to experience farewells like you who are different from us and savor every second of farewell, then it could hap-

pen that our tears would rise to a flood that no dams, even if
they had been built by the forefathers, would be able to withstand. (59)

Here the man solely dependent on himself clearly demonstrates his fear
of self-exposure and the dissolution of painstakingly maintained ego
boundaries.

A GENERATION OF MEN "WITHOUT ARRIVAL"

The young women in Borchert's stories are rarely given an individual
character, and more rarely still, a personal history. They function essentially like the mothers, that is, like the young men's projection figures.
Inherited images of women, and clichés such as that of the whore, appear with remarkable frequency. Because the woman is pictured as a
seductress, most often in a pejorative sense because she seeks material
gain from it, the question arises whether the young male narrators also
are not willingly stylizing these figures in their encounters with them as
such, because in this way erotic attraction can appear less dangerous to
the young one bound to the mother as first love. Thus the homeless
man in "Bleib doch, Giraffe" ("Do Stay, Giraffe") knows from the very
beginning what the woman will be, namely, "like all the rest," "hungry,
naked, and painted" (65). Before the erotic attraction that she exudes
overwhelms him, he forces a separation. Outwardly, it is mostly the
men's relationship to their war experiences that hinders a real encounter.
Yet interestingly enough, the preparedness for death that he experienced
at the front is not foreign to her either. In her destitution, she is now
also prepared to die: "Death, she chortled, that would be something,
you" (66). He certainly sees himself from the very beginning as being "at
the end of the world" in a "darkness" where his "own ocean" threatens
to engulf him. Here the solitary man's fear of self-exposure and self-
dissolution referred to above manifests itself again. Consequently, the
other's words cannot reach him at all. He climbs aboard the train claiming he must move on. His exclamation that follows, "Do stay, giraffe!"
refers only to the request to extend the farewell just long enough for the
train to leave the station. She refuses to take this role, however. Essentially, the ambivalent attitude typical of Borchert's young men expresses
itself in these two contradictory statements: to long for an encounter and
yet in the end to flee from it.

There are moments when Borchert's young man admits to himself that he is seeking a woman in order to find salvation from his own need. In "Im Mai, im Mai schrie der Kuckuck," this need almost leads to a successful encounter. Here again, it is the woman who takes care of the man by giving him a bed to sleep in and the opportunity to formulate his experience of loneliness and loss of identity. In the end, however, he remains a marionette still twisting on the strings of the collapsed killing-machine army. He continues to be so strongly programmed to imagine the desired liberation from his experiences as violent and bound with murder—"we murder them every night until someone saves us"—that his kisses taste of metal, and he has the "odor of blood from slaughtered soldiers in his hair" (241). As a result, man and woman must remain foreign to each other, as much as they desire to be together. In the end, both look at each other "always related and antagonistic and indissolubly lost in each other. . . . There is the door. He is already standing outside and still does not risk the first step." He takes his leave then and goes away, and "[t]hat is as it should be" (243).

The young men's identity crises render them soft and sensitive, despite all of their external roughness. Most of the time they are unable to act, due to their submission to their experience of loss and fear. They remain fixated at the point where they would have to make a decision. This is true of Beckmann, for example, who does not move beyond the moment when he must definitively decide either to walk into the Elbe or to integrate himself into society. The latter would mean taking his views on the violent nature of humanity with him into society. The impact of Borchert's texts is based on the fact that, in effect, as Andersch has formulated, they simultaneously constitute "a single question" and an appeal to choose:

> He [Borchert] sits with Büchner on the precipice of determinism, the question echoes up horrifyingly, not to be overheard; *Woyzeck* has been completed, there is no more escalation. Just as we had begun with it, we are at the end of the "homecoming literature," at the end of nihilism, at the end of inescapability.[20]

The shocking insight into their own readiness for violence apparently does not let go of these young men after the war, these men who were discharged from maternal security by the war. Beckmann asks himself, "Who protects us from it, that we do not become murderers?" (164). This question refers to the one-legged man whom he has murdered in his imagination as he usurped the man's place with the Girl. Here Beckmann's consternation results from the knowledge that he does not fundamentally differ in his readiness to commit violence from those who have made him feel excluded from society. For Beckmann, the Girl signals his sole opportunity to conquer his isolation. Yet access to her is blocked, precisely because it is only possible through "murder." The experience of existential isolation links Beckmann to Woyzeck: both experience themselves as standing at the edge of society; both compete for a woman whom they lose, Beckmann through his recoiling at the "murder" of his competitor, and Woyzeck through the murder of the woman after she has been unfaithful to him. Beckmann, on the other hand, allows his wife's infidelity to go unpunished.

Borchert's young men most often remain stranded at the level of Beckmann's cry, "Why am I living? For whom? For what?" Or they retreat with a hasty farewell: "We meet in the world and are human being with human being—and then we steal away . . . like thieves" out of "fear" of the "cry" of the "heart" (61). Arrival, which would mean the decision to attempt to locate oneself, still remains in Borchert's texts a rather empty future prospect that may only be filled with clichés, such as the "arrival on a new star, in a new life," or "under a new sun, to new hearts" (61). All the same, Borchert's men are young; they still have time and the belief that one day a new home will yet come into being. Admittedly, however, an overpowering experience of premature aging determines the present:

> And in the train stations filled with march music, they cheered us into the dark, dark country of war. And then it came. Then it was there. And then, before we could comprehend it, it was over. In that interval lies our life. And that is ten thousand years. . . . And no one can still recognize us, us grizzled twenty-year-olds, so much did the roaring ravage us. (241)

ATTEMPTING TO FREE ONESELF FROM THE "BARBS OF COMMAND"

Borchert's roaring consisted mostly of commands. This is because his young men had only reached low ranks in the military hierarchy, the highest being that of Lieutenant Fischer in "Die lange lange Straße lang." The military machinery can only function if commands are given, and if the soldier functions in a state of constant anticipation of those commands. This basic attitude is an essential component of the conversion of the individual into a part of the "totality-machine troop," as Theweleit has described it.[21] Functioning as a soldier appears to Borchert's young men, in retrospect, as utmost heteronomy and self-devaluation. Canetti observed in *Masse und Macht*: "He [the soldier] swallows command after command and whatever he may feel about it, he is never allowed to tire of them. For every command that he carries out—and he carries all of them out—a barb remains behind in him."[22] In the barb that sinks itself deep into the person, the command remains preserved in "its power, its breadth, its limit," and it can take years before this "sunken and stored part of the command" comes to light again.[23] The common soldier portrayed by Borchert must swallow one command after the other without having many opportunities to issue orders himself. According to Canetti, a dissolution of this barb of command is only possible if the situation that the command had brought about is afterward reversed. This is precisely what the former sergeant Beckmann attempts in *Draußen vor der Tür*. He was given the command by his Colonel to reconnoiter a forest with twenty men. At the end of the patrol, eleven men are missing. Beckmann thinks he recognizes the private first-class Bauer—to whom he himself gave the fatal order to remain at his post—in the person of the one-legged man who appears with the Girl. Now he wants to return the responsibility for the command and for the dead to the Colonel. Beckmann experiences the barb of the command like a foreign intruder he wants to be rid of, to give back.

> THE OTHER: Come, Beckmann. We'll take the road. We'll pay a man a visit. And you'll give it back to him.
> BECKMANN: What?
> THE OTHER: The responsibility.
> BECKMANN: Pay a man a visit? Yes, let's do that. And the responsibility, I'll give it back to him. Yes, we'll do that. I want to sleep one night without cripples. (118)

Additionally, in the dream Beckmann describes to the Colonel, he carries out an act of resisting orders, something he had not committed during the war. He causes the war dead, who have assembled before a general, and whose number has increased to incalculable proportions, to refuse the command to count off. Beckmann credits himself with this mutiny, because the general had conveyed the command to him personally. Suffering from the soldierly barbs of command, as well as the attempt to cut them out of the self and be rid of them, is characteristic of Borchert's young men. Lieutenant Fischer, in "Die lange lange Straße lang," also is unable to come to terms with his responsibility for having sent fifty-seven men to their deaths with his command. In "Die Katze war im Schnee erfroren" ("The Cat Was Frozen in the Snow"), former soldiers are haunted by the illusion of having burned a Russian village, along with its civilian population, to ashes. Here Borchert shows that, with the dissolution of the enclosed army mass, the question of personal responsibility for actions taken during the war may no longer be re- pressed, precisely because the soldiers who were previously formed into a mass are now forced, as single persons, as individuals, to take respon- sibility for their actions.

The existential need of Borchert's young men is to free themselves from their molding as recipients of commands in the military machin- ery. The male characters in "Das ist unser Manifest" are still "shooting holes into everything" with their "machine guns: the Ivans, the earth, Jesus" (312). On the other hand, they are already capable of refusing to reorder themselves in a collective: "We will never again assemble in re- sponse to a whistle or say 'yessir' in response to a bellow. . . . We will cry, shit, and sing, when we want" (308). This new self-definition is only possible for the young men, however, if they live through and work through their war and frontline experiences one more time, in order to free themselves from the deformations that these barbs have caused. No one achieves this, though. All the same, Borchert does allow Beckmann, at the end of *Draußen vor der Tür*, to overcome his fruitless attitude of denunciation, in which he sees himself only as a victim. In that he recognizes his own role in the war's murder, his own readiness to com- mit violence, he becomes a man with "bitter knowledge." His radical insight enables him to answer the questions posed at the end ("Why am I alive? For whom? For what?") in a manner such that, for himself and his environment, the walk into the Elbe becomes superfluous. As Bor- chert himself comments in a letter to Max Grantz: "Beckmann does not walk into the Elbe in the end. He cries out for an answer. . . . And he receives no answer. There is none. Life itself is the answer."[24]

THE BRUTAL HEROES OF
THE OLDER GENERATION

The men of the older generation stand in stark contrast to the young men with bitter knowledge who desire to go from being marionettes to becoming human. From the perspective of the younger generation, the older generation is primarily responsible for the crimes committed under

National Socialism and during the war, as Beckmann states in *Draußen vor der Tür*:

> They betrayed us. . . . When we were still very young, they made war. And as we grew older, they talked about war. Enthusiastically. . . . And when we were older still, they conceived of a war for us. And then they sent us into it. And they were enthusiastic. . . . No one told us, you are going into hell. . . . So they betrayed us. Betrayed so terribly. And now they are sitting behind their doors. The teacher, the director, the court official, the senior physician. Now no one sent us. No, no one. All of them are now sitting behind the doors. And they have the door tightly closed. And we are standing outside. (158)

On the basis of this accusatory stance, the men of the older generation become the product of a negating fundamental philosophy rather than a composite of contradictory attitudes. Too intense and massive is the sense of having been betrayed. In part, the son's anger at having been betrayed by his father also plays a role, as pointedly illustrated in "Im Mai, im Mai schrie der Kuckuck." This feeling of betrayal results from the fact that the fathers also contributed to the separation of the sons from their mothers and *Heimat*. Here, at the son's departure for the army, the fathers wave their hats "loudly and lustily with their lead faces": "Take care, Karlheinz—until death—take care—my boy the *Feeeheeede*" (239).

The men of the older generation in *Draußen vor der Tür*, namely, the Colonel and the Cabaret Director, are portrayed as "grotesque, caricatured human puppets" (157) by Beckmann, who, despite his gas mask, is the real seer. The Colonel has repressed his portion of guilt for the murders of the war; in fact, he remains ever the militarist who refuses to question his own role in any form. He possesses such an ironclad armor around his ego that Beckmann's concerns and his tormenting delusions simply bounce off of him. This is why he is able to be jovial and friendly to Beckmann. If the Colonel has already reintegrated himself perfectly into society, the same is true for the Cabaret Director. The Cabaret Director shares the Colonel's hard cynicism, the repression of the recent past, as well as rabid neocontinuity. Beckmann is striving for authentic conduct, while the Cabaret Director is always playing a role, evidenced, for example, by his three pairs of eyeglasses (Beckmann has only one pair). At first he presents himself as a progressive supporter of young talent; then he transforms himself into a conservative custodian of an artistic taste that seeks amnesia and entertainment. Consequently, he is too cowardly to tell Beckmann openly that he has no chance to work for him. From the Cabaret Director's perspective, Beckmann himself is responsible if he walks into the Elbe. The Cabaret Director does not count himself among the "millions who now must hobble through life and are happy if they fall." As for the Colonel, all "lower ranks [are] suspicious, turf-heads, reasonists, pacifists, water corpse aspirants" (154). For him, Beckmann would "have gone to the dogs anyway." From this perspective, Beckmann's accusation of murder against the Colonel and the Cabaret Director appears reasonable subsequently, because it unveils their latent readiness to commit violence.

"Earlier," the character of the Other states, "it could have happened that they mourned in San Francisco if a balloonist crashed near Paris." Beckmann asks, "Earlier? When was that? Today only death lists with six zeros accomplish that. But people no longer sigh under their lamps, they sleep deeply and tranquilly, if they still have a bed" (144). The collective "inability to mourn," which the Mitscherlichs convincingly described, reveals itself here.[25] Further, the Colonel and the Cabaret Director equate masculine—"human"—behavior with conformity to existing power structures and societal ideologies, with the rabid pursuit of personal gain as well as with emotional coldness and the repression of compassion toward the weak. "Masculine" behavior means exuding a sense of superiority, allowing no doubts toward one's own actions, the reproduction of an "elbow" society. Through this, Borchert makes it clear that there is no transformation in the mentality of German society before and after the "zero point." In the end, no distancing from, let alone working through, the war and National Socialist ideology has yet taken place. It is therefore no coincidence that Beckmann, who asks unpleasant questions, is considered someone whose "conceptions and reason [have been] addled by that little bit of war" (121).

Latent masculine aggression present in the older generation can certainly be transformed into overt aggression, and not only in war. This fact is demonstrated in "Alle Milchgeschäfte heißen Hinsch" (All dairy stores are called Hinsch).[26] The mildly ironic tone, which forces the reader to keep the events depicted at a distance, cannot conceal that at issue here is the critical encounter with a mentality considered masculine. This ideology regards brutality as proof of "heroism": "Heroes, even if they are idealists, heroes, . . . these heroes are never squeamish. Heroes cannot possess the cautiousness of cowards—they must be violent and brutal" (23). Concretely, the story portrays a milk truck driver who grabs the dairy store owner's daughter under her skirt so roughly—

"not particularly tender . . . (heroes can never allow themselves that!)" (24)—that the shock causes her to drop the milk can she had just raised up over her head. It is a matter of attempted rape, as the narrator himself comments. The consciously objectifying, ironic, distance-preserving language makes no attempt to deny this: "He [the hero] wanted to take Elsie like a curve which one goes into without taking his foot off the gas. He wanted to knock her over like he brought his steering wheel around, and take possession of her like a milk can with his hairy paws" (24). In a mild, entertaining tone, the story deconstructs masculine aggressive behaviors in which perpetuation beyond the "zero point" and the collapse of the Third Reich are clearly demonstrated. That the daughter still mourns the loss of the "hero" truck driver, despite the severe injuries she suffers, illustrates the acceptance of violence, even by its victims. It is through the brutal aggressor, of all people, that she feels herself awakened as a woman. Images of milk deliverers driving their wagons through the streets "like heavy artillery" or Elsie gripping a milk can "like artillery soldiers grip their grenades and find the sensation of the hard metal pleasing on their skin" (24) underscore a proximity to the past war. It is difficult to say whether the woman's acceptance of the violent act in the story portrays a brutal, male fantasy. If so, the narrator's perspective would signal his alignment with that of the milkman rather than his ironic distance. Even if one were to interpret the woman's acceptance in this manner, it would still provide document of the "brutal hero"'s mode of thought and behavior. It is well known that heroism was one characteristic propagated by the National Socialists and intended to prepare the male for battle and the deployment of his own life. According to this ideological formation, latent or overt readiness to commit violence has in fact remained intact within the brutal hero of the postwar period.

HEINRICH BÖLL'S HANS SCHNITZLER: THE ARRIVAL OF ONE WHO BARELY ESCAPED IN A NEW LIFE

Borchert's young men develop from "marionettes" into sensitive men with "bitter knowledge," while the older men remain mostly "brutal heroes." Using Heinrich Böll's unfinished novel, *Der Engel schwieg* (*The Silent Angel*), I now examine what he added to the image of this male generation. As late as 1952, Böll still proclaimed his pronounced commitment to "war, rubble, and homecoming literature," which attempted to take stock of the German mentality and existential foundations after the "zero point" of 1945.[27] Moreover, he saw its most significant representative in Borchert, who had chosen the "conflict suffered by the individual who makes and experiences history" as the point of departure for his early stories.[28] *Der Engel schwieg* was written in 1949 and 1950 but was published only posthumously.[29] In this story, Dr. Fischer, philologist, lawyer, editor of a church journal, and close confidant of the archbishop, is a figure comparable to the Colonel and the Cabaret Director in *Draußen vor der Tür*. In that he represents the Church, which conformed to existing powers, he is already the focus of Böll's radical critique of the Church. Like the Colonel and the Cabaret Director, the collapse of 1945 does not signal a "zero point" for Fischer. It is true that he was earlier a member of the National Socialist Party; nevertheless, he has obtained an edict from the archbishop exonerating him. Fischer belongs to privileged society both before and after the "zero point." As a "fisher of money, not a fisher of men" (the Doctor's characterization of him), he refuses the homecomer's request for bread; as brother-in-law to the dying Mrs. Gompertz, he illegally asserts his claims of inheritance, thus putting an end to her "humane impulses" and readiness to help the needy (105). This exercise of power belongs to his self-understanding as a man. He has an "imperious face" (182). His appearance also signals that he has learned, during changing times, always to remain near the upper strata of society: "This wide, pale, male face never changed. Neither war nor destruction could weaken it: the doughlike surface of academic impoliteness, eyes that knew that they knew something . . ." (95). Like Borchert's older generation of men, he too is a brutal hero, if Mrs. Gompertz's accusation of him is true—namely, that he has sexually abused his own daughter and forced her to have an abortion at a clinic (102). Fischer develops a strategy of barely concealed brutality and violence against the sick Mrs. Gompertz when he forbids her to give money to beggars and attempts to take over the right of disposal of her husband's money; against Hans Schnitzler, his brutality becomes overt when he tears away the testament of Mrs. Gompertz's husband—which contradicts his own claims—from Hans by pushing "him against the wall," pinning "his arms . . . while his free hand purposefully thrust[s] into the other's left pocket" (186). Even though Fischer claims to be "a good Christian," he is a stranger to "human impulses," (100) as he states to Mrs. Gompertz.

In contrast to Borchert, Böll does not primarily emphasize the contrast between the older and younger generations but rather between those who rapidly reestablish themselves, the irredeemable ones securely

positioned close to power, and the majority of the have-nots. Nevertheless, the main character, the homecomer Hans Schnitzler, is comparable
to Borchert's young men with bitter knowledge. Like the character of
Feinhals in Böll's *Wo warst du, Adam?* (*And Where Were You, Adam?*), as
well as almost all of Borchert's men, Hans was merely a common soldier
who saw himself as having been cast out of maternal security when he
was drafted into the army. It is no coincidence that his departure from
his mother is depicted in the novel's longest chapter: "This torturous
afternoon now seemed in his recollection worse to him than the entire
war" (37). Even though Böll does not portray Hans's war experiences in
detail, he does, however, make him into a deserter during the final days
of the war. But the desertion, which could be read as the expression of a
conscious decision that makes an individual out of the marionette soldier, is not described that way at all. Instead, Hans is dominated—like
Borchert's characters—by the experience of subjection, an experience
that goes along with clear devaluation and loss of self. Hans's missing
identity is symbolized by the fact, in part, that he continually took on
new names as a deserter, and is in fact given a new name after the war.
Shortly before the end of the war, Hans was to be executed for desertion,
yet the court clerk, who turns out to be Mrs. Gompertz's husband,
"robs" him of "death" by helping him escape and thereby committing
himself to the firing squad instead: "I now understand," says Hans, "that
one can give someone life by stealing death from him" (50). Gompertz
willingly offers himself as Hans's "death deflector." In contrast to the
opposing army, which functions as a "death deflector" during war, Gompertz's decision concerns itself with voluntary self-sacrifice founded upon
individual decision. Hans accepts the sacrifice yet feels devalued as a
survivor, because he cannot owe his existence to his own action. Hans's
identity crisis, stemming from self-denial and self-deprecation, leads to
an incredible exhaustion. In this condition, he is comparable to Borchert's men. More than Borchert, Böll emphasizes the corporeal: bodily
exhaustion as well as hunger. Hans spends "almost three weeks" (73) in
bed after arriving home. During this time, his new partner Regina has
long since accustomed herself to the barter economy of the day. She
trades away everything of value that she owns on the black market, in
exchange for basic necessities. Her role as a mother for Hans expresses
itself in the procurement of an identity for him, in the form of papers
from the American authorities.

   In contrast to Borchert's men, however, Hans ultimately develops
sufficient strength to engage in the first independent activities intended
to secure his life with Regina, and he thereby lives a life that remains

inaccessible to Borchert's men. That is, Hans and Regina are able to achieve a relationship that ultimately extends beyond Hans's projection of the mother role. In the world of the novel, there are the (mostly evil) haves and the (usually good) have-nots. Love, Böll shows, exists between those without possessions and symbolizes the willingness to share unconditionally with each other what little there is, as well as to construct a life together out of nothingness:

> He knew well what it would mean if he walked into the kitchen: he would have to live: assume an endless burden of days that were not payable with a few kisses; climb onto the platform of daily life, this grandstand of the black market, work or thievery, while he had thought he could slumber under the grandstand in the shadows and under the stomping of the players. (137)

For Hans, erotic attraction, in contrast to Borchert's men who are quickly tempted to project the image of the whore onto the woman, clearly regresses to that of "endless affection" (145). Additionally, Hans lacks the external brashness and roughness behind which Borchert's young men often hide their vulnerability.[30] He does not shy away, like Borchert's young men do, from giving himself to the other, from the penetration of his own armor. The affection that Hans obviously received from his mother, and still expresses as "desperate affection" toward her, is of a kind he is also able to feel toward Regina, who has accepted him as one who depends upon help because of his traumatic war experiences, as if that were completely self-understood (38).

The fragmentary nature of Böll's novel demonstrates itself in part through the fact that the time period between the powerfully portrayed separation from the mother and the punishment for the desertion is left out. Apparently Hans has not been made into a functioning element in the killing-machine army in the same manner as Borchert's men. He has attempted to make his way through the war as an individual. He attains this by changing roles within the lower echelons of the military hierarchy, as well as by hiding himself behind changing, unknown names. As he is arrested at the end of the war, his life is saved by Gompertz's own self-sacrifice. Because Hans has maintained a distance from the "competition" between life and death, he does not owe his life to his aggression against the enemy. He is therefore less deformed than Borchert's men. In contrast to them, Hans has no feelings of guilt in relationship to his participation in warlike operations. Because of his own particular history in the war, he is prepared to be taken care of by Regina, while Beck-mann is compelled to leave the Girl. Because Hans is finally prepared to climb onto the "platform of daily life . . . this grandstand of the black market, work or thievery" (138), he creates the preconditions necessary for not seeing Regina as the providing mother. Correspondingly, mutual love may lead to a marriage, whereby Hans not only acquires wine from Kaplan in order to drink to his decision to marry, but rather, in recognition of Regina's piety, arranges a church wedding.

ALFRED ANDERSCH'S WERNER ROTT: "MASCULINE FREEDOM" AS A PROGRAM

In Borchert's "Im Mai, im Mai schrie der Kuckuck," the soldier return-ing home from war remembers his soldierly cry: "into the deaf-mute heavens: and lead us not into desertion" (240). In "Jesus macht nicht mehr mit" ("Jesus Won't Play Anymore"), Borchert did depict a refusal to obey orders, but never a desertion. His male figures are, as soldiers, still too clearly marionettes, even if they do possess "bitter knowledge." It is well known, however, that Andersch placed a deserter at the center of his autobiographical "report," entitled "Die Kirschen der Freiheit" ("The Cherries of Freedom," 1952). In the following, the male figures in the story "Flucht in Etrurien" (Flight from Etruria), which first appeared in 1950 as a series of installments in the *Frankfurter Allgemeine Zeitung* and was published again in 1981, is comparatively examined.[31] This early story contains motifs that were later transformed and developed in *Die Kirschen der Freiheit*. In "Flucht in Etrurien," Werner and the young Erich desert from their troop, which is being sent to the collapsing front on the Italian coast, and which is, in fact, moving in the opposite direc-tion of the fleeing remainders of the German army. Only Werner suc-ceeds in deserting to the American side, however, while Erich is bitten by a snake and dies in agony.

Werner can be read as a foil to Borchert's marionettes and men with bitter knowledge. He is searching for the "experience of freedom," which, according to Andersch, the young generation of German men could in fact construct in opposition to the experience of the dissolution of the self within the formed army mass, as well as against the pressures of imprisonment.[32]

A night will come, Werner thought, in which I will be alone without having to wait for someone. Finally alone. Alone and

free. Outside of law and order. Taken in by the night and freedom's wilderness. . . . Nights and days between imprisonment
and imprisonment. Thus my hope begins. (103)

It is not the purpose here to delineate the obvious influence of French
existentialism and, in particular, Sartre's philosophy of freedom, on Andersch.[33] He is describing a masculine "attitude," a behavior that opposes
the mentality of Borchert's men.[34] Werner, who knows already at the
beginning of the story that the battle is for the wrong cause, breaks away
from the formed mass of his squadron—which is, in any case, showing
the first signs of disintegration—through an escape that simultaneously
makes him autonomous, seeking to determine his own fate by free
choice. The escape from the troop is already imagined in advance as an
exit from the condition of being externally determined by civilization, as
a regression into a precivilized, masculine-autonomous existence: "Moving myself cautiously, through the grass, under trees and cliffs. An Indian game. . . . Ambling hiking gait. Flowers. Sleeping out in the open
on the gorse hill. Trickling water, mute animal eyes" (103). Borchert
likewise portrays the imagination of figures who crawl back into a precivilized existence. In contrast to Andersch, however, his retrogression to
an overpersonalized, overhistoricized stream of life (*Lebensstrom*) expresses itself mostly as a flight from actual demands.

While still with the troop, Werner fights for Erich, whom he tries to
convince to desert with him. Erich truly embodies the "human marionette" who does not really want to experience the transformation into
"masculine freedom" (122). For Erich, the most important reason for
remaining with his troop lies with his fiancée Katrina, who, in the case
of a desertion, would accuse both him and herself of treason against the
fatherland: "She feels that I am not protecting her anymore. Every war is
also a battle for the women. Going away means leaving her in the lurch"
(122). In fact, Andersch is alluding to a powerful force, one that compels men to continue to fight, even for a bad and simultaneously hopeless cause. Here Andersch is constructing a motivation that is diametri-
cally opposed to the condition of Borchert's men. Whereas Borchert's
marionettes and men with bitter knowledge feel betrayed by the mothers
and brides who have let them go off to war, here the woman accuses the
man of betrayal. Through this, Katrina instills in Erich, as Werner critically observes, "a genuine bad male-conscience" (122). For Werner, a
flight from the woman's bonds is a desirable masculine decision and
extends back to the first separation from the mother. While Werner can
imagine himself as a free, wild man who plays Indian, Erich has not

completed that separation. He regards parting from his bride as a be-trayal—a central motivation for his functioning as a marionette in the war machinery up until that point. Erich further recognizes that deser-tion also constitutes a separation from his own people that would subse-quently stigmatize him as a "foreigner," even after the army's defeat. Masculinity for Werner, however, is equated with personal responsibility and individual freedom. Loneliness is to be accepted. Because of this, Erich's arguments do not impress him. Werner fights a "serious men's duel" with Alex, who wants to stay with the troop until the bitter end (this also seems to be a self-determined decision), over the weak Erich, who has not yet grown up. That Erich is bitten by a snake and dies appears in this context to be both highly symbolic and logically consis-tent. He has succumbed to the insinuations of a woman; he fears her faithlessness as a consequence of his behavior. Yet through his death, he is removed from her and the National Socialist ideology she represents. In this respect, it also is logically consistent that Werner removes the dead man's army insignia from his uniform and thus transforms him, in the end, into a deserter.

CONCLUSION

Human marionettes, men with bitter knowledge, and brutal heroes—the critical balance of Borchert, Böll, and Andersch is clearly marked by their proximity to the overpowering experiences of war. The result is an inventory of male behaviors joined with sharp criticism and negation. Therein lies the real achievement of the authors of the "young genera-tion." From their perspective, characteristics and behaviors that are not commensurate with the image of the soldier demanded by fascism and war are given value for the first time. At the same time, men with bitter knowledge insist that only a retrospective journey through one's own experiences of separation and dissolution in the war could create a "gen-eration of arrival . . . on a new star, in a new life."[35] In this respect, even Jan Philipp Reemtsma's critique, in which he provocatively characterized Borchert as a "veteran" who defends "Grandpa's machine gun" in the end, does not go far enough.[36] The figure of Werner Rott, in "Flight into Etruria," goes a good step further. He has radically decided in favor of individual autonomy and the experience of freedom, even in the face of the danger of not being recognized by the defeated Germans as one of their own. Here it must be taken into consideration that Andersch (born in 1914) is seven years older than Borchert and three years older than

Böll. In fact, Andersch does not belong to the "young generation," although he makes himself its spokesman. He experienced Hitler's assumption of power in 1933, for example, very consciously.[37] In contrast to Borchert and Böll, he possessed—influenced in part by his development in American prisoner-of-war camps—a vague political conception, namely, that of a democratic socialism, as it was represented in the journal *Der Ruf*. In addition to a political agenda, Andersch possessed a clearly defined literary program for a morally and politically engaged literature, which he formulated, for example, in his essay "Deutsche Literatur in der Entscheidung" (German literature at the crossroads, 1948).[38] Consequently, literary-programmatic elements enter into his portrait of Werner Rott more starkly than in Borchert's and Böll's works. In contrast to Böll's and Borchert's men, this man is not only supposed to invite identification but to embody an exemplary attitude as a "solution" to the "questions" posed by Borchert's men.

NOTES

1. Cf. Hermann Glaser, *1945. Ein Lesebuch* (Frankfurt a.M.: Fischer, 1995), 85 f.; Joseph Brockington, "Ein Ja in das Nichts hineinbauen: Möglichkeiten und Formen der Hoffnung in der Literatur der Nachkriegsgeneration. Wolfgang Borchert und die 'junge Generation,' *Pack das Leben bei den Haaren. Wolfgang Borchert in neuer Sicht*, Gordon Burgess and Hans-Gerd Winter, eds. (Hamburg: Dolling & Galitz, 1996); Hans-Ulrich Wagner, "'Ein Man kommt nach Deutschland': *Draußen vor der Tür* im Kontext der Heimkehrer-Hörspiele der unmittelbaren Nachkriegszeit," *'Pack das Leben bei den Haaren.' Wolfgang Borchert in neuer Sicht*.

2. Max Frisch, *Tagebuch 1946–1949* (Frankfurt a.M.: Suhrkamp, 1958), 37 f. [Translator's note: This and all subsequent translations from the original German texts are my own.—K.B.]

3. Ibid., 38.

4. *Neue Zeitung*, February 18, 1946.

5. Alfred Andersch, "Das junge Europa formt sein Gesicht," *Der Ruf*, August 15, 1946. Cited in *Der Ruf: Eine Auswahl*, Hans A. Neunzig, ed. (München: Nymphenburger, 1976), 24.

6. Dieter Wellershoff, *Die Arbeit des Lebens* (Köln: Kiepenheuer & Witsch, 1985), 203.

7. Alfred Andersch, "Das Gras und der alte Mann," *Frankfurter Hefte* 3 (1948): 929.

8. See Brockington, "Ein Ja in das Nichts hineinbauen," 22–35.

9. Wolfgang Borchert, *Das Gesamtwerk* (Reinbek bei Hamburg: Rowohlt, 1986), 313. Subsequent references to Borchert's texts will be made directly in the body of this text and cited from this edition.

10. On the determination of gender and sexuality and the concepts that underlie them, see, for example, Andrea Maihofer, *Geschlecht als Existenzweise* (Frankfurt a.m.: n.p., 1995).

11. At the same time, what separates them from the other levels of rank is their limited ability, if any, to give orders, as well as their lack of an overview of the progression of the battle itself.

12. Elias Canetti, *Masse und Macht* (Frankfurt a.m.: Fischer, 1980), 31.

13. See Klaus Theweleit, *Männerphantasien. Bd. 2: Männerkörper. Zur Psychoanalyse des weißen Terrors* (Reinbek bei Hamburg: Rowohlt, 1980).

14. Canetti, 15.

15. Ibid., 77.

16. Ibid., 83.

17. Theweleit, 211.

18. Jean Améry, *Jenseits von Schuld und Sühne: Bewältigungsversuche eines Überwältigten*, 2d ed. (Stuttgart: Klett-Cotta, 1980), 84, 82 f.

19. Peter Rühmkorf, *Wolfgang Borchert in Selbstzeugnissen und Bilddokumenten* (Reinbek bei Hamburg: Rowohlt, 1961), 44 f.

20. Andersch, "Das Gras und der alte Mann," 929.

21. Theweleit, 143 ff.

22. Canetti, 372.

23. Ibid., 360.

24. Wolfgang Borchert, *Allein mit meinem Schatten und dem Mond. Briefe, Gedichte und Dokumente*, Gordon Burgess and Michael Töteberg, eds., in cooperation with Irmgard Schindler (Reinbek bei Hamburg: Rowohlt, 1996), 195.

25. See Alexander and Margarete Mitscherlich, *The Inability to Mourn*, Beverley Placzek, trans. (New York: Grove, 1975).

26. Wolfgang Borchert, "Alle Milchgeschäfte heißen Hinsch," *Die traurigen Geranien und andere Geschichten aus dem Nachlaß* (Reinbek bei Hamburg: Rowohlt, 1962). Subsequent references to this story will be made directly in the body of this text and cited from this edition.

27. Heinrich Böll, "Bekenntnis zur Trümmerliteratur," *Erzählungen, Hörspiele, Aufsätze* (Köln: Kiepenheuer & Witsch, 1961), 342.

28. Heinrich Böll, "Die Stimme Wolfgang Borcherts," *Erzählungen*, 355.

29. Heinrich Böll, *Der Engel schwieg*, afterword by Walter Bellmann (Köln: Kiepenheuer & Witsch, 1994). Bellmann's afterword provides information on the genesis of the novel, the reasons it was not published during Böll's lifetime, and the fate of individual passages that were incorporated into other texts. Subsequent references to the novel will be made directly in the body of this text and cited from this edition.

30. Hans shares with Borchert's men both sensitivity and the inability to act. But even more than Borchert's young men, Hans lacks any kind of aggressiveness. Thus, for example, although he sees through Fischer's actions, he accepts Fischer's calculated attack totally helplessly.

31. Alfred Andersch, *Flucht in Etrurien. Zwei Erzählungen und ein Bericht* (Zurich: Diogones, 1981). Subsequent references to this story will be made directly in the body of this text and cited from this edition.

32. Andersch, "Das junge Europa formt sein Gesicht," 24.

33. Cf., among others, Gary Hay, "Die Kirschen Etruriens in der Faszination von Sartres Appell zur Entscheidung," *Zu Alfred Andersch*, Volker Wehdeking, ed. (Stuttgart: Klett, 1983), 13–22.

34. By "attitude," Andersch is referring, in "Das junge Europa formt sein Gesicht" (Young Europe forms its countenance), to the "inconsiderate abandon" of the entire person, and in the case of the German youth, "to the wrong cause." Werner pulls himself out of this, and his "masculine attitude" is his decision to choose his own individual freedom.

35. Borchert, *Gesamtwerk,* 61.

36. Jan Philipp Reemtsma, "Und auch Opas MG. Wolfgang Borchert als Veteran, '*Pack das Leben bei den Haaren,*'" 239–249.

37. It is well known that Andersch, who had previously been active in the Communist Youth Organization, was imprisoned for three months in Dachau after the burning of the German parliament. After that he was under the surveillance of the Gestapo, which forced him to relinquish all political activity and retreat into privacy. Andersch himself did in fact desert from the German army to the American side on April 6, 1944, in Italy. Andersch, Böll, and Borchert are conjoined by their opposition to the Nazi regime and militarism. This opposition is most clearly political in Andersch's case.

38. Cf. Volker Wehdeking, *Über die Konstituierung der deutschen Nachkriegsliteratur in den amerikanischen Kriegsgefangenenlagern* (Stuttgart: J. B. Metzler, 1971).

Väterliteratur, Masculinity, and History: The Melancholic Texts of the 1980s

Barbara Kosta

> In mourning the world becomes poor and empty; in melancholia it
> is the ego itself.
>
> —Sigmund Freud, "Mourning and Melancholia"

No country has been more vexed by the topic of national identity and
no country, I venture to say, has dealt as consciously with its past as
Germany. It could be said that the past continues vigorously to define
national sensibilities, identities, spaces, and debates, and that despite ongoing efforts to erase the past, it continues to wield its power from an
obstinate subconscious. Daniel Goldhagen's book, *Hitler's Willing Executioners,* serves as one example of the recent challenges to German national identity. His claim that the Holocaust was the culmination of a
long history of anti-Semitism and that Germans essentially were all willing participants in genocide sent tremors through the intellectual community and engendered a reexamination of perpetrators and the power
of discourse to fuel animosities and legitimize murder. Apart from the
critique of sloppy scholarship and high-pitched argumentation, Goldhagen's thesis called for a reevaluation of German history, thus agitating
public debate and furthering the confrontation with the horrific crimes
committed during World War II. Similarly, the furor aroused by the
exhibit "War of Annihilation: Crimes of the Wehrmacht 1941–1944"
produced yet another view of the past that cast a stark light on German
national identity.[1] This exhibit of photographs displays the army's participation in the massacre of civilians, thus incriminating "regular" soldiers
for crimes that were previously thought to be committed only by the SS.
Curious about public reception of the exhibit in Vienna, documentary
filmmaker Ruth Beckermann recorded reactions using a remarkably un-

intrusive cinema verité style in her film *Jenseits des Krieges* (Beyond the war, 1996). Her spectators were mostly men who fought in the army during World War II, and who, to a large extent, denied the army's involvement in genocide. One exhibit goer, however, who claims to have witnessed the photographed atrocities, judiciously warns against the denial of their occurrence, since generations to come need this knowledge in order to intervene in history's recurrence. A young woman, visibly shaken, adamantly refused to see the male members of her family through the lens of the exhibition. To believe these images, she protested, would threaten the economy of familial bonds—a price too high to pay.

For a number of authors who were born just before or during World War II, this price had to be paid. They took the risk of entering the minefield of memory and the painful terrain of the past, of strained family relations, and of identity, choosing one of the most intimate genres, autobiography/biography, to explore specifically their father's lives, and subsequently, their relationship to their fathers, their own identities, and German history. What emerged was a genre of *Väterliteratur* in the early 1980s in West Germany, in which sons and daughters probed their fathers' involvement in the Third Reich while creating a literary mirror for self-reflection. The appearance of this genre in West Germany in particular was concomitant with an interest in autobiographical explorations, which arguably issued from the women's movement and its call for the politicization of the private sphere in the early 1970s, and the *New Subjectivity* with the literature of the fathers as one of its subgenres.[2] Among the writers and works that define father literature are Bernhard Vesper, the earliest contributor to this genre with his groundbreaking novel *Die Reise* (The trip, 1971), followed by Elisabeth Plessen's *Mitteilung an den Adel* (*Such Sad Tidings*, 1977); Christoph Meckel's *Suchbild: Über meinen Vater* (*Image for Investigation: About My Father*, 1980); Sigfrid Gauch's *Vaterspuren* (Traces of father, 1979); Jutta Schütting's *Der Vater* (The father, 1980); Heinrich Wiesner's *Der Riese am Tisch* (The giant at the table, 1979); Peter Härtling's *Nachgetragene Liebe* (Love in the aftermath, 1980); Ruth Rehmann's *Der Mann auf der Kanzel* (*The Man in the Pulpit*, 1980); and Brigitte Schwaiger's *Lange Abwesenheit* (Long absence, 1983). These reminiscences were accompanied by a plethora of critiques and essays, with provocative titles such as "Die Macht der Väter ist gebrochen" (The power of the fathers is broken), "Auf der Suche nach dem verlorenen Vater" (In search of the lost father), and "Annäherung an den Vater" (Rapprochement with the father), which reveal a sense of loss and longing in both literature and interviews. Michael Schneider's essay, "Fathers and Sons, Retrospectively: The Damaged Relationship between Two Generations" (1981), became a veritable mapping of the painful conflict that besieged much of his generation when it looked into a collective mirror. Attuned to the interference in their relationship to their fathers, this generation, Schneider asserts, intuited the taboos that guarded the confrontation with family histories. It was not until their fathers died that their need to investigate the biography of the father could be pursued without inhibition.[3]

For the authors who engaged in intimate confrontation with the father's biography, their own identities stood ragged at the outer edge of the patriarch's sphere, more so because the legacy of the Third Reich burdens the intersection of public and private life. A troubled national identity loomed within the accounts of a strained paternal relationship and of a struggle to negotiate the emotional ambivalences and anger toward the father who figured largely in shaping personal identity. At stake was subjectivity, as it is shaped by psychosocial structures and behaviors and their entangled repetitions passed along generations, as well as by a history that for a long time was denied. Even though the personal, as the intersection of public and private practices, is central in these (auto)biographical accounts, most research has weighted the historical legacy of fascism and the public persona of the father and has overlooked the thorny issue of gender as part of this history. That is, critical analyses of this genre of father literature have seldom explored the private as gendered—except perhaps in the relationship of women to their fathers in this same genre—and rarely have they looked at the complex relationship of masculinity and history.[4] This is due, in part, to the understanding of masculinity as the norm, and to the understanding of gender, an analytical category introduced by feminism, as associated with women.

Hinrich Seeba's provocative assertion may offer a starting point for an analysis of masculinity precisely within the void that he notes in his résumé of father literature: "The popularity of father stories in the last few years betrays an obviously long repressed need to confirm one's own identity in that a fatherless generation invents the fathers it needs in order to appropriate the past, that the political reality had denied them for so long, through fiction and *ex negativo*" (emphasis mine).[5] Seeba alludes to the compensatory invention of an otherwise absent father in order to gain access to the history that was denied the postwar generation. Yet the designation of a "fatherless society" provokes. By now rendered self-evident, it is a term that has "normalized" itself in its repetitions while it betrays the most complex set of expectations, disappointments, and feelings of loss. In other words, what does the word *father* evoke in contrast to *fatherless*? What did the generation born between 1935 and 1950 associate with the concept of father, and how did his absence manifest itself? By focusing on the construction of masculinity within the anxious, (auto)biographical accounts of a postwar father-son relationship, with an emphasis on the autobiographical moments, that is, on the figure of the son, the obscure concept of fatherlessness becomes more defined. The absence reveals a melancholic relationship to the father that stems from a disturbed specular relationship, a burdened image of masculinity and a male identity derived from a bond haunted by the specter of pathology. In their biographical reflections, the writers examine the image of the father in order to distance themselves from a paternal image that threatens the very core of their own masculinity. Owing to the merging of identities in the literature of the fathers, the (auto)biographical separation between narrator and father is fragile indeed; it is as tenuous as the line drawn between (auto)biography and invention. Christoph Meckel's novel *Suchbild: Über meinen Vater* (1980) and Sigfrid Gauch's *Vaterspuren* (1979) both illustrate the porous boundary between father and son and an attachment to the father that produces an injured narcissism and a melancholic text.

THE MISSING MODEL

A discussion of father narratives and of these two novels must be prefaced by an account of the events that led up to such (auto)biographical outpourings. Before the postwar generation or those born in the 1930s (referred to as those who are "blessed by being born late") embarked on biographical explorations of their parents' lives, many felt compelled to dismiss their parents from their lives with the allegation that, "This is the Generation of Auschwitz—you can't have a discussion with them."[6] This time the Oedipal conflict, a common literary topos so often cited in psychoanalysis as a fundamental stage in male development, was immured in an unprecedented and extremely burdened context.[7] This time the fathers who were condemned as representatives of the state, as agents of history and sculptors of a fascist nation, were held accountable for the war atrocities and were first called upon to answer the difficult question of their involvement. As *Zeit* journalist Ulrich Greiner notes in a discussion of postwar father-son relationships, "Their conflict, however, knows no precedent since their fathers did something that human beings had never done in this way: the systematic annihilation of a whole group of people executed with modern efficiency."⁸ The sons and daughters who took their fathers to task were among the first generation of Germans to address openly the trauma of Auschwitz and to initiate a "fascism debate"—a radical critique of the middle class and capitalism's role in making Auschwitz possible. The West German student movement channeled the restless passions of the postwar generation into a protest against the silence that had stifled their adolescence, and against the structures that comfortably rested on an insidious fascist past. This intellectually inflamed youth dissented against the knowledge that strove to cover up, distort, deny, or forget the past. Reviewing the initial revolutionary verve of the '68 generation, Greiner remembers the discovery of an intellectual history that was exiled and burned by the Nazis and long neglected in the postwar era:

> And we discovered everything back then that National Socialism had repressed . . . and banned of leftist and critical theory: Herbert Marcuse, Wilhelm Reich, Georg Lukacs, Leo Löwenthal, Adorno, just to mention the most important. The sons were overcome by a passion for reading and debating; for engaging in critique and contradiction and finally for confronting the fathers, and this passion would not have gotten so strong if we suddenly hadn't realized that we were not only cheated of love and cheerfulness, as Vesper later wrote, but of an intellectual tradition that was extinguished by National Socialism and that was repressed again after the war in the exuberance of anticommunism.⁹

Retrospectively, Greiner succinctly describes the prevailing mood felt by a generation that had been historically, intellectually, and emotionally orphaned. His notable omission of women's part in this enterprise, symptomatic of the male Left in the late 1960s and obviously beyond, resonates generally with a pervasive discrediting of the private sphere, of the subjectivities that are shaped there and of the grave effects of emotional abandonment.

In search of an intellectual heritage, and more significantly, of emotional stability and of figures to idealize, the postwar sons replaced their family fathers with symbolic fathers. In hindsight, it is interesting that the theories that these ersatz fathers represented unwittingly cultivated a deep divide between the private and public spheres. The male student rebels retained this conceptual divide in their disregard of the personal as political. Posters of Marx, Lenin, Trotsky, Mao, Castro, and Che

Guevara decorated the walls of communal apartments, replaced family portraits, and provided "viable totemic resources" and a symbolic legacy of father figures that speciously empowered its followers and abated the pangs of melancholia and loss, if only momentarily.[10] These phantasmatic fathers served as tenuous substitutes, as it turned out, until the student movement that generated its repertoire of cultural icons lost momentum. Sons in particular were left once again without a model of masculinity that functioned as an antidote to the deficient images that they had internalized and learned to abhor. A paternal narrative of discipline, endurance, and self-control, indebted to a long psychocultural heritage, informed the model of masculinity with which they had generally been provided: the mainstay of this image of masculinity was war. If this image of masculinity was not already strained in a postwar era owing to their fathers' own damaged identities, the search for male models was further confounded by the assiduous disparagement of patriarchy in the emerging climate of the women's movement and feminism. The breakdown of traditional gender assumptions led further to a sense of disorientation and the desire to explore the private realm and the personal as it intersected with the political.

In response to the demands of the women's movement and a raised consciousness of power relations, masculinity/patriarchy came under rigorous scrutiny. A new sort of masculinity was cultivated in the 1970s— that of the "Softie," a model scorned in today's climate of backlash.[11] To be sure, the desire to reinstate new models of masculinity asserted itself, as was concluded at a psychoanalytical symposium held in 1984 in Munich. A newspaper reported that an overwhelming majority of participants expressed the need for a new father figure: "We need fathers again, more fathers and stronger ones, that is to say, masculine ones."[12] Despite the strenuous efforts to redefine masculinity, the sons appeared caught within paradigms of patriarchy exquisitely attuned to voice, privilege, and power. They were locked within a father-son relationship that required reflection, and within paradigms that hindered it.

The 1968 student generation first believed in the possibility of severing ties and in emphatically separating themselves from the parent generation. Ironically, they manufactured their own brand of *Stunde Null* (a "zero hour") much like their parents did, to demarcate the past and present and to usher in the advent of a new era while erasing the past. All the while, the psychic residue that powerfully produces similar modes of dealing with the past and the consequences of dissociating or separating oneself from a narcissistic love object were rarely acknowledged. As the standard narrative of this time period goes, it took until the late 1970s for sons and daughters to recognize that assigning the fathers culpability was ineffectual and that they too would have to work through an unmourned past and perform rigorous introspection. To merely exorcise the father signified denying his internalization and thus the continuation of his reign. The enactment of an Oedipal struggle to eliminate the father symbolically and to secure his power—an exercise in shadowboxing—only effected a further denial of the father's imprint on the subconscious and patriarchy's hold on defining experience and perception. For many writers who sought to contain in language the conflicted, melancholic relationship to their fathers, the father is associated with the heinous crimes of Nazi Germany. The already failed father-son relationship in Western culture indeed gains in complexity in Germany at this particular historical juncture.[13]

Eric Santner's *Stranded Objects*, a study of postwar German literature and films preoccupied with memory and Germany's fascist past, is a helpful starting point in deciphering the melancholic paternal biographies that appeared in the 1980s. He attributes the preponderant sense of melancholia that generally characterizes postwar German identity as a failed recognition of the processes of identification that continue to block the labor of mourning and of working through Germany's fascist past. Clearly, these texts thoughtfully construct a genealogy of German fascism through the person of the father and the consequences for the offspring. But as Santner brilliantly argues, the sons have "inherited" their fathers' inability to mourn in their denial of guilt and in their inability to intervene in the patterns of behavior that lock them in pernicious binarisms that construct an "other." Consequently, they have internalized a psychic structure that thwarts compassion or empathy for the victims of fascism.[14] He cites the overabundance of metaphors in postmodern texts and criticism of mutilation and loss that symptomatically reveal a sustained state of bereavement.

Using Freud's distinction between melancholia and mourning as a point of departure, Santner writes:

> A melancholic response to loss, the symptomology of which is a severe, often suicidal depression, ensues when the object was loved not as separate and distinct from oneself, but rather as a mirror of one's own sense of self and power. The predisposition to love in this manner obtains when the self lacks sufficient strength and cohesion to tolerate, much less comprehend, the reality of separateness. . . . What is at stake is nothing less than the constitution of the boundaries between self and other.[15]

Santner describes the perpetuation of an insular narcissistic gaze that cultivates the sense of omnipotence and impedes the ability for empathy. He calls for an initiation of the process of mourning that recognizes the lost opportunities to intervene in the patterns of behavior that are intolerant of difference and that have calcified and become enslaved to injurious repetitions. He focuses on the relationship to the victims of genocide, who remain at the margins of contemporary texts, if they are mentioned at all. In fact, it is remarkable that few, if any, autobiographical confrontations deal explicitly with anti-Semitism and its legacy.

Written upon the father's death, the literature of the fathers indeed resides within the connecting conjunction of Freud's essay "Mourning and Melancholia" and within the precarious divide between biographical and autobiographical representation. That is, the authors engage in the work of memory to mourn the loss of the parent, but also to work through their own feelings of melancholia. Revealed between the lines and in fleeting autobiographical disclosures is a profound sense of the narrator's melancholia triggered by the experience of abandonment, disappointment, betrayal, and narcissistic injury. In contrast to the work of mourning, which precludes the physical loss of an individual or object, Freud asserts that melancholia results from abandonment, "injury, and disappointment with the loved one" to whom one was libidinally attached.[16] Highlighting Freud's text with the father-son relationship in mind, the sense of melancholia that pervades these narratives, I argue, emerges as being symptomatic of the failure of the paternal function. It is not the sense of melancholia, which Judith Butler sees as intrinsic to gender development, produced from the experience of loss or from the prescriptive separations from the love object that must be grieved.[17] Instead, melancholia follows from a lost ideal, or from the experience that an object, as Freud notes, "has become lost as the object of love. . . . This would suggest that melancholia is in some way related to an unconscious loss of a love object, in contradistinction to mourning, in which there is nothing unconscious about the loss."[18] In other words, an ego ideal is lacking, which is needed to imagine the subject as "intact." Certainly these texts reveal the psychological wounds left by a parent generation whose own inability to mourn overshadowed its relationship to its offspring, as Santner points out. Yet they also reveal a profound loss of the father-image and the understanding of masculinity that he embodied and that could no longer be sustained. Underlying these melancholic texts is the desire for a self-affirming proximity to a father-image that no longer exists. This also would explain the exclusive fixation on the father in these texts and the absence of other family members.

Väterliteratur predates recent critical attention to the constructions of masculinities, since the examination of gender issues since the 1970s had traditionally been bound to women's studies. Consequently, most studies of the literature of the fathers relegate the topic of gendered identity to the background, if it is addressed at all, and feature the historical legacy of the Third Reich as the primary wound in these texts. To fully understand the melancholic text, however, the role of masculinity must be addressed in conjunction with the historical configuration. Similarly, the melancholic sensibility evidenced here cannot be attributed to the resignation of the German Left, which was disillusioned with its failure to rock the sociopolitical foundations of Germany. Rather, it stems from the specular relationship to the father and the burdened image of masculinity and male identity that is tinged with the specter of pathology. These texts reveal a crisis of male subjectivity that defines both father and son. The fathers are scarred by their own losses and are unable to reenter the dominant fiction that bestows an (untraumatized) "intact" masculinity on the sons. Moreover, it is the deep sense of betrayal the sons experienced that is linked closely to their own masculinity. It is precisely the faltering of the ideal experienced by the youthful protagonists that Greiner erroneously downplays in his deemphasis of the emotional conflict with the father, which he refers to as a lack of "love and cheerfulness." In contrast to texts that thematize the absent father, or more precisely, the inaccessible father, these texts reveal an overly present father whose image falls like a shadow on the son; this overly present father disables and burdens the authors of *Väterliteratur*. The discovery of the fathers' position during the Third Reich dramatically disrupts identification, finds the narrators irresolvably compromised, and sheds light on the melancholic sensibility that permeates these narratives. More generally, these texts confirm the general observation that Elisabeth Badinter offers of a postwar generation faced with a "wounded father"—an expression coined by Robert Bly and Samuel Osherson. These narratives establish the undeniably Herculean paternal influence on the psyche of the son. The postwar sons, Badinter aptly writes,

> have interiorized a sad image of their father, or one of a categorical and angry judge. They complain that they know nothing about him because his vulnerability is taboo. The unapproach-

able father—who seems to avoid intimate conversations with his son—rarely expresses his love verbally, because he has inherited a model of masculinity that rejects the expression of feelings of tenderness. . . . The deep need of the son to be acknowledged and confirmed by his father runs up against the law of silence.[19]

Given the context of postwar West Germany, this silence is ominous.

The (auto)biographical exploration of the complex son-father relationship, however belatedly, attempts to break the silence. Axiomatic of this genre is that this body of elegiac texts, almost without exception, was written upon the father's death, which intimates a freedom from the prohibitions of paternal law and the authority to explore the past. The timing of these narratives evidences the lingering power of the father, even into adulthood, to instill the taboo against broaching his past. It is interesting to note the sons' willingness to obey the taboo, despite the vociferous, popular rejection of authoritative institutions proclaimed by the student movement. It may suggest the internalization of a submission to authority. More likely, it reveals the fragile attachments that were at stake.[20]

For writers such as Sigfrid Gauch and Christoph Meckel, born in 1933 and 1935, respectively, the experience of their fathers began at a time when, as Badinter writes, "hypervirility displayed itself in all of its pathology."[21] In other words, traditional male values were at a premium. George Mosse sheds light on the fascist glorification of a male ideal of strength and the disavowal of the self for a greater cause. "The importance of manliness," he writes, "as a national symbol and as a living example played a vital role in all fascist regimes."[22] Not to be forgotten, as Klaus Theweleit elaborates in his book *Male Fantasies*, which was published the same year as many father narratives, is that these fathers also were trained in the spirit of such Prussian ideals as obedience, discipline, and self-control.[23] At the end of the war, the images and concepts that steadily fueled the understanding of masculinity and the cultural ideals it represented were shattered, but the residues, that is, the internalized images, could not be swept away. No open forum existed to address the emotional vacuum and disorientation, let alone the suffering inflicted on the millions of victims of fascism. An injured masculinity resorted to brutality, or expressed itself in melancholia, depression, and an obsessive desire to monitor and control. Overcompensating for their own sense of loss and emptiness, many fathers after World War II fiercely clung to familiar patterns of behavior, with the private sphere serving as the site where they struggled to restore their deeply disturbed sense of masculine subjectivity.[24] The lessons these defeated patriarchs dealt their children were perhaps more vigilantly imparted due to the fathers' psychological vulnerability at the end of a war. Again, Michael Schneider sees a common thread in many of these narratives that he links to the psychopathology of the German postwar family. Echoing the words of writer Christoph Meckel, Schneider points to the recurrent, nearly stereotypical characterization of the father in this genre of literature. The father, he writes, appears as a "a grim, tortured and tormenting man who lives by regulations and who abuses his children in order to once again feel that he is in control; the father as a too powerful, punishing, intimidating and crippling authority figure who reacts with indifference to his children's needs for love and tenderness."[25] Implicit in the family portrait Schneider sketches, however, is the perspective commonly associated with a 1960s' generation that protested against this very method of authoritative child rearing. Mingled with postwar traumatization, "poisonous pedagogy" (schwarze Pädagogik) may have been experienced more severely, but it traditionally laid the foundation of the paternal narrative. As the narratives of father literature suggest, the sons who were born in the 1930s witnessed a dramatic transformation from the heroic-omniscient-father to the defeated-father to the image of perpetrator, which left profound scars that inevitably impacted male subjectivity.

THE PATERNAL NARRATIVE GONE BAD

Among the most celebrated novels in this genre, Christoph Meckel's *Suchbild: Über meinen Vater* explores the enigma called "father" nine years after his death, prompted by the discovery of a war diary with entries dated back to Hitler's rise to power. The image of the father represented in the diary calls for a reexamination of the father's life, of the person who had eluded the son, and of the image that had settled in the archive of personal memory. As the narrator writes: "I came across the notes of a person, who I didn't know. It was impossible to know this person, even to think of him as being possible exacted too much."[26] Meckel contends that the revelations of the memoir turned his father's case into a public matter, significant as yet another piece in the puzzling history of Germany that continues to defy comprehension.

Altogether, three diary entries are included as evidence of the transformations the father underwent. The first entry, from 1933, expresses an adamant refusal to join the Nazi party and a strong antiwar stance.

The second entry recounts an unavoidable conscription into the military and reveals the progressive identification with the war cause and its insidious ideological motor—not in support of Hitler but in service to the superiority of German idealism. With a pathos stylistically reminiscent of writer Ernst Jünger, the father romanticizes the call to battle in an entry dated June 30, 1943: "[M]y soldierly heart longs for the front, for action and male adventure" (61). Increased responsibility, power, and authority within the ranks brought about a change in the poet of nature, Eberhard Meckel, whose transformation resembles Bertolt Brecht's malleable character Galy Gay's mutation from peaceful, passive fisherman to war machine in the play *Mann ist Mann* (*Man Equals Man*, 1927). As the narrator in *Suchbild* describes the change: "The aesthete who cultivated a noble language, sank into the gutter language of the army" (73). To explain the father's eventual involvement, his acquiescence to the goals and perspectives of German fascism, and his growing callousness to the atrocities he witnesses and perpetrates, the son proposes: "He immersed himself in the body of an idea" (72). A third diary entry from the time of his imprisonment on the island of Elba reflects that the father identifies himself as an innocent victim and as part of a misled and betrayed *Volk*.

In search of an explanation for the choices his father made, the narrator cites childhood experiences of humiliation and corporal punishment, and he chillingly concludes: "My father was a spewed out child." "He crawled out of the hole of his childhood beaten" (21/23). A profound existential angst defined the father who turned to nature, to the scenery of his homeland, to his family, and to literature for comfort against the feeling of the melancholia and depression that plagued him. As the author of nature poetry, Eberhard Meckel, entranced by Idealism, escaped into sentimental and romanticized, though hardly innocent, landscapes; these served as a refuge, but according to his son, they also blinded him to the political urgencies of his time and disabled critique: "Overall, he lacked an elementary sense of being horrified because he lacked insight into the way things connect together" (69). In fact, many authors of this same genre fault their fathers for an acute selective awareness that stems from their positioning within humanist traditions and their subservience to authority.[27] As a proponent of German middle-class values and ideals who was absorbed in elitist sensibilities and a nationalist at heart, the father's "deep introspection," the son speculates, "predestined" him for a blood and soil ideology (34); at the same time, the son less generously proposes that "his mediocrity made him susceptible" (92).

While the narrator is intent on performing an intellectual autopsy to determine the machinations of the banality of evil and to abstract the elusive father figure to represent postwar relationships, another economy simultaneously animates his enterprise. It reveals itself in disjointed and interspersed narrative fragments, breakdowns that relate memories of proximity and security, then breaches of trust and the feeling of abandonment, and finally, the violation of a projected identity that ultimately disrupts the father-son relationship. The sense of security the narrator felt in early childhood in his father's presence fades in the course of the narrative, yet its position at the beginning of the narrative intimates its significance as a referent for future experience: "A feeling of security and blind faith, a wonderful certainty in his presence" (9). Much later, emphasizing the father's idiom in a different typeset, the narrator imparts: "The father wanted to possess his child's heart and he possessed it. The child was attached to the father and had faith in him for a long time" (50). He presents a father whom the son experienced as unique, as an ideal he desired to emulate; the father bedazzled his child until increasingly frequent brutal rituals of physical punishment abruptly denied the son his innocent paradise. As Meckel writes: "Corporeal punishment was introduced in order to enforce a sense of what is right and in the name of order, obedience and benevolence" (56). The father compulsively repeated the familiar destructive patterns that characterized his own upbringing, and the bodies of his children became the surfaces upon which discipline and paternal will were exercised. The narrator recalls a grim turning point marked by the endurance of corporal punishment for ten days, and all for the harmless infraction of a four year old. The son remembers losing faith in the father. The glorified father-image changed again once he returned from the war wounded, defeated, and broken. The autobiographical voice recapitulates the bitter disappointment that significantly shaped his experience of his father:

> The joyous anticipation of my father was infinite. Memories of early childhood seem to have gilded his image. I flew to him in the gilded image. After a few months the radiance was gone. The disenchantment was complete, disturbing at first, and then endlessly gray. The demi-god of childhood trust had turned into a nervous man who had to satisfy his need for authority. (110)

Robbed of the internalized phantasy of a good object that forms part of the loved self, the masculine subject, the son, is deserted, left without an "unbroken" image of masculinity and thus "fatherless."

In place of the glorified patriarch, an overwrought, dispirited father struggles, upon returning from the war and internment, to reconstitute himself within the private sphere by exercising an oppressive control or self-sacrifice that strains familial ties. It is at this point that the narrator suspends memories of the father to convey, with a note of resentment, the hardship of the years immediately after the war for him and the family whose guardian was missing. Contrary to expectations, the father's appearance became associated with the claustrophobic atmosphere of the postwar period, the suffocation of spontaneity, and the unnatural silences that guarded against the floodgates of recent memory. In these years, the narrator withdrew from the father. This autobiographical narrator, who uncannily emulates his father's penchant for lists throughout *Suchbild*, inventories the aspects of family life that were missing and insists that "a fatherlessness was missing, it was missing and missing" (147). A sense of openness and lawlessness were missing that allowed for candor and emotion. On the contrary, the domain of the father remained undisturbed. The family endured the desperate paternal control and even accommodated the father in his repression of the past, and, as the narrator remarks, thus denied him the opportunity to work through the trauma and pain of past experiences. Even though the question of German guilt plagued him, he never perceived himself as being responsible. After the war, the father attempted to console himself with writing, but his once-cherished notions of homeland and nature were burdened by the Nazi past and consequently inoperable.

Throughout *Suchbild*, the son stages a gradual separation from a hurtful paternal identification. He is likewise cognizant of his latent desire to produce memories of an ego ideal, as the repository for everything it admires, in which the subject would like to see itself reflected. This desire serves as a referent for the negative father-image and for what is lacking. Despite the son's efforts to separate from the father, the father's imprint remains profound. The narrator recalls that his decision to study architecture fulfilled his father's expectations. More subtly, an uncanny resemblance in structure manifests itself at times in a subtext that is idiosyncratic. The descriptions of nature, the apparent fondness for lists, and, significantly, his engagement in the Oedipal drama in which he defeats the already defeated father, the ignominious patriarch, with analytical bravado, all convey his ensnarement in both the personal and the systemic paternal narrative. Thus the image of the son is implicated in *Suchbild* as much as that of the father, from whom the narrator self-deceptively disjoins himself. Moreover, the son sparingly reveals himself in the first person and even buffers himself against the risky business of introspection with abstractions. The allegory, as a *post scriptum* in which a man in innocent play destroys the world, further removes the narrative from the realm of personal inquiry.[28] Furthermore, the son's association with a literary tradition much different from the father's supposedly drives a wedge between father and son. Much like the father, the son turns to fictional writing, particularly to poetry, which sparks an Oedipal rivalry, the outcome of which is the son's declarative triumph, "My mere existence hollowed out his" (156). Much different from the father whose traditions were easily conscripted by fascism, the narrator identifies with an engaged, politicized literature, with a tradition of self-reflection and critique in the spirit of Brecht. Within the logic of the narrative, this type of antibourgeois literature empowers him to intervene in the structures that informed his father's history. Yet the demonstrative emancipatory intent and resolution arouse suspicion. The public-private division and the structures of identity the narrator maintains suggest the limitations of the critical tools he employs. It is only with the discovery of Eberhard Meckel's diary that the son considers the experiences of the father to be of public significance and thereby fails to grasp that the most private of gestures is political and that the division of public-private is ideological. The question that is rarely asked and that haunts these narratives is: How do the sense of crisis in the father-son relationship and the feelings of disappointment and abandonment affect masculine subjectivity, and what structures of the traditional paternal narrative are preserved? Given the magnitude of personal and political culpability contemplated within Meckel's novel, an intervention that both ventures beyond the father's personal history and works through it is urgently needed.

FATAL ATTACHMENTS

In Sigfrid Gauch's novel *Vaterspuren,* a burdensome emotional bond to a father who was a zealous Nazi and anti-Semite complicates the narrative in ways that the author of *Suchbild* is spared.[29] Gauch, however, takes greater risks than Meckel in his exploration of the father's influence. Reminiscent of Elizabeth Plessen's *Mitteilung an den Adel,* one of the earliest novels of the genre of father literature, the narrative opens with news of the father's death, the drive to his parents' home to "see" his father for the last time, and the memories of childhood. Similar to Plessen's biographical inquiry, Gauch's recollections also reveal the inordinate task of facing the emotional miasma of loss and affection for a father who supported the Nazis as a doctor and an author of racial theories. The tension the son experiences can hardly be more poignantly articulated than this: "I am all too well aware of my own schizophrenic situation: to love a father as a person and to be horrified by his personality" (135). Furthermore, the juxtaposition of the tender description upon viewing the feeble father on his deathbed with a description of his father's role in the Third Reich starkly illustrates the irresolvable conflict: "I sit down on the edge of his bed and stroke his head, kiss him on the forehead, the cheek, and stroke his shoulder, arm and hand."/"I remember long drives in which I sat in the car alone and thought about my father: the private staff sergeant physician . . . the adjutant of Heinrich Himmler, and author of 'New Elements of Racial Research,' the person the prosecution described as a bureaucratic murderer during the Eichmann trials, the person, who I knew as: my father" (9). This irreconcilable negotiation of emotions toward the father, owing to his history and his politics on the one hand, and the psychological and emotional bonds on the other hand, underpins the dispassionate description of a menacing bond. Confounded by the duplicitous image of the father, the son is caught in a melancholic bind. One need only recall the internal struggle Freud observes as a fundamental symptom of melancholia. "In melancholia," he writes, "the relation to the object is no simple one; it is complicated by the conflict of ambivalence. . . . In melancholia, that is, countless single conflicts in which love and hate wrestle together are fought for the object; the one seeks to detach the libido from the object, the other to uphold this libido-position against assault."[30] This fatiguing maneuver within the male subject is caused by the relationship to the father in *Vaterspuren*.

The exploration of *Vaterspuren*, literally the "traces of the paternal voice" in the subconscious of the progeny, resonates with Freud's use of "memory traces."[31] The recapitulation of dialogues and the recollection of images, feelings, and narrative fragments assist the protagonist in retrieving the experiences that shaped his identity. At the heart of the narrative lies the need to examine the painful rupture between the father-image and the historical father, and to explain the daunting paternal figure that extinguishes the son. Cast as a Jekyll/Hyde character, at times benevolent and vulnerable, at other times a monstrous tyrant who lacks empathy and kindness and whose miserliness verges on contempt, he denies the son a stable emotional orientation. This duality accentuates the schizophrenic experience of the father, who is also described as an overbearing, self-indulgent patriarch who entraps the son in a self-effacing dependency. While the son attends a boarding school, the father rents a room in the vicinity. The son explains, "I shouldn't be so alone, and you wanted to attend to my lessons" (28). He monitors the son's scholastic progress, stands by his side, and professes an unwavering loyalty, all of which produce an indebtedness that the son spends his life repaying. At the same time, the father prevents the son from cultivating friendships and pursuing amorous liaisons; he isolates him from his classmates, and effectually denies him the possibility of developing outside of the patriarchal gaze that engulfs him in austere demands of performance upon which affection depends. Despite his proximity, the father remains emotionally inaccessible. "You meant well, really well," the adult voice repeatedly insists, as if to redeem the image of an emotionally abusive father and to stifle the pangs of anger (35). As a captive of the father's authoritative gaze and of an emotional investment that inhibits independence, the traditional paternal function of modeling autonomy and separation is perverted.

Within the insular relationship to the father, the son constructs himself as the father's victim who has lost the Oedipal battle and who is besieged by his father's needs and egotism. The father, the purveyor of his son's masculinity, in fact "feminizes" his son to empower himself. The narrator conveys a childhood plagued by humiliation, by the anxiety to please the father and to perform. Even as an adult, the narrator is overly sensitive to the father's whims and susceptible to the emotional terror the father exerts to gain attention. His own positioning as victim is interesting in light of research on male masochism. According to Kaja Silverman, the masochistic phantasy is a subversion of the paternal function, a sort of escape from it, and a way of punishing its imposition: "What is beaten in male masochism is not so much the male subject as the father, or the father in the male subject. Masochism works insistently to negate paternal power and privilege."[32] In other words, submission to the father offers a means of resistance to the model of masculinity he represents and a complex means to assert difference. In surrendering to the father, the narrator seemingly relinquishes power, which further frames the father as perpetrator and secures the son's difference. Empowering himself, if only tentatively, the narrator also includes a panoply of voices and gestures to confirm his representation of the father figure and to assert his difference in relation to the father. At the same time, the insertion of the father's documents prevents the potential slippage between autobiographical and biographical representation and fortifies the walls of difference between father and son. These documents also offer for examination the domineering person called "father."

The father is defined prominently by his past as a soldier and a war veteran—the experience of World War I, for which he volunteered, his enthusiastic enlistment in World War II, and his love of uniforms, the props of masculinity—suggesting that male identity during this period in history is enmeshed in an image of bellicose masculinity. As his most ardent and unsuspecting audience, the adolescent son learns to idolize the father who relates exploits like that of a clever escape from a French labor camp during World War I, or of his single-handed capture of three Serbian villages whose civilians he protected from the rage of his comrades (25).

Furthermore, the inclusion of a fictional fragment that the father authored, which escaped being burned in 1945, unlike other documents he destroyed, reflects the codex of masculinity that he endorsed. It is rooted in biologism, camaraderie, nationalism, service, and honor. Such insertions as the appreciative letter of a soldier who expresses his gratitude for being under the father's command, mingled with the collection of letters from high-ranking Nazis, betray the emotional stratagem between the attraction and repulsion of a defenseless son confronted with a contested paternal image. It is not surprising then that the dutiful son, unwilling to disappoint his father's expectations, fulfills his military obligations; manhood, he is taught, depends on good performance as a servant of the state. With amazing candor, the narrator thematizes the complex internalization of the father figure. Upon visiting the site of his childhood, the narrator remarks somewhat nostalgically that his father had more experiences to boast about than his classmates' fathers, a fact that could have won him recognition among his peers except that these stories were prohibited. The author catches himself feeling flagrant pride: "I try to repress these thoughts again" (93). The question that bedevils the narrative is this: What are the consequences for a son who is unable to distance himself from the father, who readily acquiesces to his father's demands into adulthood, and who confesses that he has yet to cut the umbilical cord? (44)

The porous boundary that separates father and son in the (auto)biographical narrative alludes to an inevitable continuity of histories in public and private realms and contradicts interminable efforts to create caesuras. Even though the protagonist allows little explicit insight into the actual patterns he inherits, he presents the bewilderment of his attachment to an otherwise morally reprehensible father. At the same time, he seeks moments with which to identify so as not to slay the father figure who is part of his psychic economy. "He meant well," the narrator tells a priest who listens unresponsively, "but acted wrongly and unjustly" (53). Interestingly, he fixes on the father as a failure. "In truth," the son interprets, "you were a shirker" (14). He adds: "Certainly, you spent your whole life fighting. But you never made it through a fight. You are not a fighter by nature. You never compromised, but you never gave anything your all. Every so often you risked your life, but you never really made any great sacrifices" (67). The father was unable to live up to his own expectations and was faced with the ruins of his life. It is curious with what frequency the son calls his father a shirker, a name he overhears a relative use to characterize the father, while at the same time confessing his inability to withstand the paternal superego that rules his emotional economy and demands subordination. To be sure, the son loses himself in the father's history to justify his own entrapment and to redeem his father. A confidant cautions the narrator, "By losing yourself in such stories you are only trying to create excuses, and act like they are explanations" (109). The suggestion is made to find other models for identification in order to break through the murky cycle of apologias that stagnate development and reinforce paralyzing continuities: "Try to live with the other Germans who also existed" (108). Yet this voice hardly impacts the text, as excuses for the father's involvement in the Third Reich compulsively recur. He catches himself reciting his well-rehearsed script when he explains to the priest who will perform the funeral service: "He subordinated his uncompromising support of misunderstood humanistic ideals to a false, criminal idea" (48). It is interesting to note that both Meckel and Gauch cite a seamless transition from their father's humanistic beliefs, which inherently cultivated blind spots, to fascism.

Sensitive to the unconscious continuities of experience and knowledge, as illustrated in the father-son configuration, the deceptive concept of a "zero hour" that officially but speciously separated a postwar Germany from its fascist past is criticized in the father's excited recollection of his war experiences and his unreflected, steadfast political beliefs. The author simultaneously takes to task the lax efforts to de-Nazify West Germany in the early postwar years, exemplified by the official judgment of the father's de-Nazification (64–65). Unchanged were his anti-Semitic diatribes, which included a denial of the magnitude of the Holocaust and an offensive revision of history (55). This haunting continuity has yet to be addressed in contemporary autobiographical representations.

The work of memory, intermingled with long descriptions of the funeral preparation in the town in which the father is to be buried both literally and symbolically, represents taking leave of the father and detaching himself from his dominion. Yet with the physical end of the relationship, the emotional attachment, however tortured, persists. In contrast to Meckel's novel, the work of memory in *Vaterspuren* does not distance the autobiographical subject from the biographical referent; it draws him back into the realm of the father, who has left indelible traces. The memory work performed in the melancholic text does not free the subject unless, in Freud's estimation, "the fixation of the libido to it [the object]" abates.[33] After the funeral, the son enters the father's vacant room and takes in the remnants of his existence as though seeking an essential father untouched by history—a phantasm. In the drawer next to the bed he finds his father's eyeglasses, his medication; he slowly releases the pump on his inhalator, takes out his father's shoes from the closet, and smells his clothes in order to imprint in his senses the scent of the absent body: "This is how father smelled, I thought; I try to commit it all to memory" (149). His confidant's imperative, "Free yourself of him," nestled in the protagonist's conscience, interrupts, yet it remains external to the subject (149). The voice is not integrated in the emotional economy that constitutes him as the son of his father. The narrative ends with the son lying down on his father's bed. "That is why I'll sleep in his bed tonight" (149). The subordinating conjunction has no obvious antecedent except the narrative as a whole, and it leaves open to speculation how much power the father will retain over the son. It is likely that this sign of regression, passivity, and powerlessness concedes an irrevocable, fateful attachment. The melancholic text remains constricted in ambivalence.

Meckel and Gauch select a literary form to reflect upon their fathers and to establish a mirror for self-reflection. It is impossible to keep the father at arm's length, since the paternal voice generally commands the strong identification of the son. To impose the traditional paradigm of father-son conflict as a struggle for self-assertion would leave unnuanced its contours and deny both the historicity of emotion and the ways in which issues of gender play themselves out at specific points in time. The Freudian paradigm of an embattled father-son relationship, in which the transfer of power "naturally" passes from one generation to the next, entangles the son in a narrative of violence, reinforces such dubious notions as breaking with the past, and, in fact, assumes "some intrinsic or essential content to any identity which is defined by either a common origin or a common structure of experience or both."[34] The evocation of this traditional paradigm simultaneously sustains all-too-well-established structures of power in which these narratives, successfully or not, seek to intervene. To understand aspects of "masculinity" and, to use "Raymond Williams's term, the 'structure of feeling' to signal that emotion is a social form and not just an aggregate of individual expressions," more explorations of the father-son relationship will be necessary, ones that unsettle traditional terms and produce a more sophisticated understanding of male subjectivity.[35]

The literature of the fathers opens up what Santner calls a space "in which elegiac procedures can unfold," and the work of mourning can progress.[36] It is a space for self-invention, exploration, discovery, and reflection that uses the tension between authenticity and fiction intrinsic to the autobiographical project. Paramount to this project is the need to gain an understanding of "how we became who we are," a question that set in motion Christa Wolf's self-reflexive, autobiographical inquiry in her novel *Patterns of Childhood*. With regard to the literature of the fathers, or for that matter any autobiographical privileging of the father-son relationship, the project remains incomplete if the interplay of masculinity—that is, gender as a significant marker of identity—and German history is not taken into account. This must happen without fixing these key players within unalterable identities and without succumbing to the repetitions of the traditional paternal narrative. Given the ongoing confrontation with the German fascist past in a now-unified Germany and the continued disclosure of repressed knowledges, it will be interesting to see whether masculinity as a complex and discursive category will be subjected to a critical gaze and recognized in all of its inflections. The literature of the fathers presents only a first attempt toward unraveling the complex relationship between gender and history.

NOTES

1. The exhibit was organized by the Hamburg Institut für Sozialforschung and has been visited by well over 200,000 Germans and Austrians since 1995. In Munich, the *Bayernkurier*, a Christian Social Union (CSU) newspaper, accused the organizers of the exhibit of "einen Vernichtungsfeldzug gegen das deutsche Volk zu führen." See Matthias Arning, "Für die CSU bedrohen Historiker die Ehre der Deutschen," *Frankfurter Rundschau*, February 21, 1997.

2. This literature is characterized by introspection, resignation, and melancholia, which most notably bore a male signature. The filmmaker Wim Wenders used images to reflect on personal identity, sending his characters out on a *Bildungsreise* in his road movies, while writers such as Botho Strauß (*Die Widmung*), Peter Schneider (*Lenz*), and Peter Handke (*Wunschloses Unglück*) established its literary tradition. Handke and Wenders even collaborated on a number of films, such as *Falsche Bewegung* (*The Wrong Move*) and *Im Laufe der Zeit* (*Kings of the Road*).

3. Michael Schneider, "Fathers and Sons, Retrospectively: The Damaged Relationship between Two Generations," *New German Critique* (1984): 3–51.

4. See Barbara Kosta, *Recasting Autobiography: Women's Counterfictions in Contemporary German Literature and Film* (Ithaca, N.Y.: Cornell University Press, 1994).

5. Hinrich Seeba, "Erfundene Vergangenheit: Zur Fiktionalität historischer Identitätsbildung in den Vätergeschichten der Gegenwart," *The Germanic Review* 66 (1991): 176.

6. Gudrun Ensslin, quoted in Jillian Becker, *Hitlers Kinder? Der Baader-Meinhof Terrorismus* (Frankfurt a.M.: n.p., 1978), 35.

7. The father-son conflict is a prominent topos in German literature, most often associated with Expressionism.

8. Ulrich Greiner, "Söhne und ihre Väter: Über die Studentenbewegung als Konflikt der Generationen," *Die Zeit*, May 6, 1988: 14. "Ihr Konflikt jedoch kennt kein Vorbild, denn ihre Väter hatten etwas getan, was Menschen in dieser Weise noch nie getan hatten: die mit moderner Effizienz betriebene systematische Ausrottung eines ganzen Volkes."

9. Greiner, 15.

10. Erich Santner, *Stranded Objects: Mourning, Memory, and Film in Postwar Germany* (Ithaca, N.Y.: Cornell University Press, 1990), 45.

11. See Heino Ferch, interview, "Der Mann muß einfach Mann sein," *Der Spiegel* (December 1998): 280–282.

12. "Gesucht: Die starken Väter: Zu einem psychoanalytischen Symposium in München," *Süddeutsche Zeitung*, September 19, 1984: 37.

13. See Elisabeth Badinter, *XY: On Masculine Identity*, Lydia Davis, trans. (New York: Columbia University Press, 1995), 147. Here she cites Shere Hite, who reports after numerous interviews with fathers and sons that this relationship is rarely close and fulfilling. The damaged relationship is reflected in that "sons have trouble talking spontaneously about their fathers. But in private conversation, they complain about their fathers' humiliations, criticisms, derision, and condescension."

14. See Björn Krondorfer, *Remembering and Reconciliation: Encounters between Young Jews and Germans* (New Haven, Conn.: Yale University Press, 1995).

15. Santner, 2–3.

16. Sigmund Freud, "Mourning and Melancholia," *General Psychological Theory: Papers on Metapsychology* (New York: Collier Books, 1963), 170.

17. Judith Butler, "Melancholy Gender/Refused Identification," *Constructions of Masculinity*, Maurice Berger et al., eds. (New York: Routledge, 1995).

18. Freud, 167.

19. Badinter, 148.

20. It is interesting to note that a vocal minority among the generation that pursued a leftist politics has been accused of swinging to the Right. See the debate surrounding Botho Strauß' "Anschwellender Bockgesang."

21. Badinter, 20.

22. George Mosse, *The Image of Man: The Creation of Modern Masculinity* (New York: Oxford University Press, 1996), 155–156.

23. Klaus Theweleit, *Male Fantasies. Vol. 1: Women, Floods, Bodies, History* (Minneapolis: University of Minnesota Press, 1987, 1977); *Male Fantasies. Vol. 2: Male Bodies: Psychoanalyzing the White Terror* (Minneapolis: University of Minnesota Press, 1989, 1978).

24. Helma Sanders-Brahms's film *Germany, Pale Mother* (1980) painfully conveys the deep frustrations and anxieties that plagued the private sphere of postwar German households.

25. Schneider, 24.

26. Christoph Meckel, *Suchbild: Über meinen Vater* (Düsseldorf: claassen, 1980), 64. Subsequent page references to Meckel's text are from this edition and are cited in the body of this chapter. All translations are my own.

27. See Ruth Rehmann, *Mann auf der Kanzel: Fragen an einen Vater* (Munich: Deutscher Taschenbuch Verlag, 1980); *The Man in the Pulpit: Questions for a Father* (Lincoln: University of Nebraska Press, 1997).

28. For a discussion of the allegory, see Todd Hanlin, "A Biography for the 'New Sensibility': Christoph Meckel's Allegorical *Suchbild*," *German Life and Letters* 39:3 (1986): 235–244.

29. See Sigfrid Gauch, *Vaterspuren: Eine Erzählung* (Königstein/TS: Athenäum, 1979). Subsequent page references to Gauch's text are from this edition and are cited in the body of this chapter. All translations are my own.

30. Freud, 177.

31. Ibid., 178.

32. Kaja Silverman, *Male Subjectivity at the Margins* (New York: Routledge, 1992), 211.

33. Freud, 178.

34. Lawrence Grossberg, "Identity and Cultural Studies: Is That All There Is?" *Questioning Cultural Identity*, Stuart Hall and Paul du Gay, eds. (London: Sage, 1996), 89.

35. Peter Middelton, *The Inward Gaze: Masculinity and Subjectivity in Modern Culture* (New York: Routledge, 1992), 125.

36. Santner, 151.

Homosexual Images of Masculinity
in German-Language Literature after 1945

Wolfgang Popp

Homosexual images of masculinity are, on the one hand, images of man and masculinity as they exist in the minds and fantasies of homosexual men. They are, on the other hand, images of homosexual man and homosexual masculinity as they are present in the minds of the heterosexual social majority, where they acquire different expression in men and women. In their diverse subcultures, homosexual men develop aspects, images of man and masculinity, which may then become stereotypes or clichés: the buff, potent, dominant superman; the boyish, delicate, lascivious, faithful prince charming; or the mobile, adventurous, funny, promiscuous rogue. Such stereotypes or clichés arise not only in the minds of homosexuals, however, but also in those of heterosexual men and women. They are ideals of sexual desire with two possible functions: I want to have such a man, and I want to be such a man (and be desired as such).

These positive images of desiring men and masculinity are contrasted to images of masculinity that do not originate in desire and that signal in many ways an inversion or a disturbance of the individual's desiring structure: man and masculinity as something threatening, something to be rejected, something worthy of disgust. Specific stereotypes or clichés to which such images can condense are the sexist, misogynist, racist macho; the shrill, feminine, affected queen; the pederast. Such images of masculinity lodge themselves in the minds of homosexuals as well as in the minds of other men and women.

Aesthetic literature (belles lettres, drama) plays an essential role in the development of such images of masculinity. Male and female authors seize upon images they encounter in their everyday lives (which they correlate positively and negatively with their own images) and form them into literary prototypes. Such literary prototypes influence the imagination of male and female readers and reinforce or relativize (positively or negatively) their individual images of masculinity. If homosexual images of masculinity in literature are those that correspond both to the image of man and masculinity in the minds of homosexual men, and to the image of homosexual man and masculinity in the minds of heterosexual men and women, then the sexual ego conception of the male or female author can be important. I consciously set the term *sexual ego conception* against contested terms such as *sexual disposition* or *sexual orientation*. These terms are based on all too restricted notions of the fixity and invariability of an individual's sexual desiring structure. Although one's sexual ego conception includes one's sexual fixation or preference, which is to a certain extent ontogenetically interpretable, it extends this ego conception to the level of a "self-conception" possessing a definite individual character. As a general principle, this holds true for everyone, even if the degree to which the sexual ego conception is conscious differs in each individual.

For authors, one may assume—as a rule—that the (homosexual) characters they create are credible to the extent that they have developed for themselves a homosexual ego conception that is as clear as possible. Here, "credible" designates, on the one hand, characters in whose representation a condensation of homosexual desire exists, and on the other hand, characters who provide, or can provide, male and female heterosexual readers with an insight into this desire. As objects of (the male or female author's) homosexual desire, these characters will be depicted as prototypes of a specific conception of masculinity. The wish, however, that the character (also) be gay (and reciprocate this desire) will always more or less overtly underlie the author's conception. It certainly cannot be assumed or expected that homosexual authors who have made themselves recognizable as such will automatically or necessarily always depict homosexual images of masculinity. Likewise, it is questionable to infer the author's (hidden) homosexuality from a more or less univocal fashioning of homosexual prototypes in literary texts. However, the insistence of traditional literary criticism that the male or female author's sexuality belongs to an intimate sphere that is worth being protected and must play no role in the interpretation of a literary work is as unhelpful as the idea that the knowledge of an author's sexual intimacies automatically provides the key to understanding that which is fashioned into literature.

With these qualifying deliberations, the question of homosexual images of masculinity in German literature after 1945 can be made more concrete: the issue will be which images of man and masculinity German-speaking homosexual authors fashion as literary prototypes of the homosexual gaze, of homosexual fantasy, and to what extent their own homosexual ego conception plays a role in this.

HANS HENNY JAHNN'S SAILORS

Understood in this sense, Hans Henny Jahnn's (1894–1959) image of masculinity is characterized by three moments. In his longer novels, but also in many dramatic texts, Jahnn fantasizes and fictionalizes: (1) male couples who always live in close connection with one another throughout their lives and who sequester themselves accordingly from the external world; (2) their role as social outsiders resulting from a secret crime that binds them to each other in guilt; and (3) two men of radically dissimilar social origin, one of them intellectually introverted, the other one proletarian, naïve, radiating, and with a beautiful body. Jahnn's own biography also is marked by the experience of such a male friendship: the son of a simple Hamburg ship's carpenter, he begins a passionate friendship with Gottlieb Harms, who, two years his elder, comes from an altogether upper-middle-class home. The two break out of the constriction of their authoritarian parental homes in 1914 and roam as vagabonds through northern Germany until Harms falls ill with typhoid and must be brought back to Hamburg. During this time, Jahnn allows his friend to call him by his girl's name Henny and writes in his diary sentences such as the following: "But I am his wife!—I want his kisses!—And I want to sleep next to him!"

At the same time, he feels guilty about the illness from which Gottlieb never completely recovers. Herein could lie the biographical origins of Jahnn's fantasy, that lifelong male friendship can only come about through guilt. The two do in fact live together until Gottlieb's early death in 1931. In 1915, both go as young men into exile in Norway in order to avoid participation in World War I. In 1918, they find the idealistic, antibourgeois "believer's community Ugrino" on the Lüneburg Moors and live together with men and women in a "commune" that appears nothing short of modern. They begin one of the most important and progressive music publishing houses, the Ugrino-Verlag, and remain—becoming married men with wives and children in the meantime—together. Literary critic Hans Mayer, a longtime friend of Jahnn's, holds that—summarizing somewhat coarsely—Jahnn's life and opus consisted of nothing but collecting experiences of a "joint fate with a second man" during his boyhood and youth in order to "transfigure" them in the rest of his life and in his literary work.[1]

Harms nonetheless does not seem to have been Jahn's ideal object of desire. Early on, the diary of his youth discreetly portrays the writer suffering from his friend's refusals as a lover. This could, in fact, this had to, provoke the author all the more to fantasize this object of desire to full extent in his literary works, in the form of the radiating, naïve, and direct young man with a beautiful body, best in the function and uniform of a sailor.

In the novel *Perrudja*, published in 1928, it is the simple farmer's son Hein who learns to develop his physical attractiveness through a friendship with the dreamer Perrudja, the "richest man of the world," and who, as such, enables the elder to understand and accept himself as (homosexually) desiring. In the novel trilogy *Fluß ohne Ufer* (River without banks), which is about 2,000 pages long (written 1935–1945, published 1949–), it is the initially mysterious sailor Tutein who casts a spell over the naïve young musician Horn and encourages him to pursue a lifelong, adventurous, and outsiderish male friendship. In the novel fragment *Jeden ereilt es* (It catches up with everyone), on which Jahnn worked during the 1950s, the proletarian son of a whore, Gari, grows into the youthfully beaming, unprejudiced, and sexually potent sailor icon of homosexual desire—in the tradition of Herman Melville's *Billy Budd* or the brotherhood of Jean Genet's *Querelle*.

The poetic mechanism through which the socially heterogeneous protagonists are driven by common guilt for a crime into a unique and sheerly compulsive dual relationship is realized differently in each of the novels:

In *Perrudja*, the forest owner Perrudja at first courts the farmer's daughter Signe in a traditional manner. In order to win her, however, he must eliminate her official groom, which he does along with Signe's younger brother Hein. As a condition for marriage, however, Signe insists that Perrudja confess to the murder of the rival. When he is unable to do so, she rejects him, practically pushing him into a (homosexual) relationship with Hein in the process. In *Fluß ohne Ufer*, the sailor Tutein murders Elena, the fiancée of the musician Horn, and compels him, in the face of a shipwreck, to seal a guilt pact concealing his crime. In *Jeden ereilt es*, the shipowner's son Mathieu is rescued by the proletarian boy Gari from a "killing ritual" that a gang of boys wants to perform upon him. The two then seal their future friendship through a bloody ritual act, in which Gari chops off a finger from Mathieu and later carries it in a leather case around his neck.

Jahnn never outed himself as homosexual. He never called his literary characters homosexuals. Nonetheless, it is unmistakable that they are
homosexual figures and that the author's homosexual gaze, his homosexual desire, manifests itself in a literary guise in them. Gustav Anias Horn
thus reflects in his "record" in *Fluß ohne Ufer* on the death of his friend
Tutein in an extraordinarily bodily, sensual, and sexual manner:

> He lay there, very thin, with sunken eyes. I did not understand
> at first. I needed minutes to establish that he was no longer
> breathing. I didn't grasp it and wasn't prepared to comprehend
> its meaning. I laid my hands onto his, which were cold, but did
> not yet have the coldness of a corpse. His lids were not com-
> pletely closed; I noticed it only very slowly—as if he had
> opened them again in order to look at me once more with an
> extinct, completely inwardly directed gaze. Without reproach,
> but disturbed . . . I then raised the cover from Tutein's body,
> tore up the nightgown in which he was clothed. As I enclosed
> his appearance with my glances, the iron ring, which had kept
> my heart forged in, burst open. I did not cry immediately. At
> first a bittersweet stream of tenderness took hold of me. The
> appearance was familiar to me as ever. The dark nipples, the
> little hollow of the navel, stomach and thighs and the splendid
> forms of his sex. The hair, in which it was bedded, was not
> dead, it lived, the fine fuzz on thighs and legs lived. Even the
> emaciated extremely white hands recovered his life. I began to
> caress the body. Slowly, my eyes were filled with tears. And I
> knew again, how much I had loved him, how much I still loved
> the dead body, how singular our life had been.[2]

Notably, Jahnn portrays the friendship between the student Mathieu and
the sailor Gari in *Jeden ereilt es* as an active homosexual relationship. The
two speak here in the changing room of a swimming pool:

> "Why don't you look at me, Mathieu? Why are you crying?
> Why don't you caress me? Why don't you embrace me? I am still
> here, after all."
>   Mathieu raised his head. He saw Gari, this man, this body,
> the image of his angel, unimaginable, but for him beholdable,
> the measure of all things—the only form, softness and warmth,
> which came from eternity. And he still saw that Gari's member,
> the male pound of flesh, was highly erect—big, as he had never

seen it, no longer twelve years old. He threw himself onto his
knees, touched Gari's feet with his head. He thought nothing.
But his lips moved. "I worship," he whispered unintelligibly,
without feeling the meaning of the words.

"This is how I am," he heard Gari's voice, "big and heavy,
when the blood shoots into it.—Please, get up, Mathieu,—look
at me, embrace me, caress me—"

Mathieu obeyed, arose and saw, almost numb, delirious
with delight, close, almost distorted through the closeness, the
landscape of these thighs. In a kind of self-defense, he pressed
the disheveled blond hair of his head against the dark manly
fullness of his beautiful friend. He was not excited; it seemed to
him as if he were extinguished, taken away, sunk into the other.
Suddenly, afflicted by some sort of thought, it seemed to him as
if he had done something dishonest or forbidden. He sprang up
immediately, stood, embraced Gari, kissed his neck, sought with
his mouth the auricle.

"Caress me, Mathieu—lower too, where I am very round
and parted. I am everywhere the same; there is no difference.
There is only a difference in feeling and joy."[3]

An author can hardly formulate more clearly if he does not want to find
himself on the border of the pornographic. Jahnn's fascination with the
sailor's male beauty cannot be overlooked, and it is of an unambiguously
homosexual nature. At the same time, he succeeds in fashioning the
dilemma of homosexual fascination in a literary manner. Precisely because the sailor is so alive, fleshy, erotic, sexually real and near, precisely
because he demands of his introverted homosexual friend the perception
and appraisal of this flesh—for exactly these reasons, he becomes simultaneously a fantasy figure for the introverted friend, an unreachable
"angel" who may only, and at most, be seen, grasped, touched, in a
dream.

The fantasy of an inviolable living relationship between two men in
which one represents virile potency (beaming youth) while the other
gives intellectual depth to the relationship is probably a widespread expression of a homosexual image of masculinity among (German) gays.
Hans Henny Jahnn fashions this in literature. For this reason, I regard
him as one of the most important German-speaking gay authors. That,
to this day, he has hardly found recognition within the majoritarian
literary discourse of German-speaking societies, and even less so internationally, may be immediately connected to his central theme.

HUBERT FICHTE'S NEGROES

While for Jahnn, the unique and lifelong bond to the beloved conditions the homosexual image of masculinity, the image of masculinity of Hubert Fichte (1935–1985) is characterized by promiscuity and the never-ending search for different sexual partners. As a youth, Fichte was among Jahnn's friends and was encouraged by him to write. In his novel *Versuch über die Pubertät* (Experiment on puberty, 1974), he sets Jahnn in the guise of the writer Pozzi, a partially loving, partially critical and caricaturing monument. In contrast to Jahnn, Fichte openly admits his homosexuality and figures homosexual characters as objects of desire with reckless linguistic openness. He connects the image of the beautiful sailor with a different image of masculinity: the exotic, mysterious, "wild," dark-skinned man:

> In the aquarium of Monaco, I meet an American Negro in white marine uniform and onto the ceremonies of petty-bourgeois puberty, onto the transformations of my desires into the stone-aged, age-stoned activities of the servant, the presence of this perfect black body presses itself.
>
> Now, the magic is there.
>
> The time stands still for thirty years.
>
> .   .   .   .
>
> It is the Negro from the novels of Genet and Melville and Pozzi, that smiles at me, and I hear a pop in my ears, like after the deafness of climbing, when the hearing returns at a high altitude.
>
> Time stands still. The world shrinks together onto the center of this black body laced up in linen. The memories turn around and, prepared by times of want, the image of the smiling Negro fills me up, down to the fingertips, like he fills up his linen uniform and like I want to fill him up, penetrating him through the intestines, milt, liver all the way to the brain.[4]

Fantasies of the black man's inexhaustible and insatiable sexual potency have ruled the minds of heterosexual as well as homosexual men (and women) from the colonization of Africa through the present day—even if the attitudes toward black and dark-skinned people often carry racist traits in the everyday social reality of European societies today. Hubert Fichte provocatively ignores any "political correctness" in the usage of language: he denotes black people with the word "Negro," which has pejorative connotations today, and he indulges without inhibitions in the (racist) fantasies of extraordinary, exotic sex with the black man. Through this fantasy, he also compulsively suffers disillusionment. In the novel *Der kleine Hauptbahnhof oder Lob des Strichs* (The small main train station: Or in praise of prostitution), which was only published posthumously in 1988 as part of the voluminous *Geschichte der Empfindlichkeit* (History of sensitivity), Fichte portrays the mixture of fascination, fear, and disenchantment in the encounter of the Hamburg writer Jäcki with the "Negro" Charles, a nurse at the Eppendorf hospital:

> Charles was really completely black.
> It also didn't come off.
> Only not on the soles of his feet.
> That looked uncanny, as if something had been forgotten.
> And the palms.
> Like paper.
> Inside on the lips, very pink.
> And the tongue.
> The teeth were white.
> And the white of the eyes.
>
> . . . .
>
> The arched-up chest.
> Charles's cock stood erect like a branch.
> The skin had slid back from the shiny head, everything black.
> —Impeccable, Jäcki thought:
> —As Homer says.
> —Like a Negro prick, as they call aubergines in the free port.
> —Violet.
> —Eggplant, it is called in English.
> —Charles has black balls.
>
> . . . .
>
> Charles turns onto his stomach.
> He laid himself out as if in an old sacrificial position.
> He kneeled—the white soles turned to heaven.
> The thighs swelled upwards, like Egyptian columns, out of which a branch, a leaf still sprouts.
> Charles offered his ass as the highest, the double-fruit, the black mouth, something dark, shimmering fleece in the middle.
> Behind, Charles's back folded down onto the sheets.
> Charles propped himself with his elbows.
> Carved.

Charles waits for Jäcki to fuck him.
Jäcki had the feeling of disappearing, tiny, in Charles's black body.
—It smells like cocoa and cacti.
Charles immediately started to groan.
He laid down flat onto his back.
He contemplated again his violet giant cock.
Jäcki tried to sit as symmetrical as possible on Charles's knees and
thought about what to do with the aubergine now.
Jäcki apologized that he could not accommodate such an eggplant
in him.
Charles answered something understated, American and continued
to smile at his own thing.
—That's the greatest now, Jäcki thought.
—The blackest, most enormous, and Hui! it is already over.
—So little remains of the feeling.
—As if one were cheated.
—Then it is only a big, black sausage and the jaw hurts.
When Charles arrived in paradise, it tasted bitter and sweet to
Jäcki. Jäcki thought something devout, book of the dead,
Phtatateeta.
Jäcki thought:
Now I swallowed it and did not look if it were black.[5]

The mixture of fascination, sexual lust, disappointment, and even disgust
marks the underlying structure of desire: the necessary disjunction between sexual fantasy and the triviality of the real sexual act—here accentu-
ated in the homosexual man-man constellation and exoticized in the ambivalent black and white contrast. In *Versuch über die Pubertät,* Fichte
describes the youth's fantastic and orgiastic expectations placed on the
sexual act with another boy of the same age (in mutual masturbation):

I, I, I, I.
The all too solid flesh is molten and harder.
To kill the hate-able I!
I had thought, I would become unconscious, start to scream,
pain and consideration wouldn't mean anything anymore, we
would tear open simultaneously, our organs would lie observable,
we would hollow each other out and slide into each other.
Not the usual smells, not the usual light reflections, tones,
touches, sensations—none of that.
Before it is time, the sensations are deflected and a few

drops come and then it is already over and it smells like bri-
quette and the longing for surrender remains now as punishment, as a death sentence, that I want to execute upon myself
with horror.[6]

This is an extraordinarily compressed orgy of images of bodily violence:
killing, hating, becoming unconscious, screaming, pain, recklessness,
tearing open, hollowing each other out and slipping into each other,
punishment, death sentence, horror, execution. These images describe
no reality; rather, they are images of sexual fantasy, of sexual desire, of
expectation for the completely extraordinary and unique in the sexual
act. The sexual act itself stands in the greatest imaginable contrast to
these images of desire. Fichte describes its trivial reality with laconic
words:

We pull down the pants.
He doesn't count the thrusts.
His is fat and blunt.
It doesn't work properly.
He takes mine in his hand.
Now it is there.
It doesn't hurt.
But it isn't a pleasant feeling.
It doesn't stop again.
Klaus turns on the light. He didn't manage to finish. Something
burst on my side and his hand is full of blood and slime. Klaus
makes sure that there are no splashes on his pants.[7]

The contrast between sexual experience and sexual fantasy, which is
depicted in an almost caricaturing literary form here, certainly does not
only correspond to the real experiences of homosexuals but also to those
of heterosexuals (even if perhaps not in the same form for men and
women). But even if homosexuals and heterosexuals share the same masculine sexual fantasy of penetrating another body, the sexual fantasy of
homosexuals probably also has a further-reaching component: in it there
exists at once the wish to experience one's own "all too solid flesh" as
"molten," to become unconscious, to suffer pain and to scream, to be
torn up so that one's own organs may "lie observable," to become
hollowed out. The homosexual fantasies of violence are not so much
directed as violence against others, but rather they fantasize the extraor-

dinary, the unique, and the orgiastic—of the sexual encounter—in reciprocal violence.

The experience of the catastrophic contrast between the orgiastic sexual fantasies and the real, limited possibilities of sexual acts almost inevitably leads to a splitting between homosexual desire and actual sexual lust in the self-consciousness and self-perception of the homosexual individual. The compulsion to realize acute sexual lust destroys the integration of sexual desire with a totalizing conception of love.[8] This compulsion leads to an unending search for the Other, a search that hopes to find its distinct—and for the fantasy of many homosexuals, typical—goal in the (always disappointing) encounter with the dark-skinned or black man.

The images of masculinity that sailors and dark-skinned men have in common are that both concern themselves with societal outsiders: the sailor is phantasmatically located on the ship, in a society of men that is relatively secluded from the external and everyday world; the dark-skinned man, merely because of his "being different" and most of the time also because of corresponding discrimination, is an outsider, and in Europe, a member of a minority. By bringing themselves phantasmatically in (sexual) relation to these outsiders, through solidarity with them, as it were, homosexual readers may console and fantasize themselves over and beyond their own experiences of discrimination as sexual outsiders in the social reality of life.

There are of course also homosexual images of masculinity that point in the opposite direction. They do not orient themselves around the fantasy of the outsider but around that of the socially integrated, assimilated man.

ALEXANDER ZIEGLER'S EPHEBES

For the Swiss-German Alexander Ziegler (1944–1987), social integration and assimilation lead to literary texts with a strong trivializing tendency. Like Jahnn, he dreams of an exceptional two-man relationship for life, yet his men are not marked by social differences or bound by guilt. Instead, they are thrown upon each other through inexplicable "romantic love" and must mostly confront a considerable age difference. Ziegler's novel *Die Konsequenz* (The consequence, 1975) reached a public of millions through its screen adaptation, which was aired several times on German television.

In it, the twenty-three-year-old first-person narrator with the auto-

biographically connotated name Alexander is interned for being homosexual. In prison, he meets Thomas, the sixteen-year-old son of a penal
officer. At this point in the narrative, the love relation for which Alexander has been sentenced to prison turns out to have been an illusory,
"romantic love"; the sixteen-year-old Stefan implores the prisoner to forget him because he has meanwhile found a girl. As Alexander reflects:

> I had just turned twenty-three and believed I had found in
> Stefan a friend at whose side I could overcome more easily the
> adversities of the life of a homosexual. The many partners that I
> had loved fleetingly and had lost again had only seemed as tran-
> sitional stages on the search for a second ego, until Stefan en-
> tered my life and my love for him developed so quickly and
> without bounds that it was irrelevant to me if I violated any law
> with this love.[9]

This "search for a second ego" seems to become fulfilled for Alexander—who had been disillusioned by his experience with Stefan—
when the young Thomas almost forces his homosexual love upon him.
Thomas has himself locked up in an adventurous manner with Alexander in his prison cell, and the two experience their first intoxicating
night of love:

> Thomas leaned his head onto my shoulder and said: "Will you
> promise me that we will stay together? Perhaps one day, we will
> laugh terribly when we think back to this night."
>   I answered by stroking his hair with my hand; for the first
> time in a long time, I experienced once again something like
> happiness. And then, after a while in which neither of us spoke,
> Thomas said into the silence: "I've never loved anyone before."
>   "One doesn't love often in one's life. Twice, three times,
> perhaps, or even four times, and each time you think: this time
> you have defeated the world, now you have made it—forever.
> But this isn't so. One day you realize then that no love can last
> forever because the feelings two people have for each other de-
> pend on circumstances which we cannot determine ourselves."
>   Thomas looked at me in surprise. "You don't know what
> love is, otherwise you couldn't speak like that. When you have a
> boyfriend whom you love, there won't be anything that could
> separate you from him—not even prison."[10]

About another night of love, Alexander reflects:

> This night meant more for me than seeing each other again; I
> knew then that I could perhaps find physical gratification with
> another man, but that nobody except for Thomas was capable
> of making me happy.
> We decided to never separate. "We have a right to be
> happy," Thomas said, "and we lay claim to this right, even if
> everyone is against us."[11]

Everyone is against the lovers: at the request of the primitively
homophobic parents, Thomas is taken as a minor to an educational
institution where he is physically and psychically broken. The fateful
homosexual love, which appears as normal as any other romantic love, is
tragically destroyed by an uncomprehending, homophobic society.

The image of masculinity, developed here as a typically homosexual
one, is binary: on the one hand, the sensitive, by all means still attractive, adult, who matured through experiences of discrimination and suffering; on the other hand, the enthusiastic, passionate, inexperienced,
ephebic youth or boy. Both are only hindered from realizing their seemingly normal "romantic love" by a homophobic society. The social integration of this type of homosexual love couple fails, and it must fail,
because it is grounded in the fantasy of a conception of love and relationships that is indistinguishably equal for both heterosexual and homosexual partners.

DETLEV MEYER'S METROPOLITAN GAYS

Detlev Meyer (born in 1950 in Berlin) opposes a conception of gay love
and relationships in which social integration is based specifically on the
distinguishability of homosexual partners and their relationships from
comparable heterosexual constellations. In his novel trilogy *Biographie
der Bestürzung* (Biography of consternation), published from 1985 on,
Meyer creates a couple that embodies a distinct image of homosexual
masculinity: emancipated, self-conscious, metropolitan gays, invariably
slightly campy, shrill, and whimsical, who move primarily within the gay
subculture yet who maintain a thoroughly durable relationship in which
they deal with everyday conflicts like all heterosexual couples—at the
same time, they do so in a different manner. Meyer thus describes "one
of those conversations" of partners Viktor and Dorn,

in which the speech of one is introduced with the repetition of the last sentence or word of the other one. Following this scheme, Viktor thus says: There is nothing more to it, aha! and ends with: What you impose on me is a bit strong. To this Dorn: What I impose on you is a bit strong? What do I impose on you, can you tell me that perhaps? Then again Viktor: I can very well tell you that . . .

As always, such dialog is finished by Dorn; they agreed upon this years ago, not the fiercest quarrel can change that. It belongs to the conventions of their war that Dorn says: Come on, let's stop.

We play Strindberg for gays again. And then he must leave the room and slam the door and listen behind the door if Viktor really says his epilog. It begins: Never again with me, with me never again . . .

And then they sit for hours in their rooms and brood over the war guilt question, the modalities for the truce and the freedom in peace.

They are completely exhausted after these armed encounters, which, strangely, are always carried out in the kitchen, always at breakfast, as they fortify themselves for another day, originally with the intention of helping each other endure it.[12]

Or Meyer has Dorn thinking at the swimming pool about their relationship:

> I ask Viktor to put oil on me. He does it grudgingly and tenderly like the brushes of a car wash. He asks me if I want to roll myself out here, as I look for a shady place for my towel, gray terry cloth with black meander.
>
> He looks at the swimming trunks of the guys and boys, I look at the swimming trunks of the guys and boys, in between we exchange envious, hungry glances.
>
> I need half an hour to tame my anger over the word "roll out." If this tone must reign, so be it! I murmur behind his beautiful back which delights me as if I were seeing it for the first time, as if it were the back of a body foreign to me. If I want to be angry at Viktor, I must not look at him, especially his pectoral muscles, I don't know any more perfect ones, always urge me to reconciliation.
>
> Why, I wonder, turning away from him, doesn't a flawless

mind also live in this classically formed body, in which I can detect no mistake? Why isn't the spirit, like the body, also formed according to my ideal image?

I have thought up Viktor in an ever more suitable manner for me in the course of our years together. Why has he wanted lately to become dissimilar to my idea of him? I find that unwise, because it is irritating.

The carefree little friend doesn't exist, never did, he says. I would have to take him, thus love him, as he is, or not at all.

Oh, Viktor, how easy we could have it, if we agreed upon my definition of love and partnership. We would have so much fun!

Sure, we would have fun! says Viktor. Fun at his expense. But he doesn't bend over backward for me, doesn't bend over backward for anyone. May I please get that through my head. It probably wouldn't work, after all, if he, to give only one example, cut my hair, blew it dry, shaved my neck and lent me his most beautiful shirt, which he had of course ironed, also lent me money, what lent me money?, slipped it to me for good, called a cab for me, wished me a "good evening" and promised not to go out because I like knowing that he's home when I go check out all the bars.

Sweetie, he says, it's over!

And then he consoles me, that I am in love with Torsten and that he suffers hellishly from it.

Viktor, I say, nobody will ever love you like me.

There, I have finally said a true word, he says, indeed nobody would ever love like me.[13]

Detlev Meyer caricatures the illusions and phantasms of romantic love as they haunt the minds of gays. But he does not only caricature them, he designs with his life companions men of flesh and blood, with human weaknesses and strengths, fantasies, wishes and needs, experiences of happiness and suffering. With gays who quarrel like Viktor and Dorn, and who quarrel over such problems, Meyer presents a homosexual image of masculinity in which many prejudiced stereotypes of "gays" are to a certain extent turned against their own prejudicial character and are connected to an emancipatory message for gay readers: own up to your everyday, trivial, petty-bourgeois, and narrow-minded problems and conflicts, relinquish wanting to be like all the others—then you will be at once yourself and like all the others. Heterosexual male and female readers may perhaps recognize in between all the amusement about the oddities of gay quarrels that (and how) they are ultimately the expression of an admirable solidarity between the protagonists—and that they are, despite all the oddities, structurally not so far from their own relational conflicts and the manner in which they are carried out.

RONALD M. SCHERNIKAU'S EMANCIPATED YOUTH

While Alexander Ziegler presents the inexperienced ephebic youth as the typical object of desire of "romantic love," Ronald M. Schernikau (1961–1991) supplies him with all of the problems of specifically gay coming out during this phase of life. His strongly autobiographical *Kleinstadtnovelle* (Small town novella), published in 1980, begins with a scene in which the protagonist, "b.," is awoken by his mother:

> i am afraid, am feminine, am masculine, double. feel my body withdraw from my body, see my white hands, the eyes in the mirror, i don't want to be double who am i? want to be i, masculine, feminine, see only white. i stand across from myself, want to reach me, reach my arms out for me where am i? i see, kiss, embrace and unite with myself. sometimes lea appears, then again, in the end he perceives it consciously. b. feels: he lies in bed, it is morning, his room becomes blurred, he tries to perceive it, feels the movement of his head, doesn't steer. no hope today a good day, shit-getting-up shit-school shit-life. what habitually annoys him is his mother who tries to wake him, for years the same words, sentences, tone of voice. there is no escape from her love which also drives itself to wake him so tenderly that the waking-up is drawn out to almost unbearable length. his returning, his gathering, his being-moody is only a reaction to her deferment of reality.[14]

In this little scene, some essential moments of the homosexual's search for an ego are prismatically captured: the inquiry into the masculinity and femininity of his own identity; the problem of the doubling of the body's experience, in which his own ego steps out of the body and stands across from it as a mirror image; desires of fusion with a vis-à-vis, a you, which reduces itself to his own ego; the disturbance of the ego perception by the breaking in of social reality, here—absolutely, typically gay—in the form of the loving mother, whose tender waking ritual is experienced by the sleeper and awakener as a burdensome, destructive intrusion in his engagement with his ego.

And as capital and *leitmotiv* sentence of Schernikau's *Kleinstadt-novelle*, the phrase "i am afraid" signifies a coming-out story emerging from the context of the gay movement of the 1970s: "b.," confined by all means to the moral narrow-mindedness of small-town life and his school, but also emotionally guarded by the love of the liberal-thinking, liberal-acting mother, understands himself as a pioneer of gay emancipation in the province. His fear is not so much, and not at first, the fear of being discriminated against or criminalized. On this level of fear, he knows very quickly how to stand his ground as a gay man against his fellow students and teachers. Tomas Vollhaber makes clear in his book *Das Nichts. Die Angst. Die Erfahrung* (Nothing, fear, experience) that the homosexual's fear during the exploration of his ego lies deeper. It is the fear of experiencing nothingness: to the extent that ego identification is, likewise, always an identification taken from society and within society, the homosexual continuously experiences his ego as a nonexistent, destroyed, or disintegrated ego, one that fluctuates in doublings—and in a double life—without stability and psychosocial security.[15] In spite of his emancipated consciousness, Schernikau's protagonist "b." experiences— as Vollhaber discerningly observes—this nothingness by coming to understand that heterosexual patriarchal society does not offer any models of behavior for a love relationship between two men not determined by the general heterosexual patriarchal taboo of fear against sexual practice in general and anal sexual practice in particular.

In this way, it is precisely the youth's image of masculinity—the image of a youth growing up and contending with his coming out—that is a specifically homosexual one: it offers gay readers possibilities of identification in which real individual experiences (of suffering) can come together with an individual concept of life that appears realistic. Having finished high school, b. takes off at the end of the narration, leaving the small town for the Eldorado of gay emancipation and self-realization: the metropolis Berlin. Neither he nor the author knows what will happen to him there. This marks in a particular way the testimonial power of the story: it presents neither a (mature) narrator's retrospection of an earlier stage of life and experience (as to some extent in Fichte and Ziegler), nor does it develop phantasmic actions and characters from segments of experience (as in Jahnn and Meyer). Rather, the author is almost identical to the (invisible auctorial) narrator through auto-biographical reference and narrates in immediate biographical proximity to the experiences of the protagonist, b. This conditions the language, which often appears like the transcript of a dream in which the "day's residues" of experienced reality are filtered through imaginations of fear and transformed into alternative, self-liberating conceptions of actions. In this way, Schernikau manages to depict a homosexual image of masculinity which, though centered on the youth occupied with his gay coming out, confronts—more than the images of masculinity presented so far—the question of social identification that is at least posed by young gay readers in a problematic phase of ego searching. And by the same token, it is precisely the narration's strong autobiographical courting that may well give heterosexual readers glimpses into comprehending this difficult phase of gay development.

CONCLUSION

The authors presented in exemplary fashion and the homosexual images of masculinity developed from them differ considerably from each other. On the one hand, this may be directly explained by the fact that different images of masculinity also haunt the minds of homosexuals, and these images depend not least of all on individual expressions of homosexual ego conception. Differences also can be elucidated, however, through specific historically dependent influences.

Jahnn develops his images of sailors under historical conditions of a strong social tabooization of homosexuality and strong self-censorship. Consequently, his images of masculinity appear relatively remote from the biographically verifiable world of the author's experience. His male characters live and act in a world that is specified little in terms of real geography—they live everywhere, as it were. Nevertheless, or precisely as a result, his male characters signal an unmistakable resistance against standardized and socially accepted images of masculinity by at least claiming the ideal homosocial world of the sailor as a home and a sought-out place for homosexual desire.

Conversely, Fichte lives in a time when he can speak more openly about fascinating homosexual peculiarities of masculinity. His image of masculinity of the exotic, foreign, difficult-to-approach (and therefore mysterious) black or dark-skinned man persists, on the one hand, in the tradition of Jahnn's resistance against the heterosexual majority's standardized images of masculinity. On the other hand, however, Fichte also exposes the European's voyeuristically desiring gaze upon the "Negro" as a sexually reduced gaze that cannot gratify homosexual desire but rather allows this desire to become dissolute in the inescapability of sexual fantasy and sobering reality.

In a time when homosexuals increasingly become more public, Ziegler reacts to majoritarian offers of tolerance by presenting to the majoritarian public the drama of a gay male friendship that fails because of socially deep-rooted, yet irrational, homophobia. Unlike Jahnn and Fichte, he does not provoke the majoritarian society with a resisting image of masculinity of gay identity; rather, he adapts his gay protagonists so perfectly to the current, trivial conception of relationships that each recipient of this drama can, and must, recognize what socially and structurally conditioned injustice is inflicted upon the gay lovers.

Meyer's protagonists are placed in the metropolitan gay subculture of the present. They play with standardized gender and relationship roles, explore them in exaggeration, and invert them, thus exposing the prejudices and dispositions of power situated in them. In this manner, Meyer develops a very modern homosexual image of masculinity, which perhaps comes closest to the more recent theories and models of "queer living."

Schernikau's gay protagonist, b., however, is unable to play with the social roles given to him until he learns to see through them, to see them as mere roles. During the phase of his life when he learns this, he experiences the fear of being different, which means no more and no less than not being in, or not finding, one's own place in a society where every role is always predetermined. It is this same fear that Jahnn's and Fichte's gay narrators certainly experience with their phantasmic male images of sailors and black men, the fear that Ziegler's languishing partners in love and Meyer's queer metropolitan gays also experience and repress in different ways—repress in order to be able to live. When Schernikau's b. sets out for Berlin with this fear in his heart, it remains quite uncertain whether he will survive. The author, at any rate, will die soon, at age thirty-one. He will die of an illness, to be sure, but why did this illness nest in him?

NOTES

1. Hans Mayer, "Einleitung: Versuch über Hans Henny Jahnn," *Hans Henny Jahnn: Werke und Tagebücher in sieben Bänden*, vol. 1, Thomas Freeman and Thomas Schaufeken, eds. (Hamburg: n.p., 1974), 46.

2. Hans Henny Jahnn, *Fluß ohne Ufer II. Roman in drei Teilen. Zweiter Teil: Die Niederschrift des Gustav Anias Horn*, Uwe Schweikert, ed. (Hamburg: Hoffman und Campe, 1986), 151 f.

3. Hans Henny Jahnn, *Jeden ereilt es*, Uwe Schweikert, ed. (Hamburg: Hoffman und Campe, 1986), 124 f.

4. Hubert Fichte, *Versuch über die Pubertät* (Hamburg: Hoffman und Campe, 1974), 305 f.

5. Hubert Fichte, "Der kleine Hauptbahnhof oder Lob des Strichs. Roman," *Die Geschichte der Empfindlichkeit*, vol. 2 (Frankfurt a.m.: Fischer, 1988), 65–72.

6. Fichte, *Versuch über die Pubertät*, 92.

7. Ibid., 91.

8. Cf. Martin Dannecker, "Engel des Begehrens. Die Sexualität der Figuren in Hubert Fichtes Werk," *Der Körper und seine Sprachen*, Hans-Jürgen Heinrichs, ed. (Frankfurt a.m.: Athenäum, 1985), 15–35.

9. Alexander Ziegler, *Die Konsequenz* (Zürich: Schweizer Verlagshaus, 1975), 22.

10. Ibid., 75 f.

11. Ibid., 138 f.

12. Detlev Meyer, *David steigt aufs Riesenrad. Biographie der Bestürzung*, vol. 2 (Düsseldorf: Eremiten-Presse, 1987), 74 ff.

13. Ibid., 85 f.

14. Ronald M. Schernikau, *Kleinstadtnovelle* (Berlin: Rotbuch, 1980), 7.

15. See Thomas Vollhaber, *Das Nichts. Die Angst. Die Erfahrung: Untersuchungen zur schwulen Literatur* (Berlin: Rosa Winkel, 1987).

Neo-Nazi or Neo-Man? The Possibilities for the Transformation of Masculine Identity in Kafka and Hasselbach

Russell West

In his book *The Inward Gaze*, Peter Middleton has commented on the difficulty of heterosexual men in developing an emancipatory politics "because once made the subject of reflection upon itself, gender deconstructs almost all the founding concepts upon which theories of language, culture, and self are based. Gender is a much more radically destabilising concept than most men theorists have recognised."[1] This is so because the very concept of gender grounds subjectivity within the complex interactions of individuals, social groups, and the language by which identity is constituted. The vertiginous lack of final reference points Middleton mentions also provides, however, a surprising freedom that leaves modes of masculinity open to substantial refashioning. Both of the opportunities offered by such freedom, and the anxieties that are generated as a result, belong to our contemporary experience of a rapidly shifting gender landscape and a confusing public arena of discursive strategies and political struggles.

Representations are constructed in an unavoidably intersubjective context, as theorists as diverse as Peirce and Sartre have stressed, with signification always being signification "to somebody," and all texts "contain[ing] within themselves the image of the reader for whom they are intended."[2] Representations of gender, more specifically, the ongoing construction of masculinity, are always addressed to a social recipient. This reliance of gender construction upon a system of signs and upon a social context that receives and may or may not ratify gender representations makes gender a precarious and fluid but thereby open-ended en-

I am grateful to Vanessa Agnew and Franziska Meyer for stimulating and helpful discussions concerning early versions of this text.

tity. This is evident in the particular case I examine here, namely, that of the minor literary genre of the "letter to the father."

The larger context of this chapter is the concern felt by many men, responding to the challenges of the feminist movement, regarding the destructive effects of masculine gender practices within specific Western societies. One aspect of the perceived need to transform men's relationships with other men, with women, and with children is the reassessment of the link between fathers and sons. It is this issue that I address in examining the "letter to the father," in particular, Kafka's *Brief an den Vater* (*Letter to the Father*, 1919) and Ingo Hasselbach's *Die Abrechnung: Ein Neonazi steigt aus* (Settling accounts: A neo-Nazi quits, 1993).[3] Kafka of course needs no introduction; Hasselbach's certainly more ephemeral notoriety first arose out of his central role as a spokesman for the German post–reunification neo-Nazi movement in the highly controversial 1992 documentary film *Wir sind wieder da* (We're back again) made by Paris-based German film director Winfried Bonengel. After the virulence of his Nazi opinions in Bonengel's film, Hasselbach made a subsequent media splash by publicizing his decision to break with his neo-Nazi past in the autobiographical *Die Abrechnung*. The resulting second wave of public attention, much of it highly critical, culminated in Hasselbach publishing a sequel to his first autobiographical text *Bedrohung: Mein Leben nach dem Ausstieg aus der rechten Terrorszene* (The threat: My life after leaving the right-wing terror scene, 1996) in which he offered more information on the neo-Nazi scene and reflected more critically upon his own involvement in that microculture of violence. Curiously a somewhat lurid English version of the first autobiographical text appeared in the United States that same year with the intriguing title *Führer-Ex: Memoirs of a Former Neo-Nazi*.[4] In many ways, Hasselbach's first text is more disturbing and more revealing than the later sequel, precisely because of the unreflected spontaneity of both its form and content.

Both Kafka's and Hasselbach's texts problematize the constitution of masculine identity within a relationship to a socially endorsed figure, the father, and to language itself. Both texts dramatise, though in very different ways, the confrontation of masculine speakers with their own gendered identity in a political and personal context, and men's capacity to reflect critically upon themselves and to change. Rather than proposing a larger theoretical model or strategies for action, as offered by theorists such as Nancy Chodorow, Dorothy Dinnerstein, or Jan Horsfall, I limit myself here to examining the problematic character of filial/paternal relationships as portrayed in these texts.[5] In concentrating on fatherhood, I do not wish to espouse the restoration of traditional patriarchal role models but rather to explore to what extent writing makes available discursive and thus subjective *transformations* of such models. Nor do I intend to suggest that the examination of father-son relationships is the only way to intervene in practices of broader gender relations; reassessment of and intervention in the complex and multiple gender relationships in which men participate is needed if real change is to be achieved. In the following, however, I concentrate on father-son relationships, as it is this aspect of gender practice in particular that Kafka's and Hasselbach's texts highlight.

The two "letters," written eighty years apart, initially seem to have little in common. Kafka's text describes a reign of psychoterror orchestrated by the father at the son's expense, taking place almost exclusively within the private sphere of the family. Hasselbach's "letter" begins on a similar note of filial accusation but rapidly abandons the confines of the family to tell the story of the son's exploits as a leader of neo-Nazi political gangs, and thereafter increasingly occupies the public domain of politics and punch-ups. Kafka's father is represented as an intolerably overbearing presence from which the son only escapes with difficulty, while Hasselbach's father is almost completely absent in the son's life, except for one very short period. Kafka's text speaks of a crippled masculinity incapable of action and substituting for deeds the protective distance and doubtful efficacy of the written word, whereas Hasselbach's aggressive manhood is defined by a Nazi ideology, asserting itself in opposition to the power of the state and targeting the powerlessness of visible minorities in a newly unified Germany. To some extent, the two texts offer a profile of versions of masculinity that carry unmistakable traces of the central dramas of anti-Semitism influencing Germany's destiny in the twentieth century: for Kafka's consciousness of his status as a victim, as a "damaged man," to appropriate an expression from Sander Gilman, prefigures the contempt facism, of which Hasselbach is a latterday avatar, reserves for feminized social scapegoats and in particular for the feminized body of "the Jew."[6] The contrast of capitulating manhood to violent hypermasculinity obscures the fact, however, that the two texts share in common the form chosen by their authors, that of the epistle addressed to the father. This form foregrounds the way in which human subjectivity is decentered, created out of social and historical interactions between others. How the writing subject himself might intervene in a process of the constitution of selfhood that always precedes, and to that extent eludes the self, is the implicit question asked by both Kafka's and Hasselbach's "letters" to their respective fathers. It is not so much the

constitution of hypermasculinity upon the basis of an opposed "feminized" form of maleness that I consider here (though I return to this
issue later on), but rather the displacement of stable notions of masculinity by the very form of address chosen by the two writers.

To this extent, Kafka, though writing eight decades before Hasselbach, can function as a guide to reading the later text: on the one
hand, as a constant reminder of the way in which the autobiographical
enterprise constitutes a semiotic construction of identity, and on the
other hand, of the irreducibly sociolinguistic character of gender constitution. It will become clear that where Kafka's text enacts a smothering
paternal voice vitiating filial autonomy, in a context where language is a
mode of resistance and its own defeat, Hasselbach's narrative is governed
to a large extent by the *absence* of clear paternal discourses. The latter
text, while mourning the lack of a clear and tangible figure of identification, simultaneously opens up a space in which substitute modes of
identification emerge, and thus modes of filial enunciation, finally structured around the transformative but open-ended process of writing itself.
Kafka's apostrophe to the father, ambiguous as it is, can guide us in our
reading of the productive instability of Hasselbach's own inscription of
his gender identity. In Hasselbach's writing, the autobiographical text
becomes a powerfully ambivalent form, nonetheless holding out the
hope of gender refashioning in the context of contemporary political
struggles.

FILIAL EPISTLES AS WRITING

Kafka opens his *Brief an den Vater* with the words: "Dear Father, you
recently asked me, why I claim to fear you."[7] The centrality of discourse
in Kafka's letter can explain much about the communicative and relational functioning of Hasselbach's *Die Abrechnung* and can suggest ways
of reading it that are relevant to us as contemporaries of its author. An
important article by Walter Müller-Seidel shows how Kafka's *Brief an
den Vater* is exemplary of many preoccupations of the modernist literary
movement—among others, the displacement of objective knowledge,
the misappropriation of literary genres and generic boundaries, the use
of concepts drawn from psychoanalysis, and the displacement of the
sovereign subject as the heroic center of narration and of the narrated
action.[8] But to the extent that Müller-Seidel concentrates on the contents or thematic of Kafka's work, he neglects the form, the style in

which it is written, effectively recuperating Kafka's text for a premodern-
ist aesthetics that subordinates the signifier to the signified. The most
radical aspect of modernist textual experimentation—and the very aspect that Müller-Seidel's reading of Kafka tends to resist—was the pri-
macy of the signifier over the signified. This inversion of previously valid
aesthetic priorities gave rise to texts bristling with syntactic distortions,
neologisms, and verbal pyrotechnics; in a word, modernism fore-
grounded what Julia Kristeva has succinctly named "textual produc-
tivity."[9] Hasselbach's text is of course not a modernist text, but it does
manifest the ambivalence and instability that we have come to expect
from textual artifacts, since the implications of modernist thought began
to take effect in literary criticism. Nonetheless, it is by using Kafka as a
guide to reading the minor genre of the "letter to the father" that I
explore Hasselbach's autobiographical text as an exemplary engagement
with what Kristeva, in her work on modernist literary texts, has called
the "sujet en procès." Kristeva's expression includes connotations of productive process and of critical, juridical scrutiny; she conceives of selfhood as no longer static and unquestionable, but involved, through the
slippages of the "primary" semiotic process of representation, in a constant process of self-constitution, open to questioning and revision.[10] It is
the unfinished, open-ended nature of subjectivity that the project of
writing calls attention to, the aspect of literary activity that Kafka's text
asks us to search for in its successors.

Let us return to the opening line of Kafka's letter: "Dear Father, you
recently asked me, why I claim to fear you." The son's letter immediately
privileges the linguistic signs of another subjectivity: "Father," "you,"
and the father's activity of questioning. The filial self only appears in the
form of the accusative "me," that is, as the object of the other's linguistic
activity. Kafka's written self, in this opening phrase, is constituted, gram-
matically speaking, as the product of an external subjectivity. In this
most modernist of texts, the self-determining Cartesian ego gives way to
a mode of selfhood that is "subjected" to language and determined by
the enunciatory practice of other language users. Kafka's words arise
out of someone else's words. His writing subjectivity is preceded and
founded by a prior *paternal* language. This writing subjectivity admits to
being constituted by a prior subjectivity and linguistic practice at the
very moment of attempting to constitute itself by the act of writing. The
intensely contradictory character of writing, which embodies the tension
between self-constitution and powerlessness, is carried to the level of
Kafka's description of his own psychological disposition. Literary activity

allows Kafka to gain a degree of independence from his father, to escape from the closed-in world of family life and paternal repression: "Here, I had actually moved, independently, away from you a bit."[11] Yet at the same time, the very practice of writing in which he asserts his freedom simultaneously dramatizes and reasserts the power of the father: from the mention of "fear" in the very first line of *Brief an den Vater*, to the last pages of the letter where Kafka dramatizes the father's imagined rejoinder, in which the son's strategies of resistance are totally deconstructed and thus outmaneuvered, the text engenders its own emasculation,[12] whence the tension ever present in *Brief an den Vater*, which simultaneously performs quite contradictory strategies, on the one hand writerly self-constitution and on the other hand, determination by a prior, all-powerful subjectivity. The production of self is always undermined by the evidence it provides—at the moment of enunciation—for the production of selfhood by others.

Hasselbach's letter begins with a similar linguistic privilege accorded to a father figure: "Dear Hans!/You surely know that this time I have made my departure from the neo-Nazi scene public, and thereby irreversible."[13] Once again, the letter opens with the name of the father, with an other's pronoun "you," and with the father's act of knowledge. In the very act of initiating his own textual enterprise, the son stakes out his own ego boundaries by referring to the father's preexisting ego. The son is constituted by the father's gaze, even if invisible to the son (the "surely," paradoxically, turns the statement into a supposition, in the absence of direct knowledge and direct contact with the father). The absence of direct contact signals something, however, that is less evident in Kafka's *incipit*, powerless as it is to escape the aggressive paternal interrogation dominating the first half of the opening sentence—namely, that the father's prior, masterful subjectivity is also *created* by the son's discourse. Hasselbach's enunciation creates the paternal gaze, just as all through the narrative Hasselbach creates other father figures, reference points for his sense of self. What Hasselbach foregrounds in his writing is *his re*production of the production-of-his-self-by-another-subjectivity, an enterprise more forcefully asserted than in Kafka's text. With Hasselbach, such reproduction is a means of reworking, or reshaping, a subjectivity formed by prior influences, an impulse, in contrast, that one senses is curtailed again and again in Kafka's letter.

Both Kafka and Hasselbach after him foreground the fact of the constitution of their subjectivities by prior discourses and prior discursive actors. Yet what they choose to do with this fact gives their respective texts a radically different character. Both, for example, deny that their epistle is in any way an accusation of their fathers. As Kafka reassures the paternal recipient of his letter: "I believe that you are entirely free of guilt regarding our alienation from one another. But I too am equally innocent. If I were able to bring you to recognize that, then not so much a new life might be possible, we're both too old for that—but rather, a sort of peace, not a cessation, but a softening of your endless accusations."[14] The retraction of blame, however, is in this context an admission of powerlessness, which leads into a classic modernist topos of the loss of vitality, the failure of natural regeneration. Hasselbach's retraction of blame offers a stark contrast to Kafka's weary pessimism: "Please don't misunderstand me, this is not supposed to be a bill of indictment. It's just that I fear that what happened to you, may be repeated with me. One of my girlfriends has recently become pregnant by me. . . . I think it would be better this child not be born. I assume that things were pretty much the same with you and my mother before my birth."[15] Virile reproduction also is negated here, but rather than signaling a twilight zone in which both father and son grow old and weak, it points to a movement of repetition, of perpetuation of a destructive saga. Yet Hasselbach draws attention to this cyclical destruction not as a sign of despair but to intervene in the process of repetition. Hasselbach's writing invokes the past, indeed repeats the past, within the narrative—and by repeating it, seizes the chance to rework it. The *condition*, and at the same time the *risk* of reworking the past, is that of *repeating* the past within the narrative process, as I hope to illustrate more clearly further on in this chapter.

Thus the apostrophe that opens Kafka's *Brief an den Vater* asks the reader to consider the significance of the similar apostrophe that preludes Hasselbach's epistolary *Die Abrechnung* with his father. Whereas Kafka's text signals the impossible aporia of writing as a mode of self-determination that inevitably signals its own subjection to a prior discursive configuration, Hasselbach appears to take the imbrication of the subjectivity and subjection as the very ground of discursive action. If, for Kafka, intersubjectivity is a site where the outside world irrevocably impinges upon self-determination, Hasselbach accepts that intersubjectivity is the only place—with all of the concomitant opportunities for transformation *and* risks of failure implied—for intervention into the historical process molding the self. This difference between the two modes of epistolary address has significant implications for the rewriting of representations of masculinity today.

FROM PERSONALIZED FATHER TO
DEPERSONALIZED STATE

Kafka's "bodily" father, to expropriate Hasselbach's expression, is a being of overpowering presence, "the giant man, my father, the highest court of appeal," whose domination takes on absolute proportions: "Sometimes I imagine the map of the earth spread out and you stretching across the whole of it."[16] He is a threatening presence, a constantly vigilant, if enigmatic, figure who reduces his son to a mere nothing. Such a tyrannical paternal law gives way, in Hasselbach's narrative, to purely nominal embodiments of the law, in the first instance the Communist Party father trying to inculcate abstract socialist principles into his son, from whose life he disappears altogether after an abortive five-month acquaintance. More generally, this sketchy paternal figure is embodied by the police and their repeated indifference to criminal or violent behavior: "As so often before, the police watched from a safe distance."[17] The paternal law in Hasselbach's text no longer possesses the stifling presence of the Kafkaesque legislator but has become an absent, disembodied, and indifferent arbitrator. Alienating industrial labor and the anonymity of the modern state have frequently been identified with the loss of immediate human relations, among them an immediate, tangible experience of paternal presence. Such a vision of a lost, preindustrial fatherhood may well be purely mythological, however, as British social scientist Victor Seidler claims.[18] Yet surely the corporeal absence of fathers and the consequent reinforcement of identification with stereotypical masculinities among young boys is one very real factor in the social formation of modern varieties of masculine gender, as feminist psychoanalytical theory has pointed out.[19] Alexander Mitscherlich, in *Auf dem Weg zur vaterlosen Gesellschaft* (*Society without the Father*), offers an analysis of modern society based on what he sees as its lack of (traditional patriarchal?) role models and eroded possibilities for identification, speaking in particular of this absence of paternal figures and of the disorientation ostensibly caused for generations of men.[20] Tilmann Moser observes that, for a study written shortly after the Second World War, which diagnosed the malaise of a new generation of citizens of the German Federal Republic, Mitscherlich's book had curiously little to say about the real absence of fathers during and after the war years.[21] A similar silence can be found in Hans-Joachim Maaz's "psychogramme" of the GDR, *Der Gefühlsstau (Behind the Wall: The Inner Life of Communist Germany)*: although Maaz frequently makes claims for the catastrophic effect on children of the absence of mothers caught up in the work ethos of the new socialist Germany, he has little to say about fathers. This silence is only broken when Maaz portrays paternal presence asserting itself with a violence no longer to be ignored, as in cases of the sexual abuse of children.[22] Otherwise, fathers as a group constitute a significant absence in Maaz's text. The strange elision of fathers in Maaz's analysis, apparently invisible to the author himself, may well reflect a significant metaphorical structure common to both Maaz's and Hasselbach's texts: the assimilation of the paternal role of individual fathers to that of the paternalistic and overbearing GDR state. In his virtually fatherless text, Maaz describes the state as a father figure on more than one occasion.[23] The state is portrayed as assuming the role it confiscated from parents whose attention is no longer directed toward their children but rather toward the socialist collective, as the socialist work ethic demands. Thus Hasselbach's stepparents' entire energy appears to be absorbed by work, in obedience to the party slogans: "'All our strength for Socialism,' which didn't leave much time for the family"—producing not only the absence of mothers, as Maaz maintains, but of fathers as well: "It was no different with you, was it," Hasselbach accuses his father in a telling phrase.[24] This father is barely a real entity for the son, having been absorbed into the abstract "elsewhere" of the struggle for socialism. When Ingo's stepfather is mentioned as a real family presence, it is, as in Maaz's text, only to occur as a figure of violence: "My stepfather . . . tried to clear our problems away by means of violence."[25] Such parental absenteeism is compounded by Ingo's physical separation from his real father; when the lad does briefly move in with his father, no real communication springs up to redeem the already yawning gulf between them: "I can't remember that we ever spoke of anything except politics. Today, I think that there would certainly have been other more important things to be discussed first between a father and his son in our situation."[26] That this experience of alienation between father and son deeply marked Hasselbach is evident from the frequent mention in his text of the problematic capacity of men to speak personally with other men—a frequent topos of contemporary theories of masculinity, which by no means precludes critical attention to men's relationships with women. Briefly stated, the entire text, at times explicitly but more often implicitly, expresses Hasselbach's lament to his absent father: "How much I could have done with your presence in those days."[27] Hasselbach's text is disarmingly candid when its author states that "although I've spent no more than five whole months of all my twenty-six years with you, you have been a central figure in my life until now."[28] It is difficult to say to what extent the absconded father is myth-

ologized in direct proportion to his real absence. Be that as it may, the
father is set up as the reference point for all of the son's actions or
reactions, whether revolt or reform—despite Ingo's claims to have "almost forgotten" his father.[29] The statement is paradoxical, however, for
Hasselbach clearly states that this center of his existence is an *absent*
center: there is no one at the turning point of this filial universe. This is
the decisive difference separating Kafka's world and Hasselbach's—a difference, I argue, that is crucial in determining the contrasting character
of their respective autobiographical writings.

DESTRUCTIVE AND CONSTRUCTIVE
FREEDOM FROM THE FATHER

Kafka, if we are to believe Max Brod, ensured that his letter did not
reach his father by passing it on to his mother.[30] Similarly, Hasselbach's
letter does not seem to have reached the person to whom it was addressed, as the sequel to Hasselbach's text published several years later,
Die Bedrohung, contains no reference whatsoever to the father. The epistolary form necessarily advertises the absence of its addressee, and the
nonarrival of the text, or at any rate its temporal "inactuality," is a further function of the gap or delay in communication inherently characteristic of the apostrophic letter mode. Yet the nonarrival of these letters,
the absence of their addressees, which simultaneously necessitates and
negates the communicative act dramatized in the opening apostrophes,
appears to be based on very different experiences of the paternal universe. Hasselbach's father may be an abstraction of paternity, an existential reference point experienced as an absence. This distance does not,
however, prevent Ingo from entering into a decisive confrontation with
the ghostly father figure: "Again and again I tried to gain your recognition, and when I realized how hopeless that was, I began to attack you."[31]
In stark contrast, Kafka declares of himself and his father, "Between us,
there was never any real struggle; I was quickly defeated; all that remained was flight, bitterness, sadness, inner struggle."[32] For Kafka, however, writing appears to avoid engagement with the father, for to do so
would be to enter a paternal space in which the son would instantly lose
all sense of being—a space similar to that of his childhood exile onto
the "Pawalatsche" or balcony, where Franzicek is clearly within the reach
of paternal jurisdiction but reduced to utter insignificance.[33] In the same
way, in Hasselbach's universe the absence of the father appears, paradox-

ically, to open up a space where the son, though deprived of the support
he so yearns for, at least has room to rebel.

Hasselbach's autobiography, it seems, describes a trajectory passing
through an experience of empty images of masculinity, which nonetheless afford a degree of freedom and can subsequently be appropriated for
an alternative model of masculine identification. In the space left by the
absent father of whom Ingo "knew actually almost nothing . . . apart
from the fact that [he] was a by no means unrecognized journalist,"[34]
Hasselbach both imitates (through his public prominence) and rejects
(by the lifestyle thus enabled) the ghostly paternal model:

> Journalists from all around the world suddenly wanted to write
> stories about the house on Weitlingstrasse, and I gave up to four
> interviews most days. These interviews were always paid for.
> The price for such interviews was between two hundred and a
> thousand D-Mark. A certain amount of this income flowed into
> the Party coffers of the "National Alternative"—how much, was
> up to me. At that time, I had more money than ever before in
> my life, I could buy whatever I wanted, and naturally there was
> no need for me to go out to work.[35]

There is a clear rejection of Ingo's father's socialist work ethic in these
phrases and a shallow acceptance of West German capitalism in the
consumer flurry that devoured East Germany in the wake of the "turn to
democracy." Also significant in this statement is the assertion of a sense
of identity in which publicity, power, and money are intimately linked.

The masculine self that is erected in opposition to the absent father
figure is actually as empty as the originary paternal reference point was
invisible. The media images of these violent young men are relentlessly
fictional, consisting of visual metaphors appropriated from the mythology of the Third Reich. The day-to-day reality of the brutal confrontations between extremist left-wing "Autonomists" and right-wing "Skins"
and "Hooligans" is transformed into a constructed narrative by the bri-
colage activity of TV teams: "After seeing the film, one could not avoid
the impression that we were extremely dangerous and close to a coup
d'état, which of course didn't exactly displease some of us."[36] A party
meeting in Cottbus, during which his admired friend and charismatic
neo-Nazi leader Michael Kühnen is unexpectedly arrested before the assembled press, becomes a successful media stunt—but, comically, it also
allows Hasselbach to escape from a dreaded public speaking appearance,
heralded by the stomach pains that continue to be a recurring feature in

Hasselbach's second autobiographical text *Die Bedrohung*.[37] This is what is absent from the sensational media coverage so enjoyed by the neo-Nazis. The media images that construct the masculinity of the militant neo-Nazis elide private lives, intimate relationships, feeling bodies, and blurred gender boundaries. Rather, the hollow fictions or disincarnated images of the media rely on violent *external* confrontation with demonized others, best embodied in the neo-Nazi demagogue Ewald Althans's rallying call: "These young Europeans from Germany, Austria, England, France, Italy and Spain went off to war as idealists, and returned as men."[38] These hypermasculine pictures of "men going off to war" point, by virtue of what they so spectacularly omit, to another zone of masculine experience offering an alternative version of masculinity: one growing out of a close relationship with a male, possibly but not necessarily the biological father—precisely what the young, desperate Hasselbach misses.[39]

Yet this absence of fathers, as suggested above, offers the son a degree of freedom not without certain advantages, if wielded in a positive manner. New versions of masculinity become visible in the vacuum left by paternal absenteeism. Hasselbach recognizes one alternative model to that offered by his distant Communist Party-journalist father in the neo-Nazi comrade Michael Kühnen: "Often, I didn't speak with him at all about the 'Movement,' but rather, about quite different things," says Hasselbach, in stark contrast to the exclusively political conversations Ingo had with his father. Intimacy flows, however, directly into a willing recognition of paternalist authority: "I noticed that he liked me and that he liked talking with me. He was the only person whose authority I recognized. . . . I believe I was simply searching for an example to follow, a role which at the time no one else apart from Kühnen could fulfill. I was proud to be photographed together with him. His influence gave me a feeling of being important."[40] Kühnen is an authority in a way that the father, mouthing socialist moral platitudes rather than communicating to his son the multiple possibilities of a nascent relationship, fails to be. Rather than offering a truly transformative relationship, however, Kühnen's friendship merely confirms identification with a collective hypermasculinity. Only Kühnen's death loosens that identification: "[Kühnen's] death [in 1991] hit me so hard and unexpectedly, that at that moment I considered, for the first time, leaving the scene out of disappointment."[41]

The reliance on media images for a reinforced sense of self is thus a secondary form of social recognition, one that stands in for the more immediate and personal (paternal) acknowledgment and support that

Hasselbach's text seems to present as his pressing need. The politicized media presence reflected in the defiant assertion, "Take note: we're back again" (as Hasselbach proudly summarized his movement's impact on German society), or in the later title of Paris-based film director Bonengel's neo-Nazi documentary *Wir sind wieder da*, is thus revealed to be, in the final instance, dissatisfying.[42] The visibility claimed by the assertion of a neo-Nazi identity remains within the collective zone into which the invisible father had disappeared—in the long run, collective images leave private yearnings unfulfilled.

This regime of collective presence as a palliative for paternal absence is, however, soon made redundant by the sudden occurrence of the same expression—but with a radically altered meaning—as the expatriate film director Bonengel persistently seeks out the young extremist: "A few weeks later he was back again."[43] Bonengel keeps returning to reaffirm his interest in the young man without depriving Hasselbach of the free space to reach his own decisions and to determine the parameters of the relationship. He combines both the open space afforded—albeit by default—by the absent father and the careful attention of the alternative models of "immanent" older men present in Hasselbach's narrative.

Bonengel, unlike Kühnen, affords a more notable contrast to Hasselbach's father in his freedom from fixed ideological stances: "I had the impression . . . that this producer had not much to do with either right-wing or left-wing politics. He said to me that only people interested him."[44] In the person of Bonengel, political dogmas with their totalitarian character and their tendency to press the individual into a mold are swept out of the way by the entirely other-centered interest in the individual as unique and, precisely for that reason, attractive: "Bonengel was interested in me as a person. He said to me that I in no way fitted his stereotypical picture of a young Nazi, and that precisely because of this it was interesting to make a film about me."[45] This, in turn, becomes the basis for a transformation of the masculine subject. Hasselbach tells the father who had undertaken his "political conversion" through an imposed socialist ideology that "they [Bonengel's circle of friends] accept me just as I am, and only because of that, can I change."[46] It is the space of freedom, initially created by the retreat of the father, then kept open by the son's violent opposition to his father, and later restructured by the friendly interest of Bonengel and his friends, that allows Hasselbach to return to an emergent relationship of physical proximity to the distant father.

Hasselbach replies to the father's failure to provide a tangible role model with violence (almost the only other available mode of paternal visibility, if we are to believe Hasselbach's account of his stepfather, who had tried to resolve all "our problems away by means of violence"[47]); the ensuing violence is a primitive and purely negative mode of physical proximity. Paradoxically, violence expresses both absolute distance towards one's "neighbor," but also physical contact, *tactility* of the most perverse sort. This configuration of absence generating a proximity that is merely the explosive, destructive, and intensely *bodily* form of the *absence* of relationship is then inverted in Hasselbach's text; it becomes epistolary writing, a mode of communication posited upon corporeal absence but expressing the desire for contact with a "tangible person," embodied in an uncritical nostalgia for a "real father." It is almost as though only the appropriation (positive this time) of a mode of communication marked by absence can recast the early experiences of paternal absence and work towards a new form of filial relationship where an unprecedented intimacy may at last be achieved; it is significant that writing is for Hasselbach a mode of emulation of the paternal figure: "My mother sometimes used to say that I was so similar to you, and I think it's interesting that at my age you wrote a book."[48]

Such emulation, in contrast, is absent from Kafka's text: apparently one of the triggers for the composition of *Brief an den Vater* was the abandonment of Kafka's marriage plans, which signaled at the same time his definitive rejection of the eminently bourgeois role of paterfamilias and the authority surrounding that role. Structurally, the epistolary form presupposes and enacts the writer's distance from the addressee, a distance that is not only spatial but perhaps also ontological. The letter's nonsynchronicity underlies its possible role of creating another language rather than finding a common speech. Kafka's textual rejection of paternal bodily proximity reminds us that the physical intimacy evoked by Hasselbach's text is by no means a reality but merely posited as a possibility. For the very form of the writerly activity itself only stretches out towards the absent, implied reader: "And thus this all has become a long letter to him."[49] Hasselbach closes his "letter to the father" by an invitation to coffee—an invitation that does not yet have a reply and leaves the father as much free space as the son himself appears to need. One might well ask whether this reading of Hasselbach's autobiographical text thus far is not somewhat utopian, particularly as there is no single mention of the father in the *Die Bedrohung*. Here Kafka can once again serve as a guide for reading Hasselbach. Kafka's letter is turned back before it reaches the father, thus confirming its own avowal in the opening pages that "a new life" is impossible.[50] The lingering suspicion that the distance between humans is perhaps unbridgeable also is present in Hasselbach's "letter to the father"—but with fewer metaphysical and more immediately political implications than in Kafka's particular form of hopelessness.

AMBIVALENT TRANSFORMATION

In reading the central sections of *Die Abrechnung* describing Hasselbach's increasingly violent revolt against the GDR authorities, and his later neo-Nazi activities, one has a disconcerting sensation of reading a document very different from the beginning and end of the text. The statements of moral transformation and of personal insight that set the tone of the introduction and conclusion are replaced by an odd absence in the central sections of the text. Hasselbach's narrative of his neo-Nazi activities seems to dissolve the moral persona present in the opening and closing voice of the text, replacing it with a depersonalized, understated, and matter-of-fact neutrality. To give one example, subsequent to an armed attack on the Tacheles Artists' Colony in Oranienburger Strasse, Hasselbach reports: "Later we learnt from the newspaper, that during this attack, a woman from 'Tacheles' had been blinded."[51] No overt commentary, such as one might expect in such a "conversion narrative," is given; a less didactic, stylistic means of authorial commentary also is absent. For instance, the use of inverted commas as a means of distancing a narrating voice from elements of its own discourse functions merely to indicate a shift of semantic usages away from the customary meaning.[52] Thus, setting in inverted commas the right-wing bomb maker and professional terrorist Ekkehard Weil's "qualities" apparently carries no greater ethical significance than the use of inverted commas around "goods" in referring to a group of hooligans' booty from a drunken raid on a store.[53] This neutrality, however, is not restricted to a simple flattening of the axiological register.

Hasselbach's matter-of-fact tone is the result of a more extensive manipulation of representational strategies, depending for instance on an elision of the real brutality of neo-Nazi violence, and above all, by an almost total absence of reference to his own part in that violence. He prefers to enumerate the wounds he himself receives during a street battle in Pfarrstrasse rather than those that he himself administers.[54] Elsewhere he states, "I had the good fortune that nobody was so badly wounded, in all the armed operations that I led, as to be permanently disabled."[55] This example of self-exoneration functions by a dissociation of himself and his comrades from direct aggression towards the bodies of others (he merely "leads" the violent confrontations, and the statement elides active perpetrators of the violence—"nobody *was* wounded"—as well as presenting the violence as factitious "nonviolence"); it palliates the violence by directing the reader's attention away from the brutality itself towards the final results. The very syntax of the sentence ("I had the good fortune"[!]) privileges the self over and above the violated other.

Here the very structures of the writing itself give clues about the continued agency of neo-Nazi masculinity within the text at the moment of reading. An early passage of Hasselbach's autobiography shows how such a gendered subjectivity comes to be constituted within a "neutral" discourse. The twenty-year-old Ingo, married only a month before to a woman named Christine, received his first prison sentence for a political crime for shouting "The Wall must fall" on a public square in Berlin. After days of solitary confinement in a silent, ten-by-ten-foot cell in the cellar of the notorious Rummelsburg prison, he is visited by his wife, who confronts him with the fact that she has left him for another man. Hasselbach's only retort to her announcement is to repeat back the very words she has just used to announce her betrayal: "I lifted my hands, so that she saw my handcuffs, and repeated the last sentence: 'I've met someone, I'm living with him now too.'"[56] In the "repetition" of his wife's announcement of the end of their relationship (this strategy reoccurs, for instance, in response to a police officer's threat of violence a few pages later[57]), Hasselbach turns others' words against the persons uttering them, obviously a gesture of self-defense that converts others' attacks upon the self into the self's very weapons of defense. Yet at the very same moment, the feeling self disappears: in the repetition of others' words, there is no direct expression of feelings, no utterance of words welling up out of an "internal," affective world. Incoming aggressive statements are simply directed back at the attacker without transit through the deeply vulnerable core of the speaker's selfhood; they do not penetrate the "armour-plating" of the self thoroughly analysed by Klaus Theweleit.[58] This cordoning off of the self, producing a neutralised subjectivity, is the logical result of Hasselbach's experience of solitary confinement, during which he "killed off all feelings in myself," sank into an "absolute indifference to my surroundings and to myself"; it is the affective concomitant of the later period of detainment in the Rüdersdorf penitentiary where he "showed the other prisoners not the slightest feeling or the least weakness, for [he] could trust nobody."[59] The link between affective neutrality and subsequent neo-Nazi activism is made explicit: "I believe that these qualities, acquired in prison, are ideal for later life in the neo-Nazi world," Hasselbach continues; for the prison lifestyle is "a sort of school for the character, which trains one for an existence in a completely unscrupulous community."[60] The reader, confronted with the disconcerting sense of the narrator's neutrality, must wonder whether the "indifference" learned in prison is not still active in the text and its discursive strategies—as indeed Hasselbach himself intimates, speaking of this indifference as an "awful condition, against which I sometimes still have to struggle today."[61] Thus it is with astonishment that one reads, towards the end of *Die Abrechnung*, "I had the feeling, as often before, that nothing mattered, and that anyway, I had nothing to lose."[62] Astonishment, because despite the "as often before," such feelings have not once been mentioned in the text. Feelings are evacuated from the narrative; the self is constructed like the neo-Nazi headquarters in the Weitlingstrasse—well defended, central, visible, and housing a collective identity where intimate relationships can be elided under a communal identity.[63] In a curious observation, Hasselbach asserts that Michael Kühnen "could separate private matters and political affairs from each other very well"—in contrast, implies Hasselbach, to the other neo-Nazi comrades.[64] For the majority, the private sphere has been blended into, absorbed by, the political, neo-Nazi self, existing only as part of a militant collective organism where an individual, intimate self has no place. Identification with the militant group leaves no place for personal will or private desire, as a statement by neo-Nazi propaganda chief Ewald Athans makes abundantly clear: "With me, these disoriented youths should blend into a community in which they find everything. . . . These people should dissolve into the group completely and cannot be permitted to desire anything different."[65] Desire is oriented towards the group, obliterating awareness of the self and its difference with a consequent lack of respect for others in their difference. Clearly this mode of masculine subjectivity is not unattractive for the narrator.

Yet the fragility of Hasselbach's "neutrality" and the gendered character of that neutral selfhood become evident in speaking, for instance, about the emotional malleability of the young men drawn to the neo-Nazi movement: "Most of the youth who came to us were frustrated. They had absolutely no perspectives for the future. I gave them confidence and praised them on occasions, in order to bolster their self-respect. Such recognition made them completely dependent on the group, which we called the 'company' ['Kameradschaft']."[66] Despite having spoken earlier of the "recognition of my 'comrades'," Hasselbach does not implicate himself in his analysis of the psychological functioning of dependence on recognition.[67] Instead he presents himself in this quotation as the manipulator of others' weaknesses and as the objective, knowing speaker. Yet the photograph of himself directly next to this section of the narrative shows him standing, unsmiling and defiant, in front of a military bunker wearing a Rudolf Heß T-shirt (Heß was Hitler's right-hand man until he flew to England to persuade the British to withdraw from the war in 1941). Hasselbach's stance imitates that of Heß, his undaunted gaze into the camera is modeled on Heß', and his own identity is created out of an identification with a larger National Socialist community and its symbols. The younger man secures his own sense of self by appropriating the figure of an older, masculine authority figure. No clearer denunciation of the "neutrality" of his own discourse, and its dependent imbrication within derived images of masculinity, could be imagined. Paradoxically, it is precisely such rifts and contradictions in Hasselbach's text, and the identity it portrays, that make it exemplary of possibilities for gender transformation.

THE OPEN-ENDED SELF

What Kafka obliges us to pay attention to in Hasselbach's text is the fact that writing is always writing to someone, and thus that gendered subjectivity is inextricably constituted by *inter*subjectivity. It is when the gender influences in Hasselbach's autobiographical discourse are allowed to gain recognition, not explicitly, but rather as a result of the course of events, that a more subjective voice, abandoning the appearance of neutrality, begins to reemerge in Hasselbach's narrative. Significantly, this occurs as Bonengel, the Paris-based filmmaker who invites Hasselbach to collaborate on a neo-Nazi documentary, enters the story:

> Bonengel dared, more and more frequently, to ridicule my "comrades." He never tired of deriding my ideology, but appeared to know exactly how far he could go. I didn't hold it against him, and sometimes he even managed to get me to laugh about the stupid, affected nonsense of my "comrades."[68]

Here the masculine self finds an alternative form of solidarity to that engendered by violence. The Parisian filmmaker carefully tests out the limits of Hasselbach's still developing trust, apparently without exceeding what the relationship can tolerate. Bonengel's mockery is tolerated by Hasselbach precisely, I suggest, because the younger man senses that

Bonengel pays careful attention to his emotional signals. In dismantling Hasselbach's "ideology," he participates in the very form of subversion of imposed and rigid credos that lies behind the younger man's own revolt; even ridicule becomes a type of undeclared empathy. The presence of a respected male figure apparently allows Hasselbach's own subjectivity to flow back into the narrative, expressing his liking for Bonengel and his enjoyment of their verbal repartee. Most significantly, the stylistic distancing set in action by the use of inverted commas ("the stupid, affected nonsense of my 'comrades' "[69]) typographically signals the growing distance to the other members of the neo-Nazi scene explicitly stated in the same moment.

As the narrative nears its end, gradually approaching the fusion of the moments of enunciated action and the action of enunciation, the tone of the writing undergoes a distinct change. Strikingly, women move back into the narrative. The showing of Bonengel's documentary film, in which the son appears as a spokesman of the neo-Nazi movement, has a devastating effect on Hasselbach's mother. "It made me feel terrible," he says, "to see my mother suffering like that," and a little further on he observes, "My girlfriend had left me."[70] Femininity is present once again as a human element in the narrative, revealing a self that is attached to others by emotional ties rather than mere instrumental manipulation. A phrase at the end of the book, where he speaks of his racist and violent Nazi ideology, is particularly significant: "I sensed that what I was preaching there was false, dangerous and absurd in this world, which alone for technical and economic reasons has become a single whole to such an extent that one country can no longer exist without another."[71] Perception of the necessity of community, rather than the necessity of aggressive self-defense, is expressed in terms of "sensing" by a self no longer closed to others but aware of its own existence as a function of social relations. The narrative ends in London: Hasselbach has fallen in love with an English woman, thus signalling the reinauguration of an openness in relationship put paid to by his wife Christine leaving him while he was serving his first term in a GDR prison.

The newly found mobility and multiplicity of the self is triggered by Hasselbach's role in Bonengel's film. The documentary, starring Hasselbach as "brown rat-catcher," creates a reflexive split in the young man's perception of himself: "I was shocked at myself."[72] This process of alienation from himself as a neo-Nazi, however, had already begun during the filming. He remarks that, "I was no longer quite so keen to continue defending the Nazi credo in front of the camera. . . . I played my role to the end. Bonengel, who sensed my reservations, asked me whether I'd prefer not to appear in the film altogether."[73] What was previously an oppositional *identity* had become a *role to be played*. The documentary opened up a space, making alternative versions of selfhood possible and creating the freedom to become someone else, so that in Paris, for example, Hasselbach could say, "There, I was not only the neo-Nazi."[74] Rather than glossing over the disturbing aspects of Hasselbach's autobiography by this transition back to the utopian phase of the narrative, I would suggest that it is precisely this open-ended character of the self that makes the presence most puzzling and disturbing within the enunciation of the autobiographical text.

Thus it appears that there are several distinct discursive constructions of selfhood at work in the autobiographical discourse of Hasselbach's *Die Abrechnung*: one is built on an armoured subjectivity leading inevitably to a refusal of others' differences; another admits feeling existence within relationships, where dialogue is the condition of social community. Particularly prominent is evidence of a very potent strategy of dissociation that allows these quite contradictory modes of masculinity to exist alongside each other without any apparent signs of unease on the part of the writer. Felicity Nussbaum's clear formulation of the "'self' of autobiography" as "an effect of ideology and as mediation of its conflicts" is helpful in understanding the disturbing shifts between constructions of gender in Hasselbach's text[75]—but it does not give an entirely satisfactory answer to the question of *un*mediated modes of selfhood, which are clearly incommensurable but contiguous in the text. According to this view, the self is not an essential entity but is produced by discourses and a social environment, by the "interpellation" constitutive of identity, according to Althusser—to which, precisely, the epistolary mode, by "interpellating" or addressing an interlocutor, draws attention.[76] The discursive influence of the state in its various forms and of the family or later figures of gender identification contribute to producing the contradictory versions of masculinity at work in *Die Abrechnung*. The self active in the moment of writing is not univocal, but multiple, in a process of transformation partly occupying the discursive space of neo-Nazi masculinity reactualized by the narrative, partly occupying the space of reflective and critical self-refashioning. The voices that speak in Hasselbach's autobiography employ a mode of "contra-diction," to pilfer a term used to describe Kafka's autobiographical writing.[77] It is precisely this multiplicity that is so disconcerting in Hasselbach's autobiography. It refuses easy categorization as an example of neo-Nazi propaganda, showing as it does the disintegration of an aggressive, emotionally impoverished masculinity; it can, however, be no more easily taken as an ideologically correct conversion narrative that confirms liberal beliefs in tolerance and community, for the neo-Nazi version of masculinity is not banished from the textual enunciation.

Both the mobility of identity and the disconcerting multiplicity of its self-representation are even more evident in the expanded, somewhat lurid, English version of Hasselbach's autobiography *Führer-Ex*, with its conflicting claims of reform, its hypermasculine Nazi violence, and its stereotypical, overblown fascist slogans. In *Die Bedrohung*, Hasselbach admits that it was necessary to "rework completely" the earlier text for the American version, implying also a revision of his understanding of himself brought about by friendships with American Jews who were simultaneously themselves confronting their own families' past experiences. Thus the earlier *Die Abrechnung* could offer no absolute version of the self: "It was not possible . . . to deal with my story, in that book, in a definitive fashion."[78] *Die Bedrohung* is in many respects more carefully reflective in its personal sections and more extensively documented in its analyses of the neo-Nazi scene than its predecessor. Where Hasselbach writes of himself, the reader is offered a less violently dichotomized image of masculinity, although the ongoing transformation of gender identity continues to unfold. The portrayal of masculinity in *Die Bedrohung* is not without its tensions and displays of conflict: there is no mention whatsoever of the father to whom the earlier book was addressed, and towards the end of the narrative, the reader is informed of the failure of the relationship with Karin, the woman Hasselbach mentions at regular intervals throughout his story. The second book, far from representing masculine selfhood in a state of completion, shows to what extent the earlier narrative is a stage in a process of transformation, in which writing, and more specifically writing *to* someone, can enable the transformation of contemporary masculinities. The intersubjective character of gender constitution and representation mentioned at the beginning of this chapter becomes in these texts—to differing extents—a guarantee of social transformation.

If we are indeed to read autobiographical texts as intersubjective constructs, and thus as "locations of uncertainty and of the individual subject's shifting alliances as situated in gender and class relations," we will inevitably be led towards a social and political reading of the construction of gender and towards the recognition that narratives of the self are inextricably caught up in a historical context and are, to quote Klaus-Detlef Müller, "primarily organized in relationship to their historical object."[79] Kafka, by wielding a metaphorics of intersubjective space and power relations, opens up interpretative perspectives in reading Hasselbach, which place the discursive construction of masculinity fair and square back in the public sphere and in the political arena, in firm opposition to "archetypal" theories of masculinity promulgated by some sectors of the men's movement in the United States and Britain today. Kafka's text, by problematizing the act of epistolary writing, provides a foil allowing the reader to evaluate Hasselbach's complex and contradictory attempts to articulate a new form of masculine identity. Both texts foreground the dialogue of present and past selves in the text, existing in a conflictual continuity. Kafka and Hasselbach use autobiographical writing as a mode of combat against cycles of reiterated destruction as a way of undertaking self-fashioning in the historical context in which they are situated. Together the two texts demonstrate that change is possible through communication—with men, given the nature of these texts, but no less so with women—and that "apostrophe" also demands a response allowing the process of critical self-recognition to continue, so that individual and collective transformation of lived forms of masculinity can continue unhindered.

NOTES

1. Peter Middleton, *The Inward Gaze: Masculinity and Subjectivity in Modern Culture* (London: Routledge, 1992), 159. See also Judith Butler, *Gender Trouble: Feminism and the Subversion of Identity* (London: Routledge, 1990).

2. C. S. Peirce, "Logic As Semiotics: The Theory of Signs," *Semiotics: An Introductory Anthology*, R. E. Innis, ed. (London: Hutchinson, 1986), 5; Jean-Paul Sartre, *What Is Literature?* B. Frechtman, trans. (London: Methuen, 1967), 52.

3. Franz Kafka, *Brief an den Vater* (Frankfurt a.M.: Fischer, 1960); Ingo Hasselbach and Winfried Bonengel, *Die Abrechnung: Ein Neonazi steigt aus* (Berlin/Weimar: Aufbau-Verlag, 1993). All translations into English, unless otherwise indicated, are my own.

4. Ingo Hasselbach, *Die Bedrohung: Mein Leben nach dem Ausstieg aus der rechten Terroszene* (Berlin/Weimar: Aufbau-Verlag, 1996); Ingo Hasselbach and Tom Reiss, *Führer-Ex: Memoirs of a Neo-Nazi* (New York: Random House, 1996).

5. See Nancy Chodorow, *The Reproduction of Mothering: Psychoanalysis and the Sociology of Gender* (London: University of California Press, 1978); Dorothy Dinnerstein, *The Rocking of the Cradle and the Ruling of the World* (London: The Women's Press, 1978); Jan Horsfall, *The Presence of the Past: Male Violence in the Family* (Sydney: Allen and Unwin, 1991).

6. See Sander L. Gilman, "Damaged Men: Thoughts on Kafka's Body," *Constructing Masculinity*, Maurice Berger et al., eds. (New York: Routledge, 1995), 176–189.

7. Kafka, 5.

8. Walter Müller-Seidel, "Franz Kafkas *Brief an den Vater*. Ein literarischer Text de» Moderne," *Orbis Litterarum* 42 (1987): 353–374.

9. Julia Kristeva, "The System and the Speaking Subject," *The Kristeva Reader*, Toril Moi, ed. (Oxford: Basil Blackwell, 1986), 28–29; "La Productivité dite texte," Σημειωτιχη: *Recherches pour une Sémanalyse* (Paris: Seuil, 1969), 147–184.

10. Ibid., "Le sujet en procès," *Tel Quel* 52 (1972): 12–30; 53 (1973): 17–38.

11. Kafka, 43.

12. Ibid., 60–61.

13. Hasselbach, *Die Abrechnung: Ein Neonazi steigt aus*, 11.

14. Kafka, 6.

15. Hasselbach, *Die Abrechnung: Ein Neonazi steigt aus*, 11.

16. Kafka, 10, 57.

17. Hasselbach, *Die Abrechnung: Ein Neonazi steigt aus*, 123.

18. Victor J. Seidler, "Fathering, Authority and Masculinity," *Male Orders: Unwrapping Masculinity*, Rowena Chapman and Jonathon Rutherford, eds. (London: Lawrence and Wishart, 1996), 278–283.

19. See Chodorow, *The Reproduction of Mothering*; Dinnerstein, *The Rocking of the Cradle and the Ruling of the World*; Horsfall, *The Presence of the Past*.

20. Alexander Mitscherlich, *Auf dem Weg zur vaterlosen Gesellschaft: Ideen zur Sozialpsychologie* (München: Piper, 1982).

21. Tilmann Moser, *Politik und seelischer Untergrund: Aufsätze und Vorträge* (Frankfurt a.M.: Suhrkamp Verlag, 1993), 78.

22. Hans-Joachim Maaz, *Der Gefühlsstau: Ein Psychogramm der DDR* (Berlin: Argon Verlag, 1992), 38.

23. Ibid., 36, 85.

24. Hasselbach, *Die Abrechnung: Ein Neonazi steigt aus*, 16.

25. Ibid., 14.

26. Ibid., 20.

27. Ibid., 14.

28. Ibid., 11–12.

29. Ibid., 42.

30. Max Brod, *Über Franz Kafka* (Frankfurt a.M.: Fischer, 1977), 23.

31. Hasselbach, *Die Abrechnung: Ein Neonazi steigt aus*, 156.

32. Kafka, 33.

33. Ibid., 9–10.

34. Hasselbach, *Die Abrechnung: Ein Neonazi steigt aus*, 19.

35. Ibid., 45.

36. Ibid., 78.

37. Ibid., 79; *Die Bedrohung*, 65, 73.

38. Hasselbach, *Die Abrechnung: Ein Neonazi steigt aus*, 55–56.

39. Some theories of masculinity tend to blend notions of military hypermasculinity and homosocial *rites de passage*; see, for example, David J. Tacey's *Remaking Men: Jung, Spirituality and Social Change* (London: Routledge, 1997), 120–123.

40. Hasselbach, *Die Abrechnung: Ein Neonazi steigt aus*, 56.

41. Ibid., 56–57.

42. Ibid., 49.

43. Ibid., 142.

44. Ibid., 141.

45. Ibid.

46. Ibid., 156.

47. Ibid., 14.

48. Ibid., 157.

49. Ibid., 9.

50. Kafka, 6.

51. Hasselbach, *Die Abrechnung: Ein Neonazi steigt aus*, 72.

52. See Jacqueline Authier, "Paroles tenues à distance," *Matérialités discursives*, Bernard Conein et al., eds. (Lille: Presses Universitaires de Lille, 1981), 127–142.

53. Hasselbach, *Die Abrechnung: Ein Neonazi steigt aus*, 72, 86.

54. Ibid., 122.

55. Ibid., 155.

56. Ibid., 30.

57. Ibid., 30–31.

58. See Klaus Theweleit, *Männerphantasien*, vol. 2, *Männerkörper. Zur Psychoanalyse des weißen Terrors* (Reinbek: Rowohlt, 1993), chapter 4.

59. Hasselbach, *Die Abrechnung: Ein Neonazi steigt aus*, 27, 33.

60. Ibid., 33.

61. Ibid., 27.

62. Ibid., 128.

63. Ibid., 45.

64. Ibid., 50.

65. Ibid., 122.

66. Ibid., 121.

67. Ibid., 105.

68. Ibid., 142.

69. Ibid.

70. Ibid., 147.

71. Ibid., 158.

72. Ibid., 144.

73. Ibid., 143.

74. Ibid., 148.

75. Felicity Nussbaum, *The Autobiographical Subject: Gender and Ideology in Eighteenth-Century England* (Baltimore: Johns Hopkins University Press, 1989), xxi.

76. Louis Althusser, "Ideologie et appareils idéologiques d'Etat," *Positions* (Paris: Editions sociales, 1976), 122–129.

77. Marjanne Goozé, "Creating Neutral Territory: Franz Kafka's Purloined *Letter to His Father*," *MLA* 11: 1–2 (1987): 34.

78. Hasselbach, *Die Bedrohung*, 166.

79. Nussbaum, *The Autobiographical Subject*, xix; Klaus-Detlef Müller, quoted in Helmut Peitsch, *"Deutschlands Gedächtnis an seine dunkelste Zeit"*: Zur Funktion der Autobiographik in den Westzonen Deutschlands und den Westsektoren von Berlin 1945 bis 1949* (Berlin: Edition Sigma Bohn, 1990), 23.

Multiple Masculinities in
Turkish-German Men's Writings

Moray McGowan

What makes a Turkish-German man?[1] There can be no single, simple answer, since masculinities are fluid and contingent constructs, still more so given the multiple influences of gender and ethnicity on Turkish men in contemporary Germany.[2] Additionally, the tendency to link "masculinity" or "manhood" to colonialist dominance, or to the "hyper-virility" of fascism, becomes particularly problematic when addressing constructions of masculinity in which migrant and minority experience plays a role.[3] In the complex processes in which gender identities are generated, nurtured, discovered, explored, challenged, and subverted, individuals from migrated and minority cultures experience additional structuring pressures and, consequently, additional possibilities. Thus Turkish men in Germany find and negotiate their masculinities within frameworks where Turkish, German, and Turkish-German practices and expectations of masculinity meet, clash, and recombine. This chapter's focus on imaginative literature, which not only reflects social reality and social norms, but also exaggerates, inverts, or otherwise challenges them by exploring the desired and the feared as well as the lived, necessarily adds to the ambiguities. However, imaginative literature also is peculiarly well suited for the exploration of these multiple influences, of the complex voices in the imagined and narrated self, and of gender as performative "doing" rather than static "being."[4]

This chapter discusses factors within Turkey itself that influence Turkish-German masculinities and considers how Turkish life in Germany generates new layers of experience, expectation, and practice, which increase the complexity of these masculinities. It concludes by examining a number of literary texts that either display different facets of these masculinities or actively rehearse alternatives to them.

TURKEY AND ITS CONTRIBUTIONS TO TURKISH-GERMAN MASCULINITIES

By the 1990s, Germany had a population of just under 2 million Turks.[5] Turkish communities in Germany display many of the tensions found within Turkish society itself: between tradition and modernity, fundamentalism and secularism, right- and left-wing politics, Turkish and Kurdish national aspirations. But they also have their own complex infrastructures, part intermeshed with and part separate from the German host society.

What factors within Turkey influence Turkish-German cultural identities, specifically masculinities? Turkey is at once European and Asian, grounded in Islamic culture yet constitutionally secular, heir to numerous ancient indigenous cultures yet also a product of historical migrations. Moreover, contemporary Turkey (the world's thirteenth largest economy) is itself in socioeconomic and demographic flux, exemplified by Istanbul's growth, largely through internal migration, from a city of 1.4 million in 1961 to 10.7 million in 1992. Thus, significant differences in social and geographical origins, education, degrees of religious adherence, and motivation for emigration also will be found amongst Turks in Germany, even before we consider the variations in and effects of experience in Germany itself. Some come from village cultures where, for example, bride theft and prenuptial rape were still common as late as the 1970s.[6] Others come from modern, liberal, sometimes Westernised backgrounds. Even amongst the 90 percent of Turks in Germany who originate from rural Anatolia, factors such as whether and for how long they have experienced urban life in Turkey itself during an interim internal migration create significant differentiation. In understanding migrant experience, routes can be as significant as roots. Anatolians in Germany also reflect the ethnic diversity of their homeland: one in five Turks in Germany is actually a Kurd.[7]

As a secular state in a culturally Islamic country, modern Turkey displays great variations in its degree of religious observance. We should remember that Islam is not a church, and there are significant differences between the Sunnite majority (approximately 75 percent of the Turkish population) and the Shiite minority (approximately 25 percent). But Islamic values still constitute the principal influence on patterns of upbringing and gender relations in Turkish society, especially in Anatolia, and Turkish male identity continues to be interwoven with Islamic notions of patriarchal honour—some of them common to peasant societies elsewhere in the Mediterranean and beyond.[8] At the same time, omnipresent modern media messages accelerate processes of change and differentiation.

Besides Islamic values, a second influence on Turkish masculinities is military service. Here patriarchal masculinity and homosociality are reinforced in ways typical of most armies.[9] But often military service also gives Turks from semifeudal Anatolian villages their first direct experience of the wider world; indeed, it is often where previously illiterate villagers learn to read and write and acquire industrial skills. Army service may thus be a first step to migration and to experiences that eventually transform the masculinities such service initially serves to confirm.

TURKISH EXPERIENCE IN GERMANY

The modern Turkish migration to Germany began effectively in 1961 as a labour migration.[10] The combination of postwar boom and diminishing flows of German migration from the GDR and elsewhere in eastern Europe led to serious labour shortages, met by recruitment largely from southern Europe (Italy, Greece, Yugoslavia, as it then was, Spain, and Turkey). German society's expectation that migrant workers would not integrate was reflected in restricted legal rights and in the label *Gastarbeiter*. Euphemistically avoiding, yet also drawing attention to, the parallels to the millions of *Fremdarbeiter* ("foreign workers," many of them slave labourers), who had propped up the Nazi war economy less than two decades earlier, the term *Gastarbeiter* also held two reminders: these migrants were workers, recruited for low-status, low-paid, largely unskilled and semiskilled work; and they were to be temporary (guests do not stay). Always contentious, the term became increasingly misleading as, in the 1970s and 1980s, large numbers of migrant workers chose to settle and reunite, or else to found families in Germany. For Turks in particular, economic conditions in Turkey and the likely difficulties that returnees would face if they later sought to reenter the labour market in the European Union (of which Turkey, unlike most of the sending countries, was not a member) were strong incentives to stay. The Turkish population, 2 million strong, is still concentrated in the industrial centres of western Germany and West Berlin (as late as 1994, there were only 2,000 Turks in the whole of the former German Democratic Republic).[11] But it displays all of the socioeconomic and cultural diversification of a settled community developing over several generations. Thus though 70 percent of Turks in Germany in the 1990s were still classified as workers (compared to 40 percent of Germans), growing numbers of Turks belong to the business and professional classes.[12] Moreover, from the start, some of the Turks who came to Germany were not labour migrants as such. Intellectuals and artists in particular left Turkey for political reasons (fleeing military dictatorship, for example). By the 1990s, few Turks in Germany were *Gastarbeiter*; significant numbers, though, never had been.

Thus, any discussion of Turkish men in Germany needs to stress diversity, even when certain patterns can be identified. Turkish men of the generations who came to Germany in the 1960s or 1970s may, while in Turkey, have more or less closely embraced Islamic views on gender and masculinity. Sometimes, indeed, active dissatisfaction with Islamic values may have been one factor in their decisions to emigrate; for not even every labour migrant was simply economically motivated. Once in Germany, however, they were typically confronted with a society whose attitudes often provoked a defensive strengthening of cultural traditions. Some became more, not less, "Turkish": In 1994, 87 percent of Turks in Germany regularly read a Turkish newspaper, compared to only 30 percent in Turkey.[13] Religion, too, plays a greater role for Turks in Germany than in Turkey, for reasons more to do with ethnic reassurance than with faith.

In this first phase of labour migration, since the Turkish migrant workers typically spoke no German on arrival and lived in circumstances that encouraged segregation (often, barrack-like accommodations provided by employers), and since these first migrations were largely of unaccompanied men, the result was a further emphasis on the homosociality that usually characterises heavy manual labour, though this was neither total nor, given the exceedingly varied backgrounds of migrants from Turkey, monocultural.[14] The reduced and structurally predetermined manner of contacts with the German host culture tended to confirm and exaggerate preconceptions on both sides. In the workplace, German authority figures such as foremen and predominantly male management typically experienced and treated the Turkish workers as speechless, illiterate, and unskilled, as did the government and other agencies. "Work defines men," British sociologist Ian Harris contends.[15] But it does not define them one-dimensionally: the manual labour role may confirm traditional masculine identity yet may also undermine this identity through low status and exclusion from discursive power.

In the migrant workers' private lives, sexual contacts often featured disproportionately among their total contacts with the German host population, confirming mutual preconceptions: heterosexual Turkish men often experienced German women either as professional prostitutes

or as what their Islamic codes suggested were, effectively, equivalents—
women willing to enter into an extramarital relationship or simply appear unaccompanied in certain social situations. The severe distinctions
drawn in patriarchal Turkish villages between "family women" and
"street women" were thus sometimes perpetuated in Germany.[16] Turks
with experience before emigration in a metropolis such as Istanbul were
of course less susceptible to such preconceptions. Nonetheless, many
men retained and sometimes even intensified a simplistic and derogatory
attitude towards German women, and towards German society in general, as being culturally and ethically inferior. Their authority and patriarchal identity unsettled by general social marginalisation and the indignities of their workplace, they might turn back to these half-atrophied
Islamic roots to reassert their threatened masculinity.

Subsequent developments in their social situation might lessen this
threat, but also, given the greater contact with and competence in German language and culture displayed in many cases by their own children, might intensify it. After the German federal government's ban on
new migrant labour recruitment in 1973, far more Turkish men began
to see their migration as long-term, and thus they reunited or founded
their own families in Germany. There is of course no single model of a
Turkish family in Germany any more than in Turkey itself, but certain
trends can be observed. Many first-generation Turkish migrant men
sought to reassert Turkish and Islamic patriarchal values within the family: sharply defined gender roles, precedence rules amongst male family
members (junior males may not smoke in the presence of the head of
the family and must await permission to speak), and pressure on daughters to take Koran lessons (often taught by fundamentalist groups
banned in secular Turkey itself) to counterbalance the supposed moral
corruption of the German school.

But rarely, of course, do such measures wholly counteract modern-
isation processes or the attractions of modernity. Year by year since
1973, the proportion of Turks has grown for whom experience in and of
Germany is more central than that in and of Turkey. Further tensions
emerge, such as the second and third generations' rejection of their parents' sometimes supine acceptance of discrimination and exclusion.[17]
Much of what we have described here so far would be largely irrelevant
to the self-perception of these later generations. Increasing numbers of
Turks in Germany, whether with Turkish or German passports, have
been born in Germany and so are not migrants at all, though their
cultural environment usually remains shaped to some degree by migrant
experience. Moreover, these later generations may invoke, indeed con-

sciously adopt, elements of Turkish or Islamic culture for new reasons arising from their German experience.

Thus it is misleading to assume that there will always be a straight-forward gradient of cultural difference between the relatively "Islamic" father and the relatively "westernised" son or daughter. In some respects, of course, these children, often born in Germany and speaking German as well as their German peers, make their way more successfully in German society than do their fathers. But Turks continue to suffer significant discrimination in education, training, and employment in Germany, and the younger generations, given their higher expectations, are more readily disillusioned. While the children's sometimes fluent German and ease with Western consumer culture may destabilise and threaten the fathers' patriarchal identity, the children themselves also may invoke Islamic values or practices, whether as a deliberate provocation, as a cultivation of ethnic pride against German discrimination, or as a critique of their fathers' double standards and even, in their eyes, their fathers' ethnic betrayal. In 1996, a survey suggested that 68 percent of the 400,000 Turks in Germany ages fifteen to twenty-one saw Islam as being important in their lives, 54 percent held Islam to be ethically superior and to have privileged access to truth, 33 percent supported the fundamentalist and decidedly patriarchal Milli Gürüç (unified, new worldview) movement, and a similar proportion embraced the right-wing nationalist Grey Wolves. More than half of this cohort, itself largely secularly educated, wished to send their own children to a Koran school.[18] This young male generation's interest in Islam and the claims to superiority of its fundamentalist tendencies certainly help compensate for their treatment in their German environment. In this light, embracing Islam could be understood as a provocative revolt against a family background that they see as a bad compromise with the Western society from whose discrimination they suffer. It could, however, also offer them reintegration into their families, especially renewed contact with their fathers, from whose patriarchal regime they had become alienated at an earlier stage of teenage rebellion.

Overall, therefore, the younger generations of Turks in Germany express a complex spectrum of different combinations of Western attitudes and values, as well as Turkish ones, both acquired in the family and adopted independently or even in provocation of the family. Turkish rap, for example, blends these elements with Western pop, hip-hop, and African-American street slang.[19] The gang behaviour described in Hermann Tertilt's study of the Frankfurt "Turkish Power Boys" combines patterns familiar from, for example, W. F. Whyte's picture of immigrant groups in American cities in *Street Corner Society* (1943), with specific Turkish and Islamic elements.[20] Tertilt's ethnographic analysis of Turkish male youth illustrates how masculinities develop in a complex amalgam of subcultural peer pressures and redefined versions of the performative masculinities common in most Mediterranean cultures. Manly gestures and postures, physical strength, and permanent readiness to defend one-self are all expected. Aggressive jousts are expressed in terms of sexual coupling: *Seni sikerim* ("I fuck you") is a widely used warning to the antagonist to quit the field. But if the latter fails to react with sufficient aggression, he is an *ibne* ("faggot"): not necessarily homosexual, but not a man. The victor signifies his dominance by a simulated, apparently homosexual act, such as pretending to force the loser to fellate him. This is not, however, read by the group as being indicative of the participants' homosexual orientation. The tender, often erotic physical exchanges—embracing, kissing, hand-holding—between group members are defined as "friendship" and never linked to being *ibne,* a term of abuse reserved for those who do not defend their own territory, that is, those who let themselves be penetrated. The decisive structural opposition is then not male/female or hetero/homo, but penetrator/penetrated. The penetra-tor's heterosexual honour is not compromised by his participation in a mimed same-sex act, but indeed is confirmed by the role in it for which his greater manliness qualifies him.

To be a Turkish man in Germany in these contexts thus means facing multiple forces shaping and challenging masculinity. Origins, up-bringing, education, aspirations, relationship to the host culture—all of these interact to generate multiple permutations of male identities. And as we shall see in the following examples—which necessarily give only a partial picture—the writings of Turkish-German men both explore and expand these complex conditions governing Turkish and Turkish-German masculinities.

IMAGES OF MASCULINITY IN WRITINGS BY TURKISH-GERMAN MEN

In the early 1980s, mainstream German literary culture began to notice the emergence of work by writers who were migrant labourers, or who wrote about migrant labour, or who were simplistically associated with the latter through their ethnicity. Inevitably perhaps, this writing ini-tially attracted the label *Gastarbeiterliteratur,* though this was as inaccu-rate and discriminatory as the label *Gastarbeiter* itself, and for essentially the same reasons: it ignored the fact that many of these writers were not *Gastarbeiter*, and it marginalised this writing outside of the mainstream literary culture, implicitly or explicitly declaring it to be primarily of sociological rather than aesthetic interest.[21] Ironically, this resulted partly from the well-meaning promotion of this literature through anthologies published by an editorial team at the Munich University Institute for German As a Foreign Language.[22] The volume *Türken deutscher Sprache* (German-language Turks, 1984) documented the quantitative significance of Turkish-German writing, but the ethnic essentialism of its title and appearance in the same Munich series perpetuated the relatively simplistic context of its reception, obscuring the expanding diversity of Turkish-German experience and aesthetic ambitions in the early 1980s.[23]

But equally ironically, just as some critics were becoming more aware of the real need to resist the trivialising of Turkish-German writing as *Gastarbeiterliteratur*, feminist interest was moving the focus to women writers such as Aysel Özakin or Emine Sevgi Özdamar. This led to a new, if different, neglect of the literature of migrant labour experience, which was predominantly male and predominantly reflected in the work of male writers.[24] In focusing initially on this writing, we seek not to revive the category of *Gastarbeiterliteratur* as an unsophisticated victim literature (though such writing exists) but rather to take appropriate account of the literary responses to a significant area of Turkish-German male experience. We should stress that though 90 percent of Turkish migrants to Germany came from Anatolian villages, a disproportionate number of Turkish-German writers, if they are migrants at all and not actually born in Germany, came from the generally better educated, more cosmopolitan urban minority. Thus even texts of apparently autobiographical *Gastarbeiter* experience often are self-conscious literary constructions and, as we shall see, much Turkish-German writing has quite different contexts and aesthetic ambitions.

Many of the texts in anthologies such as *Türken deutscher Sprache* suggest masculine identities among Turkish men in Germany strongly patterned by traditional gender roles, informal sanctions, customs, and peer pressure, but also subject to the pressures and blandishments of the new host society, and to generational tensions. They explore the complicated anxieties of men living at odds with their own needs, expectations, or upbringing in a world that they do not understand, as Fakir Baykurt's "Das Telefon" (The telephone) also makes clear.[25] These anxieties are underscored in Baykurt's story by the leitmotif of "sweat," which evokes both identity-creating manual work and the discomforts of this identity's destabilisation.

The majority of the Turkish migrant workers of the 1960s and early 1970s were unaccompanied men, Herculean, exploitable, and expendable. As Kemal Kurt tells us, the worker was "quite alone/alone with his muscle power/alone with his will to work . . ./his needs have shrunk to nothing/he needs nothing, he just consumes,/and is consumed."[26] Heavy, dirty, dangerous work characterised Turkish male roles in Germany at this time, as Baykurt's story "Nachtschicht" (Nightshift) makes all too clear.[27] This work often impacts literally on the male body of the "disposable worker," which becomes a casualty of production or a currency of exchange.[28] In Aras Ören's *Der kurze Traum aus Kagithane* (The brief dream from Kagithane), one of the protagonists, Fazil Usta, driven by economic necessity, migrates to Essen, where he loses a finger between the drums of a steel rolling mill, then dies of a stress-related stomach illness.[29] Salih, in Baykurt's "Wahltag" (Election day) is prematurely aged, balding, and toothless from working too close to a foundry crucible at 1700 degrees Celsius.[30] Hasan Dewran distils these physical and psychological costs of labour migration into a single image: "One arm in Anatolia/One arm in Germany/Of the two arms/one will/remain in the machine."[31]

In the work of Aras Ören, the literal physical impact of migrant labour on the body is taken to exemplify alienation and class struggle. Ören (born 1939), who came from comfortable middle-class origins in Istanbul, was involved in theatre and left-wing politics there before emigrating to Berlin in the late 1960s. In Berlin, he was further radicalised by his experience amongst the first generation of migrant workers, and by contact with Marxist politics and the protest movement. As a result, his work embeds labour migration, including and especially that from Turkey, within a wider pattern of European working-class experience, but sees this migration also as a direct consequence of the "huge, bleeding wound" of European imperialism.[32]

This essentially Marxist perspective is combined in several of Ören's texts with a subtle metaphorical gendering of migrant male experience of the hierarchy of exploitation, echoed in Arthur Brittan's argument that migrant labourers are doubly feminised, as migrants and as labourers.[33] In the poem "Grunewald," the labourer-narrator imagines himself as the steed of a sleek white rider.[34] In *Der kurze Traum aus Kagithane*, the protagonist, Kazim Akkaya, comes to recognize that he is being milked like a "cow" by an exploitative system that stretches from his German employers to the Turkish state, eager for the hard currency he transfers home.[35] A poem in *Mitten in der Odyssee* complains that German society treats Turkish (male) workers like egg-laying battery chickens—dehumanised, but also feminised, production machines.[36]

Frequently these and other Turkish-German texts of migrant labour experience portray labourer-narrators, feminised in the sense that they are "no longer the actor, but the acted upon," compensating for their physical and psychological indignities by recourse to the hierarchies of sexual relations: "When we love our women, we love them with your brutal hands," as Ören's narrator notes in the poem "Die grenzenlose Phantasie der Gewalttätigkeit" (The unbounded imagination of violence).[37] Moreover, representations of relationships between Turkish workers and German women in Turkish-German writings demonstrate a double-edged quality: heightened experiences of indignity and the possibility of ethnic revenge. In one poem in Ören's *Privatexil*, a peep show helps the workers forget the indignity and alienation of unskilled manual labour, but also, in its joyless exploitation, it perpetuates this indignity and alienation: the workers are ripped off twice.[38] Hüseyin Murat Dörtyol's short story "So ist es, mein Sohn Kasim!" (That's how it is, my son Kasim!) describes how ethnic pride and male pride may be simultaneously wounded with fatal results: a lonely Turk, raging at his rejection by German prostitutes at the Autobahn exits, crashes his car into the Rhine. "At school they told us that the Turkish people are the greatest in the world. Here even the whores despise us!"[39] In Habib Bektaş's story "Das Länderspiel" (The international match), a Turkish nightshift worker meets an older German woman at a carnival. During their one-night stand, his months of involuntary sexual abstention explode like a bursting dam. He neither understands nor respects her pleas for him not to be "brutal." Afterwards he is satisfied, "like someone who has settled an old score."[40] The element of ethnic revenge here is reminiscent of that expressed in Richard Wright's *Native Son* (1940) or Eldridge Cleaver's *Soul on Ice* (1968). The motif of sexual violence is interwoven with the one compensatory experience afforded to his gender, namely, power over women.

The denigration of German women in some Turkish-German texts has antecedents in the genre of often semipornographic, sexually and nationally chauvinistic "Germany literature," which began to appear in Turkish in Turkey from the mid-1960s, feeding (and feeding off) prejudices and stereotypes that boastful returnees often encouraged. There are lurid tales of sex shops and of German managers offering their wives a Turkish stud as a birthday present.[41] In Fethi Savaşçi's poem "Olur mur?" (Is that possible then?), the Turkish garbageman is warned against the German girl with whom he seeks "friendship and good character," because she only wants "money and alcohol"; he is "a great Asiatic," she "a painted gossip, who carries Europe's fragmentation inside her."[42] Reflecting how hierarchies of race may conflict with those of gender, Bekir Yildiz's narrator in *The Turks in Germany* (1966) refuses to be "a German girl's plaything any more," especially one who improbably declares that what she wants from him is "the pride of the Asiatic man."[43] Complaints of racial discrimination may be embedded in a gender discrimination that the text treats as quite unproblematic, as in Mustafa Sertatas's narrator's equation of the male with the universal human in "Ich will heiraten" (I want to marry): "I am a man. An ordinary one. For my life I need that which all human beings need: food, drink, money and a woman, a normal woman."[44]

When Turkish-German writing turns its attention from the lone male to the male as head of the family, a frequent motif is the challenge to the migrant fathers' authority by their children, the second and third generations who often are better educated and more secure mediators with precisely that German environment which unsettles the fathers' identity. In Kemal Kurt's story "Ich kann dir nicht mehr in die Augen schauen" (I can no longer look you in the eye), a Turkish boy, desperate for the status that having a German girlfriend will bring him with his peers, clashes with a father who, as a prop for his challenged parental authority, applies Islamic norms more strictly than he might in Turkey and rejects German girls as being promiscuous: the text shows how patriarchy under threat fights rearguard actions on territory it might otherwise abandon with little regret. This text also exemplifies the compensatory double identity of the migrant man—downtrodden and penny-pinching in Germany in order to lord it back home—and the further generational conflict that this double identity engenders: "You should see my father in Turkey. . . . You can actually see how he takes on a second skin. He plays the successful man. Here he groans. There he's the king."[45]

Few literary texts reflect experienced reality entirely unfiltered, let alone naïvely; the act of writing itself creates and emphasises awareness of and therefore distance from the material represented. As a result, from the latter 1970s onwards, a significant number of texts that addressed Turkish-German male experience began doing so in consciously ironic and subversive ways. A central theme of Sinaşi Dikmen's satires is the double indignation experienced by the Turkish male when his patriarchal role is challenged not only by German society's paternalistic treatment of him but also by it being practised on him by women. In "Der andere Türke" (The other Turk), the Turkish narrator is visited by a

woman from the Parents' Council of his son's school, who is astonished
to find a writing desk in his flat. In "Wer ist ein Türke?" (Who is a
Turk?), a German woman on a train insists that the narrator cannot be a
Turk, as he is reading the highbrow weekly newspaper *Die Zeit*. In "Wir
werden das Knoblauchkind schon schaukeln" (roughly translated, We'll
sort out these racial problems), German women from a grassroots citizens' initiative become self-appointed guardians of the *Gastarbeiter*.[46]
Dikmen's "Der Brautbeschauer" (The bride-checker) pushes ethnic and
gender stereotypes ad absurdum in a critique of Turkish as well as German double standards. The Turkish social worker Nuri Pehlivan's public
role of furthering cross-cultural understanding is completely contra-
dicted by his private behaviour. In private, he attempts to retain patriarchal control over his family by excluding his wife—if necessary, violently—from contacts with German society. To prevent his daughter
Arzu from marrying Rolf-Dieter Grünberger, he insists that the Grün-
bergers respect Turkish traditions by appointing a "bride-checker." But
far from being put off by this as Pehlivan hopes, Herr Grünberger, who
sees his masculinity threatened by German feminism, is enthusiastic. He
converts to Islam to restore his eroded potency, and he eventually rejects
Arzu as being unsuitable for his son, since she is tainted with European
values. Thus both Grünberger and Pehlivan "bask in the patriarchal
myth of potency obtained at the expense of women's subjugation."[47]

Satirical perspectives also are central to the novels of Güney Dal,
whose work illustrates the complexity of representations of masculinity
in Turkish-German writing, underlining the fact that many writers de-
ploy sophisticated techniques, such as multiple focalisers and ironic parallels, even in those texts that appear at first sight to be primarily studies
of *Gastarbeiter* experience. Dal's 1979 novel *Wenn Ali die Glocken läuten
hört* (When the bells toll for Ali) focuses, like Aras Ören's earlier work,
on Turkish migrant labour experience in Germany in the context of
working-class struggle. But interwoven with its political didacticism is a
satirical representation of masculinity under challenge.[48] Assembly line
work, dominated by clocks and dehumanised, repetitive, mechanical
movements, contains few of the confirmations that masculinity is traditionally offered by manual work. This erosion of masculine identity is in
fact independent of ethnic origins. But Dal's Turks, as well as confirming
their manly honour through hiding feelings or repressing displays of
tenderness, echo clichés of Turkish "Germany literature" in noting the
desexualising effects of excessive work on their industrious German fellow workers: "They're a hard-working people, nothing against that. But
what do they get out of it? Work a lot, are always tired and—it's not

really polite to say this—then they can't get it up. So they leave their women to the Gastarbeiter."[49] Dal here shows Turkish workers perpetuating the same illogical stereotypes found in German images of sexually hyperactive foreigners.

This is ironically undercut, however, by the text's second narrative strand. While the political struggle proceeds at the Ford factory in Cologne, Kadir Derya, in his basement flat in Berlin, is literally unmanned by the indignities of migrant labour, his body politicised, sexualised, and gazed upon in a way rarely practised on male bodies in contemporary German writing. Herr Hartmann, the German supervisor in the laboratory where Kadir works, has given him hormone pills as a placebo for the stomach ulcers that Kadir, like many real migrant workers, has acquired from the stresses of migrant existence. The name Hartmann (hard man) suggests the virility that German society is stealing from the manual workers as it abuses their bodies and emphasises the gendered structure of the power relationship. Kadir watches in alarm as his breasts grow "as big as watermelons"[50] and "his nipples too become swollen as ripe blackberries," and he fears that his penis may drop off or grow back into his belly.[51] Kadir's moustache is no longer sufficient; only a full beard might counterbalance the threat to his gender identity: "It was as though he wanted to blaspheme and prove his masculinity to the bulges of flesh growing on his body."[52] He is obsessed with the incompatibility of being a father and having "growing breasts . . . whose origins one did not know,"[53] breasts that would collide with his wife's when they made love. Ashamed of his lost manhood, he hides away to cry.[54] To squeeze his breasts back into his body, he hatches a bizarre plan to squash them under a massive wardrobe. But lifting this would require male assistance. The friend thus made aware of Kadir's breasts might then want to "make moves to stroke them. That would not do."[55]

Kadir hallucinates, feels his heart beat like a horse racing in the sun's heat, takes the reins and rides towards the man from the house opposite. The man grabs Kadir's "ample hair," strokes it, then pulls it painfully. The man laughs, showing his teeth as much as his luxuriant moustache permits. "A hero, as far as I know, doesn't moan like a woman," he declares. Kadir reacts "subserviently." The man mounts one of the horses, digs in his spurs, and rides off.[56] In this dream, Kadir experiences the unsettling of his gender identity and, for him, the even more unsettling emergence of homoerotic desire in a series of clearly sexual images of dominance and subservience, traditional gender roles, and secondary sexual characteristics. Eventually, Kadir sets out to restore his masculinity by the most drastic means, and he amputates his right breast with a kitchen knife before collapsing.[57] The psychological scarring of migrant labour experience takes on literal form in this dark comic image, which strikingly genders the dependency of the migrant labourer on his German hosts but also mocks the panic with which a rigid heterosexual masculinity responds to the blurring of its boundaries. The stronger a Turkish worker adheres to this masculinity, the more he will experience this panic as the gendered hierarchy of the work situation threatens to feminise him. The novel thus articulates and satirises a widespread psychological phenomenon. At the same time, by turning inchoate anxieties into a comic narrative, the drastic conclusion of which the implicit male reader can be expected to find unnecessary, the novel generates a potential emancipation from an oppressively normative heterosexuality.

A decade later, in the final section of Dal's 1988 novel *Der enthaarte Affe* (The naked ape), its second narrator, a writer figure, introduces his new novel to its first narrator, Ömer Kul, as "Der enthaarte Affe": "a novel about someone [later expanded to "a man, an intellectual, a country"] who cocks a snook at evolution and at the time it takes. He's thirsting to become civilised and begs everyone he meets to tug out the hair he has inherited from his forefathers. He's ready to swallow any medication which will cause his hair to fall out, he pumps himself full of chemicals."[58] Thus the novel seems explicitly to take up and modify a theme of *Wenn Ali die Glocken läuten hört*. Whereas Kadir Derya's tragicomic regendering through medication exemplified the migrant man as a helpless victim of exploitation, *Der enthaarte Affe* displays male narrators willingly engaging in self-transformation in their enthusiasm to participate as fully as possible in (Western) modernity. They remain, though, subject to destabilising threats to their masculine identity, precisely because they cannot change as quickly as their environment.

In Dal's *Der enthaarte Affe*, Ömer Kul's incessant self-commentary also reflects a profound crisis of male identity. As a Turkish male of the older generation, he has imbibed and periodically, with ridiculous pedantry, spouts many of the leftist-liberal mores of German society, while his actual behaviour is more akin to an authoritarian Turkish father advising his son that "a boy should spread himself a bit when he sits down. For me that's simply a sign of self-confidence and of the fact that he was born a man."[59] Kul hides his social powerlessness behind his claim to see through media images of reality, and he rants in orthodox leftist fashion about Turkish and German capitalism alike. Initially, his existential agonisings send his much more pragmatic family to sleep. But as wild eccentricities emerge, including a primitive male "with the throaty cry of a savage," his family wavers between concern at his evident illness and impatience with his social dysfunctionality.[60] Ömer Kul takes extended sick leave to spend his nights writing a wall newspaper, insisting that his family read it in the morning. Its articles range from world events to a "Household Corner," in which his treatment of quotidian family matters is absurdly pompous. Compensating for his powerlessness, "editor" Ömer Kul attributes the individual articles to various reporters (named Ömer Kul) who write, for example, on James Watson Kul and Francis Crick Kul, the discoverers of DNA, on U.S. President Kul, or even, as his mind disintegrates, on concentration camp Doctor Kul.[61] In the later sections of the novel, the writer/narrator's heavy drinking, pathetic tramp-like appearance, and inability to finish his numerous novel projects offer ironic parallels to Ömer Kul's stagnation and paranoia.

Der enthaarte Affe is a comic portrait of a male subject in crisis and suggests certain ways, such as the particular form of the generation conflict, in which this crisis has been at least exacerbated by migrant experience. The complexity of the narrative structure of *Der enthaarte Affe* also reflects the more conscious self-image of the Turkish male writer as an intellectual aspirant to an avant-garde tradition, which emerges in Turkish-German men's writing in the latter 1980s and the 1990s. But from the beginning, Dal's work also shows that many male Turkish writers in Germany employ sophisticated literary techniques from an early stage, a point sometimes obscured by a sociological focus on the central thematic role of manual labour in many of their texts.

Two examples from the younger generations of Turkish-German male writing illustrate very different ways of taking issue with this writing's own accumulating traditions as well as with the respective writer's social experience and perceptions of it. Feridun Zaimoglu angrily rejects both passive victim identity and the liberal rhetoric of multiculturalism. The young Turkish male voices of his 1995 volume *Kanak Sprak: 24 Mißtöne vom Rande der Gesellschaft* (Spik speak: 24 voices from the fringe of society) are actually one voice, one performative delivery style that Zaimoglu, in his brilliantly concise introduction to the psychological stresses afflicting the second and third generations of Turks in Germany, calls the "anchor position": "arms wide, the left leg firmly grounded and taking the weight, and the right leg scraping the ground with the toe of the shoe."[62] From this position, half soapbox orator, half raging bull, Zaimoglu's young Turks reject every externally imposed identity, especially the "poor, but goodhearted Turk Ali" and the "garbageman prose" of *Gastarbeiterliteratur*.[63] Instead, like Jean Genet inverting his stigmatisation as a criminal and "pervert" into a celebration of otherness, they affirm that they are "Kanakstas" (a name that combines rap-influenced "gangsta" stances with the German racist label *Kanake*) and celebrate with electrifying, angry, linguistically inventive energy this position on the margins of a society for which they affect nothing but scorn. The twenty-four voices are linked, certainly, to a cross-section of street subculture, but Zaimoglu has self-confessedly edited their rhetoric substantially, and it may in fact be essentially fictional: it is not always easy to tell the pimp from the packer, the gigolo from the garbageman, the apprentice from the junkie, the fence from the rent boy. One voice, though, does stand out, placed last in Zaimoglu's deceptively casual but actually highly crafted composition, thus appearing as the warning summation of the various strands of this street-level view of German society: the angry indictments of its corrupt godlessness by Islamic fundamentalist Yücel.

In the work of Zafer Şenocak, work-generated masculine identity and the material and psychological costs of migrations are much less central than an experientially liberating journey through fluid ethnicities and sexual orientations. In his work, the Turkish-German man becomes postmodern, polymorphous, and androgynous, a Turkish Tannhäuser challenging the normative masculinity that would exile him from the Venusberg, affirming and exploring the dissolution of boundaries that led Dal's Kadir to self-destructive panic. Yet Şenocak's disturbingly original perspective on experienced and possible masculinities can be traced back to the complex ethnic experience invoked in his early poem "Doppelmann" (Doubleman): "The border runs right through my tongue."[64] This multiple identity is expressed in highly sensual, indeed sexualised language, extending into cultural geography: Istanbul underlines for him that "Europe is a mutant form of Asia, Asia a mutant form of Europe."[65] Cultural ambiguity and gender ambiguity intermesh. While "we men smelling of the sweat of fear/bite into raw onions," the androgynous, bisexual hero/ine of the poem, "Lu," is a man with the snakes and a woman with the bears and is fiercely insistent on his/her identity only when others seek to categorise her/him: "A dog called Lu was a cat/A wolf called Lu a lamb/but whoever called Lu a lamb had to deal with a wolf."[66]

Şenocak's literary struggle against crude binary polarisations is especially evident in his collection of essays, *Atlas of a Tropical Germany,* in which he plays with psychoanalytic categories such as temperate male orderliness versus tropical female disorder. The opening quotation from Elias Canetti declares that the German national symbol was the army, "the marching forest": German love of the forest was not simply love of nature, but of the pine forest with its rule-bound, rigid, parallel, upright trees in orderly separation one from another (the uniformed, helmeted lines of the Nuremberg rallies), in contrast to the chaos of a tropical forest.[67] Şenocak does not, however, simplistically perpetuate the "us and them" polarity of much migrant critique of German orderliness and discipline. Rather, positioning his work within contemporary German intellectual debate, he explores the—real or putative—tropical disorderliness in German culture itself.

In texts, the male body, like the female body, can be the object of history, an allegorical emblem of nation (both roles played by the Turkish male body in Turkish-German texts of *Gastarbeiter* experience), or, as in Şenocak's work, a site of heterogeneous possibilities.[68] While Şenocak rejects the self-image of the migrant as victim, traces of it can be found in the ambiguous gendering of his male narrators' encounters with German women figures. Şenocak is an intellectual at home in a Western metropolis, but also one who knows that "the Turk," the man in skirts, is charged with erotic ambiguity in the Western imagination.[69]

The title of Şenocak's volume, *Der Mann im Unterhemd* (The man in the undershirt, 1995), alludes ironically to Ernest Hemingway, the leading member of what Peter Schwenger calls "the virility school" of American writing.[70] Two stories in this volume illustrate particularly strikingly the exploration of gender possibilities in his sensual prose. "Die unterirdische Stadt" (The underground city) thinks a male fantasy through to its nightmarish conclusion: a subterranean city run by dominatrices devoted to eradicating men by killing them off through ceaseless and uninterrupted sexual activity.[71] Here, as elsewhere, Şenocak plays with pornographic language and images. In "Rolling Stones," a man allows a woman to remove his pubic hair, oil his body, and write poetry on his shaven skin, which thus, inverting conventional gendering, becomes her text. With the exchange of activity for passivity comes a loss of corporeal identity: "my body no longer had firm contours."[72] Allowing himself to be treated like a helpless baby evokes images from his past that read like a psychoanalytical sketch of male heterosexual development seen as a process of repression:

> I mounted a white mare. The horse ran on the spot. I awoke again. Waves whipped my face and my cock grew. In the night, mother's body in a transparent nightshirt loomed up out of the darkness. Sooner or later you learn to distinguish your mother

from other women. Sooner or later your aunt [who in an earlier
scene had lain beside him, caressing his penis] withdraws her
hand. Sooner or later you're totally alone.[73]

Here primal harmony with the mother is lost in the process of male
identity formation.[74] The image of the white mare may remind us that
Aras Ören's narrator in "Grunewald," feminised in his migrant labourer
role, imagines himself as the white rider's horse, and that Güney Dal's
Kadir dreams his loss of masculinity as a switch from being the rider to
being the horse. Şenocak's narrator in "Rolling Stones," in contrast, is
untroubled by, indeed celebrates, his own polymorphousness, and thus
paradoxically remains, at this specific moment of sexual and gender fantasy, in the saddle.

Şenocak's *Die Prärie* (The prairie, 1997) is a text of male and nar-
ratorial as much as migrant self-exploration, its theme echoed in its
genre-crossing form and multiple narrative perspectives. As the writer
Sascha states, "Today, everyone writes about his own sex, as though it
was about the defence of his fatherland. An obscure sexual patriotism is
spreading."[75] Here Sascha is more interested in sex and sexuality than in
his Islamic roots. His father, insistently secular in revolt against his pious
grandfather, is largely ignorant about Islam. Thus, when Sascha is com-
missioned to write a piece on the fatwa and literature, he is forced to
immerse himself in reference books; Islam "even pushes aside sex," he
notes ruefully. The "progeny of prudish protestants" in the editorial of-
fices would "rather take Islam as a theme than intercultural lust. Not
even with the added adjective 'intercultural' have I as yet been able to
arouse interest in my obsession. Otherwise it always does the trick when
you want to sell some stale topic."[76]

In *Die Prärie*, the narrator reflects on the male perception that
"women have come too close to us": whereas women are transparent (in
the sense of being open, without rigid outer boundaries), "men have at
least two skins, some are even in capsules."[77] As Kafka's *Metamorphosis*
suggests, men's own fluidity beneath their armoured carapace may be a
source of terror. Şenocak's narrator, however, positively seeks out this
fluidity. Accosted by a woman with glances "like arrows" on an empty
subway train, he allows himself to become the hunter's "booty," admit-
ting a passive role conventionally figured as feminine into the polymorphous cast of the multiple masculinity his text performs.[78] He explores the relationship between certain kinds of writing and sexuality:
the disintegration of boundaries and fixed categories, and the writer's
experience of prefiguring and preforming lived experience in texts. It is

not only women who "know that they only exist as pictures in the mirror of a man," a familiar point in the constitutive dominance of the male gaze.[79] In his relationship with the call girl Veronika, his ironic muse, who inspires him to write as many sentences a day as she has clients, the narrator experiences this indeterminacy as mutual. Gender, text, nation, and origin begin to dissolve.[80]

Şenocak's narrative plays self-mockingly with clichés of male sexuality: obsession with sex, discussion of seduction techniques, woman as mysterious Other whom it is the man's role to "entschlüsseln" ("unlock," "decipher," "explain," from *Schlüssel*, the German for "key").[81] "Men spend their lives turning the key to a woman in its keyhole. In vain. Maybe, where the lock is, there is actually no door."[82] There are several nuances here, from infantile schoolboy humour to misogynist objectification to men's imprisonment in constructions of the male self, which, by causing them to see the penis as an organ not only of gratification and procreation but also of revelation, ensure their endless puzzlement and isolation, hence their imagined longing to lay down their self-styled hero role. "The real male dream of our time is not the dream of power but the dream of powerlessness."[83] As long as it remains a dream, though, the sleeping man used by a sexually voracious woman is a male projection and does not necessitate the abandonment of patriarchal power in the waking, empirical world.

When Sascha takes a writer-in-residence post at an American college as a route to self-renewal, his Turkish-German ethnicity intensifies this experience familiar from modern German literature, as Şenocak's ironic pun makes clear: going west, Sascha loses his orientation, dis-orients himself ("die Orientierung verlieren").[84] Confronted by a homosocial hunting culture, the narrator is brought to reflect on his past sexual activity: "I had transferred my hunting instinct to women. For a long time they were the animals for me. They kept at a distance, which I had to overcome. I followed them. I lay in wait." Now he meets the first woman he has loved without feeling that he has "hunted her down."[85] In the northern woods, Don Juan mutates into Iron John; this relatively conventional motif also is part of the complex patterns of masculinity explored in Zafer Şenocak's *Die Prärie*.

Şenocak's texts suggest a poetic consciousness that has freed itself from many of the forces that have determined Turkish-German masculinities and has actively and with exploratory self-awareness addressed its own fluidity. The debt of this consciousness to some form of migrant experience is undeniable, yet not crudely fixable. Metaphors of bridges between cultures or of intercultural spaces are confronted with their own limits here, for they in fact perpetuate essentialist assumptions about fixed national cultures which, while they can be bridged or lived between, retain their dominance precisely in that fact. In a world still racked by crude nationalisms, Şenocak's strikingly original work exemplifies a dialectic whereby, out of a process set in train by Turkish migration to Germany since the early 1960s, with all of its lasting material problems, a kind of writing is emerging that has long left these origins behind; and the contribution of this type of writing to a developing postnational culture in Europe is crucially interwoven with its explorations of lived and imagined masculinities.

NOTES

1. "Turkish-German" in this essay refers to people of Turkish ethnicity living in Germany, not to people of mixed parentage. The potential problematic of the term is acknowledged. There are, it should also be noted, significant Turkish gay communities in Germany, but their specific experience, and the related constructions of Turkish gay male identity, would require a separate analysis.

2. From the extensive recent literature on masculinity, in addition to texts cited in this chapter, I have drawn on Peter Middleton, *The Inward Gaze: Masculinity and Subjectivity in Modern Culture* (New York: Routledge, 1992); Anthony Rowland, ed., *Signs of Masculinity: Men in Literature 1700 to the Present* (Atlanta: Rodopi, 1998); Lynne Segal, *Slow Motion: Changing Masculinities, Changing Men* (London: Virago, 1990).

3. These links between masculinity and colonialism and/or fascism are made, for example, in Michael Roper and John Tosh, eds., *Manful Assertions: Masculinities in Britain since 1800* (London: Routledge, 1991), 14, and in Elisabeth Badinter, *XY: On Masculinity*, Lydia Davis, trans. (New York: Columbia University Press, 1995), 20. Comparable positions are argued by Klaus Theweleit, *Male Fantasies*, 2 vols. (Cambridge: Polity Press, 1987, 1988), and George L. Mosse, *The Image of Man: The Creation of Modern Masculinity* (New York: Oxford University Press, 1996), 155–156.

4. See D. H. J. Morgan, *Discovering Men* (London: Routledge, 1992), 46–47.

5. See Eva Kolinsky, "Non-German Minorities in Contemporary German Society," *Turkish Culture in German Society Today*, David Horrocks and Eva Kolinsky, eds. (Providence: Berghahn, 1996), 71–112; here, 92. This opening section also draws substantially on Faruk Sen and Andreas Goldberg, *Türken in Deutschland. Leben zwischen zwei Kulturen* (Munich: Beck, 1994). See also Werner Schiffauer, *Die Migranten aus Subay. Türken in Deutschland. Eine Ethnographie* (Stuttgart: Klett-Cotta, 1991).

6. See Daniel G. Bates, "Normative and Alternative Systems of Marriage among the Yörük of Southeastern Turkey," *Anthropological Quarterly* 47 (1974): 270–287.

7. Moreover, some of the Kurds in Germany are not from Turkey but rather fled Iraq for political reasons from the 1950s onwards.

8. Attempts to argue nonmisogynist readings of Mohammed's views of women, such as Fatima Mernissi's in *The Veil and the Male Elite: A Feminist Interpretation of Women's Rights in Islam* (Reading: Addison-Wesley, 1991), are relatively isolated voices within Islam.

9. Güney Dal's novel *Wenn Ali die Glocken läuten hört* intriguingly suggests that migrant labourers who had done military service in Turkey continued the practice acquired there of walking in male pairs with intertwined fingers, to the nervous puzzlement of German onlookers. Güney Dal, *Wenn Ali die Glocken läuten hört*, translated from the Turkish by Brigitte Schreiber-Grabitz (Berlin: Edition der 2, 1979), 92. All translations of works into English throughout this chapter are by the author.

10. The date of the contract between the Federal German and Turkish governments on labour recruitment, part of a series of contracts between 1955 and 1968 that formed the legal framework for the arrival of the so-called *Gastarbeiter*. See Verena McRae, *Gastarbeiter. Daten—Fakten—Probleme* (Munich: Beck, 1980), 13–14.

11. Horrocks and Kolinsky, 85.

12. Sen and Goldberg, 33.

13. Ibid., 118.

14. Between 1961 and 1976, 678,000 Turkish men and 146,000 Turkish women were officially recruited for migrant labour in West Germany. See Sen and Goldberg, 60.

15. Ian M. Harris, *Constructing Masculinies* (London: Taylor & Francis, 1995), 23.

16. See Werner Schiffauer, *Die Gewalt der Ehre. Erklärungen zu einem türkisch-deutschen Sexualkonflikt* (Frankfurt a.M.: Suhrkamp, 1983), 126.

17. Broadly speaking, Turks who came to Germany as children or youths are defined as "second-generation," and those born in Germany, "third-generation."

18. See Wilhelm Heitmeyer, "Für türkische Jugendliche in Deutschland spielt der Islam eine wichtige Rolle," *Die Zeit* 35 (1996), *DIE ZEIT im Internet, ZEIT-Archiv*, <http://www.archiv.zeit.de/daten/pages/heitmey.txt.19960823.html>. See also Stefan Willeke and Kuno Kruse, "Wie anfällig sind türkische Jugendliche in Deutschland für islamischen Fundamentalismus?" *Die Zeit* 35 (1996), *DIE ZEIT im Internet, ZEIT-Archiv*, <http://www.archiv.zeit.de/daten/pages/islami.txt.19960823.html>.

19. Still more complex are multiethnic groups such as the "Sons of Gastarbeita," based in the Ruhr, whose members are Turkish, Turkish-German, Israeli-Lebanese, and German-Filipino.

20. Hermann Tertilt, *Turkish Power Boys. Ethnographie einer Jugendbande* (Frankfurt a.M.: Suhrkamp, 1996), 189–216. See also the portrait of the Berlin Turkish "Fighters" in Klaus Farin and Eberhard Seidel-Pielen, *Krieg in den Städten* (Berlin: Rotbuch, 1987).

21. A critical overhaul of this simplistic reception has been led by scholars outside of Germany in a complex debate through the 1980s and 1990s that cannot be rehearsed here. See Arlene Teraoka, "Gastarbeiterliteratur: The Other Speaks Back," *Cultural Critique* (1987): 7, 77–101; Leslie Adelson, "Migrantenliteratur oder deutsche Literatur? *Torkans Briefe an einen islamischen Bruder*," *Spätmoderne und Postmoderne. Beiträge zur deutschsprachigen Gegenwartsliteratur*, P. M. Lützeler, ed. (Frankfurt a.M.: Fischer Taschenbuch Verlag, 1991), 67–81; Sabine Fischer and Moray McGowan, "From Pappkoffer to Pluralism: Migrant Writing in the German Federal Republic," *Writing across*

Worlds: Literature and Migration, R. King, J. Connell, and P. White, eds. (London and New York: Routledge, 1995), 39–56.

22. See Irmgard Ackermann, ed., *Als Fremde in Deutschland. Berichte, Erzählungen, Gedichte von Ausländern* (Munich: Deutscher Taschenbuch Verlag, 1982), and *In zwei Sprachen leben. Berichte, Erzählungen, Gedichte von Ausländern* (Munich: Deutscher Taschenbuch Verlag, 1983); Karl Esselborn, ed., *Über Grenzen. Berichte, Erzählungen, Gedichte* (Munich: Deutscher Taschenbuch Verlag, 1987).

23. Irmgard Ackermann, ed., *Türken deutscher Sprache. Berichte, Erzählungen, Gedichte* (Munich: Deutscher Taschenbuch Verlag, 1984).

24. This point is made forcefully by Leslie Adelson, "The Price of Feminism: Of Women and Turks," *Gender and Germanness: Cultural Productions of Nation,* Patricia Herminghouse and Magda Mueller, eds. (Providence: Berghahn, 1997), 305–319.

25. Fakir Baykurt, "Das Telefon," *Nachtschicht und andere Geschichten aus Deutschland,* translated from the Turkish by Helga Dağyeli-Bohne and Yildirim Dağyeli (Zurich: Unionsverlag, 1984), 95–105.

26. Kemal Kurt, "Das Epos vom mustergültigen Ausländerle," *Türken deutscher Sprache,* 87–88.

27. Fakir Baykurt, "Nachtschicht," *Nachtschicht und andere Geschichten aus Deutschland,* 72–84.

28. "Wegwerfarbeiter" (Disposable worker) is a title of a poem in Aras Ören, *Privatexil. Gedichte,* translated from the Turkish by Gisela Kraft (Berlin: Rotbuch, 1977), 33–36.

29. Aras Ören, *Der kurze Traum aus Kagithane: Ein Poem,* translated from the Turkish by H. Achmed Schmiede (Berlin: Rotbuch, 1974), 8, 22.

30. Fakir Baykurt, "Wahltag," *Nachtschicht und andere Geschichten aus Deutschland,* 118–127.

31. Hasan Dewran, "Was wird aus uns," *In zwei Sprachen leben,* 31.

32. Aras Ören, *Die Fremde ist auch ein Haus,* translated from the Turkish by Gisela Kraft (Berlin: Rotbuch, 1980), 55.

33. See Arthur Brittan, *Masculinity and Power* (London: Blackwell, 1989).

34. Aras Ören, *Texte. Anhang. Texte aus dem Revier,* translated from the Turkish by Alp Otman, *Asphalt 6: Zeitschrift für kritische Literatur und bildende Kunst* (Wanne-Eickel: Proletenpresse, 1971), 10.

35. Ören, *Der kurze Traum aus Kagithane,* 30.

36. Aras Ören, *Mitten in der Odyssee. Gedichte,* translated from the Turkish by Gisela Kraft (Frankfurt a.M.: Fischer, 1983), 85–94.

37. Aras Ören, "Die grenzenlose Phantasie der Gewalttätigkeit," *Deutschland. Ein türkisches Märchen. Gedichte,* translated from the Turkish by Gisela Kraft (Frankfurt a.M.: Fischer, 1978, 1982), 22–25.

38. Ören, *Privatexil,* 7, 25–26.

39. Hüseyin Murat Dörtyol, "So ist es, mein Sohn Kasim!" *Das Unsichtbare sagen! Prosa und Lyrik aus dem Alltag des Gastarbeiters,* Habib Bektaş et al., eds. (Kiel: Malik, 1983), 161–166; here, 164.

40. Habib Bektaş, *Das Länderspiel. Erzählungen*, translated from the Turkish by Wolfgang Riemann (Tübingen: Heliopolis, 1991), 56–68; here, 66–67.

41. See Wolfgang Riemann, *Das Deutschlandbild in der modernen türkischen Literatur* (Wiesbaden: Harrasowitz, 1983), 82–86.

42. Quoted in Riemann, 103.

43. Bekir Yildiz, *Türkler Almanyada: Almanya'da geçen dört yilin macerasi; roman* (Baski: Bilmen Basimevi, 1966), quoted in Riemann, 72–75.

44. Mustafa Sertatas, "Ich will heiraten," *Über Grenzen. Berichte, Erzählungen, Gedichte von Ausländern*, 97–99; here, 97.

45. Kemal Kurt, "Ich kann dir nicht mehr in die Augen schauen," *Türken deutscher Sprache*, 81.

46. Sinaşi Dikmen, *Der andere Türke. Satiren* (Berlin: Express Edition, 1986).

47. Gil Michael Gott, *Migration, Ethnicization and Germany's New Ethnic Minority Literature* (Ann Arbor, Mich.: University Microfilms International, 1995), 145.

48. Leslie Adelson offers an illuminating reading of this novel in "Migrants and Muses," *The New History of German Literature*, David E. Wellbery et al., eds. (Cambridge, Mass.: Harvard University Press, forthcoming).

49. Dal, 50.

50. Ibid., 59.

51. Ibid., 26.

52. Ibid., 37.

53. Ibid., 60.

54. Ibid., 97.

55. Ibid., 36.

56. Ibid., 63

57. Ibid., 150–153.

58. Güney Dal, *Der enthaarte Affe*, translated from the Turkish by Carl Koss (Zurich: Piper, 1988), 357.

59. Ibid., 51.

60. Ibid., 52.

61. Ibid., 194–196.

62. Feridun Zaimoglu, *Kanak Sprak: 24 Mißtöne vom Rande der Gesellschaft* (Berlin: Rotbuch, 1995), 13. See also Joachim Lottmann, "Kanak Attack," *Die Zeit*, November 14, 1997, 88.

63. Zaimoglu, 12.

64. Zafer Şenocak, "Doppelmann," *Türken deutscher Sprache*, 39.

65. Zafer Şenocak, "Archivare in Istanbul," *Das senkrechte Meer. Gedichte* (Berlin: Babel, 1991), 7–14; here, 9. His novel *Gefährliche Verwandtschaft* explores a further dimension of hybridity, a Turkish-German-Jewish triangle. Zafer Şenocak, *Gefährliche Verwandtschaft* (Berlin: Babel Verlag, 1998).

66. Zafer Şenocak, *Fernwehanstalten. Gedichte* (Berlin: Babel, 1994), 25–27.

67. Zafer Şenocak, *Atlas des tropischen Deutschland* (Berlin: Babel, 1993), 5. Şenocak's volume *Atlas of a Tropical Germany: Essays on Politics and Culture, 1990–1998*, Leslie A. Adelson, trans. and ed. (Lincoln, Neb.: Bison Books, 2000) contains a selection of material different from the original German volume, but is an important introduction to his work for English-speaking readers.

68. I draw on Leslie Adelson's seminal text here, though she is discussing female bodies: Leslie Adelson, *Making Bodies, Making History: Feminism and German Identity* (Lincoln: University of Nebraska Press, 1993), 36.

69. For a more in-depth discussion on the "man in skirts," see Graham Dawson, "The Blond Bedouin: Lawrence of Arabia, Imperial Adventure and the Imaging of English-British Masculinity," *Manful Assertions: Masculinities in Britain since 1800*, Michael Roper and John Tosh, eds. (London and New York: Routledge, 1991), 113–144.

70. Peter Schwenger, *Phallic Critiques: Masculinity and Twentieth-Century Literature* (New York: Routledge, 1984), 13.

71. Zafer Şenocak, *Der Mann im Unterhemd* (Berlin: Babel, 1995), 93–103. Akif Pirinçci's *Yin* (Munich: Goldmann, 1997), a massive novel requiring a separate analysis in its own right, develops this motif still further: a man-killing virus has left behind an all-female world.

72. Ibid., 114.

73. Ibid., 116.

74. A process discussed in David D. Gilmore, *Manhood in the Making: Cultural Concepts of Masculinity* (New Haven, Conn.: Yale University Press, 1990), 27–28.

75. Zafer Şenocak, *Die Prärie* (Hamburg: Rotbuch, 1997), 9.

76. Ibid., 40–42.

77. Ibid., 7.

78. Ibid., 16–17.

79. Ibid., 6.

80. Ibid., 13. At the time of writing, Şenocak had just published *Der Erottomane* (Berlin: Babel, 1999). Its title, punning the terms *erotomaniac* and *He-Ottoman*, ironically blends his gender awareness and the orientalist image of the sensual Turk.

81. Şenocak, *Die Prärie*, 49–51.

82. Ibid., 47.

83. Ibid., 64.

84. Ibid., 69.

85. Ibid., 84.

Afterword

Michael Kimmel

I have never set foot on German soil, though it is one of the two countries that are my ancestral home. To this day, I tend to avoid buying German products. Even in my years as a hippie, it was with some discomfort—and my grandparents' explicit condemnation—that I drove a VW bus.

I do not write this out of pride; rather I experience a certain shame in confessing such a lingering antipathy. I have often imagined myself walking down a bustling German street, confronting older men, asking angrily, "What did you do during the war? Where were you?" I imagine asking men my age about what their fathers did.

Perhaps, though, this will explain why I received the manuscript for this book with some trepidation. Although I had known of the project for some time, and had been generally supportive of it, I also avoided reading it.

In my fantasy, the book would contain works by German men about how German men were reimagining, retrieving, restoring their damaged sense of manhood after their humbling—even emasculating—defeats in the two World Wars in this century. Particularly after the Holocaust, what had German men done—both in reality and in representation—to feel again like men?

I didn't especially want to know. I wasn't certain that I especially *wanted* German men to regain their sense of masculinity, even in representation, after the national complicity in planned, well orchestrated and systematic genocide—including those few distant family members of mine who had not managed to leave when my more immediate relatives did.

I wasn't fully prepared for the articulate and anguished efforts to use the emerging field of masculinity studies—which explores men's experiences through the prisms offered by feminist theory, queer theory, and multiculturalism—to explicate the experiences of German men after the war. To be sure, I knew several of the authors, either by reputation or by their writings, and so I was prepared to be engaged intellectually by formidable scholars and thinkers. As I read their rich and deeply thoughtful essays, I vacillated between exhilaration and despair.

I was, in a sense, prepared for some of the essays in this book; or, rather, for the ideas that several of the authors explore and critique. One grows weary and despondent (if ever more intransigently and piously self-righteous) reading of the resurgence of Nazi paraphernalia in contemporary Germany, or the Nazi-inflected racist attacks against ethnic minorities, Turks, and others. When I read of postwar apologists, who sought to "repress the memory of the Holocaust in a breathtakingly rapid and cynical manner," as Inge Stephan writes, it seemed familiar. I was primed to learn the schemes, both rhetorical and real, that German men had devised to "extinguish memories of the traumatic experiences of the war."

Much of that extinguishing seems to have come through the repudiation of the real fathers—the collaborative fathers, the genocidal fathers, the Nazi fathers—and a longing for new, different fathers. Instead of rejecting the regime of the fathers, many writers seem to have rejected the fathers themselves, claiming, as did one journalist in Barbara Kosta's essay, that German men "need fathers again, more fathers and stronger ones, that is to say, masculine ones." "Oy," I said to myself, "Just what I need. Stronger, more masculine German father figures."

Others, of course, do challenge the regime of the fathers, and they enter that "minefield of memory" in Kosta's memorable phrase. The writers in her essay not only ask the generic question about the responsibility of the fathers, but the specific one, they dig into their own fathers' pasts to construct what Tilmann Moser calls a "biography of reparation."

In reading these essays I was struck by two recurring themes that appear to run on parallel tracks. What is startling to me are the ways that Roy Jerome's careful framing and judicious editing enables the reader to explore both shame and silence, seeing their various dimensions, their convergences and divergences, both analytically and personally.

What we learn is that both dominator and dominated experience silence and shame, although in somewhat different ways. As Harry Brod points out in his moving personal effort to heal the chasm in his identity expressed by the hyphen between "German" and "Jewish," there is a silence in both worlds. "While the silence of the silencers translates into a voice of authority, the silence of the silenced leaves the next generation with a void rather than a voice," Brod writes.

The hallucinogenic efforts of both dominator and dominated to ignore the cataclysm, to seal off those years in a mental museum, seem now perverse, yet also plaintive. Healing, we know, can come only with language—barely audible, muffled, wrenching sighs and cries at first, perhaps, congealing only later into words, phrases, utterances.

However different these silences, I believe they both reveal an effort to cover over, to conceal, a deep shame. For the German sons of the fathers, it is the lingering shame of the complicit, the collaborator, the persecutor, the murderer. German men my age must carry a terrible knowledge of the depths of depraved cruelties that those whom they loved had been able to perpetrate.

But there is also a shame at having been the victim of the crime. For me, it was the shame of passivity, the shame of the helpless, vanquished, oppressed, emasculated. The few stories I heard growing up in the affluent New York suburbs in the 1950s were stories that filled me with self-loathing, with disgust at my own people. Stories about how the Jews stood in line at Babi Yar, waiting their turn to be machine gunned into the muddy ditches that served as mass graves. How they passively, helplessly, did everything they were told to do, despite the cynical destruction of their families, their lives. How they surrendered their families, offering up their children to the cruelest of tortures.

These few stories were among the only ones to pierce my family's silence in the early 1950s, as American Jews struggled to come to terms with what had happened, and, in a climate far more anti-Semitic than today, tried to plant the seeds of a new, free generation. My grandparents didn't want to talk much about the Holocaust out of their own fear and shame, perhaps, as if to mention it made its reappearance that much more likely.

I recall conversations with my friends about what we heard. If it had been us, we asked ourselves, wouldn't we at least take one of them with us? Wouldn't we try and escape? Fight back? Die fighting? When I looked at my reflection in the mirror I wasn't sure what I would have done. Run? Hide? Fight? What a revelation it was for me to finally find the stories of the Jews who did fight back, the armed Resistance, the militant uprisings in the Warsaw and other ghettoes, or even those who did escape, who survived.

The shame of the silenced and of the silencer. The silence of the shamed.

As I read these essays, though, I was always aware of the ways in which these emotions were also about gender, about the ways in which German and Jewish *men* experienced their respective silences and shames. Shame and silence are part of being a man in our societies, part of the quotidian compromises with gender inequality that we make to survive. How, after all, do we men respond when we see women harassed on the street, or splayed in pornographic photo spreads proudly displayed in our office bathrooms? How do we respond when we hear men ridicule or threaten gay men? How do we typically respond when other men make insulting comments about women, or laugh at sexist jokes? And what do we do when white men laugh surreptitiously at racist humor?

We are silent. Not necessarily out of complicity nor conspiracy, but rather from fear of what might happen to us if we were to break ranks, if we ourselves tried to break the silence that allows such insults, such indignities, such cruel inequality to continue. We are silent, which is how it continues. It may be done by "them," but they can do it only because they believe we support it. Which we do by our silence. It is thus done in our name. For it is not just those few men who rape, who batter, or who harass women whenever they enter the public sphere, but the silent complicity of the majority of men. (I have tried to write about this silence in an essay, "Masculinity As Homophobia: Fear, Shame and Silence in Men's Lives," published in *Theorizing Masculinities*, H. Brod and M. Kaufman, eds. (Newbury Park, Calif.: Sage, 1995)).

Our knowledge of our silence and our silencing is the source of our shame. Shame that we did not speak up. Shame that we were, ourselves, silenced.

The perspective of the emerging field of masculinity studies, then, enables me to enter the world of post-Holocaust German men, seeking to break their silence and give voice to their shame, to reconstruct a masculinity based on principles of accountability, integrity, and a shared commitment to break the silence. We can understand, for example, how the silencer is himself often silenced, and how the silenced may find some crevices in which to begin to speak.

One central principle of contemporary masculinity studies is that we explore the different definitions of masculinity as articulated by different groups of men. We understand that masculinity means different things in different cultures, and within any one culture over time. We understand that masculinity means different things to the same man as he ages, and how different groups of men in the same society may have a different set of ideas about masculinity. Making masculinity visible does not mean making race, class, nationality, ethnicity, sexuality, age, or any other variable "invisible" as a result. We theorize about *masculinities*, not about masculinity as a singular categorical essence, and a central tenet of the investigation is to explicate the different ways in which masculinities are articulated by different men. I often ask my students to imagine two different men: a 76-year-old black gay man who lives in Chicago and a white 19-year-old heterosexual farm boy in Iowa. Would they not have very different ideas about what it means to be a man?

On the other hand, would they not have some beliefs and assumptions in common, some facets of their understandings of masculinity that are similar, despite the differences? I am reminded of the admonition of the great French historian Marc Bloch (himself killed as a member of the French Resistance) who advised historians "not to attach too much importance to local pseudo-causes" while at the same time to "learn to become sensitive to specific differences."

And is that not the lesson to be learned here, that as German men agonize to theorize their shame and speak through their collective and individual silences, they do so as *German* men, with the specificity of postwar historical consciousness, and they do so as German *men*, in the ways that men must everywhere confront their own shame at their own collaborative silences in any society scarred by gender inequality.

I am Jew to their German: I am an outsider, the one whom they wanted eliminated. Now, also, I am the scrutinizer, they the scrutinized. But I am also a man to their man, linked to their struggles by some similarities in my own struggles. While I cannot yet go as far as to call us brothers under the skin, we are nonetheless closer than I had thought, joined in the terrible knowledge that illegitimate power demands a false consensus based on the silencing of all dissent.

If not, then, brothers, then at least men—and through that emerging consciousness of our flawed humanity there is, perhaps, an opportunity for me to dismantle my own wall of resistance. Perhaps a chance to reach across chasms that yawned across time and memory. Perhaps I will someday even take my son to see the land from which his ancestors came.

Contributors

Klaus-Michael Bogdal is professor of German at the Gerhard-Mercator-Universität Duisburg, Germany, where he is coeditor of *Der Deutschunterricht* and *Oldenbourg Interpretationen*. His many publications include *Historische Diskursanalyse der Literatur. Theorien, Lektüren*; *Neue Literaturtheorien. Eine Einführung*; *Literaturtheorie und Geschichte*; *Neue Literaturtheorien in der Praxis. Textanalysen von Kafkas "Vor dem Gesetz"*; *Zwischen Alltag und Utopie. Arbeiterliteratur als Diskurs des 19. Jahrhunderts*; *Willkommen und Abschied der Maschinen; Literatur und Technik. Bestandsaufnahme eines Themas*; *Weimarer Republik*; *Lektüre-Praxis, Lektüre-Vielfalt*; *Fremdheiten-Eigenheiten*; and *Männerbilder*.

Harry Brod is associate professor of philosophy and humanities and director of Humanities at the University of Northern Iowa. He is the author of *Hegel's Philosophy of Politics* and editor of *The Making of Masculinities: The New Men's Studies*; *A Mensch among Men: Explorations in Jewish Masculinity*; and (with Michael Kaufman) *Theorizing Masculinities*. His current project is a book about anti-racist white men.

Klaus-Jürgen Bruder is professor of psychology at the Freie Universität Berlin and cofounder of the interdisciplinary journal *Psychologie und Geschichte*. He has published *Monster oder liebe Eltern? Sexueller Mißbrauch in der Familie*; *Subjektivität und Postmoderne. Der Diskurs der Psychologie*; *Jugend. Psychologie einer Kultur*; *Psychologie ohne Bewußtsein. Die Geburt der behavioristischen Sozialtechnologie*; and *Kritik der Bürgerlichen Psychologie. Zur Theorie des Individuums in der kapitalistischen Gesellschaft*. His research interests include the history of psychology and psychological discourse, pragmatism, postmodernism, the culture of youth, and gender relations and discourse.

Roy Jerome received his Ph.D. in German literature. He is currently finishing a program in clinical psychology at Teacher's College, Columbia University, where he concentrates on psychoanalytic theories of masculinity, men's mental health, trauma, and violence. He also works with principal investigators at the New York State Psychiatric Institute helping mental health practitioners receive federal and private funding for mental health research. He works with prison inmates in the New York metropolitan area on violence relapse prevention and harm reduction in heroin addiction. He is also currently conducting research on violence and masculinity in American society.

Barbara Kosta is associate professor of German Studies at the University of Arizona, where she teaches twentieth-century German and Austrian literature and German film. She is the author of *Recasting Autobiography: Women's Counterfictions in Contemporary German Literature and Film.*

Moray McGowan received his B.A. and M.A. from Newcastle-upon-Tyne and his Ph.D. from Universität Hamburg. He has taught in Siegen, Kassel, Lancaster, Hull, and Strathclyde and is currently professor of German and head of the Department of Germanic Studies at Trinity College Dublin, Ireland. His research interests include modern and contemporary German and European literature and cultural studies. He is the author of *Marieluise Fleißer*; *From High Priests to Desecrators: Contemporary Austrian Writing* (coedited with Ricarda Schmidt); *Denn Du tanzt auf einem Seil. Positionen deutschsprachiger MigrantInnenliteratur* (coedited with Sabine Fischer); "German Writing in the West (1945–1990)," in Helen Watanabe-O'Kelly's *The Cambridge History of German Literature*; and numerous essays and book chapters on contemporary German literature and culture.

Tilmann Moser studied literary theory in Tübingen, Berlin, and Paris. After a journalistic education in sociology and politics in Frankfurt and Gießen, he completed his education in psychoanalysis at the Sigmund-Freud-Institut in Frankfurt. There he went on to become assistant professor of criminology and psychoanalysis in the School of Law. Since 1978, he has worked as a psychotherapist in private practice in Freiburg, Germany. His most recent publications include *Mutterkreuz und Hexenkind. Eine Gewissensbildung im Dritten Reich. Die Biographie eines*

Kindes, das ohne Absicht Juden verraten hat, die dann deportiert und ermordet wurden; Dabei war ich doch sein liebstes Kind. Eine Psychotherapie mit der Tochter eines SS-Mannes; Dämonische Figuren. Die Wiederkehr des Dritten Reiches in der Psychotherapie; Politik und Seelischer Untergrund; Strukturen des Unbewußten; Ödipus in Panik und Triumph; Der Erlöser der Mutter auf dem Weg zu sich selbst; Vorsicht Berührung. Über Sexualisierung, Spaltung, NS-Erbe und Stasi-Angst; Stundenbuch. Protokolle aus der Körperpsychotherapie; and Körpertherapeutische Phantasien.

Carl Pietzcker studied Latin, Greek, philosophy, physical education, and German in Tübingen, Rome, and Freiburg. He is currently professor of German at the Institute for Contemporary German Literature, Albert-Ludwigs-Universität Freiburg, Germany, and coeditor of *Freiburger literaturpsychologische Gespräche.* He is the author of *Einheit, Trennung und Wiedervereinigung. Psychoanalytische Untersuchungen eines religiösen, philosophischen, politischen und literarischen Motivs; Lesend interpretieren. Zur psychoanalytischen Deutung literarischer Texte; "Ich kommandiere mein Herz." Brechts Herzneurose—Ein Schlüssel zu seinem Leben und Schreiben; Trauma, Wunsch und Abwehr. Psychoanalytische Studien zu Goethe, Jean Paul, Brecht, zur Atomliteratur und zur literarischen Form;* and *Einführung in die Psychoanalyse des literarischen Kunstwerks am Beispiel von Jean Pauls "Rede des toten Christus."*

Wolfgang Popp is professor of German language, literature, and didactic at the Universität Siegen, Germany, where he is coeditor of *Forum Homosexualität und Literatur.* His publications include *Ikonen des Begehrens. Bildsprachen der männlichen und weiblichen Homosexualität in Literatur und Kunst; Männerliebe. Homosexualität und Literatur; Die Suche nach dem rechten Mann. Männerfreundschaft im literarischen Werk Hans Henny Jahnns;* and numerous articles on literary didactic, education, and homosexuality and literature.

Inge Stephan is professor of Contemporary German and chair of the Program in Gender Problematics in the Literary Process at the Humboldt-Universität zu Berlin, Germany. Her many publications include *Musen und Medusen. Mythos und Geschlecht in der Literatur des 20. Jahrhunderts; Unaufhörlich Lenz gelesen—. Studien zu Leben und Werk von J.M.R. Lenz* (with Hans-Gerd Winter); *Jüdische Kultur und Weiblichkeit in der Moderne; Die Gründerinnen der Psychoanalyse; Heil über dir, Hammonia. Hamburg im 19. Jahrhundert. Kultur, Geschichte, Politik* (with Hans-Gerd Winter); *Das Schicksal der begabten Frau;*

Frauenliteratur ohne Tradition? Neun Autorinnenporträts; and *"Wen küm-mert's, wer spricht." Zur Literatur und Kulturgeschichte von Frauen aus Ost und West.* Until 1996, she was also coeditor of the journal *Frauen in der Literaturwissenschaft.* She is currently coeditor of the series *Literatur im historischen Prozeß, Literatur-Kultur-Geschlecht,* and *Zeitschrift für Germanistik.* Her many areas of study include women's literature, femi-nist literary theory, and gender studies.

Russell West is professor of British and American Studies at the Univer-sity of Applied Sciences, Magdeburg, Germany. His publications include *Figures de la maladie chez André Gide; Conrad and Gide: Translation, Transference and Intertextuality;* and *Marginal Voices, Marginal Forms: Di-aries in European Literature and History.*

Hans-Gerd Winter is professor of German in the Department for Liter-ary Studies at the Universität Hamburg, Germany. He is the author of *Dann waren die Sieger da. Studien zur literarischen Kultur in Hamburg 1945–1950; Büchner-Opern; Pack das Leben bei den Haaren. Wolfgang Borchert in neuer Sicht; Unaufhörlich Lenz gelesen—. Studien zu Leben und Werk von J.M.R. Lenz* (with Inge Stephan); *Liebe, die im Abgrund Anker wirft. Autoren und literarisches Feld im Hamburg des 20. Jahrhun-derts* (with Inge Stephan); *Sie, und nicht wir; Die französische Revolution und ihre Wirkung auf Norddeutschland und das Reich;* and *J.M.R Lenz.* His research interests include literary history from the eighteenth to the twentieth centuries, the literary history of Hamburg, and sociological literary theory.

Index